THE NEW CAMBRIDGE SHAKESPEAR[E]

GENERAL EDITOR
Brian Gibbons

ASSOCIATE GENERAL EDITOR
A. R. Braunmuller

From the publication of the first volumes in 1984 the General Editor of the New Cambridge Shakespeare was Philip Brockbank and the Associate General Editors were Brian Gibbons and Robin Hood. From 1990 to 1994 the General Editor was Brian Gibbons and the Associate General Editors were A. R. Braunmuller and Robin Hood.

THE POEMS

This is a fully annotated edition of all the poems which can be confidently assigned to Shakespeare, excluding the *Sonnets*. It contains *Venus and Adonis*, *The Rape of Lucrece*, *The Phoenix and the Turtle*, *The Passionate Pilgrim*, and *A Lover's Complaint*.

John Roe's introduction to the two long narrative poems examines their place within the classical and Renaissance European traditions, comparing Shakespeare's poetry with that of Ovid, Livy, Chaucer, Ariosto, Marlowe, and Daniel in the light of Neoplatonic influences and courtly style.

Some of these issues extend into the discussion of the various ways of reading *The Phoenix and the Turtle*. *The Passionate Pilgrim* is a miscellany of twenty sonnets and lyrics, containing only five poems which are certain to be Shakespeare's. John Roe analyses the interesting enigma of the publisher's role in preparing the collection and the conditions in which it was produced.

Evidence for and against Shakespeare's authorship of *A Lover's Complaint* is weighed. A reassessment of the much-debated question of the poem's genre concludes that it is best treated as a narrative in the 'complaint' mode.

The commentary on these poems is attentive to their rich and varied rhetorical manner. John Roe demonstrates how in his management of formal tropes Shakespeare, like the best Elizabethans, fashions a living language out of handbook oratory. This updated edition also contains a new introductory section on recent critical interpretations and an updated reading list.

THE NEW CAMBRIDGE SHAKESPEARE

All's Well That Ends Well, edited by Russell Fraser
Antony and Cleopatra, edited by David Bevington
As You Like It, edited by Michael Hattaway
The Comedy of Errors, edited by T. S. Dorsch
Coriolanus, edited by Lee Bliss
Cymbeline, edited by Martin Butler
Hamlet, edited by Philip Edwards
Julius Caesar, edited by Marvin Spevack
King Edward III, edited by Giorgio Melchiori
The First Part of King Henry IV, edited by Herbert Weil and Judith Weil
The Second Part of King Henry IV, edited by Giorgio Melchiori
King Henry V, edited by Andrew Gurr
The First Part of King Henry VI, edited by Michael Hattaway
The Second Part of King Henry VI, edited by Michael Hattaway
The Third Part of King Henry VI, edited by Michael Hattaway
King Henry VIII, edited by John Margeson
King John, edited by L. A. Beaurline
The Tragedy of King Lear, edited by Jay L. Halio
King Richard II, edited by Andrew Gurr
King Richard III, edited by Janis Lull
Macbeth, edited by A. R. Braunmuller
Measure for Measure, edited by Brian Gibbons
The Merchant of Venice, edited by M. M. Mahood
The Merry Wives of Windsor, edited by David Crane
A Midsummer Night's Dream, edited by R. A. Foakes
Much Ado About Nothing, edited by F. H. Mares
Othello, edited by Norman Sanders
Pericles, edited by Doreen DelVecchio and Antony Hammond
The Poems, edited by John Roe
Romeo and Juliet, edited by G. Blakemore Evans
The Sonnets, edited by G. Blakemore Evans
The Taming of the Shrew, edited by Ann Thompson
The Tempest, edited by David Lindley
Timon of Athens, edited by Karl Klein
Titus Andronicus, edited by Alan Hughes
Troilus and Cressida, edited by Anthony B. Dawson
Twelfth Night, edited by Elizabeth Story Donno
The Two Gentlemen of Verona, edited by Kurt Schlueter

THE EARLY QUARTOS

The First Quarto of Hamlet, edited by Kathleen O. Irace
The First Quarto of King Henry V, edited by Andrew Gurr
The First Quarto of King Lear, edited by Jay L. Halio
The First Quarto of King Richard III, edited by Peter Davison
The First Quarto of Othello, edited by Scott McMillin
The Taming of a Shrew: The 1594 Quarto, edited by Stephen Roy Miller

THE POEMS

VENUS AND ADONIS, THE RAPE OF LUCRECE,
THE PHOENIX AND THE TURTLE,
THE PASSIONATE PILGRIM, A LOVER'S COMPLAINT

Updated edition

Edited by
JOHN ROE
Senior Lecturer, Department of English and Related Literature, University of York

CAMBRIDGE
UNIVERSITY PRESS

CAMBRIDGE UNIVERSITY PRESS

Cambridge, New York, Melbourne, Madrid, Cape Town, Singapore, São Paulo

Cambridge University Press
The Edinburgh Building, Cambridge CB2 2RU, UK

Published in the United States of America by Cambridge University Press, New York

www.cambridge.org
Information on this title: www.cambridge.org/9780521671620

First published 1992
Fifth printing 2005
Updated edition 2006

Printed in the United Kingdom at the University Press, Cambridge

A catalogue record for this publication is available from the British Library

ISBN-13 978-0-521-85551-8 hardback
ISBN-10 0-521-85551-9 hardback
ISBN-13 978-0-521-67162-0 paperback
ISBN-10 0-521-67162-0 paperback

CONTENTS

ILLUSTRATIONS

PREFACE

I should like first to acknowledge the help invariably conferred by previous editors of Shakespeare's poetry, in particular H. E. Rollins, whose monumental Variorum edition of the *Poems* has proved indispensable. I have also gained immeasurably from the efforts of subsequent editors such as Prince, Maxwell, Lever, and Wells–Taylor. The process of saluting influence in detail is cumbersome; but I have tried to do my best, and I hope that economy in acknowledgment will not be taken for neglect or evasion.

I wish also to acknowledge the help and understanding of the founding editor of this series, the late Philip Brockbank. I also wish to thank Anthony Mortimer for bringing to my attention the depiction of Venus and Adonis, by the Flemish artist Bartholomäus Spranger, reproduced on p. 15. My copy-editor, Charles Hieatt, has smoothed my path in the latter stages by his keen detection of errors and inconsistencies, and Sarah Stanton of Cambridge University Press has been always attentive to queries and misgivings.

Various friends and colleagues have in addition read parts of the manuscript and given generously of their time and energy in making comments: Marie Axton, Jacques Berthoud, the late Bernard Harris, Gwynne Evans, Anne Jackson, Robin Robbins, and Timothy Webb. Thanks, also, to John and Vanessa Lindsay Smith for the use of Cragg Cottage at a critical stage.

The library staff of the following institutions have responded cooperatively to requests and queries: the Bodleian, Oxford, the Folger Library, Washington, D.C., the John Rylands Library, Manchester, the University of Leeds, the Shakespeare Institute, Stratford, and, not least, the University of York.

My gratitude, also, to the University of Kyoto, where I spent 1990–1 on leave of absence, which allowed me the time to incorporate some late revisions and emendations.

Finally, although my wife has modestly expressed her wish not to be included here, she has been my help and mainstay throughout, and it would be truly negligent of me not to acknowledge the very great debt I owe her.

For this new edition I have extended the introduction to take account of and evaluate recent developments in scholarship, a procedure which is also reflected in the expanded Reading List. The commentary remains largely unchanged, apart from the correction of a few factual errors and the modification of the occasional note. Otherwise I have found no reason to alter things substantially. I based my commentary originally on the principle of demonstrating Shakespeare's rhetorical resourcefulness as a poet, and this continues to be my aim. For this updated edition I should like to thank the general editors, Brian Gibbons and Al Braunmuller, for their help and advice.

J. R.

University of York

ABBREVIATIONS AND CONVENTIONS

1. Shakespeare's works

The abbreviated titles of Shakespeare's plays and poems have been modified from those used in the *Harvard Concordance of Shakespeare*. All quotations and line references to works other than *The Poems* are to G. Blakemore Evans (ed.), *The Riverside Shakespeare*, 1974, on which the *Concordance* is based.

Ado	*Much Ado about Nothing*
Ant.	*Antony and Cleopatra*
AWW	*All's Well That Ends Well*
AYLI	*As You Like It*
Cor.	*Coriolanus*
Cym.	*Cymbeline*
Err.	*The Comedy of Errors*
Ham.	*Hamlet*
1H4	*The First Part of King Henry the Fourth*
2H4	*The Second Part of King Henry the Fourth*
H5	*King Henry the Fifth*
1H6	*The First Part of King Henry the Sixth*
2H6	*The Second Part of King Henry the Sixth*
3H6	*The Third Part of King Henry the Sixth*
H8	*King Henry the Eighth*
JC	*Julius Caesar*
John	*King John*
LC	*A Lover's Complaint*
LLL	*Love's Labour's Lost*
Lear	*King Lear*
Luc.	*The Rape of Lucrece*
Mac.	*Macbeth*
MM	*Measure for Measure*
MND	*A Midsummer Night's Dream*
MV	*The Merchant of Venice*
Oth.	*Othello*
Per.	*Pericles*
PhT	*The Phoenix and the Turtle*
PP	*The Passionate Pilgrim*
R2	*King Richard the Second*
R3	*King Richard the Third*
Rom.	*Romeo and Juliet*

Shr.	*The Taming of the Shrew*
Son.	*Sonnets* (Riverside)
STM	*Sir Thomas More*
Temp.	*The Tempest*
TGV	*The Two Gentlemen of Verona*
Tim.	*Timon of Athens*
Tit.	*Titus Andronicus*
TN	*Twelfth Night*
TNK	*The Two Noble Kinsmen*
Tro.	*Troilus and Cressida*
Ven.	*Venus and Adonis*
Wiv.	*The Merry Wives of Windsor*
WT	*The Winter's Tale*

2. Editions

Adams	*The Passionate Pilgrim* (facsimile of Folger copy), introduction by Joseph Quincy Adams, 1939
Benson	*Poems: written by Wil. Shakespeare, Gent.*, printed by Thomas Cotes for John Benson, 1640 (*see* Klein)
Booth	*Shakespeare's Sonnets*, ed. Stephen Booth, 1977
Boswell	*Plays and Poems*, ed. James Boswell (with notes by Malone, Steevens, etc.), 1821
Brown	*Poems*, ed. Carleton Brown, 1913
Cambridge	*Works* (Cambridge), ed. W. G. Clark and W. Aldis Wright, 1893
Cotes-Benson	*see* Benson
Craig	*Works* (Oxford), ed. W. J. Craig, 1891
Craig ²	*Poems*, 2 vols., ed. W. J. Craig, 1905
Dowden	*Poems*, ed. E. Dowden, 1903
Dyce	*Poems*, ed. Alexander Dyce, 1832
Feuillerat	*Poems*, ed. Albert Feuillerat, 1927
Gildon	*Poems*, ed. Charles Gildon, 1710
Gildon ²	*Poems*, ed. Charles Gildon, 1714
Herford	*Works*, ed. C. H. Herford, 1899
Hudson	*Works*, ed. H. N. Hudson, 1856
Hudson ²	*Works* (Harvard Shakespeare), ed. H. N. Hudson, 1881
Johnson	*Plays*, ed. Samuel Johnson, 1765
Kerrigan	*The Sonnets and A Lover's Complaint*, ed. John Kerrigan, 1986
Kittredge	*Works*, ed. G. L. Kittredge, 1936
Klein	*Shakespeare: Poems (1640)* (i.e. facsimile of Benson), introduced by H. Klein, 1979

Knight	*Works*, ed. Charles Knight, 1841
Lee	*Works*, ed. Sidney Lee, 1907
Lever	*The Rape of Lucrece*, ed. J. W. Lever, 1971
Lintott	*Poems*, 2 vols., ed. Bernard Lintott, 1709, 1711
Malone	Edmund Malone, *Supplement to the Edition of Shakespeare's Plays published in 1778 by Dr Samuel Johnson and George Steevens*, 2 vols., 1780.
Malone²	*Plays and Poems*, ed. Edmund Malone (with Steevens), 1790
Maxwell	*Poems* (New Shakespeare), ed. J. K. Maxwell, 1966
Pooler	*Poems* (Arden), ed. C. K. Pooler, 2nd edn 1927
Pooler²	*Sonnets and A Lover's Complaint*, ed. C. K. Pooler, 1918
Porter	*Poems*, ed. Charlotte Porter, 1912
Prince	*Poems* (New Arden), ed. F. T. Prince, 1960
Q1	First quarto, *Venus and Adonis*, 1593; *The Rape of Lucrece*, 1594
Q2	Second quarto, *Venus and Adonis*, 1594; *The Rape of Lucrece*, 1598
Q3	Third quarto, *Venus and Adonis*, 1595?; *The Rape of Lucrece*, 1600
Q4	Fourth quarto, *Venus and Adonis*, 1596; *The Rape of Lucrece*, 1600
Q5	Fifth quarto, *Venus and Adonis*, 1599; *The Rape of Lucrece*, 1607
Q6	Sixth quarto, *Venus and Adonis*, 1599; *The Rape of Lucrece*, 1616
Q7	Seventh quarto, *Venus and Adonis*, 1602?; *The Rape of Lucrece*, 1624
Q8	Eighth quarto, *Venus and Adonis*, 1602; *The Rape of Lucrece*, 1632
Q9	Ninth quarto, *Venus and Adonis*, 1602; *The Rape of Lucrece*, 1655
Q10	Tenth quarto, *Venus and Adonis*, 1617
Q11	Eleventh quarto, *Venus and Adonis*, 1620
Q12	Twelfth quarto, *Venus and Adonis*, 1627
Q13	Thirteenth quarto, *Venus and Adonis*, 1630
Q14	Fourteenth quarto, *Venus and Adonis*, 1630
Q15	Fifteenth quarto, *Venus and Adonis*, 1636
Q16	Sixteenth quarto, *Venus and Adonis*, 1675
Ridley	*Works* (New Temple Shakespeare), ed. M. R. Ridley, 1934
Riverside	*Riverside Shakespeare*, textual editor G. Blakemore Evans, 1974
Rollins	*Shakespeare: the Poems* (New Variorum), ed. H. E. Rollins, 1938

Rollins (1612)	*The Passionate Pilgrim* (facsimile of 1612 edn), introduction by H. E. Rollins, 1940
Sewell	*Works*, ed. George Sewell, 1725
Signet	*Complete Shakespeare*, general editor S. Barnet, 1972
Smith	*see* Riverside (poetry section, ed. H. Smith)
Steevens	*see* Malone
Wells–Taylor	*Complete Works*, ed. S. Wells and G. Taylor, 1986, with a separate *Textual Companion* (1987)
White	*Works*, ed. R. G. White, 1865
Wyndham	*Poems*, ed. George Wyndham, 1898

3. Other works, periodicals, general references

Abbott	E. A. Abbott, *A Shakespearian Grammar*, 1869
Aen.	The *Aeneid* of Virgil in *Virgil*, 2 vols. (Loeb), trans. H. R. Fairchild, 1935
Akrigg	G. P. V. Akrigg, *Shakespeare and the Earl of Southampton*, 1968
Alciati	Andrea Alciati, *Emblemata cum Commentariis*, 1531, Padua 1621 (facsimile rpt, 1967)
Alexander	*Elizabethan Narrative Verse*, ed. Nigel Alexander, 1967
Apology	Sir Philip Sidney, *An Apology for Poetry*, ed. G. Shepherd, 1965
Arber	Edward Arber (ed.), *A Transcript of the Registers of the Company of Stationers of London, 1554–1640 A. D.*, 5 vols., 1875–94
Art of Poetry	*Horace: Satires, Epistles, and Ars Poetica* (Loeb), trans. H. R. Fairclough, 1929
AS	Sir Philip Sidney, *Astrophil and Stella*, (*see* Ringler)
AV	The Authorised Version of the King James Bible (1611)
Bradbrook	M. C. Bradbrook, *Shakespeare and Elizabethan Poetry*, 1965
Breton	*The Works in Verse and Prose of Nicholas Breton*, 2 vols., ed. A. B. Grosart, 1879
Brooke	*The Works of Christopher Marlowe*, ed. C. F. Tucker Brooke, 1910
Bullough	*Narrative and Dramatic Sources of Shakespeare*, ed. Geoffrey Bullough, vol. 1, 1957
Bush	Douglas Bush, *Mythology and the Renaissance Tradition in English Poetry*, 1932
Campion	*Complete Poems of Thomas Campion*, ed. W. R. Davis, 1967

Capell MS	Manuscript corrections made by Edward Capell to his copy of Lintott's edition (Trinity College Library, Cambridge)
Carleton Brown	*Poems by Sir John Salusbury and Robert Chester*, ed. Carleton Brown, 1914
Castiglione	Baldassare Castiglione, *The Book of the Courtier*, trans. Sir Thomas Hoby (1561), ed. J. H. Whitfield, 1928
Cercignani	F. Cercignani, *Shakespeare's Works and Elizabethan Pronunciation*, 1981
Chambers	E. K. Chambers, *William Shakespeare. A Study of Facts and Problems*, 2 vols., 1930
Chambers [2]	*The Oxford Book of Sixteenth Century Verse*, ed. E. K. Chambers, 1932
Chaucer	*Works*, ed. F. N. Robinson, second edn, 1957
City of God	*Augustine concerning the City of God against the Pagans*, tr. H. Bettenson, 1972
Coleridge	Samuel T. Coleridge, *Biographia Literaria*, 2 vols., ed. J. Shawcross, 1954
Comes	Natalis Comes, *Mythologiae*, 1551, Venice, 1567 (facsimile rpt, 1976)
conj.	conjecture
CR	*Centennial Review*
CT	*Canterbury Tales* (*see* Chaucer)
Daniel	Samuel Daniel, *Poems and a Defence of Rhyme*, ed. A. Colby Sprague, 1930
De Amore	*Andreas Capellani Regii Francorum De Amore*, ed. E. Trojel, Copenhagen, 1892
Deloney	*Works of Thomas Deloney*, ed. F. O. Mann, 1912
De Luna	*see Willobie his Avisa*
Dent	R. W. Dent, *Shakespeare's Proverbial Language: An Index*, 1981
Donne	*Poems of John Donne*, 2 vols., ed. Sir Herbert Grierson, 1912
Dyer	T. F. T. Dyer, *Folk Lore of Shakespeare*, 1884
edn	edition
EH	*Englands Helicon* (1600)
ELH	*English Literary History*
Eliz. Sonnets	*Elizabethan Sonnets*, ed. Sir Sidney Lee, 2 vols, 1904
Elyot	Sir Thomas Elyot, *The Boke Named the Governour* (1531), ed. S. E. Lehmberg, 1962
Enc. Brit.	*Encyclopaedia Britannica*
Ewig	Wilhelm Ewig, 'Shakespeares *Lucrece*. Eine literarhistorische Untersuchung', *Anglia* 22 (1899), 1 – 32, 343 – 63, 393 – 455

Fairchild	A. H. R. Fairchild, *Shakespeare and the Arts of Design*, 1937
Fairchild [2]	A. H. R. Fairchild, 'The Phoenix and the Turtle', *Englische Studien* 33 (1904), 337–84
Fasti	Ovid, *Fasti* (*see* Bullough)
Feuillerat [2]	A. Feuillerat, *The Prose Works of Sir Philip Sidney*, 4 vols., 1912
Ficino	Marsilio Ficino, *Commentary on Plato's Symposium on Love*, trans. Sears Jayne, 1985
Florio	John Florio, *Italian Dictionary* (1598)
FO	Folger
FQ	Edmund Spenser, *The Faerie Queene* (1596), ed. J. C. Smith, 2 vols., 1912
Fr.	French
Franz	Wilhelm Franz. *Die Sprache Shakespeares*, 1939 (fourth edn of *Shakespeare-Grammatik*)
Fraunce	Abraham Fraunce, *The Third Part of the Countess of Pembrokes Ivychurch, entitled Amintas Dale*, ed. Gerald Snare, 1975
Genetics	T. W. Baldwin, *On the Literary Genetics of Shakespeare's Poems and Sonnets*, 1950
Geneva	Geneva translation of the Bible (1560)
Golding	Arthur Golding, *The .xv. bookes of P. Ovidius Naso, entytuled Metamorphosis* (1567), ed. W. H. D. Rouse, 1904
Gombrich	E. H. Gombrich, *Art and Illusion*, fourth edn, 1972
Gow	A. F. S. Gow, *The Greek Bucolic Poets*, 1952
Greene	*The Life and Complete Works in Prose and Verse of Robert Greene*, ed. A. B. Grosart, 15 vols. 1881–6
Grierson	*see* Donne
Griffin	Bartholomew Griffin, *Fidessa, more chaste than kind* (1596) (*see Eliz. Sonnets*)
Grosart	*The Poems of Robert Chester (1601–11). With verse contributions by Shakespeare, Ben Jonson, George Chapman, John Marston, etc.*, ed. Rev. A. B. Grosart, 1878
Gurr	Andrew Gurr, *The Shakespearean Stage, 1574–1642*, second edn, 1980
HAR	Harleian
Heninger	S. K. Heninger, Jr, *Touches of Sweet Harmony*, 1974
Heroides	Ovid, *Heroides and Amores*, trans. Grant Showerman, 1914
HL	*Hero and Leander* (*see* Brooke)
Homilies	*The seconde tome of homelyes* (1563)
Ital.	Italian

Jackson	MacDonald P. Jackson, *Shakespeare's 'A Lover's Complaint': its Date and Authenticity*, 1965
Jonson	Ben Jonson, *Works*, ed. C. Herford and P. Simpson, 11 vols., 1925–52
Kinnear	*Cruces Shakespearianae*, by B. G. Kinnear, 1883
Kökeritz	H. Kökeritz, *Shakespearian Pronunciation*, 1953
Lat.	Latin
LGW	*Legend of Good Women* (*see* Chaucer)
Livy	Titus Livius, *Ab Urbe Condita*, in *Livy*, trans. B. O. Foster (Loeb), 14 vols., 1919–59
Lodge	Thomas Lodge, *Phillis Honoured with Pastorall Sonnets, Elegies, and amorous delights* (1593)
Lodge [2]	Thomas Lodge, *Complete Works*, 4 vols., 1883 (rpt. 1966)
Mackail	J. W. Mackail, 'A Lover's Complaint', *Essays and Studies* 3 (1912), 51–70
McKerrow	R. B. McKerrow, *Printers' and Publishers' Devices in England and Scotland 1485–1640*, 1949
Marlowe	*see* Brooke
ME	Middle English
Metam.	Ovid, *Metamorphoses* (Loeb), trans. F. J. Miller, 1916 (*see* Golding)
MLR	*Modern Language Review*
Muir	Kenneth Muir, *Shakespeare the Professional and Related Studies*, 1973
Murry	John Middleton Murry, *Discoveries*, 1930
NA	*New Arcadia* (*see* Feuillerat and Skretkowicz)
Nares	Robert Nares, *A Glossary; or, Collection of Words*, 1822
Nashe	*The Works of Thomas Nashe*, ed. R. B. McKerrow, 5 vols., rev. F. P. Wilson, 1958
Neilson	W. A. Neilson, *The Origins and Sources of the Court of Love*, 1899
NM	*New Mermaids* texts of Elizabethan and Jacobean playwrights
N&Q	*Notes and Queries*
NPT	*Nun's Priest's Tale*
ODEP	*Oxford Dictionary of English Proverbs*, ed. F. P. Wilson, third edn, 1970
Odes	*Horace: the Odes and the Epodes* (Loeb), trans. C. E. Bennet, rev. 1927
OE	Old English
OED	*Oxford English Dictionary*
O. Fr.	Old French

Onions	C. T. Onions, *A Shakespeare Glossary*, 1911; rev. by Robert D. Eagleson
Ovid's Elegies	*see* Brooke
Painter	William Painter, *The Pallace of Pleasure* (1566) (*see* Bullough)
Partridge	A. C. Partridge, *A Substantive Grammar of Shakespeare's Nondramatic Texts*, 1976
Partridge, Eric	Eric Partridge, *Shakespeare's Bawdy*, 1971
Partridge, *Orthography*	A. C. Partridge, *Orthography in Shakespeare and Elizabethan Drama*, 1964
Perrow	E. C. Perrow, 'The last will and testament as a form of literature', *Transactions of the Wisconsin Academy of Sciences, Arts, and Letters*, 1913
Petrarch, *Letters*	Petrarch, *Selected Letters*, trans. Morris Bishop, 1966
Plutarch	*The Lives of the Noble Grecians and Romanes*, trans. Sir Thomas North, 1579
PQ	*Philological Quarterly*
Prose	*Francesco Petrarca: Prose*, ed. G. Martellotti and others, Milan-Naples, 1955
Puttenham	George Puttenham, *The Arte of English Poetry*, ed. G. D. Willcock and A. Walker, 1936
Ralegh	*The Poetry of Sir Walter Ralegh*, ed. Agnes M. C. Latham (Muses Library), 1951
Ren & ModS	*Renaissance and Modern Studies*
RES	*Review of English Studies*
rime	Petrarch, *rime sparse*, trans. as *Petrarch's Lyric Poems* by R. M. Durling, 1976
Ringler	*The Poems of Sir Philip Sidney*, ed. W. A. Ringler, 1962
Robertson	J. M. Robertson, *Shakespeare and Chapman*, 1917
Salzman	Paul Salzman, *An Anthology of Elizabethan Prose Fiction*, 1987
SB	*Studies in Bibliography*
Sarrazin	G. Sarrazin, *William Shakespeares Lehrjahre*, 1897
sc.	*scilicet*
Schmidt	Alexander Schmidt, *Shakespeare-Lexicon*, 2 vols., 1874–75
Schoenbaum	S. Schoenbaum, *William Shakespeare: A Compact Documentary Life*, 1977
SEL	*Studies in English Literature*
Shakespeare's England	*Shakespeare's England*, ed. Sir Sidney Lee and C. T. Onions, 2 vols., 1916
Simpson	P. Simpson, *Shakespearian Punctuation*, 1911
Sisson	C. J. Sisson, *New Readings in Shakespeare*, 2 vols., 1965

Skretkowicz	*Sir Philip Sidney: The Countess of Pembroke's Arcadia (The New Arcadia)*, ed. V. Skretkowicz, 1987
Slater	Eliot Slater, 'Shakespeare: word links between poems and plays', *N&Q* 220 (1975), 157–63
Small Latine	T. W. Baldwin, *William Shakspere's Small Latine & Lesse Greeke*, 2 vols., 1944
SMP	Edmund Spenser, *The Minor Poems*, ed. E. de Selincourt, 1910
Sp.	Spanish
Sprague	*see* Daniel
SpS	*Spenser Studies*
Spurgeon	Caroline Spurgeon, *Shakespeare's Imagery and What It Tells Us*, 1935
SQ	*Shakespeare Quarterly*
S. St.	*Shakespeare Studies*
S. Sur.	*Shakespeare Survey*
Staunton	Howard Staunton, 'Unsuspected corruptions of Shakespeare's text', *Atheneum*, 14 March 1874
subst.	substantively
Surrey	*Poems of Henry Howard Earl of Surrey*, ed. Emrys Jones, 1964
TC	*Troilus and Criseyde* (*see* Chaucer)
Tilley	M. P. Tilley, *A Dictionary of the Proverbs in England in the Sixteenth and Seventeenth Centuries*, 1950 (references are to numbered paragraphs)
TLS	*Times Literary Supplement*
TSE	*Texas Studies in English*
Walker	W. S. Walker, *A Critical Examination of the Text of Shakespeare*, ed. W. N. Lettsom, 3 vols., 1860
Weelkes	Thomas Weelkes *Madrigals To 3. 4. 5. and 6, voyces* (1597), in E. H. Fellowes, *English Madrigal Verse*, 1920
Whitney	Geoffrey Whitney, *A Choice of Emblemes*, Leiden, 1586 (ed. H. Green, 1866; reissued 1967)
Willobie his Avisa	*The Queen Declined, An interpretation of Willobie his Avisa, with the Text of the Original Edition*, by B. N. De Luna, 1970
Willoughby	Edwin E. Willoughby, *A Printer of Shakespeare*, 1934
Wyatt	*The Complete Poems of Sir Thomas Wyatt* (Muses Library), ed. K. Muir, 1949

INTRODUCTION

This edition contains the following works of poetry: *Venus and Adonis, The Rape of Lucrece, The Phoenix and the Turtle, The Passionate Pilgrim,* and *A Lover's Complaint.*

In the early 1590s Shakespeare may have felt that he was destined for a career as a poet rather than in the theatre. His two big narrative poems, written within a year of one another in 1593 and 1594, both carry fulsome dedications to the Earl of Southampton. These are the only two works Shakespeare is known to have dedicated to anyone. Securing the patronage of a rich and influential nobleman would have seemed the obvious and most direct way to preferment, and the evidence suggests that this is what he was bent on doing. Yet in the middle of the decade, following the reopening of the theatres after their closure because of the plague, his stage-writing gathered fresh impetus, and he never again wrote narrative poems of the length or ambition of *Venus and Adonis* and *The Rape of Lucrece.*

At the same time as he was writing *Venus and Adonis* he began his sonnet sequence, which was not, however, published until 1609. (The scope and ramifications of the *Sonnets* warrant a separate editorial volume.) Eagerness on the part of contemporary readers to encounter them (we know from Francis Meres's 1598 remark about the 'sugred Sonnets' that they were circulating in manuscript) may well have occasioned the publication of an odd collection calling itself *The Passionate Pilgrim* in 1599, reprinted with additions in 1612. Although it was published under Shakespeare's name, it appeared almost certainly without his authority. This miscellany of twenty sonnets and lyrics contains only five poems which are positively by Shakespeare. Some of the other pieces have been ascribed either with certainty or conjecturally to other authors, and the rest, about half the volume, are by persons unknown. The number of sonnets in the collection on the theme of Venus and Adonis testifies to the enormous popularity of that poem while hinting that the love of Venus for Adonis may have been thought to be the principal subject of the sonnet sequence. Of particular interest is that the two opening sonnets of *The Passionate Pilgrim* are indeed Shakespeare's, since they constitute close enough versions of Sonnets 138 and 144. What gives the collection its continuing value, despite much pseudo-quality, is that it should have included these two examples ten years before any of the other sonnets saw print.

1601 witnessed the appearance of yet another curious collection. This was Robert Chester's *Loves Martyr*, dedicated to Sir John Salusbury and put together by various hands, the most strenuous contributor being Chester himself. The volume contains poems by Ben Jonson, George Chapman, John Marston, and Shakespeare, who contributed *The Phoenix and the Turtle*. It is a further mystery how Shakespeare came to be involved in this poetic symposium, and even harder to decide what his intentions were in the poem itself (see the arguments below, pp. 41–50). It is unique in the

Shakespearean canon and appeared nowhere else in his lifetime (apart from the second printing of Chester's book in 1611); but few have ever doubted his authorship.

Although Shakespeare's *Sonnets* were among the first of his poetic compositions, they were the last of his non-dramatic works to be published, and there is evidence that he continued writing them into the 1600s. When they did finally appear in 1609 they were followed in the same volume by a narrative poem entitled *A Lover's Complaint*, which the publisher also attributed to Shakespeare. For a long time its authenticity was strongly contested. But recent scholarship has made emphatic advances in favour of its being by Shakespeare, and the poem is now confidently regarded as his. Its date of composition is still under dispute, estimates ranging from the mid-1590s to as late as the year of publication, though a majority prefers the beginning of the 1600s. Arguments have recently been put forward favouring a return to the formula of its first publication, i.e. placing it once again with the *Sonnets* (see below, p. 61). However, one of the principles of the present edition is to observe the generic links and similarities between the poems; from this perspective, bearing as it does the dual influence of the Ovidian and complaint traditions, *A Lover's Complaint* stands interestingly between *Venus and Adonis* and *The Rape of Lucrece*.

The poem of ninety-five lines that begins 'Shall I die?', and that had hitherto existed in manuscript only, has been included by Wells–Taylor in the new Oxford *Complete Works* and in their *Original-Spelling Edition* as an authentic Shakespearean piece. Following the poem in the same scribal (Secretary) hand appears the signature 'William Shakespeare'. The early seventeenth-century manuscript collection which contains it is Rawlinson Poetical MS 160 in the Bodleian Library.

The confident endorsement of the poem's attribution by Taylor (*TLS* 20 December 1985) gave rise to a keen scholarly exchange. For the debate see *TLS* 20 December 1985–31 January 1986, in particular R. H. Robbins's reply of 20 December 1985. Wells–Taylor marshal the arguments in favour of the poem's authenticity in their *Textual Companion* (pp. 450–4). For opposing arguments see Donald W. Foster, '"Shall I die?" Post mortem: defining *Shakespeare*' (*SQ* 38 (1987), 58–77), and Thomas A. Pendleton, 'The non-Shakespearian language of '"Shall I die"' (*RES* New Series, 15 no. 159 (1989), 323–51).

I have not included the poem in this edition because I am not persuaded it is Shakespeare's.[1]

The danger of including works of dubious attribution is that habit builds on habit. The inclusion of the 'Shall I die?' verses by Oxford has in turn made way for the adoption as canonical of various slight funerary verses popularly, but with no great plausibility, ascribed to Shakespeare from the early seventeenth century. One of these, the epitaph on Elias James, is also found in the Bodleian manuscript, from which Malone printed it for its curiosity value in his Prolegomena to the 1790 *Plays and Poems*. It is

---

[1] When this edition first appeared the only other editor to have had time to respond to Wells–Taylor's proposals was the Penguin editor, Maurice Evans, who printed the verses, though evidently with some reluctance. See *William Shakespeare: The Narrative Poems* (1989), pp. 62–6. Since then other editions have appeared, all of which, with one exception, have opted for various reasons to print them, either centrally or in an appendix. See below, pp. 79–80.

therefore all the more interesting that he should have ignored the manuscript's other attribution. As for this and other epitaphs and the like verses (see also below, p. 46), it still seems sensible to share Chambers's caution (I, 550–5); accordingly they have not been reproduced here.

The themes treated by the two long narrative poems exercised an extraordinary power over the Renaissance artistic imagination. The illustrations included in this edition serve as iconographic comments on certain of the significant and dramatic moments in the poems.

Venus and Adonis

THE POEM

By virtue of its exuberant stylistic confidence, *Venus and Adonis* has always been recognised as a leading example of the erotic narrative tradition. It shares with Marlowe's *Hero and Leander*, with which it is often compared, a brilliance and accomplishment which other poems in the genre imitate but do not match. With these two effortlessly fluent masterpieces English poetic *sprezzatura* comes of age. Discerning compatriots would have leafed through their pages with feelings of incredulous admiration and pride. Later, Romantic poets such as Keats and Coleridge gave special praise to *Venus and Adonis* for its quickness of wit, imaginative bravura, and liveliness of detail.

Sidney's belief in the power of art over nature, a dominant credo of the period, finds itself repeatedly vindicated.[1] Take for example the famous stanza describing Adonis's horse:

> Look when a painter would surpass the life
> In limning out a well-proportioned steed,
> His art with nature's workmanship at strife,
> *As if the dead the living should exceed–*
>   So did this horse excel a common one,
>   In shape, in courage, colour, pace, and bone,   (289–94; my italics)

The purpose of such descriptions is to bring out the life of things in such a way as to exceed even the power of life itself. Keats writes to his friend Reynolds on the celebrated snail image (1033–4) that Shakespeare 'has left nothing to say about nothing or anything' (see commentary). Coleridge puts a similar point differently when he commends Shakespeare's subtlety in rendering vivid detail: 'You seem to be told nothing, but to see and hear everything.'[2] Such observations suggest that not a little of the poem's appeal lies in its convincing evocation of a living moment. Yet the argument that life as portrayed in poetry excels natural life brings us back to the poem's art. Much of its power derives from its verbal dexterity, not just in hitting off successful details such as

---

[1] See *Apology*, p. 100. Sidney develops Horace (*Art of Poetry*, lines 408–15) who sees the two as necessary to each other.
[2] Coleridge, II, p. 15.

the evocation of the horse (259–300), or the snail simile (1033–34), but in the way in which words play on each other.

Much of this has to do with the role played by rhetoric in shaping the poetic character of *Venus and Adonis*. For the Elizabethans rhetoric constituted one of the great discoveries of antiquity. Perhaps 'the application of rhetoric' is a better way of putting the matter, since the precepts of classical orators such as Quintilian and Cicero had been available throughout the Middle Ages. What is curious about the application of rhetorical principle in Elizabethan poetry is that it differs in manner even from the ancients whose principles it revives. Latin poets such as Virgil, Ovid, and Horace indisputably observe the relations of words to each other and produce effects comparable to those described and recommended in theories of oratory. Yet the Elizabethans' self-conscious display of wit in creating verbal effects exceeds anything in classical literature and is probably greater than in contemporary Europe. Petrarch certainly knew how to pun, as his wordplay on the name Laura makes clear, but Elizabethan poetic punning seems to be of unprecedented intensity. Not only the pun but the stylish use of a wide range of rhetorical tropes characterises the poetry of the 1590s. Even Wyatt, who puns frequently, does not display anything like the variety of figures of speech which occur in the opening sonnets of *Astrophil and Stella*. And of course this dexterity is not confined to the genre of poetry: verbal virtuosity is the distinguishing mark of *Love's Labour's Lost* (written probably between 1593 and 1595). Neither ancient comedy nor the comedy of another contemporary European literature demonstrates wordplay on so sophisticated a scale. The fact that linguistic principles in Spain, Italy, or France were at the time comparatively more settled may account to some degree for the uniqueness of the English position. As studies of Shakespeare's vocabulary have shown (see below with respect to *A Lover's Complaint*), the English language was expanding at a considerable rate and its grammatical and syntactical character undergoing fundamental modification.[1] Culturally England had absorbed the impact of the Reformation and was a strong independent Protestant country within a geographical alignment of states dominated by Catholicism. In such circumstances it is not surprising that the trope of oxymoron, or antithesis, inherited from Petrarchan poetry, should register changes in how it was used and a marked increase in frequency. Punning similarly indicates division or unsettled meaning. When Venus pleads for a kiss from Adonis she puns on the different senses of the word 'seal':

> Pure lips, sweet seals in my soft lips imprinted,
> What bargains may I make still to be sealing?   (511–12)

The word means variously the sign of authority which certifies a document and the conclusion of a bargain. Hinted at is the idea of things being sealed in silence, or made impermeable. Such punning works antithetically in that it enables a range of meanings to be comprehended at once (which no other deployment of language can do), while

---

[1] The claim being made here is not that English possessed greater resourcefulness than other contemporary literary languages (the writings of Rabelais would sufficiently rebut that), but rather that certain tropes, and above all the habit of punning, occur in English at a special rate and in an accentuated manner.

reminding us pointedly that meanings contradict and conflict with each other. Sealing a bargain denotes an agreement between equals, whereas the privileging seal of a king denotes inequality; the official pomp and display of a documentary seal differs from the furtive sealing of lips to keep a secret. The pun accordingly signals the ideal capacity of language to bring different and discordant meanings together while yet underlining the divisions that exist in reality. Poetry such as that of *Venus and Adonis* keeps uppermost in mind the relationship between the word and the world. The differences separating Venus and Adonis, differences of temperament, inclination, and disposition, differences in ethical outlook (including each's own internal contradictions), cannot be resolved by the debating parties within the poem nor in the judgement of its readers. Attempting to take a consistent ethical reading of, for example, Venus's sensuality is bound to fail. The play of language in the poem sees to that. The subversions of wordplay are no trite affair, nor are they mere surface merriment. For wordplay is not, as we have just seen, only divisive (though current fashions in linguistic theory concerning instability would insist that it was). It provides the only solution there is – an aesthetic one, which is beyond the scope of continuous, unfinished, formless action. The language of the poem encapsulates human reality, fragmented, inconclusive, and frustrating, and submits it to the order of art. If we are to see an ideal principle in the poem it is this: not an approved human choice as represented by one of the protagonists more than the other, for the poem does not ultimately evaluate such things, but a balanced contemplation of feelings, motives, and actions from contrasting or opposing angles.

Venus and Adonis is both a tragic and a comic poem. Because people are affected differently by it, and differently at different times, responses vary; we have already noted some of them. Like all poems which seem in any way to advocate sexual licence, its sensuality is held against it. Venus has powerful detractors, such as C. S. Lewis and Don Cameron Allen,[1] who argue that Shakespeare expects us to disapprove of her. We cannot do that any more than we can disapprove of Adonis. If we were to reverse allegiances, for instance, and say that Venus expressed the poem's essential spirit of exuberance, then we would be forced to include Adonis's courser along with her, the logic of this being, to adapt Sidney, 'to wish ourselves a horse' (*Apology*, p. 95). It is important, therefore, to distinguish between the overall character of the poem and locally occurring statements or appeals.

But how does the poem affect us by and large? It works by contraries, celebrating the principle of erotic pleasure embodied in Venus while countering this with that refinement of spirit expressed in Adonis. Between the two polarities degrees of approximation can be observed. Adonis's integrity is tempered by his childish petulance over the loss of his horse (325–6); but such chafing and lowering of brows is none the less attractive, as Venus finds. Venus's voluptuous appeal is qualified by her disingenuousness; yet that aspect of her too finds an answering chord in the reader who is no longer sexually innocent. The erotic principle, embodied in Venus, is never confused with mere lasciviousness, as it is in Marston's more voyeuristic poem, *The Metamorphosis*

---

[1] See Lewis, *English Literature*, pp. 498–9; and Allen, 'On *Venus and Adonis*' in *Elizabethan and Jacobean Studies*, pp. 100–11.

1   Titian's *Venus and Adonis*

of Pigmalion's Image. Nor, despite attempts to link the poem with Nashe's salacious *Choise of Valentines* (see below, p. 12), is there much to satisfy pornographic inclination. The closest the poem comes to this is the moment when Venus sketches for Adonis a picture of sensual possibilities:

> 'Fondling', she saith, 'since I have hemmed thee here
> Within the circuit of this ivory pale,
> I'll be a park, and thou shalt be my deer:
> Feed where thou wilt, on mountain or in dale;
>   Graze on my lips, and if those hills be dry,
>   Stray lower, where the pleasant fountains lie.   (229–34)

Even as she holds out the prospect of her body as a place in which to graze she turns the grazer from an eager scavenger into a timid animal finding refuge from 'tempest and from rain'. The duality of such imagery keeps a constant balance between the twin appeal of erotic enjoyment and tender restraint, the poem shifting back and forth easily between the two. Its success depends on neither principle's becoming dominant.

But there is a moment when the balance may seem to be upset and the ethical question matter more. This comes when Venus manages to prolong her kissing of Adonis, enacting for herself something of the enjoyment she promises him in the stanza quoted above:

> Now quick desire hath caught the yielding prey,
> And glutton-like she feeds, yet never filleth;
> Her lips are conquerors, his lips obey,
> Paying what ransom the insulter willeth,
> > Whose vulture thought doth pitch the price so high
> > That she will draw his lips' rich treasure dry.
>
> And having felt the sweetness of the spoil,
> With blindfold fury she begins to forage;
> Her face doth reek and smoke, her blood doth boil,
> And careless lust stirs up a desperate courage,
> > Planting oblivion, beating reason back,
> > Forgetting shame's pure blush and honour's wrack.   (547–58)

These stanzas touch on the more troubling side of sexuality, namely the process whereby possession leads to loss, or, in this precise instance, how the grip of desire removes rational control, which constitutes human dignity. The description matters less as an account of Venus's attempt to ravish Adonis, and more as an indication of how the self is lost as brute instinct gains ground – 'reason', 'shame', and 'honour', all signs of self-consciousness, being temporarily obliterated. Such moments derive their inspiration in part from the *Metamorphoses*, which repeatedly shows characters undergoing transformation as a result of a sexual encounter, most famously in the pursuit of Daphne by Apollo in Book I. This frightened virgin escapes her fate at the god's hands by being changed into a tree; the subsequent flowering symbolises the irresistible force of sex, which, though denied its immediate object, does involve an enforced change in her condition: Daphne gives up her maidenly freedom to come and go as she pleases, and takes root. Without going so far as to enforce a physical change in his protagonists as they experience passion (Adonis only flowers in death), Shakespeare none the less portrays the powerful psychological transformation which a person temporarily undergoes in the grip of sexual longing. The same argument is applied more despairingly in *The Rape of Lucrece* and in *Sonnet* 129:

> Savage, extreme, rude, cruel, not to trust,
> Enjoy'd no sooner but despised straight,
> Past reason hunted, and no sooner had,
> Past reason hated,

and further,

> Mad in pursuit, and in possession so,
> Had, having, and in quest to have extreme,
> A bliss in proof, and prov'd, a very woe,
> Before, a joy propos'd, behind, a dream.   (*Sonnet* 129. 4–7, 9–12)

The difference between these observations and those of the passage quoted from *Venus and Adonis* is that Venus never experiences the 'having'. She is on the point of but never possesses 'bliss'. However furiously her face may reek, such 'desperate courage' never fully confronts conscience, for the sexual act remains unconsummated, 'unhad'. Within a couple of stanzas of her leaving off kissing him Adonis tells Venus that tomorrow he means to hunt the boar:

> whereat a sudden pale,
> Like lawn being spread upon the blushing rose,
> Usurps her cheek; she trembles at his tale,
> And on his neck her yoking arms she throws.
> She sinketh down, still hanging by his neck;
> He on her belly falls, she on her back.   (589–94)

At this point the poem fully recovers its tone of tender comedy and pathos, and the recovery is made possible by the fact that desire remains unglutted. The voracious Venus of only a moment before adopts a more passive posture. Even as she 'devours' Adonis the narrative varies the significance of her action and its effect upon him by introducing images which would be unthinkable in a sonnet such as 129 and inappropriate to *The Rape of Lucrece:*

> Hot, faint, and weary with her hard embracing,
> Like a wild bird being tamed with too much handling,
> Or as the fleet-foot roe that's tired with chasing,
> Or like the froward infant stilled with dandling,
> He now obeys.   (559–63)

Taming is injurious to a wild bird, though it is kind to calm a tetchy child; a deer at the beginning of a chase is eagerly hunted, but when seen at the end, exhausted, it arouses pity. This process of revising analogies places a check on those images which maintain an idea of the brutality of appetite, so that not only do they modify the impression of a threatened Adonis conjured earlier, but at least one of them even justifies Venus's attentions.

One of the poem's most discerning and judicious critics, Hallett Smith, finds that the provincialism of such images makes it the inferior of *Hero and Leander* for sophistication:

There is nothing like the variety of color, of surface finish, that Marlowe's poem exhibits. And curiously, Shakespeare's queen of love herself seems considerably less divine than the semi-human figures of Hero and Leander.   (*Elizabethan Poetry*, p. 86)

The maternal Venus observed above supports Smith's impression, as does the occasional gawkiness of Adonis. Yet while Shakespeare's poem may defer to Marlowe's on the point of surface accomplishment (Hero's costume and Leander's anatomy are both richly evoked in comparison with the largely undescribed persons of Venus and Adonis), as a poem of atmosphere and mood rather than of expressive detail it shows a capacity for introspection lacking in the earlier work. This has again to do with Coleridge's instructive observation (quoted above), 'You seem to be told nothing, but to see and hear everything', but also with Shakespeare's more sympathetic narrative stance, which shares the hopes and frustrations of Venus equally with the youthful, naive idealism of Adonis. By contrast, Marlowe's amused and caustic commentator keeps a knowing distance from both his protagonists, whom he regards as equally untutored. His point of view (to invoke a Jamesian term) is provided by the mature, homosexual Neptune, whose desire for Leander is more self-confident than desperate. Marlowe gives the impression of knowing all the answers, whereas Shakespeare's narrator shows slightly more concern to explore the questions. Shakespeare, who allows freer play to instinct, filtering his theme less than Marlowe through the lens of scepticism, creates a dimension of pathos as the action moves from the common Marlovian ground of inadvertent slapstick to that of the brutality of chance and accident at the moment in which the boar catches Adonis unawares. In their different and opposing ways both Venus and Adonis exercise the freedom nature offers to take one's pleasure according to one's inclination. But what she senses, and what he is still too young to have learnt, is equally true: nature's freedom recognises no distinction of value or intention; violent accidents or impulses also share it. The world that acknowledges the force of Venus's sexual appeal is the same one that includes the boar's mindless savagery. This is not to say, as is often claimed, that the two are identifiable, or that the boar stands as an allegory for an essential destructiveness in Venus's passion; but they are in some respects coextensive: what nature permits the one she must allow to the other.

The effect of pathos is realised variously in the depiction of the two principals, partly in the not-altogether callow innocence of the youth (see for example Adonis's condemnation of lust in lines 793–810), but also in Venus herself, who renounces her procreative advocacy following the death of the boy, prophesying instead that love will henceforth act cruelly and arbitrarily. To some degree Shakespeare follows the practice of classical authors in observing this contradictory behaviour of a deity: a goddess being still a woman and therefore subject to whim might turn petulant when crossed, acting out of character and even contrary to her own interests. But that does not sufficiently explain the force of Venus's dire prediction, which issues in a spirit of lament as much as threat, as if she is discovering that things have changed beyond her control. It is not Adonis now but fate that has crossed her, and, understanding this, she declares her new-found opposition to love as much in terms of a submission to destiny as an edict of her own rule:

> Since thou art dead, lo, here I prophesy,
> Sorrow on love hereafter shall attend;
> It shall be waited on with jealousy,
> Find sweet beginning, but unsavoury end;
>   Ne'er settled equally, but high or low,
>   That all love's pleasure shall not match his woe.   (1135–40)

In the attempted 'rape' scene, as the prospect of raging sexuality gradually fades, it is followed by a series of statements which appear to vindicate Venus in terms of *carpe florem*:

2   Giorgione's *Sleeping Venus*. 'For on the grass she lies as she were slain' (*Ven.* 473)

> What wax so frozen but dissolves with temp'ring,
> And yields at last to every light impression?
> Things out of hope are compassed oft with vent'ring,
> Chiefly in love, whose lease exceeds commission:
>   Affection faints not like a pale-faced coward,
>   But then woos best when most his choice is froward.
>
> When he did frown, O had she then gave over,
> Such nectar from his lips she had not sucked.
> Foul words and frowns must not repel a lover:
> What though the rose have prickles, yet 'tis plucked.
>   Were beauty under twenty locks kept fast,
>   Yet love breaks through, and picks them all at last.   (565–76)

As she sinks fainting at the news of what he intends the next day, she finds herself at last lying beneath him; this is enough to revive her, but to no avail:

> Now is she in the very lists of love,
> Her champion mounted for the hot encounter.
> All is imaginary she doth prove;
> He will not manage her, although he mount her:
>   That worse than Tantalus' is her annoy,
>   To clip Elizium and to lack her joy.   (595–600)

The broad comedy secures the complete release of the poem from the darker effects that temporarily cloud it. In *The Rape of Lucrece*, as we shall see, such disturbances are not negotiated so lightly, and there is to be no similar recovery of equilibrium; but *Venus and Adonis* maintains its tone by restricting blame to fortune and the laws of mortality while steadily reducing the role of conscience.

It would be overstating matters to say that the poem presents us with a vision of the golden age longed for by Tasso, in which 'S'ei piace, ei lice' (i.e. 'if it gives pleasure, it is lawful'). Like the *Aminta*, from which this statement of pleasure as natural law comes, Shakespeare's protagonists experience the frustration that characterises the pastoral mode. In a true golden age pleasure is indeed lawful and according to the will of nature; but in a fallen age nature works contrarily, encouraging pleasure on the one hand while denying it on the other.

Venus might be regarded less as a goddess than as a creature from a perfect world who has strayed into a lesser one, and has to adjust to different principles. 'Nature never set forth the earth in so rich tapestry as divers poets have done; neither with pleasant rivers, fruitful trees, sweet-smelling flowers, nor whatsoever else may make the too much loved earth more lovely. Her world is brazen, the poets only deliver a golden' (*Apology*, p. 100). Sidney reminds us that what is golden is the *poem* which takes command of the fragmentary nature of experience and gives it perfect expression. Coleridge speaks of 'the power of reducing multitude into unity of effect, and modifying a series of thoughts by some one predominant thought or feeling'. The rhetorical, self-conscious, artificial style of *Venus and Adonis* succeeds in rendering instinct more instinctual and life more lively than our inchoate responses perceive it to be.

The poem ends in the only way that will permit unqualified sympathy for each of the protagonists: Adonis dying pointlessly and prematurely, Venus grieving for him but still unloved. Differences of moral outlook are settled in the grim destiny which, as nothing else can, draws them close to one another. It is not exactly that we should now discount the ethical debate which was so prominent earlier; but we are shown that the moral sense is too closely bound up with the experience of living to be able to judge it in detachment.

Coleridge long ago laid the ghost of the moral problem (though it is never entirely still):

Hence it is, that from the perpetual activity of attention required on the part of the reader; from the rapid flow, the quick change, and the playful nature of the thoughts and images; and above all from the alienation, and . . . the utter *aloofness* of the poet's own feelings, from those of which he is at once the painter and the analyst; that though the very subject cannot but detract from the pleasure of a delicate mind, yet never was a poem less dangerous on a moral account.

(Coleridge, pp. 15–16)

As the examples cited from the text have perhaps made clear, Shakespeare feels closer to his protagonists than Coleridge, bound by a more stringent public morality, dares to allow. We need no longer look for excuses on this account. But Coleridge is entirely right in directing attention to the spirit and energy which inform artistic principles, and in reminding us that the imperfections and contradictions experienced by human nature find in art a sustaining fullness of meditation.

BIOGRAPHICAL CONSIDERATIONS

The first and by no means the least significant observation to make about the two narrative poems, *Venus and Adonis* and *The Rape of Lucrece*, is that Shakespeare wrote them when he was on familiar terms with the Earl of Southampton in 1593 and 1594. This much we know from the two letters of dedication printed at the head of each poem. Southampton was a coming man in the decade of the 1590s, and Shakespeare was not alone in regarding him as a promising Maecenas. The lexicographer John Florio dedicated his *Worlde of Wordes* (1598) to him, and Barnabe Barnes commended his sonnet sequence *Parthenophil and Parthenope* with a further sonnet extolling Southampton's 'gracious eyes' ('Those heavenly lamps which give the Muses light'), thereby exhorting the earl to 'view my Muse with your judicial sight'.[1]

In the lower reaches of the literary trade, Thomas Nashe fortified his risky venture of publishing a sensational prose romance, *The Unfortunate Traveller*, with a flattering epistolary account of Southampton's helpful attitude; and he may also have made him a gift of his pornographic poem *A Choise of Valentines*.[2] Nashe appears to follow Shakespeare in writing a letter (rather than the more formal sonnet) in craving the earl's indulgence, his dedication to *The Unfortunate Traveller* even imitating some of the stylistic flourishes of Shakespeare's address to Southampton at the beginning of *Venus and Adonis*.

Akrigg in his biography suggests that Southampton had set about establishing a literary circle which would emulate the one which had held sway a generation before, namely that of Sir Philip Sidney and the Countess of Pembroke, whose family he joined in a remote connection by marrying Essex's cousin.[3] A young man of undoubted charm and promise (he was still only nineteen when *Venus and Adonis* was published), assuredly more in tune with the dawning era of the theatre than Sidney's moralistic sister, and privileged by his sex to associate with men of the stage, Southampton seemed an ideal patron for figures like Nashe and Shakespeare, in their pursuance of the uncertain, often perilous profession of letters. In the event, things did not work out so well. The earl came to show more of an interest in a military and political career than in the arts, and, unlike Sidney with whom he had soldiership in common, he was no poet himself. More to the point, he was often in debt and unable to make the financial returns hoped for by sycophantic authors (which may explain why Nashe's dedication disappears from

---

[1] Akrigg, p. 184.
[2] The poem carries sonnets addressed to 'Lord S'. Some editors think this must be Southampton, but others incline to Ferdinando, Lord Strange (see Akrigg, p. 38). Nashe may have been prompted in his choice of Southampton by the 'racy' *Venus and Adonis*: as Gabriel Harvey commented. 'The younger sort takes much delight in Shakespeare's Venus and Adonis: but his Lucrece, & his tragedie of Hamlet, Prince of Denmarke, have it in them to please the wiser sort' (*Shakspere Allusion-Book*, 1, 56).
[3] See Akrigg, pp. 184–5. In 1596 Thomas Wilson dedicated to Southampton his translation of Montemayor's pastoral romance *Diana*, which had exercised a strong seminal influence on Sidney's *Arcadia*.

the second edition, published the same year).[1] On coming of age late in 1594 (the hour of Nashe's and Shakespeare's expectancy), he was saddled with two large expenses: one a payment to the Crown for the transfer of his lands, the other a fine for the staggering sum of £5,000 which he was obliged to pay Lord Burghley upon failing to honour a contract to marry the latter's granddaughter (Akrigg, pp. 38–9).

It was probably the closure of the theatres in 1593, consequent on the outbreak of the plague, that caused Shakespeare, who was already the author of several plays, to turn to poetry and Southampton's patronage in the first place. Coinciding with this is the point that Shakespeare in the early 1590s, the time of the sonnet vogue, could not yet be certain that his future lay in the theatre. As an erotic narrative, *Venus and Adonis* imitates the form made popular by Lodge (*Scillaes Metamorphosis*, 1589) and cultivated by Marlowe, who, despite his dramatic successes, put a good deal of creative energy into *Hero and Leander* (1593; published 1598), thought to be his last work. The sonnet and the narrative poem together held the field in the early 1590s. However, an entry in the Queen's treasurer's accounts for March 1595 identifies Shakespeare as a member of the Lord Chamberlain's players who had performed before her Majesty the previous Christmas.[2] The theatre was active again, and Shakespeare had resumed his career as dramatist and performer. He and Southampton were going their separate ways.[3]

Yet this is not the last sighting we take of the earl in connection with Shakespeare, for the poem itself appears to convey a few hints.

Within the impersonal concerns of theme and artistry, a few possibly biographical notes may be struck. Adonis is treated throughout the poem with a mixture of humour and affection which might suggest that Shakespeare had a real person in mind. The Hilliard portrait leaves us in no doubt as to Southampton's youthful beauty. Further significance may attach to the use of the name of Narcissus, invoked by Venus as she despairingly urges him to follow his procreative instincts.[4] Southampton's reluctance to marry Burghley's granddaughter (already mentioned in connection with financial difficulties) possibly struck contemporaries as a sign of fastidiousness. Did, as some have supposed, Burghley's employee John Clapham write his Latin poem *Narcissus* (1591) as an indirect rebuke to the young ditherer (see Supplementary Notes to *Venus and Adonis*)? But along with Shakespeare's teasing of the boy goes a certain measure of regard for the principles he espouses. His expostulation on love, which he insists to Venus is not at all the same thing as lust (see *Ven.* 787–804), portrays an Adonis who

---

[1] In fairness to Nashe and Shakespeare it must be said that they did try to cultivate a personal relationship, unlike some authors who cheerfully used the scattershot principle of dedicating their work to everybody who might prove useful (e.g. Henry Lok, who in 1597 published a sequence of religious verses with commendatory sonnets to Southampton and fifty-nine other worthies).

[2] See Schoenbaum, p. 184.

[3] In the seventeenth century, following a change in the cultural climate as well as in his personal fortunes, Southampton received works of a more overtly religious nature, such as Sylvester's *Memorials of Mortalitie* (1615) or one Thomas Ailesbury's *Paganisme and Papisme* (1624) (Akrigg, pp. 150 and 172).

[4] Shakespeare applies this very argument to the young man of the *Sonnets* (specifically 1–17), which naturally raises the question whether Southampton may be identified with him. The evidence is strong but by no means conclusive, and other plausible candidates exist. It may also be that, as with certain of Shakespeare's plays, an idea once engendered (whether through a biographical impulse or not) recurs as a theme elsewhere.

is both touchingly naive and yet admirably pure of heart. Is Shakespeare tempering whatever criticism may be implied by the Narcissus analogy with a more flattering appraisal? The picture he presents of Adonis is more complex than that of Ovid's thoughtless young blood who indulges the goddess's passion but then recklessly goes off and gets himself killed hunting the boar (*Metam.* 10. 708ff.). And the requiem for the youth sung by the Shakespearean Venus, who insists on his Orphic qualities (see below and 1093–1104n), similarly exceeds any claim that Ovid makes on his behalf. Yet even to introduce Ovid into the discussion is to acknowledge that arguments concerning the biographical aspects of *Venus and Adonis* are limited in the information and insights they afford, and it is to the literary questions posed by the poem that we need to turn.

THE LITERARY CONTEXT AND TRADITION

Popular from the thirteenth century onwards, Ovid came into new and vital contact with English poetry as a result of Arthur Golding's translation of the mythologically exciting *Metamorphoses* in 1567. Further editions followed in 1575, 1584, and 1587, attesting to the impact of Golding's work. Unlike an epic such as the *Aeneid*, Ovid's poem conveniently divides into numerous discrete episodes involving perennially fascinating topics such as frustrated passion, incest, rape, and murder, all of which, including the last, are aspects of its erotic character. In addition, the overall theme of transformation or change of identity makes for keen psychological interest. With Ovid the epic's customary sphere of action broadens to include something of a more reflective dimension, so that the poet seems not merely to be presenting a startling event but also musing on what may underlie its occurrence. The sonnet, first in the hands of Petrarch and as adopted subsequently in England by Wyatt, Sidney, Spenser, Shakespeare, and notably John Donne, had already shown a disposition towards psychological reflectiveness, and the Ovidian epyllion (as these erotic narrative poems have become known)[1] made such explorative possibilities further available. What masterpieces in the form such as *Hero and Leander* or *Venus and Adonis* typically show is the encounter between two lovers, or would-be lovers, and the invariably tragic aftermath of their *innamoramento*. Tragedy, rather than romance, is the other main element of the epyllion, and is the stuff of such plays as *Romeo and Juliet*, which Shakespeare could have written either before *Venus and Adonis* or, more likely, a year or two after *The Rape of Lucrece*. The poems deal exclusively in terms of the amorous encounter, omitting the social and political framework,[2] but, like the drama, they depict the lovers as two characters who in their separate ways register the effect of passion upon them. The fullness of characterisation, especially as undertaken by both Shakespeare and Marlowe, far exceeds anything contemplated by Ovid, as is shown by the length of the Elizabethan treatment of the fable which characteristically extends Ovid's one or two hundred lines into a poem of over a thousand. At the same time, it must be recognised that the Elizabethan poet did not limit his adaptation of Ovid to the *Metamorphoses*. *Hero and Leander* derives not from this poem but from Ovid's *Heroides* (Heroic Ones), the theme of which is the writing of love epistles. Usually, the letters are sent by despairing women

---

[1] 'Epyllion' is in fact a nineteenth-century descriptive term and means 'little epic'. The Elizabethans, who did not distinguish genre so precisely, used variously such terms as 'history', 'fable', or 'poem'.

[2] *Lucrece* belongs to the 'complaint' rather than the Ovidian genre – see below, p. 38.

3   Bartholomäus Spranger's *Venus and Adonis* Spranger's painting followed the publication of Shakespeare's poem by a couple of years, though it is unlikely that he knew it. His self-confidently voluptuous goddess, who all but eclipses her mortal lover, resembles the Venus of the early part of the poem where she is at her most enticing. By contrast, Titian's matronly, beseeching goddess is more like the Venus of the poem's latter stages

to men who are either fickle or indifferent; but in a few cases, notably in that of Hero and Leander, the expression of love is mutual.[1] In these imaginary lovers' epistles Ovid fully depicts the anguish and passion of the human heart, giving Renaissance poets such as Marlowe and Shakespeare plenty of instruction in the form.

Another point at issue is that the *Heroides* treats of love affairs conducted between mortals, as is the case with Hero and Leander. Venus and Adonis differs from this in that one of the principals is a goddess. Notwithstanding, Shakespeare's treatment of Venus's passion for Adonis closely resembles Marlowe in spirit, while his shrinking-violet boy represents the kind of male beauty Marlowe extols in Leander. Similarly, Leander, while swimming to Sestos to keep his assignation with Hero, finds himself in the embrace of the sea-god Neptune, who has something of Venus's single-minded approach to love. Marlowe, like Shakespeare, freely mingles gods and mortals in his poem; in so doing both Elizabethan poets observe the ease with which ancient Greek and Roman deities inhabit a human landscape. The differing status of Venus and Adonis matters less than the gulf in passion that divides them, Venus's superiority as a divinity underscoring the irony and pathos of her plight as a beseeching wooer.

Venus and Adonis draws on various characteristics of Ovid, and while Ovid recounts this tale in the *Metamorphoses*, it is his talent for developing a mood of erotic hope and suspense in the *Heroides* (where the writers of the letters do not of course yet know the outcome of their passionate hopes) that Shakespeare drew upon for such episodes as Venus's attempt to seduce Adonis in the early part of the poem and her terrified intimation of his fate at the end.

Comparing Shakespeare and Marlowe (who was an accomplished classicist and trans-lator, as his version of Ovid's *Amores* demonstrates) brings up the vexed question of Shakespeare's own prowess as a translator and the problem of his apparent dependence on Golding for his understanding of the *Metamorphoses*. Baldwin has shown decisively that Shakespeare had a good reading knowledge of Roman poetry and would have been capable of reading the famous episodes of Ovid without an intermediary.[2] What, then, was Golding's function? To some extent he undoubtedly did make the task of reading Ovid that much easier; and if, as is fairly sure, Shakespeare used him as a crib, he would not have felt abashed by it. But Golding is more interesting as an inspiration than as a source; and it is in his role as a model of stylistic emulation rather than as a purveyor of classical tales that he deserves to be considered.

In the first decade of Elizabeth's reign, English poetry had a considerable distance to travel before it could claim to be the equal of other contemporary European literatures, to say nothing of the classics. Yet it is precisely the spirit of emulation which we see at work as the age begins that produces such treatises as Sidney's famous *Apology for Poetry* and Samuel Daniel's *A Defence of Rhyme*. Beginning with Italy, each of the major literatures which can be counted a part of the European Renaissance had to undergo the process of absorbing the influence of the ancient literature it sought to emulate

---

[1] As it is also, for example, in the letters between Paris and Helen, translated by Thomas Heywood and included in the expanded 1612 edition of *The Passionate Pilgrim* (see below, pp. 58–9).
[2] See *Small Latine*, 2.417–55.

while at the same time breaking the shackles which such an influence imposed. To do as the Romans was no good if that merely produced a stale, inkhorn imitation of the original. The solution was, as Bembo in Italy and Du Bellay in France both argued, to renew the vernacular in such a way as to incorporate the most characteristic strengths of the imitated language while enabling the native tongue to realise its own identity, and in particular its capacity for sophistication.[1] The results were mixed and sometimes controversial, but, as we know, the enterprise succeeded. European literary languages did gradually come into their own as the fifteenth and sixteenth centuries progressed, and as a way of exhorting his countrymen to emulate recent Italian successes, Daniel pointed to the example of Petrarch:

his twelve Æglogues, his *Affrica* . . . with his three Bookes of Epistles in Latine verse, showe all the transformations of wit and invention, that a Spirite naturally borne of the inheritance of Poetrie & iudiciall knowledge could expresse: All notwithstanding wrought him not that glory & fame with his owne nation, as did his Poems in Italian, which they esteeme above al whatsoever wit could have invented in any other forme then wherein it is.[2]

Correspondingly, what Golding offered to his contemporaries was not merely an aid to reading Ovid but also a means of emulating him, of realising the potential of the English language to accomplish poetic performances which had previously seemed dauntingly sophisticated. Ezra Pound, pronouncing with characteristic impatience, has made the point that Golding's fourteeners (his equivalent of Latin hexameter) proceed with anything but the monotony traditionally associated with the form.[3] Golding's supple handling of line as well as his ability to keep pace with the amount of material Ovid packs into his hexametric verse can easily be demonstrated:

> Yea even from heaven she did abstain. She lovd *Adonis* more
> Than heaven. To him she clinged ay, and bare him companye.
> And in the shadowe woont she was too rest continually,
> And for to set her beawty out most seemely to the eye
> By trimly decking of her self. Through bushy grounds and groves,
> And over Hills and Dales, and Lawnds and stony rocks she roves,
> Bare kneed with garment tucked up according to the woont
> Of *Phebe*, and she cheerd the hounds with hallowing like a hunt,
> Pursewing game of hurtlesse sort, as Hares made lowe before,
> Or stagges with loftye heades, or bucks. But with the sturdy Boare,
> And ravening woolf, and Bearewhelpes armd with ugly pawes, and eeke
> The cruell Lyons which delight in blood, and slaughter seeke,
> She meddled not. And of theis same shee warned also thee
> *Adonis* for too shonne them, if thou wooldst have warned bee.   (Bullough, I, 167)

The careful and varied pointing of enjambement and caesura keeps the reader constantly attentive, while the quiet shift from third person to direct address, as the poet

---

[1] See Bembo, *Prose della Volgar Lingua* (1525); Du Bellay, *Deffence et illustration de la langue francoyse* (1549); and in England, Spenser's *Shepheardes Calender* (1579), particularly the 'glosses' provided by E. K.

[2] Sprague, p. 141.

[3] *ABC of Reading* (1934), pp. 126–7.

delivers Venus's warning to Adonis, illustrates Golding's agility in deploying his protagonists alternately as bearers of narrative consciousness or as mere players in the scene. Although Marlowe and Shakespeare exceed him in the poise and confidence they bring to the iambic pentameter line, Golding none the less gives the later poets an idea of what can be done and the confidence to bring it off. His contribution, then, is that he provided something far more than a translation; he showed that it was possible to make English, a language that was yet to be formed when Ovid first rendered his myths into Latin, capable of transposing them into a new idiom.

But with all this it also matters precisely what kind of poem Golding decided to translate. Previous sixteenth-century translators, such as Surrey or Thomas Phaer, tended to choose the noble *Aeneid* as the representative Latin epic. Golding's choice of poetic narrative, the theme of which is for the most part not at all clear, and in which characterisation emphasises the dark and often perverse side of the human psyche, carried startling implications for the state of culture in which he wrote and into which Shakespeare (three years old when Golding's book appeared) had recently been born.[1]

The *Metamorphoses* provides a model for depicting psychologically interesting human dramas, and the *Heroides* shows how to bring a dimension of pathos to them. Shakespeare and his contemporaries drew freely on both works to create the amorous sub-genre to the epic, the epyllion or erotic narrative, as it is now more generally called (see above, p. 14, n). Epic poetry celebrated warlike deeds ('Arma virumque cano' is the *Aeneid*'s opening statement) and, as in the case of Virgil, occasionally further ennobled these by making them the basis for a celebration of national destiny. In the Renaissance, all epic tended towards the metaphysical, seeking to understand and explain the relationship of things through the actions depicting them. Yet a sceptical counter-movement also occurred. Love, which orthodox epic viewed as a distraction, or diversion at best, finds a curious centrality in Ariosto's brilliant romance epic, the *Orlando Furioso*, which shows a knight of Charlemagne's court pursuing a ludicrous, distorted passion. Ariosto challenges the humanist confidence in heroic ideals by showing they can be subverted by the slightest whim or impulse. Once enamoured, the knights can think of nothing else, just as Venus, having been pricked by her son's arrow (a detail of the legend rather than of the poem), longs insatiably for Adonis. Even apparently heroic actions such as the Saracens' assault on Paris can be seen as merely frustrated erotic feeling.

Yet the *Orlando Furioso* is regarded as a great humanist triumph, despite its mockery of ideals, and the reason for this is that it portrays in its own balance and composure, its even-tempered, good-humoured tone, the achievement of another ideal: *mediocritas*. *Mediocritas* is that avoidance of extremes which is the sign of a mature, reflective civilisation. According to this ideal, the mind that can weigh opposing or contradictory arguments and impulses without being overwhelmed by them is the best

[1] Gordon Braden (*The Classics and English Renaissance Poetry*, pp. 8–16) argues that Golding's increasingly Puritanical cast of mind accounts for his discontinuing to translate pagan classics after his successful publication of the *Metamorphoses*.

equipped to deal with the tricky, unnerving conduct of human fate and its affairs. It
marks the survival and modification of the stoic impulse in a stabler, more spacious
and expansive world in which capricious fortune is as likely to reward as persecute.
The balance maintained by the *Orlando Furioso*, like that of *Hero and Leander* and
Venus and Adonis, deploys itself in every aspect of its form. Ariosto understands the
power of erotic impulse and even sympathises, like Shakespeare and Marlowe, with the
torment it brings; but, like them, he gives equally good reasons for deriding it. *Mediocritas*, then, with its circumspect, charming formulations of scepticism or disbelief,
shapes and controls a good deal of *Venus and Adonis*, especially the middle sections
where the two protagonists find themselves engaged in an amorous controversy in
which reason as much as passion dictates the terms. Yet it does not account for everything, least of all for the mood of pathos which adds a curious dimension to the erotic
energy of so many of the stanzas or tempers the wit and humour of the prevailing
argument.

   Possibly the final answer lies with yet another Italian text. Written at about the same
time as the *Orlando Furioso*, and adopting much the same perspective, Castiglione's
Book of the Courtier presents a sequence of dialogues between various courtiers at the
palace of Elisabetta Gonzaga. It was translated into English by Sir Thomas Hoby in
1561, and it rivals Golding's *Ovid* in the influence it exerted on Elizabethan authors.
Its sophisticated, assured, good-humoured, courteous, and above all graceful conversational sequences demonstrate that evenness of tone and well-tempered balance that we
have already touched upon. Castiglione in particular commends the art of doing difficult things (dancing, horsemanship, playing a musical instrument) seemingly without
art, almost negligently; and the word he uses to express this is *sprezzatura*, meaning the apparent dispraising of one's own efforts, as if the achievement which others
admire hardly merits attention.[1] Several of Ariosto's courtly episodes depict the kinds
of pursuits that are discussed in Castiglione's book, love being a prominent topic. It is
easy to imagine the appeal Venus's arguments would have for the sophisticated young
men of Elisabetta's court, though Adonis would equally find a defendant there for his
loftier viewpoint. None the less, we are not prepared for the temporary abandonment
of refined Ariostan scepticism, which Castiglione maintains over the first three books,
in favour of a statement of Neoplatonic ideals as Cardinal Bembo takes up the argument in Book IV. Responding with undoubtedly greater sympathy than Ariosto to the
intellectual principles of the Florentine Academy of the late fifteenth century, whose
two leading philosophers were Marsilio Ficino and Giovanni Pico della Mirandola,
Castiglione expresses through Bembo, himself the author of a Ficinian treatise (*Gli
Asolani*), a vision of love as aspiring towards pure mind. Bembo's arguments, and above
all the faith which maintains them, find no counterpart in the rest of the dialogue. Even
those spokesmen who represent a more positive attitude towards human motivation
(for example, Giuliano de' Medici) refrain from accompanying Bembo in his flight of
Platonic fancy. Bembo does not in fact have quite the last word, though his powerful
appeal is so placed as to leave the reader with an abiding impression of it as he closes the

---

[1] Hoby renders the word as 'disgracing' (Castiglione, p. 46).

book. The Lady Emilia Pia gently tugs at the impassioned Bembo's sleeve, reminding him that his place is still on earth, and the court delivers a few ironic comments at his expense. Castiglione seems to be giving full rein to the Neoplatonic love ideal while acknowledging its inevitable obstacles.

The relevance of this to Shakespeare and Marlowe is that they combine in their narratives most if not all the qualities identified in the authors so far mentioned. The fascination and pathos of an Ovidian story mingles with the measured judgement of Ariostan humanism, whether as depicted in the versatile poise of the Italian poem or in the mature debate of Castiglione's pages. And *The Courtier* adds a further element beyond the scope of *mediocritas*; this is its vision of ideal love. It is questionable whether this element can be said to be present in *Hero and Leander*, though Chapman continued Marlowe's poem supposing that it was; but *Venus and Adonis* does contain it in some degree.

The difference between *Hero and Leander*, as it stands in Marlowe's version, and Shakespeare's poem is that the hero of the latter meets his death. This contributes the Ovidian pathos which we have already described; but it may do more. Once all possibility of fulfilling her desire has gone, Venus pays tribute to the qualities in Adonis which she claims first caused her to fall in love with him. She singles out his power to enchant wild beasts (1093–1104) and identifies Adonis as the unique source of 'true, sweet beauty' (1080) in a manner which anticipates claims made for the Platonic lovers in *The Phoenix and the Turtle*. Similarly, Venus bitterly prophesies that without Adonis's inspiring example love will be incapable of rising above its familiar low condition of fickleness and torment (1139–64). These are not aspects of Adonis that Venus seems to care much for while Adonis is alive and so to speak within her grasp, and we may accuse her of having a conveniently selective memory. Furthermore, during their initial debate, she parodies Platonic instruction, according to which the lover proceeds from the grosser senses to the more refined by reversing the order, starting with sight and culminating in taste:

> But O what banquet wert thou to the taste,
> Being nurse and feeder of the other four. (445–60)

Despite this, the mood of expansive tenderness developed by the poem in its closing phase supports Venus in her exaggerated claims. If these are not precisely true to how she loved Adonis or to his real relation to the world and other creatures (we suspect, for example, *pace* Venus, that the boar was not in fact trying to kiss Adonis when he gored him), they present a vision of him that is necessary to the poem's tragic statement. Venus's appeal to the court of inspired love resembles closely that of Cleopatra (with whom she is often compared) as she reflects upon Antony:

> But if there be, nor ever were one such,
> It's past the size of dreaming. Nature wants stuff
> To vie strange forms with fancy; yet t' imagine
> An Antony were nature's piece 'gainst fancy,
> Condemning shadows quite. (*Ant.* 5.2.96–100)

The uniqueness of Antony, argues Cleopatra, is that while he is – or was – a mere mortal, a product of nature, he seems a being that only the imagination, the sphere of the ideal, would create. Now that Antony is remote and intangible, it appears that, for the first time, Cleopatra is able to understand what he truly represents. But seeing it requires a concentration of mind that grief alone can induce. In the same way, Venus seems to accept that Adonis's reluctance was not after all a mark of narcissism but fidelity to a principle of self-realisation:

> To grow unto himself was his desire.   (1180)

This statement, though slightly ambivalent, does not carry a negative intention: it suggests both a retreat from the material world and a process of self-nurture. As such it is perfectly consistent with a Neoplatonic view of love, which places the attainment of an ideal condition above all other things, including the possession of the lover who has been its inspiration. For Venus, Adonis finally becomes such an object of love, but only after he is dead. While life and emotional turmoil exist, the pressure to enjoy the moment inhibits such absolute contemplation. Death alone makes it possible. Much though some readers would like her to, Venus sees no reason to feel remorse at her physical desire for Adonis or to regard the boar's fatal action as a symbol of the true end and nature of her passion.[1] In this she is right. The poem's imperatives are not those of rationally constructed ethics but of nature, in whose world love is often unreciprocated and beauty perishes before it knows itself (in mockery of Adonis's confident reproach to Venus in line 525). The Neoplatonic vision, which is glimpsed sporadically and, in the main, comically earlier in the poem, functions seriously at the close not as its own triumphant principle but as an enhancement of tragic pathos.[2]

The Rape of Lucrece

THE POEM AND INTERPRETATION

The Rape of Lucrece is the antithesis of *Venus and Adonis*. Sexual desire, which aggressively yet also touchingly and humorously characterised Venus, returns to its familiar role as the preoccupation of the male; chastity, so ill-suited to the improbably coy Adonis, recovers its conviction in the person of Lucrece. *Venus and Adonis* is a poem of the fresh outdoors, which salutes procreative energy even as it recognises its inevitable shortcomings. *Lucrece* is a poem of interiors, of physical and spiritual darkness. The corridors down which Tarquin stalks, illuminated by his own 'lightless fire', lead into a

---

[1] For example, see Bradbrook (p. 63), and Heather Asals, '*Venus and Adonis*: the education of a goddess', *SEL*, 13 (1973), 31–51.

[2] It is, as Lennet Daigle argues, possible to view the entire poem according to a systematic Neoplatonic programme (see '*Venus and Adonis*: some traditional contexts', *S. St.* 13 (1980), 31–46). This would mean that the sensual nature of Venus's initial appeal is to be seen as a first stage in her eventual progress towards pure love. But it is doubtful whether Venus, as the poem depicts her, would have rejected the erotic if Adonis had lived; and the humour with which Shakespeare demonstrates how ideal arguments serve personal interests (Adonis after all does not need to subdue an unruly passion in himself – he simply does not want her) reminds us that *mediocritas* keeps a firm grip on interpretation.

4 Titian's *Tarquin and Lucretia*

circle of complexity, at the centre of which he meets the innocent but no less confused Lucrece.[1]

The poem starts with Tarquin, ruminates on his quickly conceived lust, and, like *Macbeth*, contemplates his inexorable pursuit of an aim that can only destroy him. But unlike *Macbeth* it ceases to concentrate on the perpetrator, once he has done the deed, and switches attention to the victim. As soon as the rape has been accomplished it is clear that the poet intends to devote the rest of his story to vindicating the heroine. The comparison with *Macbeth* (a play which contains echoes of the poem, including references to Tarquin) illuminates the different sort of progress *Lucrece* follows after the offence. Whereas Macbeth purges his guilt within and through his own fate, the discarded Tarquin cannot fulfil this function himself. The purgation comes instead through Lucrece, who sheds her own blood. Does this make her Tarquin's counterpart in guilt, or does it merely mean that fate is unfairly forced on her as a sacrificial victim? The very change of direction in the poem, so different from the inexorably logical sequence of *Macbeth*, helps explain both the quandary experienced by Lucrece as victim and the uncertainty and confusion into which interpretation tends to fall.

This brings up first of all the question of the poem's moral perspective, in particular the nature of Lucrece's 'self-slaughter' and her motive in performing it.

St Augustine attacked the Lucrece of classical legend by reminding her supporters that a truly clear conscience had nothing to fear. He was concerned to dispute the morality of suicide, and argued that if Lucrece were truly an innocent victim she should not have killed herself: killing an innocent is also a crime.[2] If on the other hand Lucrece secretly consented to being raped, she was no heroine. The paradox as Augustine presents it is indeed a thorny one since it involves the notoriously difficult and contentious issue of victim complicity in sexual aggression. Shakespeare however avoids this spectre by inviting his readers to think further along the lines of the rape victim's own attitude to her experience. Unlike Augustine, Shakespeare does not ignore the cultural imperatives and taboos of an ancient society, in which pollution, even of an utterly innocent family member, brings shame on the family, shame which the victim's death is believed to cleanse. At the same time, Shakespeare is writing in a Christian culture, in which the law forbade suicide. The resulting moral debate arises from the Christian emphasis on the supreme importance of the individual soul, whereas classical Roman culture gave greater importance to the family and, under certain circumstances, allowed suicide.

A significant passage occurs at what might be described as the moment of 'transference', that is, following the rape when Tarquin slinks away and leaves Lucrece musing on the event:

---

[1] One critic has recently argued that the antithesis which opposes the two antagonists to each other also works by producing an unexpected resemblance between them. See Dubrow's account of the poem's syneciosis ('strange harmony', as the Elizabethan stylist John Hoskyns called it), in *Captive Victors*, esp. pp. 80–142.

[2] *City of God*, 1.19.19–20.

Ev'n in this thought through the dark night he stealeth,
A captive victor that hath lost in gain;
Bearing away the wound that nothing healeth,
The scar that will despite of cure remain;
Leaving his spoil perplexed in greater pain.
　　She bears the load of lust he left behind,
　　And he the burden of a guilty mind.

He like a thievish dog creeps sadly thence;
She like a wearied lamb lies panting there.
He scowls, and hates himself for his offence;
She, desperate, with her nails her flesh doth tear.
He faintly flies, sweating with guilty fear;
　　She stays, exclaiming on the direful night;
　　He runs, and chides his vanished loathed delight.

He thence departs a heavy convertite;
She there remains a hopeless castaway.
He in his speed looks for the morning light;
She prays she never may behold the day:
'For day', quoth she, 'night's scapes doth open lay,
　　And my true eyes have never practised how
　　To cloak offences with a cunning brow.　　　　　　　　　　　(729–49)

Like any rape victim Lucrece feels that she has been contaminated and finds it hard, in fact impossible, to distinguish between Tarquin's culpability and her own personal shame. Even though pollution has been foisted on her ('the load of lust'), she cannot help regarding it as her own. As the poem proceeds towards its dénouement a chorus of voices urges her to believe in her innocence; but Lucrece has resolved on suicide as the only solution long before her husband and countrymen arrive on the scene, and there is no wavering on her part. Medical science, at least in Shakespeare's application of it, seems to bear out her sense of contamination, for her spilt blood divides into pure and corrupt elements:

Some of her blood still pure and red remained,
And some looked black, and that false Tarquin stained . . .

And ever since, as pitying Lucrece' woes,
Corrupted blood some watery token shows,
　　And blood untainted still doth red abide,
　　Blushing at that which is so putrified.　　　　　　　　　(1742–3, 1747–50)

However inviolate her mind, the blood is evidence of those 'accessary yieldings' (1658) to which the body, despite its owner's will, succumbs (Chaucer – see below, pp. 37–8 – maintains that she was unconscious throughout, which clears her of even involuntary physical participation). Augustine would say that none of this matters; but it is plain that Shakespeare took the body–soul dualism seriously, as *Venus and Adonis* shows. In the earlier poem the two are kept separate by careful contrivance (the man's inclination to chastity being decisive), but in *Lucrece* the act of sex brings them together: a chaste mind finds itself occupying a defiled body, and the resultant confusion will not be dispelled except by drastic action. The poem accordingly salutes her suicide as a triumphant release of her soul from its circumstances of defilement:

> Even here she sheathèd in her harmless breast
> A harmful knife, that thence her soul unsheathèd:
> That blow did bail it from the deep unrest
> Of that polluted prison where it breathèd.   (1723–6)

There is no evidence that Shakespeare wishes to think the matter out more subtly than this. Indeed, he probably sensed that he did not need to. While culpable in the view of the Church, suicide performed with such a fine and conscientious regard to personal honour would undoubtedly strike a chord of sympathy with the laity (hence Tyndale's worries over Lucrece's popularity).[1] Shakespeare has thoroughly integrated this Roman lady (who in line 1694 appeals to her kinsmen as 'knights') in a familiar chivalric context, one which is characteristically adept at blurring theological principle and, with whatever effect on logic, regarding the actions of sympathetic characters in a morally favourable light.

From this perspective, the distinction between stoical Rome and contemporary England is not very marked. Of responses on the page, we have only those of Lucretius, Collatine, and Brutus to judge by, the rest standing 'stone-still, astonished with this deadly deed' (1730). Lucretius deplores her action as an inversion of the natural order, as a result of which children now predecease the parents, depriving fathers like himself of the consolation of survival through progeny. This cannot be enlisted as a Christian objection to what she has done, and indeed it too closely resembles one of Lucrece's own laments on the disorder of things to do much more than supplement her own plaintive rhetoric. Collatine feels uxorious rage at Tarquin's violation of his spouse, but soon falls to a futile competition with his father-in-law over who has greatest claim to grief – a further stylistic means of emphasising the pathos of her loss. Brutus criticises her for having plunged the knife into the wrong culprit, less a measured judgement of Lucrece and more a clever rhetorical means of establishing a case against the Tarquins. In each spokesman, style and performance hold sway over the finer points of moral inquiry, the effect taken as a whole contributing to the depiction of a Lucrece who has behaved in a sombre but laudable manner in conformity with Sidney's commendation of 'the constant though lamenting look of Lucretia, when she punished in herself another's fault' (*Apology*, p. 102).

In his overall handling of the theme, then, Shakespeare shows greater interest in the requirements of style – and in particular genre – than ethics, further supporting evidence for this being that the formal character of *Lucrece* can be traced to his activities

---

[1] St Jerome had extolled the courage and resolve of Lucrece and saw her as a worthy example for Christians to follow – even though she was a pagan. Tertullian further commented that concern for personal glory was acceptable to God if it accorded with his design. The Augustinian position, however, was alive and well in Shakespeare's day thanks to the efforts of Tyndale. See Donaldson, *The Rapes of Lucretia*, pp. 34 and 174–5.

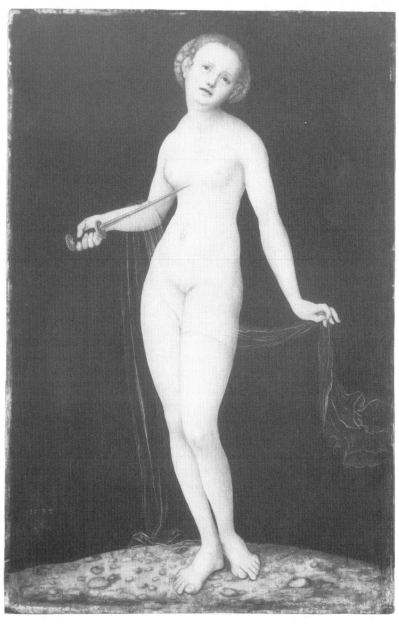

5   Cranach's *Lucretia*

in the theatre. He had lately completed the dynastic first Tudor tetralogy (echoes of which can be heard in some of the lines of *Lucrece*), which concerns itself with the transmission of guilt from one generation to the next by inherent curse or pollution; as well as this, his tragic instinct was shaped by the code of revenge drama, with its insistence on the extirpation or purgation of guilt through blood, to which his own recent Roman tragedy *Titus Andronicus* – again echoed sporadically by the language of the poem – belongs. (All of this is connected with the contemporary practice of putting Senecan ideas on to the Elizabethan stage.) The solution Shakespeare finds for the dilemmas confronting and expressed via Lucrece is the formalist one of subduing the abstract puzzles of conscience to the emotive force of the complaint genre, on the reasonable assumption that the pathos it produces will take care of any lingering ethical doubts.

To a large extent he succeeds. Readers generally object less to contradictions in the handling of the morality of the subject and more to the extended apostrophes of such bleak personifications as Night, Time, and Opportunity (what William Empson has described as 'the Bard doing five-finger exercises in rhetoric at the piano', *Signet*, p. 1670b). Despite the Augustinian school's suspicion that here is a lady protesting too much, the more obvious danger of such speeches is their inordinate length unsupported by a viable dramatic context. Shakespeare does all he can to elicit sympathy for the heroine as victim, but the lengths to which he goes risk an over-exposure of technique, sometimes culminating in stridency.

As Lever (p. 28) points out, we need to remember the circumstances of the time. Similar rhetorical extravagance had already worked on the stage in Kyd's *Spanish Tragedy*, which was to enjoy a later revival. Compared to this, Lucrece's speeches are not at all excessive. Also, the poem enjoys the advantages of being read in solitude, which makes for a different experience altogether from the reception of dramatic utterance. The demands of naturalism constantly forced the theatre to renew its style, and Shakespeare himself contributed decisively to the modification in rhetorical habit which was taking place on the stage. By contrast, the spaciousness of the narrative mode allows the mind to absorb the immediate drama and to contemplate at length the metaphysical condition which it expresses. Nowhere is this more powerfully done in such poetry than in the stanza just prior to the rape, where we witness the helplessness of the victim and the terrible (again Ovidian) transformation that has taken place in her attacker:

> Here with a cockatrice' dead-killing eye
> He rouseth up himself, and makes a pause;
> While she, the picture of pure piety,
> Like a white hind under the gripe's sharp claws,
> Pleads, in a wilderness where are no laws,
>   To the rough beast that knows no gentle right,
>   Nor aught obeys but his foul appetite.   (540–6)

Such descriptions never lost their appeal for Shakespeare's contemporaries, for the poem went into at least six editions in his lifetime, including one in the year he died.

But a modern readership needs, to some degree, to recover the technique of appreciating the principles by which such a passage functions.

It is accordingly from the perspective of rhetorical practice that we must judge how theme and action are presented, and in particular how the heroine is perceived. In the early part of the narrative Shakespeare impresses upon the reader Lucrece's artlessness and simple good faith. Such unsuspecting honesty of disposition is hard to render without running the risk of making its possessor appear naive or unintelligent. Anyone else would suspect Tarquin was up to no good arriving unannounced and without a prior word from Collatine. But in order that she should epitomise uncomplicated virtue, Shakespeare has her accept the visit as quite natural; suspiciousness in her at this stage would cloud our impression. The antithetical structure of the poetic argument enables Shakespeare to present matters in extremes, ideal chastity opposed to base lust:

> This earthly saint, adorèd by this devil,
> Little suspecteth the false worshipper;
> For unstained thoughts do seldom dream on evil;
> Birds never limed no secret bushes fear.
> So guiltless she securely gives good cheer
>   And reverend welcome to her princely guest,
>   Whose inward ill no outward harm expressed. (85–91)

As the last line shows, antithesis works internally in the case of Tarquin, indicating his inner turmoil and self-division, whereas Lucrece shows no such innate contradiction.[1] Tarquin has the devil's view of the sleeping, innocent Lucrece as he enters the sanctity of her bedchamber at a narrative moment in which the playful effects of the description trouble some readers as inappropriately precious:[2]

> Her lily hand her rosy cheek lies under,
> Coz'ning the pillow of a lawful kiss;
> Who, therefore angry, seems to part in sunder,
> Swelling on either side to want his bliss;
> Between whose hills her head entombèd is,
>   Where like a virtuous monument she lies,
>   To be admired of lewd unhallowed eyes . . .
>
> Her hair like golden threads played with her breath,
> O modest wantons, wanton modesty!
> Showing life's triumph in the map of death,
> And death's dim look in life's mortality.
> Each in her sleep themselves so beautify,
>   As if between them twain there were no strife,
>   But that life lived in death, and death in life.

---

[1] Pursuing the notion of syneciosis (see above, p. 23, n), Dubrow argues that the contradictoriness involves Lucrece in terms of motive as it does Tarquin, and appears to see this as part of Shakespeare's design. But if this is what happens, it is more likely to be an incidental and unplanned development, since the poet bases his account of Lucrece's triumph on her resistance to compromise. See Dubrow's conclusion, p. 168.

[2] Consider Lewis's objection: 'The conceit which makes Lucrece's pillow 'angrie' at 388 would have been tolerable in *Hero and Leander* but is here repellent' (p. 499).

Her breasts like ivory globes circled with blue,
A pair of maiden worlds unconquerèd,
Save of their lord no bearing yoke they knew,
And him by oath they truly honourèd.
These worlds in Tarquin new ambition bred,
  Who like a foul usurper went about
  From this fair throne to heave the owner out.   (386–92, 400–13)

Doubtless for the modern reader, more accustomed to expect moments of unbroken dramatic plausibility, such narrative pauses seem an artificial and stilted slowing of the action. But their function is to state and recall to us the poem's governing themes. Lucrece, in this image of her, has the power to resolve contradictions which in Tarquin, as in ordinary sinners, are only exacerbated. Differences of life and death are annulled, as they were in paradise, which knew no mortality. The outcome of anger is sweetness, and so on.

In addition, the picture does contain a significant element of erotic psychology, whereby an unconscious, innocent posture calls forth a voluptuous response. Shakespeare takes his cue for this from Ovid, whose original description of Lucrece as the dutiful housewife at her loom he has carefully adapted to the dramatically charged bedroom setting. (By contrast, Ovid spends few preliminaries on the rape.) A comparison shows how Shakespeare incorporates something of Ovid's delicacy of physical description and suspenseful erotic anticipation in his description of Tarquin's stealthy advance on his sleeping victim. John Gower's awkward verse translation of 1640 (the first in English) renders the Roman passage as follows:

Her lilie-skin, her gold-deluding tresses,
Her native splendour slighting art him pleases.
Her voice, her stainless modesty, h'admires:
And hope's decay still strengthens his desires.
Day's horn-mouth'd harbinger proclaim'd the morn;
The frollick gallants to their tents return.
His mazing fansie on her picture roves;
The more he muses still the more he loves:
Thus did she sit, thus drest, thus did she spin,
Thus plai'd her hair upon her necks white skin;
These looks she had, these rosie words still'd from her,
This eye, this cheek, these blushes did become her
As billows fall down after some great blast,
Yet make some swelling when the wind is past:
So though her person from his sight was tane,
Yet did that love her person bred remain.
He burns; and prick'd with spurs of basest lust,
Against her chast bed plots attempts unjust.   (Bullough, 1, 194)

Whereas Ovid's Tarquin turns these images of Lucrece over in his mind while still in the camp, Shakespeare, as the above passage shows, weaves them into the scene in which he beholds her in bed without her knowledge. The conceits are entirely appropriate to the complexity and contradictoriness of the situation whereby chastity kindles lust and the mutually inimical instincts of modesty and lasciviousness find themselves drawn indivisibly together.

There is a rhetorical purpose to Shakespeare's rearrangement of source material, and that is to concentrate all the particulars of the tragedy in these few strategically placed stanzas. The artistic conceit of life alternating with death in the image of the sleeping woman announces the eventual fate of Lucrece, which is, again paradoxically, made beautiful by its quality of heroic sacrifice. Like the Troy ecphrasis (see below, p. 31), though on a smaller scale, the picture given here summarises in concentrated form the thematic concerns to be demonstrated in the course of the action. Far from merely contributing an elusive and momentary lyric voice to the sombre epic tale, the stanzas signal the dimension of tenderness and pathos which unify the whole experience. An Elizabethan audience, looking less for naturalism of mood and more alert to the demands of thematic contemplation, would enjoy the manner in which these conceits maintain their fragile, delicate play while encompassing a wider significance.

While the device or strategy is more characteristic of narrative poetic art, Shakespeare none the less sometimes makes use of it in his mature tragic dramas, an interesting example occurring in *King Lear* (Quarto version) where the description of Cordelia given by the Gentleman to Kent fulfils, even to the evocation of her sympathetic tears, all the requirements of the ecphrasis mode of concentrated pity:

KENT. Did your letters pierce the Queen to any demonstration of grief?
GENT. Ay, [sir], she took them, read them in my presence,
    And now and then an ample tear trill'd down
    Her delicate cheek. It seem'd, she was a queen
    Over her passion, who, most rebel-like,
    Sought to be king o'er her.
KENT. O then it mov'd her.
GENT. Not to a rage, patience and sorrow [strove]
    Who should express her goodliest. You have seen
    Sunshine and rain at once; her smiles and tears
    That play'd on her ripe lip [seem'd] not to know
    What guests were in her eyes, which parted thence,
    As pearls for diamonds dropp'd. In brief,
    Sorrow would be a rarity most beloved,
    If all could so become it.
                                  (*Lear* 4.3.9–24)

Another relevant example occurs in Macbeth's description of the murdered Duncan immediately upon rousing his household (lines which have often puzzled later generations of critics and readers):

                Here lay Duncan,
  His silver skin lac'd with his golden blood,
  And his gash'd stabs look'd like a breach in nature
  For ruin's wasteful entrance.
                                  (2.3.111–14)

The use of non-naturalistic epithets to describe the King's face and blood enable the play (even allowing for the duplicity of the speaker) to raise in a single image one of the central themes, the sacredness of kingship, for which gold and silver are appropriate epithets. Johnson's observation that Macbeth's seemingly odd choice of diction plausibly depicts a hypocritical mind trying to feign innocence is attractive but incorrect. The audience would have recognised that even in the mouth of a perjurer and murderer (indeed, especially in such a mouth) these words capture precisely the reverence and awe of majesty. The appearance in plays of such vigorous temper as *King Lear* and *Macbeth* of images so firmly rooted in narrative poetic art bears testimony to the easiness, for Elizabethan readers and playgoers alike, of the artificial mode.

After the rape, Lucrece for the first time experiences antithesis as self-division – which Tarquin has known all along. The poem is ready now to dispense with him and concentrate fully on her. Lucrece registers her new-found sense of topsyturviness by railing on Time, Night, and Opportunity, all of whom appear to her to behave perversely. A psychologically effective moment occurs when Lucrece, gazing with suspicion on the blushing groom (1338–44), discovers that she can no longer distinguish innocence from evil. The play on faces uneasily reddening contrasts with the earlier artless blushing of Lucrece that so appeals to Tarquin when he pays his furtive visit (50–77).

Aware of self-division, another expression for her fallen condition, Lucrece chooses not to live. This is the tragic hero's decision, and it comes as no surprise; anything less would be unheroic. At this point Shakespeare introduces the much-debated Troy *excursus* (or *ecphrasis* – see Supplementary Notes). Despite arguments favouring political allegory, the Troy passage functions most obviously and effectively as a means of providing Lucrece with an appropriate heroic dimension: she sees her own fate, as we are meant to see it, depicted in the 'skilful painting':

> At last she calls to mind where hangs a piece
> Of skilful painting, made for Priam's Troy,
> Before the which is drawn the power of Greece,
> For Helen's rape the city to destroy,
> Threat'ning cloud-kissing Ilion with annoy;
>   Which the conceited painter drew so proud
>   As heaven, it seemed, to kiss the turrets bowed.   (1366–72)

The last line in particular indicates the tragedy's attempt at assuming cosmic proportions which its bedroom and palace-chamber setting have so far inhibited. The allegory explored by the painting is explicable entirely in personal rather than political terms: Lucrece finds herself in Hecuba and her husband and father variously in both Priam and Hector, while Tarquin is clearly represented by Sinon but also by Pyrrhus. The armies on either side, as well as the city and its fortifications, recall and expand those many images of 'servile powers' (295), 'ranks of blue veins' (440), 'round turrets' (441), 'sweet city' (469), and 'troops of cares' (720) which have previously represented the bodies, feelings, attitudes of mind, and souls of rapist and victim.

But some recent criticism, as well as abandoning the old Augustinian dilemma, would dissent from the reading just proposed. Among the more interesting of these are the attempts at a political interpretation (i.e. closer to the spirit of Livy than Ovid) put forward first by E. P. Kuhl in a seminal article and revived again by Michael

Platt.[1] Kuhl argues that the main purpose of the poem is exemplary: it intends to demonstrate to Southampton the dangers of abusing power and status. Tarquin's initial scruples, as he nerves himself up, over unlawful possession and betrayal of trust (not unlike Macbeth's prior reflections on the duties of kinship) are repeated to him by Lucrece as she tries to reason him out of his determined course. Quite apart from the patent embarrassment that would be likely to issue from so close an alignment of Tarquin with Shakespeare's patron, the limitation of this idea is that it largely ignores the sufferings and reactions of Lucrece herself, which take up about two thirds of the narrative.

Platt, on the other hand, attempts to demonstrate the political meaning of the poem in terms of its overall structure, and shows great ingenuity in doing so. Despite his title he does not in fact see Shakespeare as advocating republicanism, even indirectly, but rather as pleading for responsible government. (Like Kuhl he belongs to the advice-to-a-prince school.) Platt bases his argument on the device of synecdoche: a partial statement or observation stands for something larger, as in the stanza in which Achilles' spear represents the warrior (1422–28). Correspondingly, the indulgence of individual passion symbolises the abuse of political power and consequent instability. Platt's interpretation of the Troy ecphrasis is more or less the opposite of the one given above. Gazing on the picture (1366–1568), Lucrece sees her own rape in the rape of Troy, and vice versa (Platt, pp. 65–66). But in the picture she also sees Hecuba, with whose sufferings she empathises, and she looks in vain for Helen – whose beauty she would destroy if by so doing she could prevent the awful fate incessantly visited on woman-kind as punishment for its power to attract men. While it is possible to read political meanings into individual actions, as Platt does, the poem insists on confronting us with the sufferings and predicament of the heroine as a woman, and only incidentally as a political symbol.

As might be expected, by her very sex Lucrece has attracted to the poem an increasing number of feminist studies. These take a different political line from Kuhl or Platt in examining the role of Lucrece within a patriarchy (where, it is argued, her body is perceived as an emblem of territorial possession rather than as a thing of her own). In such a perspective there is little that distinguishes the rapist from the other men in the poem: Collatine's original foolishness in boasting about his wife has kindled Tarquin's lust even more than her beauty; Lucrece is regarded by both men as an extension of male identity; the dispute between husband and father as to whose grief is the greater (1793–1806) is a selfish one with little genuine concern for the victim; the rape itself demonstrates Lucrece's essential passiveness, which is her condition in marriage, with the result that she is compelled to see her violation primarily as an offence against her husband; Brutus, like the others, indulges in suspect oratory and makes opportunistic use of Lucrece's death.[2]

---

[1] See Kuhl, 'Shakespeare's *Rape of Lucrece*', *PQ 20* (1941), 352–60, and Platt, '*The Rape of Lucrece* and the Republic for which it stands', *CR 19* (1975), 59–79.

[2] See variously articles by Coppélia Kahn, 'The rape in Shakespeare's *Lucrece*', *S. St.* 9 (1976), 45–72; Nancy Vickers, '"The blazon of sweet beauty's best": Shakespeare's *Lucrece*', in Patricia Parker and Geoffrey Hartman (eds.), *Shakespeare and the Question of Theory*, 1985, pp. 95–115; and Catherine R. Stimpson,

Curiously enough, such studies resist implicating the author himself in the patri-archal conspiracy and prefer, like old-fashioned criticism, to keep him aloof from the vice of artifice practised by his characters, even though his poetic manner seems prey to it. As one interpreter puts it, not altogether plausibly, 'Shakespeare moves in two directions at once: he dramatically calls into question descriptive fashion while amply demonstrating that he controls it.'[1]

One need not be a feminist reader to concur with some of the positions described above. Collatine's behaviour at the beginning of the poem is ill-advised (though not as foolish as that of Posthumus Leonatus, in *Cymbeline*, who wagers on his wife's fidelity), and one wonders what Lucrece's reaction might have been had she learned that her husband was partly responsible for her predicament. But as with other politically angled interpretations, most feminist readings ignore the fact that the poem concentrates so much of its imagination on Lucrece herself, on her inner woe, and only a relatively small amount on her context. Context, indeed, where it is registered, acts mainly as a foil for the heroine's personal drama. Collatine and Lucretius are inadequate not because they selfishly cultivate their own grief, even if this is what they do, but because helplessness is expected of them: theirs is the role of the traditional grieving chorus, powerless to assist the main tragic figure.

Like *Venus and Adonis*, from which in so many other respects it differs, *The Rape of Lucrece* ends on a death and strikes a note of pathos. The determination expressed by the Romans to oust tyranny is merely chorus to this effect. This at least appears to have been Shakespeare's artistic solution; but as we have seen, the poem has not been received in so unexceptional a fashion. The pathos he succeeds in wringing from the theme does not wholly dispel the ethical disquiet caused by Lucrece's dilemma and the answer she finds to it. And though readers sympathetic to the poem's rhetorical principles will respond to its carefully orchestrated moods of sorrow and reflection, a majority will doubtless always prefer the brio and dispatch of *Venus and Adonis*. Donaldson concludes his excellent chapter on Lucrece as follows:

> Behind the lengthy rhetorical laments of the poem, one senses some uncertainty in Shakespeare's handling in particular of the principal issue of the poem, that of the proper course of action for a 'dishonoured' woman to take; an issue to which he was to return with greater thoughtfulness in the work of his maturity.   (Donaldson, p. 56)

In fact, no woman of Shakespeare's mature period confronts dishonour on so immense a scale: Desdemona and Hermione, two paragons of domestic loyalty, are beset with smears and suspicions but never literally violated. To treat of rape was always going to be difficult. In *Titus Andronicus* Shakespeare attempts to communicate the pathos ensuing from its violence by emphasising the visually horrific. In *The Rape of Lucrece* he adopts a more bearable introspective formula, without entirely succeeding, as he had superbly with *Venus and Adonis*, in subduing the poem's troubling ethical questions to the requirements of form. In this matter, indeed, he may not be so far

---

'Shakespeare and the soil of rape', in *The Woman's Part: Feminist Criticism of Shakespeare*, Carolyn Ruth Swift Lenz, Gayle Green and Carol Thomas Neely (eds.), 1980, pp. 56–64.

[1] Vickers, '"The blazon"', p. 109.

adrift of his practice in certain of the great tragedies. Eliot accused him of resorting to stoicism for the ending of *Othello*, and in *Hamlet* Shakespeare brings a *feeling* of satisfaction to the close while perhaps leaving some of the questions posed by the theme of revenge still unanswered.[1] But the historical fame of the Lucrece story and the fact that it has received such careful theological scrutiny more than usually expose the poet's customary habit of making his resolutions only partially answerable to the requirements of rationally conceived ethics. Be that as it may, henceforward the greatest outrages his heroines had to suffer were the insecurities and perversities of men's minds – complex enough matters in themselves, but artistically easier to solve.

THE SOUTHAMPTON CONNECTION

In offering *The Rape of Lucrece* to Southampton in 1594, Shakespeare seems to have fulfilled his promise to present him with a work which would qualify as that 'graver labour' foreseen at the time of the publication of *Venus and Adonis*. The dedication to *Lucrece* is even more fulsome and self-confident in its artificial self-abasement, and it has often been taken as a sign of the growth of intimacy between poet and patron. Yet we know nothing of Southampton's response. We may imagine that he liked its erotic predecessor, or Shakespeare would not have risked a second venture. But whether the poet thought it his own moral duty to try to educate the earl in more serious matters of conscience and statecraft, as some scholars have imagined,[2] is a more dubious proposition. For one thing, Shakespeare would hardly have dared tell Southampton how to behave in so public a poem; for another, the implicit identification of the earl with Tarquin would be rashness of a quite un-Shakespearean kind. It would hardly come under the humanist heading, 'education of a prince', since such treatises, fairly popular in the sixteenth century, assume a certain artlessness, and even innocence, in the pupil and limit themselves to general political matters while particularly warning against ill advisers.[3] Echoes of such things can be heard here and there in the poem, but not in a sustained, programmatic way. By contrast, artful tacticians of moral flattery such as Ben Jonson adopted the foolproof ploy of applauding their superiors for already possessing virtues they hoped they would acquire. Giving one's patron a stark lesson in self-damnation is hardly the way to keep open preferment's door; we may suppose rather that Shakespeare intended the poem as a compliment to the sage and serious part of Southampton's character. Whereas *Venus and Adonis* may well have accommodated in-jokes and personal references without losing its poise, the nature of *The Rape of Lucrece*, with its strong mixture of traditional morality, makes for a stiffness and solemnity which are quite the reverse of the more malleable myth of Eros. Besides all this, the main emphasis falls not on Tarquin, who effectively disappears about a third of the way through the poem, but on the feelings and fate of the heroine. In expressing such interest Shakespeare is not alone.

[1] See T. S. Eliot, 'Shakespeare and the Stoicism of Seneca', in *Selected Essays*, 3rd edn, 1951, pp. 126–40; and Philip Edwards, *Hamlet*, New Cambridge Shakespeare: 1985, pp. 60–1.
[2] See Akrigg, p. 200, and Kuhl, 'Shakespeare's *Rape of Lucrece*', pp. 352–60.
[3] See below on *Mirror for Magistrates*, p. 38.

A woman whose story has exercised fascination from its occurrence at an early formative point in western history, Lucrece has been subjected to fearsome scrutiny: examined as a political figure, extolled as a suffering heroine, and alternately revered and denigrated for her chastity and actions of conscience. The treatments preceding Shakespeare's which have bearing on his version need to be considered.

SOURCES

The two main Roman sources are Livy's history of Rome, *Ab Urbe Condita*, and Ovid's *Fasti* (or 'Festivals'). Livy's account takes up the relatively short space of three chapters in the first book of his historical narrative, and forms part of a series of significant events in the story of the city. In particular it serves Livy's political sympathies, since in his interpretation it plays an important role in the transition from monarchy (or tyranny as Livy describes it) under the Tarquins to republicanism. Lucrece (a heroine of the sixth century BC) receives nothing in the way of psychological depiction but assumes the person of a martyr to the cause; an almost equal emphasis is placed on Lucius Junius Brutus, who leads the successful revolt against the Tarquin family. Painter made a fairly close translation of Livy in his *Pallace of Pleasure* (1566),[1] which the author of 'The Argument' (see commentary), whether Shakespeare or another, drew upon in some detail. The rape is described in military terms (though not in the elaborate poetic metaphor of Eros as siege and invasion), and Tarquin regards his victim as a 'conquest'. Livy gets in a crack about his easily satisfied heroic instinct which glories in overcoming a woman's honour ('profectusque inde Tarquinius ferox expugnato decore muliebre');[2] Lucretia in turn grieves as if over a larger-than-life calamity or public disaster ('maesta tanto malo'). However, Livy does make a point of distinguishing between the evil that has befallen her body and her inviolate mind.[3] As she claims purity of conscience, which none of her listeners dreams of denying her, she forestalls the possibility of subsequent female backsliding by identifying her suicide as a defence of the name of (Roman) women:

though I cleare my selfe of the offence, my body shall feele the punishment; for no unchast or ill woman shall hereafter impute no dishonest act to Lucrece.[4]

This appears in Shakespeare's poem as,

> 'No, no', quoth she, 'no dame hereafter living
> By my excuse shall claim excuse's giving.'   (1714–15)

Her resolve matches the tenor of public responsibility which Livy is eager to cultivate, and emphasises that personal conscience accords with devotion to the good of the patria. Similarly, Tarquin's selfish pursuit of pleasure destroys confidence in his virtue

---

[1] See Bullough, 1, 196–9.
[2] The detail is not in Painter.
[3] See Donaldson's careful analysis of the various treatments of the rape both before and following Shakespeare (chs. 1–2, 4–5).
[4] Painter (Bullough, 1, 198).

(or, to be exact, his father's virtue) as a ruler. The importance of rape as a personal action is second to its meaning in the political sphere, and this is the line Livy follows.[1] Although, as we have seen, some critics have tried to interpret *The Rape of Lucrece* also primarily in political terms, Shakespeare is on balance more interested in depicting personal conscience and its part in individual fate; and to that extent he draws more fully on Ovid than on Livy.

Ovid throughout creates a characteristic atmosphere of beauty and horror, even down to the detail of macabre pathos as the deceased Lucrece apparently signals her support of Brutus's resolute vow:

> She at his words her sightless eyes doth move,
> And shook her head as seeming to approve.   (Bullough, 1, 196)

Like the *Metamorphoses*, the *Fasti* has for its ultimate purpose the glorification of Roman destiny. Following the lead of Livy, who never misses an opportunity to enlist supernatural endorsement of the events he considers favourable to the cause of Rome, Ovid accords the death of Lucrece the status of a portent which Brutus interprets correctly by calling for the end of Tarquinian tyranny (the spirit of Lucrece giving its blessing). Livy chooses the less extraordinary miracle of the astonishing transformation in Brutus's character from a seeming dolt and party-liner to a man of decision and initiative ('stupentibus miraculo rei, unde novum in Bruti pectore ingenium': Livy, 1.59), Despite clear differences in emphasis, such as his customary fascination with the mentality of the sexually obsessive, Ovid shares, then, his compatriot's intention to justify the progress of Roman history.

The fame of Lucrece was to outlive such temporal concerns, however, and later treatments such as Chaucer's (in *The Legende of Good Women*), though based closely on Ovid's text, concentrate more on chastity as a virtue in itself. What survives in Chaucer's estimate is not so much Roman triumph as Lucrece's own good name as a type of wifely devotion:

> But for that cause [ie. the Roman] telle I nat this story,
> But for to preyse, and drawen to memory
> The verray wife, the verray trewe Lucresse,
> That for hir wifehood, and hir stedfastnesse,
> Not only that these payens hir commende,
> But he that y-cleped is in oure legende
> The grete Austyne hath grete compassyoun
> Of this Lucresse that starf at Rome toun.   (Bullough, 1, 184)

Chaucer overstates St Augustine's compassion, but in concentrating on Lucrece as an emblem of universal female virtue, he breaks the domination of historical and

---

[1] It is worth remarking, as the question of justifiable suicide arises, that taking one's life was not a matter of indifference to the Romans. Cicero argues that only if God has summoned one is it permissible, or if one is sure God has given a valid reason (as in the case of high-minded men such as Socrates or Cato). (See *Tusculan Disputations* 1.30.73–4.)

political perspective. Brutus's role as an inspired republican matters little to Chaucer, who ends the account by a pointed comparison between the dispositions of men and women, drawing together the poem's twin themes of male treachery and female integrity:

> For wel I wot that Christe himselfe telleth,
> That in Israel, as wyde as is the londe,
> Nat so grete feythe in al that londe he fonde,
> As in a woman; and this is no lye.
> And as for men, loketh which tirannye
> They doon al day, – assay hem whoso lyste,
> The trewest is ful brotil [brittle] for to triste.   (Bullough, 1, 189)

As he acknowledges at the beginning of his account, Chaucer merely touches on the 'grete' (outline) of the political and historical dimension. Similarly, it may be that 'The Argument' of Shakespeare's *Lucrece* functions as a framework from which the poem selects certain details. Being a prose account, 'The Argument' naturally follows Livy – or more probably Painter (see Supplementary Notes). The proportion of narrative it gives to the historical question certainly exceeds that afforded by the poem; and in this Shakespeare may be re-employing Chaucer's tactic of using Roman history as a source of something which survives it. The fate of Tarquinius Superbus poses a special problem for any poet living under a monarchy, but Chaucer solves this by suggesting that the Tarquins have brought a curse upon themselves in offending against divinity (the one authority earthly kings must kneel to):

> Ne never was ther kynge in Rome toun
> Syn thilke day; and she was holden there
> A seynt, and ever hir day y-halwed dere.   (Bullough, 1, 188)

There is a touch of fairy-tale to this, not unlike the Pied Piper's punishment of the townspeople of Hamelin by depriving them of their children. If kings misbehave, they may be lost to their subjects. Lucrece's saintliness, however, might not be acceptable to those who think that the very nature of Tarquin's offence to some degree involves her complicity, however unwilling.[1] Chaucer, as well as disingenuously (and disarmingly) enlisting the authority of a chief member of the opposition – Augustine – deals forthrightly with sceptics by insisting on her complete and utter senselessness at the moment of violation:

> That, what for fere of sklaundre, and drede of dethe,
> She lost attones both wytte and brethe;
> And in a swowgh she lay, and woxe so ded,
> *Men myghten smyten of hir arme or hed*,
> She feleth nothinge, neither foule *nor feyre*.   (Bullough, 1, 187; my italics)

---

[1] Lucrece herself seems to subscribe to this view – see above, p. 24.

Chaucer, then, produces a particularly sympathetic defence of Lucrece, and the forceful nature of his assertions on her behalf suggests that he knew that his choice of her as a typical 'good woman' would not go unquestioned – hence the conciliatory gesture towards the Augustinian viewpoint. Something of this problem is to appear later in Shakespeare.

Politics and conscience were to be brought together in a new formula at the end of Mary Tudor's reign, and more pertinently at the start of Elizabeth's, in a series of stern, lugubrious poems collectively known as *The Mirror for Magistrates*, which continued to be published until the early seventeenth century. The theme connecting these poems is that of implacable fortune enacting the will of God in bringing individuals down from whatever brief height of happiness or triumph they may enjoy. The idea is a familiar medieval one and derives from the teachings of 'tragical morality'.[1] The poems in the *Mirror* collection confront the reader with a figure who unfolds an exemplary tale of personal woe. The speaker is invariably a ghost or spirit who complains of the particular event, action, or circumstances that have caused his doom. While often a king or potentate, he may equally be a rebel or political misfit (along with the confessions of Richard II we hear those of Owen Glendower and Jack Cade); and sometimes the figure is a woman, as most notably in the case of Jane Shore whose story Thomas Churchyard contributed to the collection, with a shaping effect on later poems in the 'complaint' genre, including of course *Lucrece*.

As with all Elizabethan narratives, *The Mirror for Magistrates* keeps an eye on past performances, a noteworthy sign of this appearing in the introductory poem (or 'Induction') to the sequence, in which Sorrow takes the poet on a journey to Pluto's hell and there presents to him, along with other scenes of human malady and folly, a view of the destruction of Troy:

> But Troy, alas! methought above them all,
>   It made mine eyes in very tears consume,
> When I beheld the woeful weird befall,
>   That by the wrathfull will of gods was come;
> And Jove's unmoved sentence and foredoom
>   On Priam king and on his town so bent,
>   I could not lin [cease], but I must there lament.   (Chambers[2], p. 125)

Scenes like this no doubt acted as a prompt to Shakespeare when he in turn led Lucrece to the painting which depicted the fall of Troy and the sorrows of Hecuba (1366–1568). A source for all such depictions is the second book of Virgil's *Aeneid*, in which Aeneas explains to Dido how his city fell to the Greeks. More specifically, Marlowe's description in *Dido Queen of Carthage* exercised an undoubted influence on Shakespeare in his choice of images or words describing the sack and carnage.[2] Influence builds on influence, and *The Rape of Lucrece* is accordingly a poem in which many previous voices can be heard mingling with and modifying one another, making it difficult to decide

---

[1] See Lever 'Shakespeare's narrative poems', p. 123.
[2] See Bush, *Mythology*, p. 152n. and *Luc.* 1554n.

where to attribute a particular effect or to determine how much conscious selection has been at work. However, as in Chaucer, though at much greater length, the main emphasis falls on Lucrece and our judgement of her.[1]

Responsibility for this may lie particularly with Samuel Daniel's *The Complaint of Rosamond*, published only a short while before in 1592. Daniel's poem derives quite clearly from the *Mirror* narratives in that it confronts the reader with the ghost of a woman who has fallen prey to misfortune. The nature of her transgression is her untimely love (for a king no less), the punishment for which has been undertaken by the jealous wife and queen. In developing his story, Daniel transforms the homiletic sternness of the *Mirror* tradition into the romantic genre of the complaint; other examples quickly followed, dealing in the main with sorrowful heroines whose tearful confessions begged pity rather than censure.[2] Daniel establishes sympathy for Rosamond by depicting her as an unwilling victim of her own fate. She too is an object of lust, though this is the rather melancholic, hesitant lust of an older man who asks a matron of the court to intercede for him. This woman explains the king's interest to Rosamond, who accepts him as her lover. Henry's eventual grief on discovering the poisoned corpse of his mistress is genuine and meant to be redemptive. All this of course we have only from the mouth of Rosamond herself, but there is nothing in the poem to suggest that we should distrust her. Daniel gives his heroine a voice in which to keen at length, and in adapting the tactic for his poem Shakespeare for the first time presents a version of Lucrece in which the victim expresses her own motives and misery. Until then she had been a silent witness to the statements made about her by poets and historians.

Shakespeare's poem resembles Daniel's in a good many respects: each uses rhyme royal, and a similar rhetorical play of argument occurs in both, so much so that certain stanzas could be transferred from one to the other without detection. The moral argument or conscience-wrestling undertaken by Rosamond interestingly makes her combine in one person elements of both of Shakespeare's protagonists, as if a more sympathetic version of Tarquin were to meet with a less resolute Lucrece:

> But what? he is my King and may constraine me,
> Whether I yeelde or not I live defamed:
> The world will thinke authority did gaine me,
> I shal be iudg'd hys love, and so be shamed:
> We see the fayre condemn'd, that never gamed.
>   And if I yeeld, tis honorable shame,
>   If not, I live disgrac'd, yet thought the same.[3]

One further detail linking Daniel to Shakespeare is the casket, a present to Rosamond from Henry, who hopes that its richly inwrought erotic motifs will nudge her thoughts in the direction of desire. But Rosamond notes rather the pathos of those women who represent seductive beauty:

---

[1] Furnivall suggests that Shakespeare combines the theme of *The Legende of Good Women* with the style of extended lament characteristic of *Troilus and Criseyde* (Rollins, p. 419).

[2] See the section on *A Lover's Complaint*, pp. 61–3, below.

[3] *The Complaint of Rosamond*, lines 337–43 (Sprague, p. 50).

The day before the night of my defeature,
He greets me with a Casket richly wrought:
So rare, that arte did seeme to strive with nature,
T'expresse the cunning work-man's curious thought;
The mistery whereof I prying sought.
  And found engraven on the lidde above,
  Amymone how she with Neptune strove.

Amymone old Danaus fayrest daughter,
As she was fetching water all alone
At *Lerna*: whereas Neptune came and caught her,
From whom she striv'd and strugled to be gone,
Beating the ayre with cryes and pittious mone.
  But all in vaine, with him sh'is forced to goe:
  Tis shame that men should use poore maydens so.

There might I see described how she lay,
At those proude feete, not satisfied with prayer:
Wailing her heavie hap, cursing the day,
In act so pittious to express despaire:
And by how much more greev'd, so much more fayre;
  Her teares upon her cheekes poore carefull gerle,
  Did seeme against the sunne cristall and perle.   (372–92)

As well as the overall similarity, a number of verbal parallels connect this passage with Lucrece's larger survey of the Trojan scene. While civil strife and the horror of war and bloodshed make for a different emphasis from this small-scale story of seduction, rape underlies Lucrece's need for solace in the first place. Both accounts draw on a classical and mythological source. The interest in 'curious' workmanship is common to each; and each of them dwells on the relationship of art to life and on the power of representation to affect the spectator. Verbal details, as in phrases like 'There might I see' (386), recur in *Lucrece* (e.g. 1380, 1388, etc.), and a phrase like, 'how she lay/At those proud feet' (386–87) seems echoed in the line, 'Which bleeding under Pyrrhus' proud foot lies' (*Lucrece* 1449). The sheer bloodiness of the Troy scene limits its similarity with the casket depiction, but elsewhere the picture of the grieving Lucrece strikes a common chord with Daniel's poem. Compare lines 391–92 (quoted above) of *Rosamond* with the following description of Lucrece and her maid:

A pretty while these pretty creatures stand,
Like ivory conduits coral cisterns filling.
One justly weeps, the other takes in hand
No cause but company of her drops spilling:
Their gentle sex to weep are often willing,
  Grieving themselves to guess at others' smarts,
  And then they drown their eyes or break their hearts.   (1233–9)

Rosamond is moved at the sight of another woman's tears (albeit artificial ones), just as Lucrece's maid responds to her mistress's sorrow. What both descriptions have in common is that they effect a moment of contemplative pathos centred on a female figure (or figures) or conveyed through a female sensibility. This brings us back once more to the question of the conflicting demands of rhetorical practice and dramatic or psychological plausibility. Another Shakespearean instance, already touched on, is the delicate tableau of the sleeping Lucrece, a picture of purity in her (literal) unconsciousness of Tarquin's gaze (386–420). Such moments, asking from the reader a tender awareness of the beauty of pathos, function ecphrastically (though in a briefer space than the Troy scene) as a statement of the overall pitifulness expressed by the main theme. The extent to which they detach themselves from their immediate context enables them to encompass the feelings and ideas of the poem as a whole. Such distillations of pity summarise the concern the poem wishes to establish over the eventual fate of the heroine, its registration at an earlier narrative point bearing on the mood intended to be dominant at the end.

The Phoenix and the Turtle

THE HISTORICAL CONTEXT

Not least in presenting problems for interpretation is the fact that as well as possessing inherent complexity, *The Phoenix and the Turtle* is only one[1] of several poems by various hands collected by Robert Chester, himself the fullest contributor, in a volume called *Loves Martyr* which was published in 1601.[2] Attempting to puzzle out internal and external correspondences calls to mind the predicament of the man in a sequence of *New Yorker* cartoons who, after contriving to arrange various floating jigsaw shapes of land into an island on which he triumphantly stands, sees approaching other men on their islands with whom he must now attempt to form a peninsula. Before looking at the poem in specific detail, we need to address the question of its place in the wider context of historical, especially personal, allegory, which in turn means surveying the main arguments that have been presented over the past century.

A. B. Grosart, who published an edition of *Loves Martyr* in 1878, was convinced that throughout the book the Phoenix stood for Queen Elizabeth and the Turtle for the Earl of Essex. While the identification appears to strike him as so obvious as not to require proof, he was soon challenged by Furnivall, who, in rejoinder to Grosart's sentimental observation of 'the great Queen's closing melancholy and bursts of weeping with the name of Essex on her lips', pointed out that she did not stick at ordering the

---

[1] Matchett (*'The Phoenix and the Turtle': Shakespeare's Poem and Chester's 'Loves Martyr'* p. 77) thinks that it might be intended as two poems (the threnos being the second), in keeping with the paired contributions of the other poets in the group apart from Chapman. Despite some questionable conclusions, Matchett's full-length study is very informative on matters of tradition and context.

[2] *Loves Martyr: or, Rosalins Complaint. Allegorically shadowing the Truth of Love, in the constant Fate of the Phoenix and Turtle* (London, 1601). In 1611 the old sheets of Chester's book were reissued with a different publisher with a new title page: *The Anuals [sic] of great Brittaine*, the only known copy of which is in the British Library. Shakespeare's poem is unheaded; 'The Phoenix and the Turtle' first appears as a title in the Boston editions of Shakespeare's *Poems* and *Works* (1807). Some editors prefer to omit the second 'the' (see Rollins, pp. 559–61).

earl's execution.[1] Even if we were to accept such death-bed accounts as authoritative, they could not have been anticipated two years earlier. The poem, after all, shows the Phoenix and the Turtle dying together. But despite these objections the theory continues to command a small following, the most appealing recent proponent being William H. Matchett, who concludes that Grosart was right even if the dates were wrong. Elizabeth effectively died with the earl: 'Though the Queen lived on, in losing Essex she had, it might be thought, lost her future.'[2]

Other scholars, while much less convinced of Essex's part in the allegory, still maintain that the Queen is the Phoenix. Elizabeth Watson, writing principally about Chester's contribution (and assuming that Shakespeare followed his lead), proposes the identification with the Queen and then says that the Turtle need not represent anyone particularly: 'the allegory operates on the spiritual plane . . . the emphasis is on the consummation of the Phoenix's virginal nuptials in death rather than on any personal relationship of the Queen's'.[3] Marie Axton, applying the ideas of Ernst Kantorowicz's book, *The King's Two Bodies*, brings attention back to Shakespeare's poem and argues that the key relationship of *The Phoenix and the Turtle* is that of the Queen to her subjects, *both* parties being represented by either bird.[4] Her argument corresponds effectively to the two-in-one strategy which carries the poem's central thrust and gains, like Watson's, in not tying the Queen to the fate of a particular contemporary. However, like all attempts to decode the allegory of a poem which remains wilfully elusive on the point of human identifications, this attractive idea carries an irreducible element of speculation.[5]

In a somewhat different corner is the bizarre identification of the Turtle with Giordano Bruno, who, whatever his relationship with Elizabeth, has the undeniable allegorical advantage of having been burnt in fact.[6]

Yet another proposal, and one which, if it had not already been expressed, somebody would be bound to put forward, is that Shakespeare himself is either the Phoenix

---

[1] *The Poems of Robert Chester (1601–1611). With verse contributions by Shakespeare, Ben Jonson, George Chapman, John Marston, etc.*, ed. Rev. A. B. Grosart (1878), p. 239. For Furnivall, see Rollins, p. 669.

[2] Matchett, p. 193. He goes on to suggest (p. 202) that this is why Shakespeare and other former supporters of Essex wrote no elegies for the Queen in 1603.

[3] 'Natural History in "Love's Martyr"', *Ren & ModS* 9 (1965), 124.

[4] 'The Phoenix is at the same time a figure for Elizabeth and for the monarch's body politic in which the poets see their own political identity as subjects. The Dove is at once a symbol for the love and fidelity of the monarch in her capacity as a natural woman, and for the love and fidelity of her subjects' (*The Queen's Two Bodies: Drama and the Elizabethan Succession* (1978), p. 119).

[5] Marie Axton is followed, with slight qualification, by Anthea Hume, who explores the framework of *Loves Martyr* as a whole to find evidence, especially in Chester's contribution, of a deliberate discrediting of Essex as false love, the earl thus being seen as a false turtle in contrast to Grosart's true one ('*Love's Martyr*, "The Phoenix and the Turtle", and the aftermath of the Essex rebellion', *RES* New series, 40 (1989), 48–71). While carrying some plausibility, this reading allows Chester more subtlety than is normally attributed to him in claiming that he was trying to assess the Queen's state of mind following the rebellion (p. 63); she is also forced to disregard the argument put forward compellingly by Carleton Brown for placing the poem's dedicatee, Sir John Salusbury, at the centre of *Loves Martyr's* interest (see below, pp. 44–5).

[6] See Roy T. Eriksen, '"Un certo amoroso martire": Shakespeare's "The Phoenix and the Turtle" and Giordano Bruno's *De gli eroici furori*', *SpS*, 2 (1981), 193–215.

or the Turtle. The idea is at least as old as Alfred von Mauntz, who interprets the poem as symbolising Shakespeare's break with Southampton.[1] Kenneth Muir and Sean O'Loughlin were to adapt and modify von Mauntz's identifications, placing greater emphasis on the poem as an expression of its author's creativity and capacity for self-renewal. While keeping biographical aspects in mind, they see *The Phoenix and the Turtle* essentially as a phase in Shakespeare's imaginative development.[2] Along roughly similar lines is G. Wilson Knight, who, in an argument apparently favouring Platonic bisexuality, asserts that 'the Turtle signifies the female aspect of the male poet's soul'.[3]

All the above readings, based wholly or in part on eminent contemporaries, pay in the view of some scholars insufficient regard to the role of *Loves Martyr*'s dedicatee, Sir John Salusbury (or Salisbury). Such is the opinion of Carleton Brown, who edited the poems (though not *Loves Martyr*) of both Chester and Salusbury, giving detailed consideration to the biographies of both men.[4]

The 1601 title page has as its heading 'Loves Martyr: or Rosalins Complaint', which recurs on an inner page as 'Rosalins Complaint, Metaphorically applied to Dame Nature at a Parlament held (in the high Star-chamber) by the Gods, for the preservation and increase of Earths beauteous Phoenix'. What follows is a long account interweaving natural and patriotic history. The patriotic part consists of the story of King Arthur, which the person of Nature recounts to the Phoenix.[5] Following this she gives a lengthy account of mineral, plant, and animal life, with special attention to their properties both real and supposed. A section on birds, which may well have inspired Shakespeare when he came to the chorus of mourners in his own poem, leads into a dialogue between the Phoenix and the Turtle as the latter helps in the preparation of the Phoenix's funeral pyre and at last joins her on it. The pelican sings a funeral lament and Chester's generous contribution finally closes with some 'Cantoes' of prayers and vows made for the Phoenix by her 'Paphian Dove'.

In Brown's eyes, the Turtle is Salusbury and the Phoenix his wife, Ursula Halsall, or Stanley, the illegitimate daughter of the Earl of Derby. They married in 1586 and soon had two children, a daughter called Jane (the recreated Phoenix) in 1587, and a son named Harry in 1589. Brown meets objections that two is one child too many for the self-reproducing Phoenix by arguing that Chester may have composed the essential part of *Loves Martyr* not later than 1587. Not everything need be that early; some poetry unrelated to the Phoenix story, such as the interpolated verses on King Arthur,

---

[1] 'Shakespeares lyrische Gedichte', *Jahrbuch*, 28 (1893), 274–331.

[2] *The Voyage to Illyria* (1937), pp. 131–2.

[3] *The Mutual Flame* (1955), p. 185.

[4] *Poems by Sir John Salusbury and Robert Chester*, EETS, Extra Series, n. 113, 1914 (for 1913). Brown challenges Grosart's identification (pp. vii–x) of Chester with the Hertfordshire JP, resident at Royston, and favours Robert Chester of Denbighshire, who appears with Salusbury and Ben Jonson in Christ Church MSS 183 and 184. This lesser luminary is a more likely candidate for patronage; Brown thinks he may have been chaplain to the Salusburys (pp. xlvii–liv).

[5] It is here that Elizabeth Watson finds that Chester's purpose is to offer an allegorical tribute to the Queen, Arthur initiating a line which culminates in Elizabeth (see Watson, pp. 124–5).

may have been finished shortly before publication, when it is generally assumed that Jonson, Shakespeare, and the other contributors wrote theirs, and *when*, as Brown neatly observes, Jane Salusbury at the age of fourteen would be reviving memories of her mother, the Phoenix, in her prime.[1] Brown further comments (p. lxxii) that the contributors who swell the volume at the end generally concur in this view of family succession, only Shakespeare appearing to dissent from it. Leaving aside the other poets' role in the enterprise, Brown turns to the question why Chester would have written *Loves Martyr* with its accent on mourning in 1587. A marriage has been celebrated, a child born; where is the grief in all this? Chester in fact describes two mourning phases in his verses: the first concerns the Turtle, who 'wanders seeking of his love' and who informs the Phoenix that 'my teares are for my *Turtle* that is dead' (Grosart, pp. 131–3), and the second involves the Phoenix with the Turtle upon their resolving to die together on her funeral pyre.[2] Mention of a second turtle complicates matters, as we may imagine, but Brown is equal to answering this. The records show no sign of a former wife or mistress; indeed, had one existed Ursula Stanley may well have demurred at appearing as her replacement. The person the Turtle grieves for, according to Brown, is not a woman but a man: this is Sir John's brother Thomas, executed for treason in September 1586, three months before John and Ursula were married.[3] This works perfectly well in terms of dates and significant events: Chester writes (in 1587) a poem of private consolation which expresses hope for future good cheer. In 1601, when the recently knighted Sir John's fortunes were at their height (Brown, p. xviii), the moment seemed suitable to bring out a volume in tribute to the way the Salusburys had weathered their setbacks. Chester duly collected together what he had written, scribbled out a bit more, and then enlisted the services of Jonson and his fellows to give the book a few degrees' extra sophistication.[4] Where Brown's argument runs into difficulties is over the matter of poetic style; it is hard to believe that the amorous courtliness underlying the passages between Chester's Phoenix and Turtle (even if tending more towards Platonic than erotic love) was in reality intended to include sentiments about a dead brother. The surface reading is the more likely one: the Turtle is grieving over his mate, and the Phoenix, recognising the virtue of true devotion, opens her breast to him. They expire together in a passionate observance of the ideal of chastity which they both share:

> Then I command thee on thy tender care,
> And chiefe obedience that thou owst to me,
> That thou especially (deare Bird) beware

---

[1] What Brown does not tell us is that the Salusburys had eight more children after Jane and Harry. See Matchett (p. 119), who uses the point (not such a strong one) against him and in support of Grosart.

[2] The spirit in which this occurs is not far removed from Shakespeare's poem, and it is easy to suppose that he sifted through Chester's laboured poem, organizing its dissipated drift into his own gnomic stanzas. Evidence that he consulted *Loves Martyr* is produced by A. H. R. Fairchild in '*The Phoenix and Turtle*: a critical and historical interpretation', *Englische Studien*, 33 (1904), 337–84.

[3] Brown, pp. lxiii–lxiv.

[4] Jonson's association with the Salusburys is confirmed by the presence of writings of his in the family papers (see above, p. 43, n, and Brown, p. civ).

Of impure thoughts, or uncleane chastity:
  For we must wast together in that fire,
  That will not burn but by true Loves desire.[1]

None the less, Brown's argument that *Loves Martyr* pays allegorical respect to the Salusburys' hopes, misfortunes, and achievements is by and large acceptable, despite the persisting awkwardness of the missing Turtle's identity. As he points out, the other poets who make up the 'Chorus Vatum' subscribe to the terms of flattery laid out by Chester. Jonson refers affectionately to 'our *Dove*', and Marston speaks of the new Phoenix, 'arising out of the Phoenix and Turtle Doves ashes', which is 'now growne unto maturitie' (Brown, p. cxxi). Such details convince Brown that the Salusburys' first daughter plays a key role in Chester's poem. Marston also takes care to paper over the cracks glaring in the edifice of Shakespeare's contribution: these are that the pair of birds vanish 'leaving no posterity'. As he follows him, Marston delicately points out that Shakespeare, despite his good intentions, has not quite told the truth about them:[2]

O twas a moving *Epicidium*![3]
Can Fire? can Time? can blackest Fate consume
So rare creation? No; tis thwart to sense,
Corruption quakes to touch such excellence,
Nature exclaimes for Justice, Justice Fate,
Ought into nought can never remigrate.
Then looke; for see what glorious issue (brighter
Then clearest fire, and beyond faith farre whiter
Then *Dians* tier) now springs from yonder flame?

It may of course be that Shakespeare deliberately bows off stage, enabling Marston to make the corrective gesture, as Empson supposes (*Signet*, p. 1676a), but such a move is at odds with the self-contained nature of his poem; Marston has to struggle a bit to get things going again. Brown is probably right to feel that Shakespeare is out of step with the other members of the chorus in not genuflecting in the Salusburys' direction. Empson (p. 1674a) trenchantly argues the reverse on the grounds that ignoring a patron's wishes would be unthinkable at the time. That *would* have been true for Shakespeare in 1593 or 1594 (as we have seen); but would it now? Of the 1601 contributors, Shakespeare was undoubtedly the feather in the Chester–Salusbury cap. Jonson was

---

[1] Grosart, pp. 135–6. The Phoenix symbolised constancy and chastity, and Chester's stanza makes it clear that the fire is that of passion finding its true consummation in a pure heart.

[2] Some scholars think that this poem is anonymous because it is unsigned; but the title page describes the 'new compositions' as being by authors 'whose names are subscribed to their several workes', which means presumably that a poet's name follows the group of poems he has submitted. Marston's name follows the fourth poem after Shakespeare's and all four poems seem to be interlinked. Ben Jonson's name occurs twice, each time after two poems. Chapman, like Shakespeare, appears to have contributed a single poem. The name 'Ignoto' appears only once, following two short poems on the nature of the phoenix which precede Shakespeare's. It may be assumed that these were convenient generalised descriptions borrowed from an author of unknown identity. Jonson, Chapman, and Marston all seem to be working as a team reinforcing each other's praise of a particular lady's virtues.

[3] Grosart, p. 185. 'Epicidium' means 'funeral ode' and would appear to refer to Shakespeare's immediately preceding threnos.

still establishing his career; despite successes with his first plays, he had not reached the pinnacle of fame he was to achieve with *Volpone* and the great comedies of 1606 to 1614. Besides, as we have already observed, he appears to have had a close connection with the family. Marston's fortunes were always checkered, and he was not in a position to sneer at patronage. Another contributor, George Chapman, was a careful man who had helped bring *Hero and Leander* to posthumous birth under the auspices of the Walsingham family; he was not likely to miscue the possibility of profitable self-ingratiation with the reviving Salusburys. The publication of *Eastward Ho!* (1605), written by all three, shows in addition that Jonson, Marston, and Chapman were all collaborating closely with each other. But Shakespeare was on a different plane, being known by now as the creator of Falstaff, of the second tetralogy, of *Twelfth Night*, and very possibly, by this time, *Hamlet*. He had also written the mysterious 'sugred Sonnets', which everyone knew about but which few people had seen (see introductory section on *The Passionate Pilgrim*). It is entirely probable that Chester's patron would have been glad to have Shakespeare in the volume on the latter's own terms. Apart from Southampton, this knight of the shires was the only man in England who could boast of possessing Shakespeare's name.

Despite Shakespeare's disconnectedness from the family part of the exercise, it is likely that he took his theme from Chester's Phoenix and Turtle story, and that he even, as Fairchild tries to demonstrate (see above, p. 44, n), examined the relevant stanzas of *Loves Martyr* quite closely. Shakespeare, as any survey of his sources at once makes clear, drew inspiration from other literary works rather than directly from history, politics, or philosophy (a practice which in its way bears out Sidney's argument in *The Apology for Poetry* for literature's supremacy over other disciplines). Chester's dialogue between the Phoenix and the Turtle on passionate chastity, and the Pelican's following verses, are among the best things in his overlong poem and at least state lucidly and readably, and with a sense of drama, the arguments on ideal love which were normally confined to prose treatises – all of which, including even Hoby's Castiglione, tend towards dry abstraction. Shakespeare probably found them interesting enough to respond to them with his own poem. This is to argue that his subject is neither the Queen nor anything to do with historical allegory, but the paradox of pure eros, or passionate propriety, and the measure to which Neoplatonic solutions (already touched on in our account of *Venus and Adonis*) may enter human affairs.

However, before turning to the poem proper we should at least consider one other recent attempt to make sense of Shakespeare's poem in connection with the part played in *Loves Martyr* by Chester and the Salusburys.

This is E. A. J. Honigmann's study, in which he follows Brown very closely in giving prominence to the Salusburys. The main difference from Brown is that Honigmann argues for the closeness, even intimacy, of Shakespeare with the family. To find the connection he revives a speculation of E. K. Chambers' that Shakespeare was the William Shakeshafte who belonged to the Lancashire Hoghton household.[1] If this

---

[1] Chambers, *Shakespearean Gleanings*, 1944, pp. 52–56. Chambers elsewhere mentions the verses on the Stanley tomb at Tonge Church which William Dugdale ascribed to Shakespeare in 1644 (see Chambers, 1, 551ff.).

were true it would help link him with the Derbyshire Stanleys in the early 1580s – a period which gives otherwise virtually no clue as to Shakespeare's whereabouts and activities.[1] If Shakespeare did know the Stanleys this early, then he would be on the scene for Ursula Stanley's marriage to Salusbury, and able to join Chester in his poetic enterprise. This, then, is Honigmann's most original contribution to the debate: far from accepting a commission for Chester's volume only in 1601, and then according to Brown in a distant, disengaged manner, Shakespeare wrote from a position close to the household. Honigmann largely accepts Brown's theory about the lost Turtle being Thomas Stanley but thinks that Shakespeare wrote his piece in 1586, before the birth of Jane Salusbury, and possibly even before the wedding had taken place.[2] This is because Shakespeare's poem salutes the death as so final, whereas Chester's 'Conclusion' celebrates a 'new uprising bird' (Grosart, p. 142), which Brown, as we have seen, identifies as the Salusburys' daughter Jane.

Honigmann's attempt to connect Shakespeare intimately with the Stanleys in the decade before the 1590s weaves a more than usually elaborate conjectural tissue; but space precludes doing more than raise a quizzical eyebrow at it here. However, some important objections (which he anticipates without really answering) occur to his method of accounting for the writing of the poem at such an early stage. *The Phoenix and the Turtle* belongs to the group of poems described on the title page as 'new compositions'. Honigmann's contention that this meant modern, as distinct from such older material as that of the 'venerable Italian' Torquato Caeliano (whom Chester, giving his work an antique flavour, purports to have translated), does not convince. It was a customary publisher's device to tempt readers by advertising work as the most recent done by a poet.[3] Then there is the question of stylistic conception. Would Shakespeare have written such a poem in the mid-1580s? Honigmann imagines that it is enough to answer this question by pleading Shakespeare's undoubted virtuosity by the age of twenty-two, citing the youthful accomplishments of such as Milton in support. But that ignores the rather more significant doubt whether the form is characteristic of the kind of poetry being written in 1586, the year of Sir Philip Sidney's death. Sidney, indeed, provides a good yardstick, for he had produced at least one poem which resembles at points *The Phoenix and the Turtle*. This is the 'Eighth Song' from *Astrophil and Stella*, the following stanzas of which may have influenced Shakespeare as he wrote (allowing for some metrical differences, e.g. the use of heptasyllabic metre in the first couplet and octosyllabic in the second of each stanza, as opposed to Shakespeare's use of outer and inner rhyming quatrains, with nearly perfect heptasyllabic metre until the threnos):

> Sigh they did, but now betwixt
> Sighs of woe were glad sighs mixt,
> With armes crost, yet testifying
> Restless rest, and living dying.

---

[1] E. A. J. Honigmann, *Shakespeare: The 'Lost Years'*, 1985, pp. 59–60.
[2] Honigmann, pp. 105–9.
[3] See the discussion on *The Passionate Pilgrim*, p. 58.

Their eares hungry of each word,
Which the deere tongue would afford,
But their tongues restraind from walking,
Till their harts had ended talking.

But when their tongues could not speake,
Love it selfe did silence breake;
Love did set his lips asunder,
Thus to speake in love and wonder. (Ringler, p. 218)

But Sidney is much more bound by the restrictions of the pastoral narrative mode he adopts, his song overall bearing a more obvious, hence more reduced referential focus than the enigmatic, emblematic terms of Shakespeare's poem. As the latter supersedes Sidney's straightforward effect of pleasing melancholy, it produces a comparatively more sophisticated, assured marshalling of complex ideas, while its lapidary, gnomic manner is characteristic rather of slightly later Metaphysical poetry than the school of Astrophil.

Because of its uniqueness within the Shakespearean canon, it is hard to establish stylistic parallels between *The Phoenix and the Turtle* and his other work. But, as Heinrich Straumann observes, at about the time of the publication of the poem, Shakespeare's belief in the human (predominantly female) embodiment of such qualities as beauty, truth, and 'grace in all simplicity' seems to falter; figures such as Ophelia, Cressida, Desdemona, and Cordelia can for various reasons no longer offer that inspired confidence in love that the heroines of the great comedies optimistically promised.[1] 1601 seems an appropriate date for a poem which, while still pledging faith in an ideal love, despairs of its earthly incarnation.

Honigmann, like the majority, if not all, of those scholars who look for a personal or historical key to the poem's meaning, pushes speculation to the limits in order to secure his argument. None the less, he is surely right to argue that Shakespeare consulted Chester's verses and incorporated their 'mystical-allusive' manner in his response (Honigmann, p. 109), though he probably did not do so until Ben Jonson showed him Chester's miscellaneous compilation. If *The Phoenix and the Turtle* points anywhere outside itself, the direction it indicates is doubtless a literary one.

THE POEM AND LITERARY TRADITION

Because the tone of *The Phoenix and the Turtle* is 'detached and impersonal', it does not follow, as Brown assumes, that it is 'frigid and perfunctory' (p. lxxiii). On the contrary, recent commentary has found that it possesses great resonance; the quarrel turns rather on matters of emphasis. Whereas Robert Ellrodt finds it to be 'throughout funereal', Prince, whose imagination it particularly fired, describes even its analytic terminology as having 'a kind of ethereal frenzy'; Peter Dronke agrees with him, though in more muted

---

[1] Straumann, *Phönix und Taube*, Zurich, 1953, pp. 50–2.

accents, in finding the mood of the poem exhilarating.[1] Then there is the question of what traditions combine in *The Phoenix and the Turtle*. Ellrodt (pp. 100–8) gives a broad survey of the classical, Platonic, and Petrarchan influences, while J. V. Cunningham tries to show that the central part, or anthem, reflects the medieval scholastic refinement – and consequent displacement – of Platonic (specifically Plotinian) thought. Again, there is the matter of the birds' emblematic value: how much of this is received wisdom, and how far is it original to Shakespeare?

As I have already argued, Shakespeare seems to take some of his cues from Chester; but Fairchild, who demonstrates this aspect thoroughly, also sees evidence of Chaucerian influence (Fairchild, pp. 360–2). The bestiary, specifically avine, tradition is well represented in Chaucer's *Parlement of Foules*; this poem contains all the birds Shakespeare mentions, and its fuller, pleonastic description of them may help explain some of the later poet's apparently enigmatic paraphrases. For example, Chaucer speaks of 'The wedded turtel with hir herte trewe' (line 355), which tells us why the Phoenix and the Turtle are ideally mated in Shakespeare's poem. (The observation is of course also made by Chester.) But, concerning the phoenix especially, there are ancient traditions which may be operating through or separate from Chaucer as well as Renaissance modifications of the bird's legend. Early Christian poets, such as Lactantius in the *De Ave Phoenice*, adapted the description of the phoenix given by Herodotus to religious purposes and identified it as a type of chastity in opposition to the cult of Venus.[2] This was no doubt influential in producing the already noted Renaissance (and Shakespearean) insistence on the bird as an example of rarity or chastity rather than on its capacity for self-renewal from its own cinders. But precisely how such influence exerted itself is much less clear. Petrarch, a strong force on later Renaissance poetry, sometimes referred to Laura as a phoenix, which doubtless suggested to his imitators that the bird was an ideal symbol for a mistress who combined beauty and virtue. In 1593 a miscellany called *The Phoenix Nest* was published, in which appeared Matthew Roydon's elegy for Sidney. The poem displays a number of birds which listen to a (human) speaker's lament for Astrophil (Sidney); this elegist commends the rare love of Astrophil and Stella (though he does not call either of them phoenix or turtle)

---

[1] Robert Ellrodt, 'An anatomy of *The Phoenix and the Turtle*', *S. Sur. 15* (1962), 99; Prince, p. xliv; Peter Dronke, '*The Phoenix and the Turtle*', *Orbis Litterarum* 23 (1968), 220. Authenticity has long ceased to be a problem, despite the poem's unusual and even unique appearance within the Shakespearean canon. The fact that it was twice published unchallenged under Shakespeare's name in his lifetime, while none of the attributions to Jonson et al. in the same volume have drawn dissent, argues strongly for his authorship. Malone had no doubt that it was genuine, though the mid-nineteenth century experienced a current of scepticism which persisted until Grosart published his edition (here at least his influence has been positive). Furnivall doubted it was Shakespeare's in 1877, but later changed his mind. Lee, in successive editions of his *Life of Shakespeare*, moved from doubt and disapproval to firm acceptance. Though a few dissenters survived earlier this century, recent opinion is almost unanimous in its conviction and admiration. See Rollins, pp. 561–3.

[2] *Lactantius: the Minor Works*, trans. Sister Mary Francis McDonald, O. P., in *The Fathers of the Church*, LIV (1965), 219. Baldwin connects Shakespeare via Lactantius to Ovid, *Amores* 2.6. Ovid's bird is in fact a parrot, but Baldwin observes that in *Metam.* 15 he treats of a phoenix and argues for a combination of sources (see *Genetics* pp. 363–73).

and impresses upon his audience that such a love is unlikely to be seen again. Elements of Roydon's poem suggest similarities with both Chester[1] and Shakespeare; but it also departs from Shakespeare (in particular) in some of its ideas. Such is the prevalence of the phoenix-as-rarity motif in Elizabethan poetry that identifying influences or sources is a daunting task.

ARGUMENT AND STYLE

The Phoenix and the Turtle does not in fact display the supremacy of any one particular tradition; its very succinct use of emblem allows it to integrate and exchange meanings without (as a longer narrative might be compelled to do) opting for one over another. In this way the poem maintains variety, charging its statement with various degrees of meaning which in turn reward the tone.

Variety expresses itself as the poem alternates between poles of significance. The birds named in the opening stanzas contrast and complement one another: the acceptable music of 'the bird of loudest lay' opposes the harsh voice of the screech-owl; the eagle registers its own distinctions, commanding, yet not tyrannical; the white swan alternates with the black crow. Underlying the choice of choric birds may well be the scheme of the four elements, since the Phoenix represents fire, the soaring eagle the empyrean or air, the swan water, and the crow earth.[2]

Various, too, are the interpretations invited by the opening line. Is this the Phoenix or some other bird? Mention of the 'sole Arabian tree' indicates but does not confirm that the Phoenix is intended.[3] Other candidates are the 'crane, the geaunt, with his trompes soune' (*Parlement of Foules*, line 344), the cock, the lark, and the nightingale.[4] In fact no bird may be particularly signified, only aspects of birds. If we read the lines metonymously, the 'herald' announces not himself but some great person whom he serves. This is not to deny outright the possibility that the Phoenix may be its own trumpeter but to stress that function rather than identity is what matters. Similarly, the synecdoche of 'chaste wings' seems to indicate the Turtle (on the evidence of Chaucer's example – see above, p. 49). Attempts at exclusively identifying the 'bird of loudest lay' tend to ignore that the Turtle is equally relevant to the opening statement, since the poem concerns itself with its relationship with the Phoenix and nowhere else in the first five stanzas does the Turtle appear. The summons accordingly issues on behalf of the Phoenix and is heard and understood primarily and most naturally by the Turtle. The opening stanzas' modification, fashioning, and refinement of emblematic allegory is what gives the poem its air of confident self-possession.

---

[1] Those interested in Brown's theory of the dates of composition of *Loves Martyr* should consult Rollins's edition of *The Phoenix Nest*, where it is shown that Roydon most likely composed his elegy shortly after Sidney's death in October 1586, early enough for Chester to have consulted it for his own poem on the Salusburys. See *The Phoenix Nest*, ed. H. E. Rollins, 1931, pp. 115–18.

[2] Compare *Luc.* 1009, 'The crow may bathe his coal-black wings in mire.'

[3] Baldwin (*Genetics*, p. 368) and Dronke (p. 208) both argue in favour of the phoenix and cite Lactantius, who describes the bird as being distinguished for sweetness, though not power, of voice.

[4] For respective arguments see Ronald Bates, 'Shakespeare's "The Phoenix and Turtle"', *SQ* 6 (1955), 23–6.

Once this pattern of fluent alternation has been established, the poem is ready for its painless shift into abstract, antithetical terminology. Concepts replace creatures as the anthem begins (line 21): love, constancy, distance, essence, possession, property, reason, confusion. Love affirms itself by contradiction, with its traditional opponent, reason, apparently acquiescing in the manoeuvre, as propositions find their formulation according to an inexplicable yet infallible logic. In fact, the notion that distance should not defy love but reinforce it is quite familiar. John Donne's poem 'A Valediction: forbidding mourning' carries an asssurance from lover to loved one that,

> We by a love so much refin'd
>   That ourselves know not what it is,
> Inter-assurèd of the mind,
>   Care less, eyes, lips, hands to miss.   (Grierson, p. 50)

Donne's poem informs the reader sufficiently of its context, a temporary separation between lovers as one of them leaves to go on a journey, whereby a Neoplatonic argument can be seen to meet an immediate need for consolation. We may assume that once he has returned the lovers will again experience the physical union that absence for the moment denies them, though the poem shows too much delicacy to make this an obvious part of its promise. But Shakespeare's Neoplatonism thrives on no such human assurance; the Phoenix and the Turtle are dead and gone for ever. It is not a question of a little bit of abstinence being good for the soul. All that it has to feed its faith is its own supreme confidence in its power of expression. Pared down to essentials, the poem seems hardly more than an exercise in declamation; what makes it all the more formidable is its ability to find a tone equal to Donne's in expansiveness without enjoying similar terms of recovery and return.

Although the abstract middle stanzas are brilliantly turned, everything they achieve lies within the Renaissance habit of antithesis and its stylistic deployment of oxymoron. None the less, they convince the reader that what they describe is rare and astonishing. Whether the art of paradox does this alone or whether thematic depth is sounded is not easy to decide. Critics have run their irony detectors over its surface without coming up with anything positive.[1] If *The Phoenix and the Turtle* achieves its statement without the dramatic personal underpinning of 'A Valediction: forbidding mourning', it also does without the ironic advantage of a poem such as Andrew Marvell's 'The Definition of Love', which is similarly patterned on antithetical clauses. Those who believe, for example, that Shakespeare joined Chester's enterprise perhaps reluctantly find the poem discreetly mocking; but others are equally convinced that he made use of the occasion to address a national concern. The poem's control of allegorical method allows us to summon forth a number of competing readings without providing us with the assurance that any one of them holds the key. The critical practice of regarding the poem as a meditation on its own stylistic medium (which at one time was applied to *all* poetry) has long been discredited; but here is one poem which appears none the

---

[1] Alvarez reminds us that all this lamentation is over a couple of 'dead birds'; but such an observation signals the beginning rather than the end of speculation. See A. Alvarez, 'Shakespeare, *The Phoenix and the Turtle*', in *Interpretations*, ed. John Wain, 1955, p. 16.

less to benefit from such an analysis.[1] Even so, to take the line that the poem regards itself as its subject still seems not to be enough to account for all that it achieves. We should broaden such self-reflexive terms, despite the self-enclosed appearance of the work, and acknowledge rather that its subject is love which finds an ideal expression of itself in the poem. Such a love is to be despaired of in life, as the threnos with its emphatic negatives makes clear, but the capacity of art to contemplate it helps partially to overcome the disillusion.

Much of the success of the poem derives from its engendering fresh images for stale terms, a facility which in turn mirrors both the generative power and regeneration. No little part of this virtuosity lies in its two subtle shifts in key: first from the invocation to the anthem, then from the anthem to the threnos. The threnos's triple rhyme introduces a new elegiac cadence without abandoning the argumentative procedure which has so far maintained antithesis. Two-in-one becomes three-in-one as the ideational pattern of the opening line of the threnos ('Beauty, truth, and rarity') demonstrates. But duality, the necessary medium for expressing hopes of recovery or redemption, persists as a part of the design, even as the earlier antithetical clamour gives way to a mood of sadness and surrender. Take, for example, the tripartite pronunciation of the following stanza:

> Death is now the phoenix' nest,
> And the turtle's loyal breast
> To eternity doth rest. (54–6)

Are they or are they not both dead? The antithesis 'Death' – 'nest' (taking 'nest' to be a place of nurture) modulates through the concept 'loyal' and comes to 'rest' in 'eternity'. The birds have died, but the Turtle's loyalty survives. Do they in some sense live on in it, or are we to see such loyalty as something which, though expressed through them, also transcends them? It is important that the dualism should be formulated in this broader syllogistic pattern: for, while maintaining an antithetical nature, the argument *appears* like a synthesis to evolve. The beauty of the solution is that it manages to strike a note of affirmation in its final prayer, assimilating but not discounting the persistently negative rejoinders.

As with death, so with sex:

> Leaving no posterity,
> 'Twas not their infirmity,
> It was married chastity, (59–61)

strikes some readers as a light-hearted Falstaffian quip on a prim pair,[2] and others as a compliment in good faith. Of course it is natural for marriages to require chastity, but that means barring access from outside, not within. Yet the point of the lines lies perhaps in the Platonic distinction between the reality of physical reproduction and its idea. It is not entirely true that the Phoenix and the Turtle leave no posterity, since all those who are 'either true or fair' (line 66) are in some degree

---

[1] Walter J. Ong provides a good example in, 'Metaphor and the twinned vision', *Sewanee Review* 63 (1955), 193–201.

[2] See Bates, p. 28.

descended from them. Unhappily, the true and fair appear not to be one and the same, for the line reads 'true *or* fair'. This ironic observation is not one that disables the ideal side of the poetic argument, since it follows logically from what has been stated previously. According to Platonism, a beautiful appearance signifies an inner spiritual goodness (fairness indicates truth); but according to the poem, only ideally is this so. With the death of the Phoenix and the Turtle the ideal conjunction is severed. None the less, the birds remain as an inspiration to anyone who is true or fair to try to restore it, so that disbelieving reason might once more see division grow together.

The reading of *The Phoenix and the Turtle* offered here detects a good deal of familiar Platonism, which in turn brings us back to the point made about the Renaissance revival of Platonic ideas in connection with *Venus and Adonis*. Such philosophy had a pronounced effect on the love poetry of the period. But Platonism, or Neoplatonism, enters the literature of Renaissance England on special terms. We have observed that Venus speaks in Platonic accents only when Adonis dies (see above, p. 21); the poem of John Donne's quoted in this section offers a Platonic solution as consolation for an unbearable separation. One of Donne's most heartfelt poems 'A Nocturnall upon St Lucies Day' strikes a Platonic note against sensual love in an effort to come to terms with the overpowering nihilism induced by his mistress' death (see particularly lines 37–41); and in Sidney's *Astrophil and Stella*, which has sometimes been subjected to Platonic analysis, the lover moves from a vision of erotic delight into a more spiritual phase, none the less intensifying rather than overcoming his feelings for the love object. Platonism often applies itself to literary statements in an irreducibly personal and even tragic manner. Far from transcending sensuality, as pure Platonism requires, much of the poetry brings it into new and sombre focus. *The Phoenix and the Turtle* differs in this respect from the examples just quoted, since it treats its argument with relaxed assurance and keeps aloof from personal anguish by dealing only in emblems. Notwithstanding, it views its Platonism from the perspective of a tragic denouement and regards its subject as a melancholy one. And yet its tone is buoyant. The curious effect of producing a mood of triumph and exhilaration in treating of loss and disillusionment brings further evidence of the transformations literary Platonism underwent as it put down English roots.

The Passionate Pilgrim

With *The Passionate Pilgrim* we come to poems of dubious ascription. This sequence of twenty poems, only five of which are certainly by Shakespeare, fascinates much more by its publishing history than by the value of its contents. The most plausible account of its genesis (given by both Edwin E. Willoughby and Joseph Quincy Adams)[1] is as follows. The printer William Jaggard, who later brought the First Folio into the world, most likely got hold of a common-place book (i.e. a collection of poems in manuscript) which contained two of what Francis Meres in 1598 referred to as Shakespeare's 'sugred

---

[1] See Willoughby, pp. 47–51, and Adams, introduction to the *PP* facsimile edn, 1939.

Sonnets'.[1] Both Willoughby and Adams conjecture that Jaggard shrewdly arranged his collection to look as if it might be Shakespeare's sonnets by placing the only two Shakespearean sonnets from the collection he had (corresponding to numbers 138 and 144 of Thorpe) at the beginning and then following up with other sonnets, including three from *Love's Labour's Lost*. In fact, the last of these three (number 16) is a song rather than a sonnet, but more of that in a moment.

The order of the sonnets following the two genuine 'sugred Sonnets' runs: (3) 'Did not the heavenly rhetoric of thine eye' (*LLL*), (4) 'Sweet Cytherea, sitting by a brook', (5) 'If love make me forsworn' (*LLL*), (6) 'Scarce had the sun dried up the dewy morn'. Then with number 7, 'Fair is my love, but not so fair as fickle', we meet with a sonnet which is not in fourteen lines but takes the form of three six-line stanzas. Conventionally, this still qualifies as a 'sonnet' (a term loosely applicable in Elizabethan poetry to any short lyric), despite the dominance gained by the fourteen-line version that we now acknowledge as the proper sonnet form and to which almost all of Shakespeare's 1609 collection adheres. In 1599, a prospective purchaser who knew only that Shakespeare's poems were called 'sonnets' would leaf through most of the volume without becoming any the wiser.

Then follows number 8, the poem from the Barnfield volume, which is in fourteen lines; number 9, a poem in fourteen-line form with one line apparently missing (see collation and commentary); number 10, in two six-line stanzas; number 11, another fourteen-line sonnet; number 12, which is in twelve lines; number 13, in two six-line stanzas; and number 14, a longer poem of five six-line stanzas. Despite these variations, the fourteen poems would appear to be a collection of sonnets, which, as Adams points out, is their intention.

All his editors agree that Jaggard was practising a deception on the reader; but how seriously and with what effect on Shakespeare it is difficult to determine. Let us first complete our description of the poems in the volume. Following the close of number 14 there surprisingly appears a second or supplementary title page, 'Sonnets to sundry notes of Musicke' (see Textual Analysis). Why this title page exists where it does is a mystery. According to Willoughby it was intended 'to enable the latter portion of the work to be sold separately should the sale prove slow' (p. 50). Adams (pp. xxxv–xxxvi) thinks that its presence has more to do with Jaggard's wish to appease Shakespeare, who may have proved difficult over the printing of some of his poems without his consent as well as the attribution to him of several more which he certainly did not write. Plausible as this conjecture is, it ignores Jaggard's apparent repetition of the offence in 1612 (see below, pp. 58–9).

Either Jaggard introduced the division to do what Willoughby has suggested (though against this it must be objected that the poems in the second part are less interesting on

---

[1] See *Shakspere Allusion-Book*, I, 46. Poem number 8, 'If music and sweet poetry agree', was published a year earlier by Jaggard's brother John in Richard Barnfield's *Encomium of Lady Pecunia*. It is a speculative point whether this poem also belonged to the putative commonplace book or came from a separate source, though its very dissimilarity from the others would argue against careful compilation on the part of the publisher (see below, p. 00). Number 20, from the second half of the volume, was also printed in Barnfield's collection (see *PP* 20.0 n).

the whole than those in the first) or he felt compelled to do it for the reasons Adams has proposed (though, again, one poem, number 16, is also by Shakespeare, which would suggest that if the bookseller was trying to make his peace with him by marking off his compositions from the rest, neither he nor the poet was concerned with accuracy). Or, another reason, he was concerned that the customer should not complain at the perpetration: the volume did have poems by Shakespeare, but it had other poems, too, which it did not pretend were his. It is yet further possible, given the already observed flexibility of terms, that Jaggard was exploiting Meres's uninformative phrase, 'sugred Sonnets', to imply that while some of them followed the fourteen-line pattern, others adopted a freer lyrical or song form (as in Donne's *Songs and Sonets*). All that we know is that each part of the volume has its distinct character, the poems of the first resembling a sonnet sequence while those of the second appear to be a medley of songs, which is perhaps why 'On a day' (from *LLL*) drifted into this section. This still leaves us with the question concerning the make-up of the first or more Shakespearean part of the volume, both how the poems relate to one another and which of them are his.

To take the second aspect of the question first: so far, only four of these poems have with any certainty been ascribed to Shakespeare (number 16, we remember, being the fifth). Several others may be described in one sense or another as 'Shakespearean': numbers 4, 6, 9, 11, all of which are on the 'Venus and Adonis' theme, each of them fixing on some moment which occurs, actually or in spirit (depending upon one's interpretation), in the narrative poem; for example, Venus attempting to woo Adonis (4 and 11), warning him against the boar (9), or (number 6) watching him bathe naked (not an incident in the poem, but one which derives from the view of Venus as lustful and Adonis as beautiful). These poems all strike a fairly lascivious note – even number 9, in which she attempts to deter Adonis from the hunt ends on a bawdy *double entendre*. Shakespeare could arguably have written any of them, but they more likely came about in response to his success with *Venus and Adonis*, just as any great literary *coup de foudre* inspires its often scurrilous and irreverent imitations – the more so if irreverence is seen as one of its own characteristics. *Gulliver's Travels* spawned a shoal of petty imitations paying homage to its iconoclastic spirit, notable among the rest being Pope's 'Mrs Gulliver to the Captain'.

The author of these four acts of homage to the nature of Venus is quite possibly Bartholomew Griffin, mainly on the evidence that number 11 (or a version of it) exists in his *Fidessa* (1596). If we attempt to compare the four sonnets with each other, it may be seen that none of them strikes a reflective mood in the manner of Shakespeare's sonnets but describes or narrates an action which comes to an invariably amusing climax. If one of them stands apart from the others, it is number 6, which seems to have a homosexual readership in mind with its contemplation of Adonis's physique. This sonnet resembles the progress of Ovid's *Elegy* 1.5, a poem of heterosexual passion in every respect, except perhaps for the detail that it was rendered into English with characteristic zest by the homosexual Marlowe (see commentary).

To cut many fruitless lines of inquiry short, it is most likely that Jaggard either found these four poems collected together in the common-place book of Willoughby's theory or he contrived to put them together from various manuscript sources. Griffin's printed version of number 11 is completely rewritten in lines 9–12, which suggests the intervention of a manuscript variant. It is less likely that Jaggard commissioned them 'to look like Shakespeare', since, allegations of piracy notwithstanding, he probably did not intend to perpetrate an outright hoax,[1] and whereas in attempting to pass itself off as an edition of Shakespeare's *Sonnets* the collection lacks due sophistication, the number of Venus-inspired lyrics available in manuscript would have been enough for Jaggard to make up his volume without having recourse to out-and-out fakery.[2]

Shakespeare's best known or best loved poem in 1599 was *Venus and Adonis* (which, as we have seen, had been reprinted more than once). The *Sonnets*, of course, were more known about than known. It is not surprising therefore that sonnets on the theme of Venus and Adonis should masquerade as the real thing, since, in lieu of any very precise information, a reader may naturally have supposed that the sonnets further explored Venus's love for the young man. It is also perhaps significant that number 1 (a 'real' Shakespearean sonnet) should contain the phrase 'some untutored youth' (line 3), which, while it does not describe the speaker as he sees himself, only as he hopes she might see him, provides a link with the Adonis theme of the other sonnets. Similarly, number 2 describes a young Adonis-like 'man right fair' being preyed upon by a 'woman coloured ill', which again adequately describes the lascivious Venus of some interpretations. Since number 3 addresses itself to a goddess, it might be supposed that we are listening to the voice of an Adonis who has been tempted by Venus. This leads into number 4, the first of the light-hearted Venus sonnets. Then comes the more sombre, conventional anguish of number 5, which in the sequence reads like a companion piece to number 3 (both of them being taken from *LLL*). But number 5 is too coloured by the play's ideas (as witness lines like 'study his bias leaves') to lend itself convincingly to the themes of *Venus and Adonis*. Number 7 breaks from any possible connection with the Venus theme, but it does interestingly echo some of the arguments of *A Lover's Complaint* (especially in such painful musing lines as 17, 'Was this a lover or a lecher whether'). Number 8 is, as already indicated, an undoubted interpolation from Barnfield's collection, to which the Jaggard family had the copyright.[3] Number 10 is an elegy for a youthful 'fair flower' and may recall Venus's lament for the dead Adonis. Number 12 has something of Venus's appeal to Adonis on the grounds of youth, and partly echoes her abhorrence of decrepit age (lines 133–44). Number 13 reads like a rebuke of this, condemning beauty's superficiality in the same suspicious temper

---

[1] Swinburne is the most damning accuser of Jaggard, calling him an 'infamous pirate, liar and thief' (*Studies in Prose and Poetry*, 1894, p. 90) – a charge from which Willoughby gallantly and with some success tries to exculpate him.

[2] It is worth reminding ourselves that uncertainty of attribution does not at this period mean intention to deceive the public. That form of hoax-making is a later eighteenth-century occupation. The apparent indifference with which many professional authors treated their works once in print attests (quite apart from their subsequent lack of control over publication) to how much more they valued the interest of an influential patron such as Southampton than the approval of a larger reading public.

[3] Copyright law was mainly confined to publishers/booksellers, who were sometimes also the printer. (*Venus and Adonis* was initially both printed and sold by Richard Field.) An author was to some degree protected by common law with regard to *unpublished* works; but once their publication had been authorised their copyright belonged to the bookseller, who had the right to sell or transfer copyright to another publisher, the author having no further say in the matter. (In 1594, Field transferred the copyright of *Venus and Adonis* to John Harrison, for whom he also printed *Lucrece*). The law remained in this state until 1709.

Adonis shows when resisting Venus. Finally, from this section, number 14 turns on the theme of the lover lying awake in anguish and hoping against hope that his beloved will give him the time of day tomorrow. Despite the reversal of sexes, the poem recalls Venus's beseeching mood as she and Adonis say goodnight to each other. Interestingly, there are verbal and circumstantial echoes with *Lucrece*, particularly the reference to Philomela in lines 17–18 and the use of 'descant' in line 4 (compare *Luc.* 1134, 'While thou on Tereus descants better skill').

The conclusion from this survey seems to be that while some of the sonnets speak directly of Venus and Adonis, others do so in an oblique way, while one or two touch on other matters. Only number 8 has nothing at all to do with the concerns of the narrative poem. In their different ways all the other poems can be said to respond to its theme, even allowing for the rather obvious objection that such a theme is anyway common to erotic narratives and sonnet sequences alike.

The appearance of the first fourteen poems, then, gives the impression of a sonnet collection, or even a sequence, on the theme of Venus and Adonis, while including other motifs. Whether the arrangement is Jaggard's or one that came to hand is hard to tell; as likely as not the common-place book compiler had done Jaggard's work for him, the printer astutely spotting the marketing advantages of the sequence.

The 'sonnets' following the supplementary title page, while formally different, claim to be sonnets none the less; and the inclusion among this second group of number 16 contradicts Adams's theory that Jaggard was trying to square things with Shakespeare by not attributing all the poems to him (see above p. 54).

What is Shakespeare's role in all this? The short answer is: probably not much. As indicated above, copyright was much more a bookseller's affair than an author's. Poets who wished to apply common-law copyright would be in the curious and contradictory position of trying to avoid publication. The lack of a dedication more or less announces Shakespeare's indifference to the event of publishing, and since most of the poems were not his he would of course subsequently have looked rather foolish had he, along with Jaggard, tried to pass them off as his own. Although nobody seems to have seriously argued that Jaggard really thought the collection was the 'sugred Sonnets', it is not impossible that he did for a brief time imagine that he had got his hands on the genuine article. But the thought is an unlikely one, and he would more probably have used Meres's description for his title instead of making up another one as Rollins conjectures.[1] How we interpret this point depends partly, as I have suggested, on whether we think he published them as he found them or whether he devised his own arrangement.

Shakespeare may well have had his reasons, beyond a *de facto* powerlessness, for saying nothing: the *Sonnets* were the most personal and in many ways the most painful things he ever wrote, and despite the vogue for sonnet sequences during much of the decade of the 1590s, and notwithstanding the success of the two narrative poems, he seems to have made no attempt, with or without a patron's help, to offer them to the world. (This argument, which bears on Shakespeare's attitude in 1599, is not affected by the possibility that in 1609 he may have given his assent to their publication.) The *Sonnets*,

---

[1] See Rollins, p. 524. *The Passionate Pilgrim* may of course have been the title of the putative manuscript common-place book.

which had started off comfortably enough, soon began to run into difficulties: not of a stylistic but a personal nature, and they end on the most troubled and stricken note imaginable. They stare straight, if not straightforwardly, into Shakespeare's conscience and touch awkwardly though powerfully on such vexed matters as personal betrayal (in which accusations of a then no doubt identifiable kind are not held back) and of course on sexuality. It may have served Shakespeare very well if the larger world beyond the privileged few who had seen his manuscripts were given only the light-hearted and superficial bawdy of the Venus sonnets in the *Passionate Pilgrim* collection. The two stray 'dark lady' sonnets heading the collection lack the ramifying force they possess in the sequence of 1609.

All this, it need hardly be said, is conjecture and can be opposed by equally valid or invalid hypotheses. But it is helpful to try to account for Shakespeare's silence over publication, a silence he did not break, apparently, until 1612; and then we have only Thomas Heywood's word that he spoke out.

It was in this year, when the *Sonnets* of Shakespeare were now known, that Jaggard brought out his third and final edition of *The Passionate Pilgrim*. A change of tack was called for, and so he gave the collection a completely new appearance by adding to it a number of poems by Heywood. These included two lengthy Ovidian love epistles, translated by Heywood from the *Heroides*, 'Paris to Helen' and 'Helen to Paris'. These and the other newly included poems made the third edition much weightier than its predecessors, but for the first time to our knowledge their presence caused Jaggard a certain amount of trouble.

This time he was filching from himself, since he had published Heywood's poems in 1609 in a collection called *Troia Britanica*. As Rollins shows (*PP* 1612, p. xxix), Jaggard printed the Heywood poems from the 1609 edition, not from manuscripts. Typography, spelling, and accidentals are the same as in *Troia Britanica*. And this is what raised Heywood's ire. The printing of *Troia Britanica* had given Heywood grounds for complaint on account of its poor workmanship. Not only that, but in reprinting Heywood's poems Jaggard made not a single correction, and now here he was including them in the new *Passionate Pilgrim* as if they were not even Heywood's but Shakespeare's. A look at the 1612 title page does not quite give the impression that Jaggard is brazenly offering Heywood's verses as Shakespeare's, since the latter's name is carefully printed half-way down the page, underneath which we read: 'Whereunto is newly added two Love-Epistles', etc. None the less, the unsuspecting reader might have imagined that the new Ovidian poems had been added from Shakespeare's stock, and some editors point to the fact that the 1612 edition appears with two different title pages, one bearing Shakespeare's name and one not, as evidence that Jaggard prepared a cancel title page while still printing in order to silence protests from the Shakespeare camp (see Willoughby, p. 91, and Adams, pp. xxxix–xlii).

At any rate, the only recorded objector to the 1612 *Passionate Pilgrim* was Heywood, who in the same year brought out his *Apologie for Actors*, appending to the volume a letter addressed to his friend, Nicholas Okes, in which he accuses Jaggard of injurious practice. Speaking of the faults in the printing of *Troia Britanica* (Willoughby, p. 92, considers these to be 'grossly exaggerated'), Heywood declares:

Here likewise, I must necessarily insert a manifest injury done me in that worke, by taking the two epistles of *Paris* to *Helen*, and *Helen* to *Paris*, and printing them in a lesse volume [i.e. *The Passionate Pilgrim*], under the name of another, which may put the world in opinion I might steale them from him; and hee, to do himself right hath since published them in his owne name.

(*An Apologie for Actors*, in *Shakspere Allusion-Book*, I, 231)[1]

Shakespeare's silence remains unbroken. We have an inkling of his dissatisfaction with Jaggard through Heywood's hearsay ('so the author I know much offended with M. Jaggard (that altogether unknowne to him) presumed to make so bold with his name'), but nothing more. If Shakespeare was annoyed, evidence suggests that he objected on this occasion only. Shakespeare's name by now carried authority and not just brilliance in literary circles, and Jaggard was perhaps putting himself at risk by reissuing this swollen version of the miscellany. But if Shakespeare had grown in stature since the late 1590s, so too had Jaggard, since he and his son Isaac, along with three other booksellers and publishers, were in 1623 given the prestigious task of bringing out the First Folio. No serious alienation from Shakespeare appears to have been effected. Nor does the kind of piracy practised by Jaggard seem to have much mattered, and Willoughby (pp. 3–4) even suggests that it was rather run-of-the-mill.

In Shakespeare's writing lifetime a significant change was taking place which gradually transferred authority for literary works (religious and political is a different matter) from patrons such as Southampton to printers and booksellers such as Jaggard, whose social status increased accordingly. Along with the many things the existence of *The Passionate Pilgrim* conceals, the modification of the roles of patron, author, and publisher (including especially the activities of the latter) is something on which it sheds a little light.

A Lover's Complaint

STYLE AND AUTHENTICITY

There is no record of contemporary responses to *A Lover's Complaint* (which was published by Thomas Thorpe in the same volume as the *Sonnets* in 1609), nor can we be sure for that matter that the *Sonnets* excited upon publication the interest that they would certainly have had ten years earlier when sonnet writing was still sufficiently in vogue. While *Venus and Adonis* and *The Rape of Lucrece* continued to appear, though at increasing intervals, *A Lover's Complaint* and the *Sonnets* had to wait until 1640 and Benson's hotch-potch edition before seeing print again. Since that time, the *Sonnets* have continued to tease and fascinate, their appeal having grown stronger in the last two centuries, while *A Lover's Complaint*, despite Malone's admiration of it as comparable

---

[1] It seems necessary to make clear that 'hath since published them in his owne name' is governed by the subjunctive mood and means that it might be *thought* that Heywood stole the love epistles from Shakespeare, pretending they were his own in *Troia Britanica*, and that Shakespeare in retaliation had Jaggard bring out a new edition of *The Passionate Pilgrim* which would indicate whose the poems really were. In other words, the argument does not go beyond *The Passionate Pilgrim*. But a number of scholars have casually assumed that Heywood was referring to the 1609 *Sonnets*, which if it had been true would have complicated matters considerably (see Rollins (1612), pp. xxx–xxxii).

with Spenser for 'simplicity and pathetick tenderness' (Rollins, p. 586), has fallen into neglect. Malone's description of the poem as Spenserian and his praise of its style give rise, however, to two separate speculations. Did Shakespeare in fact write it, and how good a poem is it?

From early on, beginning with Hazlitt (Rollins, p. 586), doubt fell on Shakespeare's authorship, though until 1850 or so most scholars accepted that he was the poet. Also, most early commentators responded favourably to the style, albeit with a feeling that some allowances had to be made. Charles Knight, for example, wrote in 1841:

> It is distinguished by that condensation of thought and outpouring of imagery which are the characteristics of Shakespeare's poems. The effect consequent upon these qualities is, that the language is sometimes obscure, and the metaphors occasionally appear strange and forced.
>
> (Rollins, p. 586)

But in 1912 J. W. Mackail published an essay which was to set the tone of response to the poem for the next half-century: not only did he not much care for it, but he questioned more thoroughly than anybody before him whether it was really by Shakespeare. Mackail attacks the congested, artificial style of the language, in which he discerns a 'forcing of phrase . . . due to pedantry, to the artificiality of a contracted, and ill-digested scholarship; sometimes to mere clumsiness' (Mackail, p. 60). He deplores, too, the flat, dragging opening so unlike the energy of the beginning of both Shakespeare's earlier narrative poems. On the strength of this Mackail doubts the poem's authenticity but explains the Shakespearean connection by the improbable hypothesis that the rival poet mentioned in the *Sonnets* is the author.[1] On the other hand, he (p. 61) convincingly conjectures that the poem, whoever wrote it, belongs to the style of the later rather than earlier Shakespeare; and although a few voices still sound their dissent, most recent commentators (e.g. Muir, Maxwell, Jackson, Partridge, and Kerrigan) think it is contemporaneous with *Hamlet* or *All's Well That Ends Well*, Jackson (p. 13) even supposing that it was written 'possibly not long before . . . publication'.

In the 1960s the case for Shakespearean authorship was resumed by Kenneth Muir, arguing persuasively on points of style, and in a more thoroughgoing manner by MacDonald P. Jackson (see Reading List). Jackson's comprehensive analysis of phraseology and, in particular, diction has been subsequently borne out by two statistical surveys performed by Eliot Slater in the 1970s, especially that of 1975, and another by A. C. Partridge (see Reading List)[2]; as a result of all of these studies the case in favour of Shakespeare seems more or less assured (but see below, p. 78).

What these recent researches demonstrate, indeed reinforce, is our sense of the constant growth in Shakespeare's vocabulary. As a consequence it is not enough to say,

---

[1] Mackail, pp. 66–70. Robertson, following up the idea, confidently identifed the author as Chapman (pp. 9–95); but he was refuted within a year (see Jackson, p. 19).

[2] Partridge, pp. 176–7, observes that it 'was a belated experiment in Spenserian pastoral' and 'that the coined archaisms were attempts to capture (if not parody) the artifice of *The Shepheardes Calender*'. This is true of some though not all of the poem's diction (a proportion of which is truly neologistic), and it leaves out of account its interesting psychological portrayals. Partridge seems to subscribe to Mackail's and Robertson's view that the poem's genesis lies in the principle of emulation rather than in Shakespeare's interest in dramatic portrayal.

in attempting to disprove his authorship, that much of the diction is not Shakespearean since the vocabulary in any of the plays after 1600 differs in some respects from the rest. While similarities exist, they lie more often in phrasing and rhythm, than in words. What we may provisionally affirm, rather, is that while word count alone does not establish authorship, only a certain number of words need be common to the plays to suggest common ground. Whereas the diction of *A Lover's Complaint* does not occur in the plays it seems not to appear in the work of any contemporary either, which supports the argument that here as elsewhere Shakespeare is adding to his considerable vocabulary.

GENRE

The poem's title clearly signals the tradition of the complaint genre, to which, like *The Rape of Lucrece*, it belongs. It looks back therefore to other poems of the early 1590s: Daniel's *Complaint of Rosamond* (see introductory section on *Lucrece*, p. 39), Spenser's *The Ruins of Time*, and Thomas Lodge's *The Complaint of Elstred*, all published when the genre was at its most popular. Both Daniel's and Lodge's poems have drawn additional comment because they were published with preceding sonnet sequences, demonstrating that difference of genre in the same volume is no argument against authorship by a single poet.

In fact, recent scholarship has tried to put matters very much on an alternative footing, arguing that the examples of Lodge and Daniel favour keeping the *Sonnets* and the poem together. The decision of this series to keep them apart may well strike some readers as obstinate, or at least unduly conservative.[1] Katherine Duncan-Jones, making some astute observations on Daniel's arrangement in particular, has demonstrated that there are clear formal and thematic links between the different poetic genres brought together in such a volume, and that by extension Shakespeare's sonnet sequence and complaint poem probably reflect a similar interconnectedness of kinds.[2] In this she is strongly supported by Kerrigan, both of them adducing further examples, including Spenser's *Amoretti* and *Epithalamion* (not a complaint poem but one which stands in an undoubtedly significant relationship with the preceding sonnets).[3]

The question is whether contemporary readers would have responded to Thorpe's arrangement of material in the way they most likely did to Daniel's. A look at the different title pages may be instructive. Daniel's (1592) is as follows: '*Delia.* / Contayning certayne / Sonnets: with the / complaint of / *Rosamond*'. The name Delia not only heads the page but its letters are twice the size of those of Rosamond, establishing the higher regard in which the poet holds the one lady over the other. Below this stand Propertius' verses: '*Aetas prima canat veneres* / *postrema tumultus*', which may be translated as follows: 'Let youth sing the joys of love and maturity vicissitude.' Coming where it does on the page, this attention to contrast and change corresponds

---

[1] The trend is not new, since Pooler's Arden text of 1918 prints them together. However, the editor presumably takes his cue straightforwardly from the 1609 publication and does not support his arrangement with anything like the considered arguments put forward by Kerrigan. See also Malone's conjectures (1790).

[2] Katherine Duncan-Jones, 'Was the 1609 *Sonnets* really unauthorized?' (*RES* 34 (1983), 168–71).

[3] Duncan-Jones, pp. 168–69; Kerrigan, pp. 13–14.

effectively to the volume's alternating subjects: first the confident and unassailable Delia, next the sorrowful and salutary Rosamond. To round out matters, Daniel has his two poetic mistresses communicate with one another across the pages of his book, the abject ghost of Rosamond sending both a tribute and a warning via the poet to Delia:

> Yet ere I goe, thys one word more I pray thee,
> Tell *Delia* now her sigh may doe me good,
> And will her note the frailtie of our blood.
> And if I passe unto those happy banks,
> Then she must have her praise, thy pen her thanks.
>
> (731–5)

The careful and instructive arrangement of Daniel's title page has no equivalent in Thorpe's, which mentions only 'SHAKE-SPEARES / SONNETS' and says nothing of the narrative poem. A reader would have carried on to the end of the sonnets, namely to sig. KI^v, before coming across the following drop-title: 'A Lovers complaint. / BY / WILLIAM SHAKE-SPEARE.' Would contemporaries then have read the volume '*as* a volume' (Kerrigan, p. 14), given the lack of any such direction on the initial title page? Daniel's careful celebration of the triumph of one of his heroines *explicitly* through the sad fate of the other finds no parallel in the Shakespearean volume. All that need be said in answer to the claim that the young seducer of the poem and the sonnet-poet's young friend are in some way connected (Duncan-Jones, p. 170) is that echoes and resemblances abound everywhere in Shakespeare's work (see below, pp. 69–70). In the absence of a clear reference by one poem to the other, and given the omission of the narrative poem from the *Sonnets'* title page, the case for parallelism or counterpointing in the manner of Daniel is less certain than may at first appear.

Both Katherine Duncan-Jones and John Kerrigan explore the boundaries of poems such as Daniel's and Spenser's and the material that links them. Shakespeare's Cupid sonnets (153 and 154), with which his sequence signs off, can be compared to the Anacreontic odes with which Spenser, Lodge, and Daniel closed their sonnet sequences and used as tonal bridges to introduce the new matter of either the complaint or, in Spenser's case, marriage poem which was to follow. They each used the ode in a dual fashion. But, again, a difference exists between their deployment of the Anacreontic mode and Shakespeare's. Daniel's ode, which acts as a coda, combines sonnet ideas (the still pleading, always despairing lover) in a more relaxed, melodious tone which eases the transition between verse forms. While thematically belonging to the sonnet sequence, it detaches itself adequately from it and stands formally between that and the narrative poem. But Shakespeare's two sonnets, functioning as a coda, and Anacreontic in character, none the less *belong formally to the sequence*. The shift in tone which they register is not enough to set them apart or equip them with the bridging function that can be claimed for the odes of, for example, Daniel or Spenser.

Generically, both as a narrative in rhyme-royal stanzas and as a complaint poem, *A Lover's Complaint* bears a closer formal resemblance as well as a more evident thematic likeness to *The Rape of Lucrece* than to the *Sonnets*. This affords a sufficient argument for placing it in the present volume. None the less, it was published originally with the *Sonnets*, and the case against continuing to place it with them is, as recent editorial decisions have made clear, far from being closed.

THE COMPLAINT

Each of the non-Shakespearean complaint poems that we have mentioned shares important characteristics with *A Lover's Complaint*. In all of them the tragic speaker is a woman (usually a spirit); and in all of them she underlines her helplessness in the circumstances in which she has been caught up. By the 1590s, love is the dominant complaint motif (perhaps inspired by Churchyard's example – see above, p. 38), and shows a tendency on the part of the genre to reflect in sombre fashion its sister mode – the Ovidian erotic narrative – naturally concentrating on women (as Racinian drama was to do later) as the principal means of expressing the sadness and suffering that results from unchecked, illicit sexual impulse.

In Lodge, as in Daniel, the woman was a king's mistress who eventually fell foul of the jealous wife. Lodge published his poem a year later than Daniel and evidently imitates him in theme and detail. Typical of *Mirror for Magistrates* inheritance, the lament turns partly on the question of the responsibilities of kingship, the nature of power, and the inexorable effects of an impersonal fortune which seems to prey on individual attempts at happiness. It is notable that in these two poems the monarch has tried to keep his mistress safe by hiding her away: in Daniel's case in a secret bower, while Lodge, recalling Greek mythology, goes one further and has his king construct another Cretan labyrinth for the hapless Elstred. Of course neither precaution succeeds against the workings of fortune. Spenser, in whom fortune also counts significantly, writes a rather different poem. The opening stanzas of 'The Ruins' bear a resemblance to those of *A Lover's Complaint* and may well have inspired its beginning (as Malone seems to have supposed).

Spenser's complaining lady turns out to be not a woman at all but the allegory of a city, the vanished city of Verulam which formerly stood on the site which is now St Albans. Verulam's own ruin forms the prelude to a general lament for the vanishing of things before, focusing on the chief loss England has recently borne: that of Sir Philip Sidney, who is of course the true subject of the lament. The political theme and the praise of the Sidney family outweigh and indeed efface any question of personal suffering, or guilt, on the part of either the poet or his female complainant. None the less, despite its different emphasis, *The Ruines of Time* shares Daniel's and Lodge's observation of an inscrutable fortune, Spenser modifying this agency gradually into the person of a severe but ultimately just and consoling God.

THEME AND CHARACTER MOTIVATION

By contrast with all of them, *A Lover's Complaint* is spoken by a still living woman who never discloses her identity. The poem makes none of the expected allusion to a familiar legendary story, as does Daniel. As if impatient with the historical and political dimensions of other examples it goes immediately and exclusively to the theme of seduction and betrayal. Perhaps the explanation for this is that Shakespeare is now more interested in the process of seduction and its aftermath than in cultivating a mood of sorrow, as the genre normally does and as he himself is inclined to do in *The Rape of Lucrece*.[1] If so, then the situation confronting the reader is one more familiar in the plays, where dramatic and psychological conflict takes precedence over narrative dénouement. Whereas a speaking ghost necessarily posits an action which is concluded, a living character indicates one that is continuing, involving decisions yet to be taken: the process going on. The young man is particularly interesting from this point of view. We hear him only by report, but she renders him extraordinarily and vividly present to us. Indeed, the success of his portrayal in the poem depends on the integrity of the maid's account – a point we shall come to shortly. Nor is the young man's speech a matter of straightforward seduction dialogue. Rather, his complaint-cum-apology mingles dubious pleading with apparent confession (as if the Tarquin who has resolved upon rape and the Tarquin beset by conscience were presented in one and the same voice).

But before proceeding further along this line, let us examine briefly what happens. First to speak is the poet, who overhears a plaintive maid. This is conventional enough, though not, as we have seen, strictly within the 'ghostly' complaint convention,[2] for she is telling her story not to the poet but to a man of reverend years, addressed by the maid as 'father' (a term apparently without religious connotations). Apart from receiving a couple of appeals which she interjects into her narrative, this elderly man seems hardly to be present, and he is never called upon to offer advice or reply to her lament (despite the identification of him as 'a blusterer that the ruffle knew/Of court, of city' – suggesting a relevant personal history which the narrative might, but does not, in fact, later draw upon). The poem largely consists of the maid's account of her downfall, in the course of which she reports verbatim her seducer's words of courtship – a speech lasting just over 100 lines, or almost a third of the poem. This speech concludes at line 280, a climactic moment, for the maid confesses her submission two stanzas later. The remaining four stanzas merely repeat her earlier claim, though with some growth in intensity, concerning the irresistibility of her wooer and his power to wreak large-scale harm. In the last line she acknowledges the depressing truth that despite all she has learnt from this cruel deception, she would probably succumb a second time if the occasion arose. The narrative bears her out in this, for the young man curiously makes it a central part of his wooing strategy to demonstrate not just his promiscuity but his unrivalled record at breaking hearts. (Normally the Don Giovanni figure leaves it to the likes of Leporello to read out the list of conquests to his Donna Elvira, and then only *after* he has succeeded with her.) But still the maid is not put off, in spite of the disquieting account of the 'sacred nun' (260) whom he claims to have seduced at first sight.

Such an odd presentation of character or speaker can be explained in one of two ways: either the poem as we have it represents a first version or preliminary draft, which on revision would have incorporated such figures as the 'reverend father' more fully, or, as

---

[1] Lucrece also speaks as a living woman, though of course her story is well known. Thomas Middleton was to relocate her thoroughly within the complaint convention with his poem *The Ghost of Lucrece* of 1600.

[2] The situation at the opening resembles rather that of an Ovidian erotic poem such as Lodge's *Scillaes Metamorphosis*, where the poet, in wretched mood himself, hears the laments of the lovesick Glaucus.

we have hinted above, it signals an attempt at developing narrative technique, searching for a method of narration which is more in line with the practice of the plays than with anything seen earlier in Shakespeare's long poems. That is, it abandons or reduces the scope of those elements we normally find in narrative – situation, location, description, action – and concentrates on character motivation. What dialogue there is does not follow the conventional pleading-and-rejection kind of either *Venus* or *Lucrece*, but follows a confessional line: first the maid to the 'father', and then the young man to the maid.

A comparison with Shakespeare's other narrative poems may be useful here: each of them is far less ambivalent than *A Lover's Complaint*. Venus and Adonis represent opposite but clear-cut principles (equally viable and defensible); they function in this respect less as characters and more as points of view. There is no disagreement in ethical terms between Tarquin and Lucrece. But the situation is no less clear; he acknowledges that his action is wrong, yet cannot stop himself. In *A Lover's Complaint* the maid finds herself drawn towards a man whom ethically she knows she should avoid; and he appears to plead with her to save him from himself while practising her ruin. The antithetical formula, similar to that of the other poems, deepens the issues without quite clarifying them, making us ponder both the usual (if not exclusive) female impulse to self-sacrifice – which invariably fails in its reforming zeal – and that restlessness characteristic of men whose appetites pall as they devour. In contrast to the spirit of conviction with which *Lucrece* presents the issues of right and wrong, *A Lover's Complaint* is a poem which stares on in bemused, appalled fascination.

She can be, and has been, likened to Ophelia in so far as she will succumb to pressure and be destroyed,[1] whereas he combines the impulsive vanity of Bertram de Rossillion with the calculating deceit of Angelo in *Measure for Measure*. What is remarkable about his wooing of her is the awe with which the seducer contemplates his success with women in general, making it a basis of his plea that all those hearts which are already in bondage to him can only be redeemed by her favour. The apparent artlessness with which he negotiates his ill repute manages to turn even conscience into a piece of strategy. Whatever reservations we may entertain about the poem's artistic success (and there are a number of those), there is no doubt as to the compelling nature of its theme: a seducer who openly displays his moral weakness, excusing his powers of attraction as if he himself were their victim rather than those whom he ensnares in his 'craft of will' (126).

The poem's examination of motive gives it that dualism that we associate with the mature plays. How far such a dualism extends is a moot point: Kerrigan, for example (pp. 59, 395–6), argues that the maid is as subject to judgement for bad faith as her seducer. In illustration, Kerrigan points to the appearance of 'fickle' in line 5 – 'a fickle maid full pale' – to describe the maid's distraught state, and claims that its meaning extends further than the apparent contextual sense of being agitated (see line 5n), involving the girl in precisely the kind of deceitfulness practised by the man as an

---

[1] Snider quotes as a parallel Ophelia's lines, 'And I, of ladies most deject and wretched / That sucked the honey of his music vows' (Rollins, p. 586).

example of 'the poem's bad doubleness'. But this is to put a good deal of weight on a word which comes at the beginning and finds no resonance later on – unless we are prepared to see it, and then very late, in the last line: 'And new pervert a reconcilèd maid' (Kerrigan also suggests that 'maiden-tongued' of line 100, while applied strictly to the young man, puts subversive pressure on the maid's sincerity). But emphasis falls on the irresistibility of seduction rather than women's complicity in it. If it succeeded by connivance, its power would be less awesome and disturbing. This is a poem in which the theme of female frailty is taken to desperate lengths without at the same time accusing women. Not just the maid but equally the 'sacred nun' has a weakness which a clever seducer may exploit – a weakness which the poem presents as an aspect of nature rather than as a moral defect. Hamlet, sensing the natural imperative, advises Ophelia to retreat to a nunnery, though this poem counters that women are not secure even there.

Hamlet itself usefully illustrates those differences of male and female psychology which the poem ponders and enumerates. In Act 1, Scene 3 Laertes cautions Ophelia not to be too free with Hamlet, lest she lose her reputation; she takes his advice to heart but equally warns him to follow his own precept regarding honour rather than prove a hypocrite – advice which Polonius expands on. (The exchange is particularly interesting since it contains words like 'cautels' and 'credent', which are common to the poem but used sparingly or not at all elsewhere.) Laertes says:

> Then weigh what loss your honour may sustain
> If with too credent ear you list his songs,
> Or lose your heart, or your chaste treasure open
> To his unmast'red importunity.
> Fear it, Ophelia, fear it, my dear sister,
> And keep you in the rear of your affection,
> Out of the shot and danger of desire. (29–35)

To this Ophelia replies:

> But, good my brother,
> Do not, as some ungracious pastors do,
> Show me the steep and thorny way to heaven,
> Whiles, like a puff'd and reckless libertine,
> Himself the primrose path of dalliance treads,
> And reaks not his own rede. (46–51)

What we have here is a reflection on weak female nature, specifying circumstance, followed by a reflection on weak male nature, emphasising inclination. Neither speaker is invulnerable to temptation, and they each should heed their own advice. Similarly in the poem, the two speakers in their different ways expose the kinds of weakness to which men and women are prone. Just as the speeches of Laertes and Ophelia reflect on each other's susceptibilities, the speeches in *A Lover's Complaint* point up successively the incapacity of the woman to resist and the man to desist.

His defence of his conduct with former mistresses is singular enough to raise doubts whether he expects to be taken seriously. Yet he does, and is:

> "All my offences that abroad you see
> Are errors of the blood, none of the mind.
> Love made them not; with acture they may be,
> Where neither party is nor true nor kind.   (183–6)

All of this is spoken with a mixture of pride and awe. Its logic resembles Venus's attempt to appease Death, whom she has previously maligned, in her fear for Adonis's safety, the word 'acture' recalling her distinction between 'act' and 'author':

> "'Tis not my fault the boar provoked my tongue;
> Be wreaked on him, invisible commander.
> 'Tis he, foul creature, that hath done thee wrong;
> I did but act, he's author of thy slander.   (*Ven.* 1003–6)

While ringing false to the reader, the young man's words ring true to the maid, for she believes his claim never to have been truly affected by another woman's passion. Instead of taking this as evidence of an egotistical, manipulative disposition, she sees it, as a well-meaning and consequently vulnerable young woman will see it, as a challenge to her power to save him from himself. Nothing is so seductive as the apparently sincere confession of past wrongs. Instead of heeding the warning, she imagines that her task is to redeem him with love, convinced that his 'maiden-tongued' (100) protestations represent a kind of purity which he has not lost, whatever his lascivious lapses:[1]

> "Among the many that mine eyes have seen,
> Not one whose flame my heart so much as warmed,
> Or my affection put to th' smallest teen,
> Or any of my leisures ever charmed.
> Harm have I done to them, but ne'er was harmed;
>   Kept hearts in liveries, but mine own was free,
>   And reigned commanding in his monarchy.   (190–6)

This peculiar and paradoxical claim (pretending to be at once lascivious and chaste) is psychologically persuasive, which makes it the most interesting thing in the entire poem. Kenneth Muir discounts the seducer's rhetoric, saying that she was won 'before he began to woo' (p. 163); but this underestimates both the subtlety of the lover's tactic and the originality of the observation.

The young man dangles a double-edged bait: she is to be his first real love while being the last of many. Not only is she offered the blameless emotional virgin that Venus found in Adonis, but she is also asked to redeem a fallen heart from sin. The

---

[1] The young man's seduction technique is the classic one practised by such rakes as Valmont on the innocent Présidente de Tourvel in *Les Liaisons Dangéreuses* or by Don Giovanni on Donna Elvira. Indeed, Elvira's recognition in Mozart's opera that despite previous betrayals she still loves Don Giovanni resembles the frame of mind of the maid in the last line of the poem, when she acknowledges that her lover would still have the power to tempt her.

history of literary examples shows that such a combination, especially its latter aspect, proves more successful in proportion to the virtue of the woman. Kerrigan argues (pp. 395–6) that 'seduction is never one-sided'. But does this mean that we should censure virtue when it succumbs to cunning? The maid's disposition is far from that of the mistress who engages the poet in mutual duplicity in *Sonnet* 138. Rather, the poem confirms the compassionate reading that it is possible to have of Hamlet's cry, 'Frailty, thy name is woman!'; for such an observation when applied to *A Lover's Complaint* means that even the best of women is defenceless against an unscrupulous clever man. The balance-sheet is only properly drawn up when in making her eventual reply to the young man's disingenuous 'Where neither party is nor true nor kind' (186) – meaning that their faith was no more binding than his own – she affirms,

> 'That not a heart which in his level came
> Could scape the hail of his all-hurting aim,
> Showing fair nature is both *kind and tame*.'   (309–11, my italics)

The dismissive phrase 'nor true nor kind' finds a fitting rejoinder in the description of those of generous ('fair') nature as 'kind and tame' (i.e. gently accommodating). The hunting metaphor drives home the difference between his calculating, and at the same time reckless (since he appears to use grapeshot), behaviour and the creature-like bewilderment of his victims. It is of course true that we have only her word for it, this being a 'complaint' poem; but as with Rosamond (see p. 39), nothing in the text or tone encourages us to practise an ironic scepticism as we listen to her (unless we are prepared to accept as evidence the interpretation of two or three words out of the entire poem – see above, p. 66). Her 'complicity' is rather the compliancy of natural virtue.

To summarise this part of the poem, then, the young man's strategy can be seen as threefold: firstly, he presents himself as a sinner in need of redemption; secondly, he presents himself as emotionally untouched and therefore chaste, a male virgin, no less; and lastly he presents *her* as a redeemer – not only of himself but of all those wounded hearts who have suffered through him. It is not by chance that he makes use of the story of the nun who merely succumbed to his charms without rescuing him from his peril. This is just the sort of thing to appeal to a pure-minded potential victim. What she learns too late is not so much the falseness of his words but the bitter personal truth that she is indistinguishable from any other woman. Not that these 'other women' are to be lightly dismissed. Had he written off his former loves as so many strumpets or inn-keepers' daughters he would have fared less well, since that would have looked like mere lust. But desire for a chaste or virginal woman can be seen as pursuit of virtue's ideal, as the Platonists themselves argue. Why should a virtuous woman doubt the sincerity of an erotic impulse? Just such logic is applied by Sidney's Astrophil as he sets out to seduce Stella:

> I sweare, my heart such one shall shew to thee,
> That shrines in flesh so true a Deitie,
> That *Vertue*, thou thyself shalt be in love.   (Ringler, p. 167)

Thus the young man's deception works its inglorious, inevitable magic.

ECHOES OF THE PLAYS

What adds to the poem's interest is the variation it offers on a theme which has already been treated several ways in Shakespeare's works. Plays which have occasioned comparison with it, mainly though not exclusively in terms of their common diction (the easiest of comparisons to make statistically), include, along with those mentioned above, *Troilus and Cressida*, *King Lear*, and *Cymbeline* (see Slater). Each of these plays (perhaps *Lear* less so) has themes in common with *A Lover's Complaint* which might account, in part, for the number of words they share. That is, even an overall change in lexical and syntactic manner will still produce similar collocations and verbal echoes as thematic concerns recur. In *Hamlet* and *All's Well* we have instances of female innocence (Ophelia, Helena) being subjected to unkind treatment from men. Hamlet's brutal remarks to Ophelia, which appear to bear a partial responsibility for her suicide, result from his deep disillusionment with the female sex and can therefore be defended as, in their peculiar way, moral.

Bertram's case is not the same. He is indifferent to Helena while lusting after Diana. (In this respect, Hamlet is untypical of the unreliable lover, since, despite Polonius's fears, sexual exploitation is the last thing the play accuses him of.) Yet Bertram, a priggish and not particularly wily egoist, is no match for the seducer of the poem in duplicity and craft. This figure is closer to Iachimo in *Cymbeline* for bedchamber cunning, except that Iachimo – as the theme makes clear – has no prospect of seducing Imogen, and succeeds in his furtive, partial victory only in vindicating her. Indeed, the degree to which the lexical similarity of this play to the poem may also disclose a thematic resemblance still has to be established, since in other important respects the two works differ from each other, *Cymbeline*, a late romance play, showing a measure of recovered confidence on Shakespeare's part in the concept of youthful female purity. Finally, *Troilus and Cressida* has its minor seducer (Diomedes), but what connects this play thematically to the poem is the pervasive sense of unease in sexual matters, communicated once more through the insecurity of woman, especially from the point of view of her material circumstances.

These various examples remind us that in the plays sexual duplicity may find expression through either men or women. (Cordelia's sisters are devious in contrast to her, but no more so than their male counterpart, Edmund, and his treachery, along with that of Goneril and Regan, finds a sexual focus in the triangular, adulterous relationship that binds them.) In *A Lover's Complaint* the plight of the maid would suggest that the guilt lies, as it does in *Lucrece*, with the man, and that she is culpable only in that she succumbed to blandishments rather than setting out actively to beguile.

Rakishness is not allowed to prosper, or go unpunished, in Shakespeare's theatre. Bertram is led to see the error of his ways with little harm done in *All's Well*, a sign of the faith Shakespeare, in his romantic comedies, places in women's power to redeem men. At the same time, if the formula of redemption is to satisfy the romance convention, it is important that the women save the men from falling rather than reassembling them after they have collapsed. Men like Orlando, Sebastian, Benedick, and Bassanio seem, if not virginal, at least not sexually dissolute. Bertram is a would-be rake rather than the thing itself; it is ironically fitting that he should be side-tracked into pursuit of a woman called Diana. When such a man finally returns to take the heroine as his wife, the play does not leave us with the sense that he does so at the expense of some former love who has been conveniently pushed to one side. What the Shakespearean romantic heroine typically does is save a situation the dangers of which she sees more clearly than the man: the two of them in other respects resemble each other for innocence. But such heartening positions yield to this poem's scepticism. Not only is the man already many times fallen, the woman has no power to bring him back. And if she had, her victory would none the less seem tainted. In recognising that the power of true love does not work miracles, *A Lover's Complaint* sounds a more desperate note than in any of the comedies up until 1600, a fact which alone encourages dating it around the time at least of *Hamlet* if not later.

The *Sonnets* present us with female duplicity illustrated in a number of indisputable examples, but they contain no maidenly protagonist. The poet interestingly enough represents himself in the exchanges both with the dark lady and the youth as a fairly passive participant, concentrating such male duplicity as there is in his unspecific charges against the young man. If we transfer the terrain from the *Sonnets* to the narrative complaint, then it emerges that female sincerity – which is what is newly depicted here – has no defence against male dissembling. We may wish to see the seeds of the maid's downfall as existing partly within herself, as Hamlet could not resist seeing that Ophelia would grow into Gertrude; but the poem does not encourage us very much in that view. What makes for despair is the perception, not that innocence wills its own destruction, but that it cannot overcome treachery. The self-sacrificing nature of love, usually seen as heroic, is mocked by the emptiness of the sacrifice.

Even Rosamond, Daniel's heroine, receives the tribute of Henry's sincere grief at her death – the usual fate of such penitents. One can imagine, following the rules of the genre, the maid finally committing suicide or dying from a broken heart, and the 'father' to whom she speaks preparing a modest grave and weeping wise tears in a passage of concluding pathos. But, simply as it stands, the narrative denies its reader the expected conventional dénouement. The maid's last-line confession, that the injury and her response to it seem destined to recur perpetually even if circumstances could be repaired, removes any possibility of a gesture towards formal consolation and insists on the power of betrayal as an ultimate statement.

STRUCTURE AND EXPRESSION

These reflections regarding final statements bring us back inevitably to the question whether or not the poem is 'finished'. It can be argued to its credit that the ending, although abrupt, reflects the inner, thematic sense of bleakness and irrecoverability.[1] Yet, too many details – character, narrative circumstance – are introduced only to be left hanging and unresolved for it to be formally satisfying. The economy with which the poet has got to the centre of his theme, in the process discarding the usual

---

[1] Snider seems to come to this conclusion, despite his overall criticism (see below), when he compares it to Michelangelo's unfinished torsos (Rollins, p. 600).

narrative framework, might argue in its favour. But such starkness still seems sketchy rather than bold or emphatic. And we should be wary of assigning to what has been plausibly described as an early draft (Muir, p. 166) the merit of evolving a new narrative technique when that technique appears nowhere else in the work of Shakespeare or his contemporaries, nor in modern literary practice for a very long time. A further disabling point is that, in contrast to the apparently boldly sketched dénouement, the narrative moves rather sluggishly, without either the facility of *Hamlet*, in the dialogue we have earlier observed, or the superseded fluency of the earlier narrative poems. It is not easy to discount Mackail's objection that the narrator, like Don Adriano in *Love's Labour's Lost*, 'draweth out the thread of his verbosity finer than the staple of his argument' (p. 67), or Snider's that two characters, the narrator and especially the 'reverend man', are introduced in some detail only to be 'thenceforth dropped without a word' (Rollins, p. 600). The neglected development of this figure at a point when some, however slight, contribution might be expected from him remains curiously unexplained.[1]

In the plays, a framework to any speech can always be found: in the dialogue between Ophelia and Laertes (see above, p. 66) Hamlet himself provides the point of reference for what they each say, while for Hamlet in dialogue with Ophelia the framework is his mother's relationship with Claudius. In the dramatic works, then, although nothing produces so clear a narrative outline as that of *Venus and Adonis* or *Lucrece*, speeches none the less find a point of focus beyond themselves. *A Lover's Complaint* lacks this perspective, which is perhaps why a reflective speech, which in a drama would be substantiated by a significant crisis or pause in the action, seems to have insufficient underpinning – despite our recognition of the convention or decorum which fashions it.

Problems also persist at the level of language or expression. Every commentator, including Kerrigan, who makes the best and most compelling case for the poem's appeal, has remarked that the syntax is contorted and its imagery opaque. *A Lover's Complaint* does not read easily; and while we can point to many examples of phrasal awkwardness in the later plays, such defects matter less in them because the dramatic situation helps to concentrate the meaning. The syntactic patterns of the drama, liberated from the constraining obligations of the poem's rhyme royal, and freely adopting rhythms patterned on natural speech, energise and integrate the many phrases, nonce-words, and neologisms which analysed out of their context look grammatically or semantically recalcitrant. By contrast, the lack of narrative flow or forcefulness in the poem exposes its odd and unfamiliar words and curious phrases as ill-digested and infelicitous. Therefore, while its theme signals a novel departure in the familiar Shakespearean territory of sexual betrayal, and its experimental-looking sparse structure might arguably contribute to its desolate rumination, the poem's imperfect balance of narrative manner and expression leaves it a good deal less readable, and artistically less assured, than Shakespeare's other verse narratives.

---

[1] Kerrigan, whose mistrust of the maid's professed motives largely determines his interpretation of the poem's form, attributes its unfinished appearance to her 'intense and human inconsistency' which takes her 'beyond the conventions which enclose her' (p. 425).

Recent critical interpretations

Since this edition was originally published in 1992, a sizeable number of contributions have been made to the study of Shakespeare's poetry. I will cover the more significant items in the various sections listed below. In addition the Reading List has been expanded to accommodate these and other interesting contributions which space precludes dealing with here. (The Reading List should be consulted where a complete reference is not given in the text.) Apart from the new and developing line in manuscript and print culture, the poems continue to be considered from fairly obvious viewpoints: the political (mainly republicanism), feminism, and now Catholicism. But neither does the question of attribution seem to abate. Following an initial gambit to place a slight lyric, 'Shall I die', in the canon there has come a sustained effort to establish recognition of *A Funeral Elegy* by W. S. as Shakespeare's. Conversely, the authenticity of *A Lover's Complaint*, which had largely been accepted as Shakespeare's, and indeed will be the subject of a volume of essays (edited by Shirley Sharon-Zisser), is coming once more into question. In more general terms – and most encouragingly for admirers of Shakespeare the poet – recent years have seen a tendency to argue strenuously for placing the poems on an equal footing with the plays, rather than seeing them as mere antecedents to the latter. One consequence of this is the forthcoming *Cambridge Companion to Shakespeare's Poetry* (edited by Patrick Cheney). Not least among recent contributions is a rival volume to this edition, Colin Burrow's *Complete Sonnets and Poems* (in the Oxford series), marked by an informed, judicious commentary, and bearing the impressive distinction of being the first fully annotated, combined edition of the sonnets and poems since that of George Wyndham in 1898. The poems are making their mark, not as an isolated group of writings, but more and more in terms of their thematic interaction with the plays.

Of books generally on the poems, three deserve particular mention. These are A. D. Cousins's *Shakespeare's Sonnets and Narrative Poems* (2000), Peter Hyland's *An Introduction to Shakespeare's Poems* (2003), and Sasha Roberts's *Reading Shakespeare's Poems in Early Modern England* (2003). The first two of these studies follow fairly traditional critical paths by concentrating on Shakespeare's intentions as a poet, and serve as very helpful introductions to the undergraduate reader, in particular. Perhaps, of the two, Hyland provides a little more contemporary context. Sasha Roberts, on the other hand, passes the initiative to the contemporary reader and asks questions about audience response by examining copies of the poems known to have been owned by certain identifiable individuals. She presents her credentials in her opening chapter, beguilingly entitled, 'Ladies reading "bawdy geare": Shakespeare, *Venus and Adonis* and the early modern woman reader', where she examines the marginalia in Frances Wolfreston's copy (which happens to be the 1593 edition). Of course there can be no certainty that Wolfreston drew the tell-tale marks alongside the 'sweet bottom-grass' passage, but Roberts speculates very much in the spirit of print-culture scholarship, which has challengingly called attention to such matters as reader intervention.

VENUS AND ADONIS

Venus and Adonis has drawn particular scrutiny over the past decade and has begun to compete with some of the plays in the canon by virtue of the kind of attention expended on it. Principally, there is Anthony Mortimer's fine book-length study, the first monograph that the poem has received.[1] Mortimer concentrates on the rhetorical art of the poem, but this does not mean that he treats it as a prolonged contemporary exercise in persuasion. He is very much alive to the texture of the verse, and if his book provides his readers with less of a historical or classical context than some of them would like, he makes up for this by the sensitivity and sharpness of his judgment of tone and intention. He does not burden the poem with theoretical analysis but he shows himself to be no mean psychologist when it comes to character motive, especially that of Venus. He brings a poet's ear to the verse, for he happens to be an excellent translator of Petrarch and Michelangelo, and he appropriately provides a valuable chapter on 'Shakespeare and the Italian tradition of Venus and Adonis'.

Secondly, there is a particularly rich volume of essays arranged to good effect by Philip Kolin, who has clearly responded to the growing popularity of the poem; surveying the field of commentary from Coleridge onwards, he includes excerpts from older introductions to editions, such as those of Wyndham and Sidney Lee, reproduces some of the more distinguished essays of the twentieth century, and adds several new pieces for the occasion.[2] The editor's own introductory essay, 'Venus and/or Adonis among the critics' is balanced and judicious, and includes a useful section dealing with the relationship of the poem to Shakespeare's plays. Kolin also includes reviews of dramatic adaptations, such as that performed (with *Lucrece*) at the Almeida theatre in Islington in 1988. His anthology concludes with an illustrated, enjoyable essay by Georgianna Ziegler, 'Picturing Venus and Adonis: Shakespeare and the artists'.

Kolin reproduces Catherine Belsey's influential Lacanian study of desire in the poem, 'Love as *trompe-l'œil*: taxonomies of desire in *Venus and Adonis*', originally published in the *Shakespeare Quarterly*. Elsewhere (in 'Shakespeare's eager Adonis') Lauren Shohet also takes on the 'discourse of desire' but by contrast makes it amenable to the values of Adonis as a proponent of the phallic order of the hunt. (See Reading List for both essays.) The Shakespearean hunt generally engages Ralph Berry, who includes an informative chapter on the poem in his book, *Shakespeare and the Hunt* (2001).

Jonathan Bate, meanwhile, writes on 'Shakespeare's sexual poetry' in an assured and highly influential comparison of the poet with one of his key classical sources.[3] Bate brings out every conceivable Ovidian angle, some of which perhaps are more convincing than others, in an argument that engages the reader's imagination throughout. He shows a good command of Ovid's *Metamorphoses* and its applicability, though he can press allusions or echoes too far, as when he over-argues, in my view, the significance of Adonis's mother Myrrha and her incestuous story as 'an ironic, darkening pre-text' (Bate, p. 54). This is in keeping with his overall interest in transgressive sexuality. But,

---

[1] *Variable Passions: A Reading of Shakespeare's 'Venus and Adonis'* (2000).
[2] Philip C. Kolin (ed.), *'Venus and Adonis': Critical Essays* (1997).
[3] *Shakespeare and Ovid* (1993).

as Mortimer points out, such an echo in fact comes to nothing in Shakespeare's poem, where his development of Venus's sexuality owes little to the Ovidian original (Mortimer, p. 139). As always, such questions turn on how much of the original myth the Elizabethan poet expects his audience to read into his own adaptation. More Ovidian essays come courtesy of A. B. Taylor's anthology, *Shakespeare's Ovid* (2000), including Pauline Kiernan's lively demonstration of Shakespeare's poetic decorum, '*Venus and Adonis* and Ovidian indecorous wit' and my own comparison of the poem with that of Marlowe, against an Ovidian background, 'Ovid "renascent" in *Venus and Adonis* and *Hero and Leander*'. Kiernan's enjoyable essay, 'Death by rhetorical trope: poetry metamorphosed in *Venus and Adonis* and the Sonnets' (see Reading List), demonstrates how Shakespeare draws upon Ovid to muse on poetic identity. Further, on the comparison with Marlowe, Maurice Charney insists on regarding Shakespeare as Marlowe's pupil, while comparing the male protagonist of each poem in terms of sexual immaturity (unlike the approach taken by Shohet above), in 'Marlowe's *Hero and Leander* shows Shakespeare, in *Venus and Adonis*, how to write an Ovidian verse epyllion' (see Reading List). The contemporary context inserts itself in a characteristically flamboyant way in Richard Wilson's allegorical reading in favour of the poem's sympathetic treatment of Roman Catholic martyrs.[1] Wilson's essay is included along with several interesting and challenging pieces in the anthology edited by Jean-Marie Maguin and Charles Whitworth, *William Shakespeare, 'Venus and Adonis': Nouvelles Perspectives Critiques* (1999). Katherine Duncan-Jones explores a different kind of contemporary relevance from Wilson's, in 'Much ado with red and white: the earliest readers of Shakespeare's *Venus and Adonis* (1593)' (see Reading List).

THE RAPE OF LUCRECE

Republican readings have begun to circulate in earnest around this poem. They are of course not new, for both E. P. Kuhl and subsequently Michael Platt put forward such interpretations quite some time ago (see above, pp. 31–2). But the argument is back with renewed vigour. For those who look more to literary tradition (which is rich in material on this subject) than to contemporary politics, Shakespeare's focus throughout is on Lucrece's condition and predicament as a woman, indeed as an heroic woman. The tradition of writing and thinking that stands behind her story, from St Augustine's condemnation through to her veneration in the Legends-of-Good-Women accounts of Boccaccio and Chaucer, all of which were readily available to Shakespeare, insist that its principal concern is with the nature and reputation of women. In this respect, the poem can, like *Venus and Adonis*, find correspondences with the plays. Those dramatic protagonists who suspect, and therefore attack, women most uncompromisingly, are the heroes of some of the great plays: Lear, Othello, Hamlet, Antony. In all of these plays, as a result of the tragic experience, women achieve redemption, wholly or in part. After these comes the drama of Leontes, whose arraignment of his wife for her supposed infidelity leads to a more positive statement of female redemption, in that she recovers a life that had appeared lost. Similarly, Lucrece commands the reader's admiration and

---

[1] See 'A bloody question: the politics of *Venus and Adonis*', in *Secret Shakespeare* (2004), pp. 126–43.

pity as an example of self-sacrificing nature, irrespective of the political circumstances of her story. Whether Shakespeare ought to show her in this light is another matter, and one that in its turn continues to furnish debate, but that at least is his intention. The emphasis falls on pathos: it is as the 'lamenting Lucretia' commended by Sidney (see above, p. 25) that she fulfils her tragic destiny.

None the less, Andrew Hadfield makes a bold bid to change the minds of those who continue to resist political interpretation. His argument comes in his book, *Shakespeare and Renaissance Politics* (2004), in particular in the chapter 'Republicanism and constitutionalism: "Tarquin's everlasting banishment"',[1] where he seems both to allegorise Elizabeth as a Lucrece whose chastity is under threat from foreign invaders (so far so unexceptionable) *and* to see her as an example of monarchy that has come to the end of its time and must cede to republicanism: 'Shakespeare's poem shows a chaste wife honourably dying and letting a small group of men take over government, a political transformation that the poem endorses' (p. 120). Is this reading perhaps contradictory? As always when it comes to political deduction, much depends on what is understood as vehicle and what as tenor. Does the number of allusions to a monarch's status merely serve to illustrate the abuse of power in an emotional context, as when a man forces a woman to submit to his desire, or does it call into question the role and purpose of monarchy as such, thus revealing the poem's motivation to be principally political, indeed republican? Barry Nass follows a line very close to Hadfield's when he argues that Shakespeare queries the 'legitimacy of official Tudor doctrine and monarchical rule', in 'The law and politics of treason in Shakespeare's *Lucrece*'. Readers are likely to be divided on this question indefinitely.

In all such debates a good deal turns on how one interprets the moment of Lucrece's death and the reactions of those around her, notably Brutus, that is, the moment that recalls the situation in Livy. Also offering a strong political reading, Annabel Patterson affirms that Brutus's ploy in appropriating Lucrece's fate to revolutionary ends wins the poet's unqualified approval.[2] Heather Dubrow, in her measured consideration of the incident, especially with respect to her overall theme of mourning, still finds Brutus's action 'self-serving', though she is willing to accord it more approval than in her earlier book, *Captive Victors*.[3] Dubrow argues that narrative strategy gives the victim some control over eventual loss or indeed death, and she invokes Hamlet's instructions to Horatio on how to tell his sad story.

Two essays that in their different ways try to demonstrate the degree of control over her destiny that Lucrece, despite everything, manages to secure, and which also make comparisons with *Hamlet*, are Mary Jo Kietzman's 'What is Hecuba to him or [s]he to Hecuba?: Lucrece's complaint and Shakespearean poetic agency' and my 'Pleasing the wiser sort: problems of ethics and genre in *Hamlet* and *Lucrece*'. Both essays draw upon definitions of genre and rhetoric for their perspective, and in different ways rhetoric also finds prominence in more avowedly feminist essays, such as Margo Hendricks's

---

[1] A version of this chapter was published earlier in *Parergon* 19:1 (2002), 77–104.
[2] *Reading Between the Lines* (1993), pp. 301–9.
[3] See the chapter, '"The forfended place": burglary', esp. pp. 45–61, in her book, *Shakespeare and Domestic Loss* (1999).

"'A word, sweet Lucrece": confession, feminism and *The Rape of Lucrece*",[1] Lynn Enterline, '"Poor instruments" and unspeakable events in *The Rape of Lucrece*",[2] and Philippa Berry's 'Woman, language and history in *The Rape of Lucrece*'. Hadfield finds support for his interpretation of the political Lucrece in Berry, who declares: 'Shakespeare's poem casts Lucrece as a more important principal actor than Brutus, suggesting that she is the truly virtuous republican figure who liberates Rome.'[3] Notwithstanding, at the end she declares her motive for killing herself to be concern for her reputation for chastity, rather than for the future government of the city (see lines 1714–15). A. D. Cousins would seem to argue as much in an unusual but refreshing piece of writing in which he gives Collatine a position of unexpected prominence in the poem's debate (see his essay in the Reading List).

Print culture obtrudes interestingly again in connection with both *Lucrece* and 'A Lover's Complaint', in Wendy Wall's study, *The Imprint of Gender: Authorship and Publication in the English Renaissance* (1993), where she deliberates on the anxieties surrounding the status of print and accordingly represents the text as female before the male gaze, along the lines of the Diana–Actaeon myth. She argues for what she calls the 'simulated dispersal' of speakers' voices throughout the Sonnets and 'A Lover's Complaint' in order to demonstrate continuity between them.

THE PHOENIX AND THE TURTLE

As might have been predicted, a good deal of subsequent scholarship takes the form of finding, or attempting to find, fresh allegorical readings to explain the enigmatic nature of this poem. Incidentally, Colin Burrow in his edition resists the traditional title and calls the poem by its first line, 'Let the bird of loudest lay'. His justification for this is that that title did not appear at the head of Shakespeare's poem until 1807, and was borrowed anyway from the supplementary title to Chester's *Loves Martyr* (see above, p. 43). This is a logical enough position in itself, but it is always questionable whether there is much mileage in trying to displace a title that has become so familiar, even if on contestable grounds. The poem is untitled simply because it is one of a number of poems making up Chester's anthology. It is so obviously *about* the Phoenix and the Turtle that it has always seemed perfectly natural to call it after them, and this is how it's been known for two centuries. Furthermore, there have been a number of attempts at re-titling Shakespeare (see the Oxford–Norton proposal to substitute the quarto title for that traditionally known by the Folio in some of the Histories) and it is maybe time to call a halt. Burrow seems not to be driven by questionable political readings. On the other hand, if he succeeds, then he will at least have removed one other problem that besets the traditional title – and which has caused a long-running and tiresome debate – whether to call it 'The Phoenix and *the* Turtle' or simply 'The Phoenix *and* Turtle'. As for interpretation, the poem itself continues to divide readers on whether it finds its true bearings in the literary tradition itself, which celebrates

---

[1] In Dympa Callaghan (ed.), *A Feminist Companion to Shakespeare* (2000), pp. 103–18.
[2] In her *The Rhetoric of the Body from Ovid to Shakespeare* (2000), pp. 152–97.
[3] Hadfield, p. 116.

the idea of a chaste, impossible love, with numerous examples from the Petrarchan to the Platonic, or whether its allegory directs itself to a particular, historical situation, inviting, or rather teasing, the reader to find contemporary names to fit the birds of the poem.

Given the recent renewal of interest in Shakespeare's religious affiliation, arguments have been advanced in favour of Roman Catholicism. Clare Asquith, for example, finds a coded reference to Palm Sunday, and to Aquinas's Latin poem, 'Lauda, Sion, salvatorem' (*Shakespeare Newsletter* 50 (2001)). For her the pair of lovers stands for two Jesuit Martyrs, Robert Southwell and Henry Walpole. Such speculation leads elsewhere to a truly bizarre identification of them as man and wife martyrs, Roger and Anne Line. This idea is proposed by two law professors, John Finnis and Patrick H. Martin, in their article, 'Another turn for the Turtle' (*TLS* 18 April 2003, 12–14). The authors attempt to demonstrate how the name Line is punned on, verbally and mathematically, in the poem. The obvious objection to this conjecture must be that if Shakespeare had wanted to hint at the significance of 'Line', he would have found a place for the name in the poem. Even the most arcane of Elizabethan allegorists (and Shakespeare was hardly one of those) did not expect readers to triple-guess the meaning. Of all the words asking for convenient yet tactfully unobtrusive expression in verse, 'Line' must be one of the easiest to accommodate; and yet it appears nowhere in the poem. (In a website entry the authors promise that all will be substantiated in a forthcoming book on an Elizabethan professor of philosophy at Oxford, *The Agent*.) Meanwhile John Klause directs attention to Catholicism via the Salusburys. Sir John Salusbury's elder brother Thomas was tragically involved in the Babington plot, and the family is urged to display respect for him by not backsliding from the faith. It is something of a strained argument that shows the poet advocating Catholicism not flatteringly but by reprimanding a dedicatee who appears not to want to know.[1] Barbara Everett, on the other hand, attacks the Catholic-Lancastrian school and turns attention firmly back to prosody in 'Set upon a golden bough to sing: Shakespeare's debt to Sidney in "The Phoenix and Turtle"' (*TLS* 16 February 2001). In comparing the metrics of the poem to those of the Eighth song in *Astrophil and Stella* she seems to be unaware of the argument put forward originally in this edition (see above, pp. 47–8).

Otherwise, it is a case of Essex rides again. Richard McCoy finds a new means of connecting the poem to him, even though earlier proponents of the Essex theory have been subjected to thorough-going scepticism (see above, pp. 41–2).[2] Also taking her cue from self-immolation, Alzada Tipton revives the case for Essex via the popular ballads and letters that support the claim that Essex must be the 'self-sacrificing' phoenix (in 'The transformation of the Earl of Essex'). There is something about the romantic appeal of the earl that makes it impossible for him just to lie down and die.

---

[1] '"The Phoenix and Turtle" in its time', in Thomas Moisan and Douglas Bruster (eds.), *In the Company of Shakespeare: Essays in Honor of G. Blakemore Evans* (2001), pp. 206–30.

[2] 'Love's martyrs: Shakespeare's "Phoenix and Turtle" and the sacrificial Sonnets', in Claire McEachern and Debora Shuger (eds.), *Religion and Culture in Renaissance England* (1997), pp. 188–298.

THE PASSIONATE PILGRIM

Very little new work seems to have been done on this miscellany. Certainly no fresh attributions have been proposed since the present edition first saw print. The situation regarding authorship of the poems appears to be about as established as it can be, pending a new discovery or theory. I have developed an argument, hinted at in this edition, on the relationship of *PP* 18 ('When as thine eye') to *Willobie his Avisa*. I claim that the miscellany poem is a riposte to canto XLVII in *Willobie*: 'it parodies [*Willobie*'s] terms of "advice" [to the lover] as well as mocking its unreal assumptions about female chastity' (Reading List). John Huntington finds fault with my argument for not taking sufficient account of the social questions raised by the author of *Willobie*. In arguing the importance of the relations between classes, Huntington champions this pedestrian poem on the grounds that it has a moral lesson both for Shakespeare and for the upper-crust readers of *The Rape of Lucrece*.[1]

A LOVER'S COMPLAINT

Controversy over *A Lover's Complaint* threatens to break out anew as two very different books prepare for publication. The first is Shirley Sharon-Zisser's edited volume of essays (due in 2006), all the contributors to which assume that Shakespeare is the author of the poem. Such is far from the case with Brian Vickers's new book *Unapproved Witness*, which Cambridge University Press is preparing for publication. The thrust of Vickers's argument is that the case for Shakespearean authorship, which was made formidably by Macdonald P. Jackson in his celebrated short monograph, is ill-founded (see above, p. 60). In his characteristically energetic way, Vickers takes on the various proponents of Shakespeare-as-author and engages with particular vigour those who, like John Kerrigan and Katherine Duncan-Jones (and now Colin Burrow, ed., pp. 140–1), maintain that there is a close connection between the poem and Shakespeare's Sonnets (see pp. 61–2 of the present edition). Burrow acknowledges himself to be particularly indebted to Kerrigan's discussion of how the poem functions. Vickers argues that both on grounds of style, language, metre, and so on, and from the point of view of merit, the poem cannot be Shakespeare's. It is hardly characteristic, and it isn't good enough. What is called for is an author who writes like the poet of *A Lover's Complaint* and whose work reflects a similar degree of mediocrity: the choice falls on John Davies of Hereford.[2] It has to be said in his favour that, even as he makes due use of computer analysis, Vickers does the work of judging himself, while showing an astonishing capacity for voluminous, intricate detail.[3] Whether he has done enough to carry the point remains to be seen; Jackson's arguments in favour of Shakespeare still seem to me to be strong. Nonetheless, Vickers gains support from a stylometric study by W. E. Y. Elliott and R. J. Valenza, 'Glass slippers and seven-league boots: C-prompted doubts about ascribing *A Funeral Elegy* and "A Lover's Complaint" to Shakespeare'.

---

[1] *Ambition, Rank, and Poetry in 1590s England* (2001), 24–37.
[2] Vickers has already put this view forward in an article, 'A rum "do"', published in the *TLS* 5 December 2003.
[3] I am grateful to the author and his publishers for being able to consult the book prior to publication.

Leaving such debates aside, we may note briefly Katharine A. Craik's 'Shakespeare's "A Lover's Complaint" and early modern criminal confession', in which an unexpectedly wider context, including that of the criminal community, is proposed for the poem. The question of genre comes under inspection in J. Laws's interestingly argued 'The generic complexities of *A Lover's Complaint* and its relationship to the Sonnets in Shakespeare's 1609 volume'. Acceptings the arguments for the arrangement of the volume put forward by Duncan-Jones et al., Laws none the less emphasises pastoral lyric rather than Ovidian complaint as a defining characteristic of the poem.

OTHER ATTRIBUTIONS

There is in fact only one questionable attribution that need detain us, and that appears to have been happily resolved. Readers who have bothered at all with such questions as 'finding a hitherto unattributed Shakespearean poem' will not need reminding of *A Funeral Elegy*, which held out rather longer than 'Shall I die' as being possibly by Shakespeare.[1] In 1996 Donald W. Foster published an edition of a poem called *A Funeral Elegy in Memory of the Late Virtuous Master William Peter of Whipton near Exeter*, in *The Shakespeare Newsletter* 46 (1996), pp. 35–9. Foster had been preparing his case as early as 1989, though it is hardly worth giving the earlier references, as the argument in favour of Shakespeare was to collapse spectacularly. The suggestion of a Shakespearean link had depended on the initials W. S. appearing twice on the title page, once under the title itself, and again following the letter of dedication. First, G. D. Monsarrat demonstrated that John Ford was a much more likely author, in '*A Funeral Elegy*: Ford, W. S., and Shakespeare'. Monsarrat plausibly explains the initials W. S. as being those of the deceased's friend who had commissioned Ford to write the elegy on his behalf (Monsarrat, pp. 199–201). Immediately following this came the indefatigable Brian Vickers's enormous, extraordinarily detailed monograph, which also effectively demolished the case for Shakespeare as author, while substantially building up the case for Ford. Vickers ends his book with a trenchant, salutary chapter on 'The politics of attribution', where he rehearses the age-old question, which seems to have become relevant again, concerning the conflict between disinterested scholarship and the desire to believe.[2] As soon as Monsarrat's essay was published both Foster, and his chief supporter on *A Funeral Elegy*, Richard Abrams, acknowledged that the case for Shakespeare as author could no longer be maintained.[3]

Where, then, does this leave editors? Rather in the position of those rival boxing organizations (WBA, IBF, WBC, etc.), each of which presents its own champion at various weights. Presumably the Riverside Edition (2nd edn, 1997) will eventually withdraw the poem, as must Norton. (Foster is the Riverside editor for *A Funeral Elegy*.) Norton in other respects follows the Complete Oxford, inevitably so given that Norton bought Oxford's text. But while Oxford has correctly and resolutely resisted the case for *A Funeral Elegy*,[4] the trivial 'Shall I die' carries on sharing the billing with

---

[1] However, though frail, this little poem isn't quite dead yet. See below.
[2] '*Counterfeiting' Shakespeare*, pp. 422–65.
[3] See the electronic discussion group SHAKSPER (SHK 13.1514, 13 June 2002).
[4] See Stanley Wells, '"A Funeral Elegy": obstacles to belief', *S. St.* 25 (1997), 186–91.

The Phoenix and the Turtle in the section called 'Various poems', placed strategically in the middle of both the Oxford and Norton complete texts. This remains the case despite the authoritative demonstration of the non-Shakespearean expression of the lyric given by Thomas A. Pendleton (see above, p. 2). Doubtless it is the personal investment in this poem by one of the Oxford editors that accounts for its refusal to be dislodged.[1] Colin Burrow, the Oxford editor of the Poems and Sonnets, breaks with the house line by publishing it under 'Poems attributed to Shakespeare'. I have given previously my reasons for thinking that this is not a good idea (see above, pp. 2–3). Burrow justifies including the poem (which he does not believe to be by Shakespeare) on the grounds that the manuscripts containing it belong to the 1630s and that the one that makes the ascription accordingly sees Shakespeare as a Caroline poet (Burrow, pp. 151–2), which he feels carries its own interest. This is a plausible hypothesis in itself, but it assumes as scribal conjecture what may be merely unaccountable scribal error. Arden 3 (forthcoming) is preparing to include the poem under 'Ascriptions'. The policy of the present edition continues to be not to include the poem at all, nor any of the funerary verses, etc., that long ago became 'Shakespearean' either by hearsay or association.[2]

---

[1] See Vickers, *'Counterfeiting' Shakespeare*, pp. 1–53.

[2] This is also the position of Jonathan Crewe, the editor of the American Penguin edition of *The Narrative Poems* (1999).

NOTE ON THE TEXT

Since this is a modernised text, it should be expected that every word will take a form immediately familiar to modern readers. This is almost the case. In a few places the Quarto printers' habits have been adopted, as, for instance, where a weak verb-ending such as 'er' or 'en' in the past participle form shows syncope of 'e' occurring before the final syllable (e.g. in *Ven.* 'batt'red', 104, 'murd'red', 502, 'check'red', 1168). The advantage of this is to mark the dissyllabic nature of the word clearly and so help with the metre. But nothing is ever simple, and compositorial inconsistency occurs. In such cases readings are regularised, except where fluency argues retaining the Quarto's reading, even though inconsistent.

The Rape of Lucrece, which was also printed by Richard Field and displays similar compositorial habits, affords some examples: e.g. 'whisp'ring' (769), 'smoth'red' (783), 'wand'ring' (839). But see 'still-slaught'red' (188), which Q1 prints as 'still slaughtered', while on the other hand printing 'self-slaughtred' (1733). They are here regularised with medial elision. In addition, Q1 prints 'characterd' (807), where trisyllabic words seem to elide the final syllable. Also, soft or voiced stem finals seem to take final rather than medial elision, (e.g. 'sepulcherd', *Luc.* 805). But it avoids syncope following the vowel in 'unconquered' (408), which metrically requires all four syllables to be sounded, as well as in the disyllabic 'conquered' (482). On the other hand, the latter, and 'still-slaughtered', may result from the compositor's carelessly applying prose convention, whereby the final '-ed' is never stressed (see Partridge, *Orthography*, p. 70). Given such uncertainty, the editor must to some degree follow his instinct, as in deciding how to resolve the following peculiarity: 'Thou smotherst . . . thou . . . murthrest' (*Luc.* 885). The practice of this edition is to regularise except where ungainliness would result; i.e. avoiding 'charact'red', 'conqu'red'.

Where rhyming words ending in '-t' are modernised to '-ed', practice is to treat them as monosyllabic. Some consistency has to be enforced here since Q1 *Ven.* has 'fixt . . . mixt' (487, 489) whereas Q1 *Luc.* prints 'fixed . . . mixed' (561, 563). Where '-ed' endings accept modern pronunciation and produce a decasyllabic line, it may seem unnecessary to insist on the final syllable, yet the number of hendecasyllabic lines resulting from feminine rhymes (e.g. 'thither . . . weather', 113, 115) or from undisguisable archaic forms ('smiteth . . . lighteth', 176, 178) warrants doing so. *Lucrece* in particular affords many such opportunities. Accordingly, 'arrivèd . . . strivèd' (*Luc.* 50, 52) is preferred to 'arrived . . . strived', and so on. However, 'entitulèd' (*Luc.* 57) is naturally observed.

The remaining three poems or collections were printed by different houses, and so reflect varying habits. Where possible, useful principles adopted from Field's house are applied to the other poems for the sake of overall consistency. Otherwise, all the poems are printed according to the principles recommended for the New Cambridge series.

Principles of collation

Venus and Adonis and *Lucrece*

Both of the long narrative poems represent a remarkably clean text in their first printing (Q1), subsequent editions declining by and large from Q1's standard either by introducing corrupt readings and errors or changing readings without warrant (see Textual Analysis). Occasionally, a later edition rationalises a spelling in accordance with modern practice, Q1 of *Venus and Adonis* has only two substantive errors, in lines 1031 and 1054, both on the inner forme of sheet G, and *The Rape of Lucrece* has one, in line 1731.

Because there are no grounds for believing that Shakespeare came back to either poem with second thoughts (indeed the evidence gathered in the Textual Analysis points to the contrary), little of value can be gained by giving a full collation. There is even an argument for dispensing with the collation altogether, apart from listing the substantive errors of Q1. This would be consistent with the general principles of the series, which require for the plays that only readings with any claim to authority be recorded. However, readers might find it interesting to observe when corruptions and vulgarisations are introduced, and how much they sometimes influence subsequent printings. Q5 of *Venus and Adonis* introduces a number of corrupt readings, some of which are plausible while others are nonsensical. The 'better' readings often persist. Similarly, Q6 of *Lucrece*, which was entirely reset (see Textual Analysis), influences Q7 through to Q9. No reading following the quartos is collated except when the text adopts it, e.g. *Venus and Adonis* 466, and *Lucrece* 879 and 1662. The selection is indicative rather than explanatory (for some conjectures see Textual Analysis). A full collation is given by Rollins.

Examples (from *Venus and Adonis*):

54 murders] murthers Q1; smothers Q7+

This means that Q1's reading persists until Q6, and then Q7's reading takes over for the rest of the quartos until Q16 (Q9 in the case of *Lucrece*). Otherwise, interruptions in subsequent quarto listings signal Q1's occasional, silent return, e.g.:

325 chafing] Q1; chasing Q5–8, 12, 16.

A single quarto reading means that it uniquely challenges Q1, as in:

213 contenting] Q1; contemning Q5.

On the other hand, when Q1 occurs alone, this means that its reading continues throughout the quartos.

The lemma is sometimes expanded to make consultation easier, e.g.:

75 still he] Q1; still she Q4–6.

Readings are given substantially except where it seems useful to compare spelling or word forms; additionally, Q1 spellings which may contribute to wordplay are noted, and punctuation where this has helped interpret syntax.

The Phoenix and the Turtle and *A Lover's Complaint*

There are no rival quartos for *The Phoenix and the Turtle*; the 1611 edition was printed from the sheets of that of 1601, and Benson obviously set the text contained in his *Poems* (1640) from one of these. It carries no disputed readings. *A Lover's Complaint* is on the other hand less straightforward; while 1609 was the sole edition to appear in Shakespeare's lifetime, a number of its readings are either clearly corrupt or confusing. The present edition collates the first recorded reading of any emendation it adopts as well as signalling occasional conjectures.

The Passionate Pilgrim
This collection was issued in three octavos (all from the same printer), which in places disagree with each other; the printed readings are further challenged by important manuscripts and by other printed miscellanies. A full collation is accordingly given.

Venus and Adonis

VENUS AND ADONIS

Vilia miretur vulgus: mihi flavus Apollo
Pocula Castalia plena ministret aqua.

To the Right Honourable
Henry Wriothesley, Earl of Southampton,
and Baron of Titchfield.   5

Right Honourable,

          I know not how I shall offend in dedicating my unpol-
ished lines to your Lordship, nor how the world will censure me for choosing
so strong a prop to support so weak a burden. Only if your Honour seem but
pleased, I account myself highly praised, and vow to take advantage of all idle   10
hours till I have honoured you with some graver labour. But if the first heir of
my invention prove deformed, I shall be sorry it had so noble a godfather,
and never after ear so barren a land for fear it yield me still so bad a harvest. I
leave it to your Honourable survey, and your Honour to your heart's content,
which I wish may always answer your own wish, and the world's hopeful   15
expectation.

Your Honour's in all duty,
William Shakespeare.

2–3 From Ovid, *Amores* 1.15.35–36. Marlowe
translates as, 'Let base-conceited wits admire vile
things, / Fair Phoebus lead me to the Muses'
springs.' By invoking Ovid the poem may be signalling the rarefied eroticism that is to follow (see
Introduction, pp. 14ff).

9 **prop . . . burden** This may imply the image
of the vine, in keeping with the ideas of growth
and fruitfulness presented early in the poem (see
Ven. 1n).

10–11 **idle hours** Probably a conventional
expression of personal unworthiness, which may
however refer to the temporary closure of the theatres because of the plague (see 508n).

11 **graver labour** A hint that Shakespeare had

already conceived of *Lucrece*, published in the following year and also dedicated to Southampton?

11–12 **first . . . invention** Either he means his
first verse composition or he is deliberately ignoring his plays, some of which would already have
been produced.

12 **so . . . godfather** For Southampton's status
see Introduction, pp. 12–14.

13 **ear** sow (with likely wordplay on 'heir'). The
metaphors of human and natural growth, although
commonplace, have bearing on the subject of the
poem.

15–16 **hopeful expectation** Echoed by Venus –
though to a more specific end (see 757ff., and pp.
12–13).

VENUS AND ADONIS

Even as the sun with purple-coloured face
Had tane his last leave of the weeping morn,
Rose-cheeked Adonis hied him to the chase;
Hunting he loved, but love he laughed to scorn.
  Sick-thoughted Venus makes amain unto him,   5
  And like a bold-faced suitor gins to woo him.

'Thrice fairer than myself', thus she began,
'The field's chief flower, sweet above compare,
Stain to all nymphs, more lovely than a man,

1–6 The poem opens at a fast pace and takes us into the heart of the action (the wooing of Adonis), as recommended by Horace in the *Art of Poetry* (see Introduction p. 3). Both protagonists are introduced immediately, and their contrasting attitudes and desires made apparent by the compound epithets which describe them and by the overall movement of the stanza, which enacts in miniature the conflict that is about to take place.

1 **Even as** Just when. But it may also carry the force of 'just like', so beginning the stanza on a simile which culminates in Adonis at mid-point; Venus sustains a similar movement over the second part of the stanza, which rounds it out chiastically, or ab> <ba. The rhetorical compass of the poem shows itself at once.

1 **purple-coloured** red, blushing. The word has classical origins (Lat. *purpureus* meaning brightness or vividness of colour – usually though not necessarily red) and described, for example, the splendour of imperial garments (the status of the sun-god is accordingly underlined). It also occurs in the classically derived genres: in tragedy or epic poetry it describes the colour of blood (invariably shed in a noble action), whereas in lyric or erotic poems it may denote passion or even voluptuousness. Here it may carry several shades of meaning from regality down to embarrassment, especially through associations of debauch, purple being the colour of the grape which signifies the god of excess, Bacchus.

2 **tane** taken.

2 **last** lingering.

2 **weeping** dewy. The metaphor equivocally suggests the morning's distress either at the loss of the sun's attentions or from his abuse of her. In this way it anticipates both Venus's argument in favour of sexual energy and Adonis's preference for modesty.

3 **Rose-cheeked** Contrasting pointedly with the sun's 'purple-coloured' to bring out the freshness and innocence of Adonis. Compare Marlowe: 'The men of wealthy Sestos, every year / For his sake whom their goddess held so dear, / *Rose-cheeked Adonis*, kept a solemn feast' (*HL* 1.91–3). See also pp. 8–9.

3 **hied him** hurried.

4 The chiastic pattern of the line reflects that of the stanza (see 1n).

5 **Sick-thoughted** Lovesick.

5 **makes amain** hurries. Change of tense from past to historic present for dramatic emphasis, as here, is a constant tactic of the poem.

9 **Stain . . . nymphs** i.e. his beauty makes theirs seem tarnished. Marlowe also uses the word 'stain' effectively: e.g. 'Her kirtle blue, whereon was many a *stain* / Made with the blood of wretched lovers slain' (*HL* 1.15–16), which plays on 'stain' as 'sign of guilt' and as 'embellishment'. Both he and Shakespeare exploit the dual capacity of the word.

9 **more lovely . . . man** The female element in Adonis's beauty registers thematically more than once in subsequent passages, for example in the exchanges between him and Venus, in which he extols the virtues of modesty, and in Venus's reading of his fatal encounter with the boar (see particularly 1115–16).

More white and red than doves or roses are: 10
    Nature that made thee, with herself at strife,
    Saith that the world hath ending with thy life.

'Vouchsafe, thou wonder, to alight thy steed,
    And rein his proud head to the saddle-bow;
    If thou wilt deign this favour, for thy meed   15
    A thousand honey secrets shalt thou know.
        Here come and sit, where never serpent hisses,
        And being set, I'll smother thee with kisses;

'And yet not cloy thy lips with loathed satiety,
    But rather famish them amid their plenty,   20
    Making them red, and pale, with fresh variety:
    Ten kisses short as one, one long as twenty.
        A summer's day will seem an hour but short,
        Being wasted in such time-beguiling sport.'

With this she seizeth on his sweating palm,   25
    The precedent of pith and livelihood,

---

14 rein] raine Q1; reigne Q7–10; reine Q11, 13+   24 time-beguiling] Q1; time-beguilding Q5

---

10 white . . . red The contrast of white and red occurs in a number of combinations, both in this poem and in *Lucrece*, the purpose being not only decorative but thematic, e.g. passion conflicting with innocence.

11 with . . . strife in competition with herself. Nature as artist was a standard Renaissance idea (just as in *WT* 4.4.86–97, which speaks of 'great creating nature'); as such she has tried to outdo her own best efforts in fashioning Adonis.

12 the world . . . life when you die so will the world. Probably with a double implication: (1) nature has no further purpose, having achieved the perfect form, (2) without Adonis the world will not survive.

13 alight alight from.

14 A method of curbing the horse to prevent it from straying.

14 saddle-bow 'the arched front part of a saddle-tree or of a saddle' (*OED*).

15 meed reward, with a pun on 'mead', whose basic ingredient is honey (see next line).

17 where . . . hisses Venus has just spoken of imparting knowledge (see 16), which in effect gives *her* the tempter's or serpent's role. Too much ought not to be made of this irony, since Venus is conceived of (by the poem at least) as more than just a temptress; but the remark's dual purposefulness is worth noting. As other examples show almost immediately, Venus is closer to Cleopatra

(who imagines that Antony sees her as his 'serpent of old Nile' – *Ant.* 1.5.25) than to any of Shakespeare's other women. See also 19–20n.

18 set seated.

18 smother Intended by Venus as an inducement, the word clearly signals an aspect of her that Adonis finds repellent. Through such choice of diction the poem contrives to speak both for and against the goddess.

19–20 Compare Enobarbus's comment on Cleopatra: 'Other women cloy / The appetites they feed, but she makes hungry / Where most she satisfies' (*Ant.* 2.2.235–7).

23 an . . . short but a short hour.

24 wasted spent, consumed. Her meaning is that time lies heavy and could be made more interesting – speeded up; but summer's time is already short compared with winter's time (for which her suggestion would be more appropriate). This is another of Venus's temptingly phrased ideas which carry negative connotations (see 18n).

26 The . . . livelihood The sign of vigour and vitality. For similar examples of hints of lubriciousness see *Ant.* 1.2.52–3: 'if an oily palm be not a fruitful prognostication', and *Oth.* 3.4.36–9: *Oth.* 'This hand is moist, my lady. / *Des.* It [yet] hath felt no age nor known no sorrow. / *Oth.* This argues fruitfulness and liberal heart: / Hot, hot, and moist.'

And trembling in her passion calls it balm,
Earth's sovereign salve to do a goddess good.
 Being so enraged, desire doth lend her force
 Courageously to pluck him from his horse.   30

Over one arm the lusty courser's rein,
Under her other was the tender boy,
Who blushed and pouted in a dull disdain,
With leaden appetite, unapt to toy:
 She red and hot as coals of glowing fire,   35
 He red for shame, but frosty in desire.

The studded bridle on a ragged bough
Nimbly she fastens (O how quick is love!);
The steed is stallèd up, and even now
To tie the rider she begins to prove.   40
 Backward she pushed him, as she would be thrust,
 And governed him in strength, though not in lust.

So soon was she along as he was down,
Each leaning on their elbows and their hips;
Now doth she stroke his cheek, now doth he frown   45
And gins to chide, but soon she stops his lips,
 And kissing speaks, with lustful language broken,
 'If thou wilt chide, thy lips shall never open.'

28 sovereign salve most precious ointment. Extending the meaning of 'balm' (27), Venus flatteringly invokes the practice of ceremonially anointing the head of a new-crowned monarch (as in *H5* 4.1.26off.). The symmetry and alliteration of 'sovereign salve' and 'goddess good' demonstrate the art of wordplay so integral to the poem. Not only do the phrases seem to insinuate an etymological connection within themselves, 'sovereign' echoing 'salve' and so appropriating a part of its meaning (similarly 'goddess' with 'good'), the *legitimate* affinity between 'sovereign' and 'goddess' and 'salve' and 'good' assists Venus's disingenuous proposal of a natural link between herself and Adonis.

29 enraged worked up (with passion rather than anger).

30 Courageously i.e. both boldly and lustfully, as the context makes clear. (See 276 and 294.) 'Courage' as animal lust was a common meaning in the period.

31 lusty Here the meaning is principally 'vigorous', but the sexual point is never far away (consider the horse's behaviour at 265ff.). The parallelism of 31 and 32 brings the word into relation

with 'tender', emphasising the innocence and inexperience of Adonis.

34 unapt (1) disinclined, (2) incapable (with play on 'appetite').

34 toy play amorously.

35–6 Varying the red–white motif (see 10n).

37 ragged rugged.

40 prove try, attempt.

42 lust (1) will, inclination, (2) sexual desire. Although stronger than Adonis, Venus is unable to subdue him to her will, which is for physical enjoyment.

43 along lying close beside him. Compare Golding 10.646: 'And lying upward with her head upon his lappe along'.

47 with . . . broken i.e. she is kissing and speaking by turns, the one action interrupting the other. The expression 'lustful language' could apply separately to both words and kisses. Shakespeare's formula is rhetorically more sophisticated than its presumed original in Ovid ('sic ait ac mediis interserit oscula verbis' – *Metam.* 10.559) or in Golding's version ('and in her tale shee bussed him among' – 10.647).

He burns with bashful shame, she with her tears
Doth quench the maiden burning of his cheeks;   50
Then with her windy sighs and golden hairs
To fan and blow them dry again she seeks.
    He saith she is immodest, blames her miss;
    What follows more she murders with a kiss.

Even as an empty eagle, sharp by fast,   55
Tires with her beak on feathers, flesh, and bone,
Shaking her wings, devouring all in haste,
Till either gorge be stuffed or prey be gone –
    Even so she kissed his brow, his cheek, his chin,
    And where she ends she doth anew begin.   60

Forced to content, but never to obey,
Panting he lies and breatheth in her face.
She feedeth on the steam as on a prey,
And calls it heavenly moisture, air of grace,
    Wishing her cheeks were gardens full of flowers,   65

---

54 murders] murthers Q1; smothers Q7+   **62** breatheth] Q1; breathing Q5+   **63** prey] pray Q1

47, 48 broken, open For similar examples of assonance replacing pure rhyme, see 451, 453 and *Son.* 61.1–3, which uses the same rhyme.

50 maiden burning This paradox (characteristically uniting innocence with passion) further extends the trope already noted at the beginning of the poem and which recurs continually as a contrast between, for example, the colours red and white (as at 10 and *passim*). We may even visualise his red cheeks turning pale under the cooling effect of her tears. By constantly varying its expression, the poem keeps basic ideas in play from beginning to end – a feature of its rhetorical virtuosity.

53 miss misdemeanour, offence.

54 murders . . . kiss The paradox of violence with gentleness raises the question whether a single motive can be ascribed to the character – or characterisation – of either Venus or Adonis. The following stanza seems to develop Venus's rapaciousness; yet this effect is soon offset by her more lyrical aspirations (see 64–6): although passion propels Venus, and Adonis practises restraint, each of them registers more than a single impression.

55 sharp by fast ravenous through hunger.

56 Tires Tears, pulls. A term used in falconry; from Fr. *tirer*.

61 to content to be content. It may also have the transitive sense, 'to content her' (i.e. submit to her).

63 prey Shakespeare's spelling (see collation) may have suggested to him a pun on prayer, thereby giving rise to the images of line 64ff. The combination in the same image of gross devouring and heavenly grace brings out the material and spiritual aspects of the theme, which operate as contrast and balance throughout. The irony that the goddess Venus is of more earthly instinct than the mortal Adonis contributes to the deliberate comedy with which such oppositions are managed.

64 air of grace i.e. freely given as an act of heavenly mercy. The poetic idea is possible because Adonis must at least bestow his breath, even though he withholds affection.

65 cheeks . . . flowers The idea of physical – particularly facial – features as landscape is popular in Elizabethan poetry, and recurs in *Luc.* 11–14 and *passim*. (Compare, for example, Thomas Campion's poem 'There is a garden in her face.')

So they were dewed with such distilling showers.

Look how a bird lies tangled in a net,
So fastened in her arms Adonis lies;
Pure shame and awed resistance made him fret,
Which bred more beauty in his angry eyes.   70
    Rain added to a river that is rank
    Perforce will force it overflow the bank.

Still she entreats, and prettily entreats,
For to a pretty ear she tunes her tale.
Still is he sullen, still he lowers and frets,   75
'Twixt crimson shame and anger ashy pale.
    Being red, she loves him best, and being white,
    Her best is bettered with a more delight.

Look how he can, she cannot choose but love,
And by her fair immortal hand she swears   80
From his soft bosom never to remove
Till he take truce with her contending tears,
    Which long have rained, making her cheeks all wet:
    And one sweet kiss shall pay this comptless debt.

75 still he] Q1; still she Q4–6

66 So Provided that (see Abbott §133).

66 distilling showers i.e. the breath forming into fine drops. (*OED* defines 'distil' as 'to issue forth in drops or in a fine moisture'.)

67 Look how Just as. An archaic form introducing or inviting a comparison, but especially appropriate in a poem which puts such emphasis on visual presentation. For variations on the form see 289, 299, 529, 815, and 925.

69 awed resistance i.e. the will to resist is checked by fear. (The phrase is paradoxical, balancing 'pure shame'.)

70 Malone compares *TN* 3.1.145–6: 'O, what a deal of scorn looks beautiful / In the contempt and anger of his lip!'

71 rank full to overflowing. The word suggests the luxuriant or innocently lascivious effect of Adonis's beauty. (See Onions for examples of coarse or lascivious connotation.)

72 Perforce Inevitably; also contributing to play on 'force'.

73 prettily entreats Venus discards her predator's role for something more traditionally feminine – an example of her varied approach and of our changing view of her.

74 ear Malone's conjecture 'air' was challenged by Steevens and has been subsequently resisted. If

allowed, Malone's reading would obscure the necessary reminder of Adonis's special kind of beauty.

75 lowers frowns; normally used to describe the sky – a further indication of the cosmic physiognomy at play in the poem (see 65n).

76 i.e. shame and anger make his face appear red and white in turn (see 10n). The conceit serves the humorous point that in Adonis even negative emotions take on (for Venus) a desirable aspect.

78 more greater.

79 Look how Compare this expression with its different use at 67. The comic effect here owes something to its apparent but not actual repetition of the formula.

81 remove withdraw (in the military sense, as, for example, in the lifting of a siege – *OED* sv *v* trans. 1b, 2 and 3c); this introduces the military idea of 82.

82 contending i.e. battling against him. Since 'contend' implies force and 'tears' submission or supplication, the phrase is additionally oxymoronic.

84 comptless countless. The word takes its significance partly from 'tears' (82) and yields two meanings: (1) inestimable, infinite, and (2) not subject to counting. Venus opportunistically grounds the logic of (1) on the fact of (2) in order to increase Adonis's obligation (as the cause of her weeping).

Upon this promise did he raise his chin,   85
Like a dive-dapper peering through a wave,
Who being looked on, ducks as quickly in;
So offers he to give what she did crave,
    But when her lips were ready for his pay,
    He winks, and turns his lips another way.   90

Never did passenger in summer's heat
More thirst for drink than she for this good turn.
Her help she sees, but help she cannot get;
She bathes in water, yet her fire must burn.
    'O pity', gan she cry, 'flint-hearted boy,   95
    'Tis but a kiss I beg, why art thou coy?

'I have been wooed, as I entreat thee now,
Even by the stern and direful god of war,
Whose sinewy neck in battle ne'er did bow,
Who conquers where he comes in every jar;   100
    Yet hath he been my captive and my slave,
    And begged for that which thou unasked shalt have.

'Over my altars hath he hung his lance,
His batt'red shield, his uncontrollèd crest,
And for my sake hath learned to sport and dance,   105
    To toy, to wanton, dally, smile and jest,

94 her fire] Q1; in fire Q7+   106 toy] Q1; coy Q4+

86 **dive-dapper** dab-chick. Shakespeare uses the full form (rather than the dialect 'didapper') for its expressive wordplay.
87 **Who** Which, as at 306, 630, 857, 956, and 968. Abbott (§264) notes the frequency of usage in similes where animals are compared to men.
89 **pay** payment (of the debt).
90 **winks** (1) blinks, (2) winces (suggested by Wyndham). Compare *Luc.* 375. But see 121–2 below, where 'wink' implies connivance.
91 **passenger** foot-traveller.
92 **good turn** i.e. (1) the deed that would relieve her, (2) his skilful evasion (which augments her suffering – 'thirst for' then becomes 'thirst as a result of').
93 **Her help** What would help her.
94 The conceit probably develops from the image of 86, with Adonis now representing the element in which Venus immerses herself unsatisfied. However, Malone's reading of 'water' as 'tears' has some appeal, given Venus's tears at 82 and the

present line's play on a familar Petrarchan paradox in which tears and passion are invariably depicted as water and fire. (Prince plausibly recalls the myth of Tantalus, which had just been given memorable treatment by Spenser in *FQ*, II, vii, 57–60). See also *Luc.* 858.
97–102 See supplementary note.
100 **jar** combat, discord. The word may suggest the impact of a charging animal (see 97–102n).
102 **unasked** without asking.
103–114 These stanzas exemplify the myth of Mars and Venus, the common interpretation of which was that manly prowess squandered itself when directed to lust. Among contemporary literary examples is Spenser's Bower of Bliss in *FQ* 2.12, where the witch Acrasia transforms her lovers to swine; and Shakespeare himself later addressed the theme in *Antony and Cleopatra*. But the passage also shows how the erotic and the heroic may appear to share a common set of values, love poetry using the *same* imagery as the language of war,

Scorning his churlish drum and ensign red,
Making my arms his field, his tent my bed.

'Thus he that overruled I overswayèd,
Leading him prisoner in a red rose chain;   110
Strong-tempered steel his stronger strength obeyèd,
Yet was he servile to my coy disdain.
  O be not proud, nor brag not of thy might,
  For mast'ring her that foiled the god of fight.

'Touch but my lips with those fair lips of thine –   115
Though mine be not so fair, yet are they red –
The kiss shall be thine own as well as mine.
What see'st thou in the ground? Hold up thy head.
  Look in mine eye-balls, there thy beauty lies:
  Then why not lips on lips, since eyes in eyes?   120

---

119 there] Q1; where Q5+

especially at 108 and 114, which identify amorous 'combat' with that of the battlefield. The resolved opposition between love and heroism furnishes the strategic logic with which Venus encircles Adonis.

103 altars Virgil refers to Venus's temple with its hundred altars ('templum illi centumque . . . arae' – *Aen.* 1.415–16).

104 uncontrollèd i.e. which has never been forced to submit.

105 sport engage in erotic play.

107 churlish drum Referring to the drum's rough sound and suggesting that the feelings it stirs are inferior to the refined sentiments of erotic dalliance.

107 ensign red i.e. signalling blood or anger; preparing for the contrast at 110.

108 The heraldic play on 'arms' and 'field' (i.e. background to a coat of arms) leads into the exuberance of 'tent . . . bed' as well as showing how love and strife can be joyfully resolved (see 103–114n).

110 The image continues the 'love as war' conceit (see 103–114n). The persistence of the colour red introduces the floral imagery which Malone suggested might derive from Ronsard: 'Les Muses lièrent un jour / De chaines de roses Amour' (*Méslanges*, 1555); but just as likely an influence was Thomas Lodge: 'Else I with roses every day / Will whip you hence / And bind you, when you long to play / For your offence' (*Rosalynde*, 1590).

111 Strong-tempered Punning on 'well-made' and 'resolute'. The play on steel is metonymic and imbues him with corresponding steeliness (no matter whether the implied blade is his own or an adversary's), in contrast to his submissiveness in the following line.

112 coy disdain disdain which is calculated to attract (hence paradoxical).

113–14 Venus's feigned warning directs Adonis to think in terms of a strictly martial contest (to which, as she knows, his nature inclines), whereas with characteristic sophistry she is really tempting him to enjoy a victory of the heart – just the sort of engagement that Adonis is anxious to avoid.

114 foiled beat, overcame. The term is from (1) wrestling (as in the contest between Orlando and Charles in *AYLI* 2.2.14) and, probably, (2) fencing (*OED v.* 2). Both sports emphasise agility, though Venus implies mental as much as physical finesse.

117 kiss . . . own i.e. in kissing her he receives a kiss.

119 there . . . lies The argument from reflection, while straightforward, may be prompted by the ideas of Castiglione's *Courtier* (especially Book IV), in which the perception of the beloved's beauty inspires the lover to absorb her form through his eyes. But Elizabethan poetry abounds in such conceits, which, to be appreciated, do not require knowledge of a coherent philosophy of love.

'Art thou ashamed to kiss? Then wink again,
And I will wink; so shall the day seem night.
Love keeps his revels where there are but twain;
Be bold to play, our sport is not in sight.
    These blue-veined violets whereon we lean   125
    Never can blab, nor know not what we mean.

'The tender spring upon thy tempting lip
Shows thee unripe; yet mayst thou well be tasted.
Make use of time, let not advantage slip;
Beauty within itself should not be wasted.   130
    Fair flowers that are not gathered in their prime
    Rot, and consume themselves in little time.

'Were I hard-favoured, foul, or wrinkled-old,
Ill-nurtured, crookèd, churlish, harsh in voice,
O'er-worn, despisèd, rheumatic, and cold,   135

---

123 are but] Q1; be but Q2, 4+ *(Q3 defective)*   **126** not] Q1; they Q7+   **134** Ill-nurtured] Q12; Il-nurtur'd Q1; Ill-natur'd Q9–11, 13+

121 wink close your eyes (see 90n).

122 Solipsistic arguments by which lovers combat threats of exposure or assert their power over their situation characterise poetry of this time. Compare John Donne's 'Thy beames, so reverend, and strong / Why shouldst thou thinke? / I could eclipse and cloud them with a winke' – 'The Sunne Rising'.

124 play (1) frolic amorously, (2) gamble (from 'bold' and 'sport').

124 not in sight unobserved.

125 blue-veined Suggesting closed eye-lids (perhaps prompted by the eye-imagery introduced at 119.) For a similar association, see *WT* 4.3.120–1: 'violets, dim / But sweeter than the lids of Juno's eyes'. Violets were a traditional emblem of modesty, which Venus interprets as ingenuousness (126).

126 See 125n.

127 tender spring youthful moustache. Human features are constantly depicted in terms of nature and the natural cycle.

128 unripe Given Venus's confident qualifying remarks, 'unripe' is probably opposed to 'over-ripe' or 'over-blown' rather than 'ripe', and is the likely equivalent of the Italian word 'acerbo' ('coming to ripeness').

129–32 The injunction to make use of time, and so defeat it, was a favourite *topos* of both classical and Renaissance love poetry, and permeates

the first seventeen of Shakespeare's *Sonnets*, which were written at about this period. The *Sonnets* emphasise beauty's obligation to procreate itself, whereas 'use' in Venus's more classical argument seems to emphasise lovemaking. Compare *Hero and Leander* 1.327–8: 'The richest corn dies if it be not reaped, / Beauty alone is lost, too warily kept.'

131 prime *OED* sb 1 (8 and 9) gives (1) the 'springtime' of human life, and (2) the period of greatest perfection or vigour (which is sometimes placed later). (1) is more likely, given 'unripe' in line 128.

133–6 Parodies of the praise of feminine beauty with similar emphasis on the details of ugliness and decrepitude were a long-established literary tradition, sometimes offered merely for fun, but also with the more serious reminder that all beauty comes to this in the end. See, for example, Petrarch, *Secretum (Prose)*, pp. 136–9). Venus may as a rhetorical tactic be appropriating her opponents' argument in order to defuse it.

133 hard-favoured harsh of feature. Compare 931 and *Luc.* 1632.

134 Ill-nurtured Ill-bred, coarse.

134 crookèd deformed.

135 O'er-worn worn out.

135 despisèd. Perhaps with a pun on 'despiced' = 'unsavoury'.

Thick-sighted, barren, lean, and lacking juice –
   Then mightst thou pause, for then I were not for thee;
   But having no defects, why dost abhor me?

'Thou canst not see one wrinkle in my brow,
   Mine eyes are grey and bright and quick in turning,   140
   My beauty as the spring doth yearly grow,
   My flesh is soft and plump, my marrow burning.
      My smooth moist hand, were it with thy hand felt,
      Would in thy palm dissolve, or seem to melt.

'Bid me discourse, I will enchant thine ear,   145
   Or like a fairy trip upon the green,
   Or like a nymph with long dishevelled hair
   Dance on the sands, and yet no footing seen.
      Love is a spirit all compact of fire,
      Not gross to sink, but light and will aspire.   150

'Witness this primrose bank whereon I lie:
   These forceless flowers like sturdy trees support me;

142 plump] plumpe Q1; plumbe Q5–6; plum Q7–10, 12

136 **Thick-sighted** Blurry-eyed.
136 **juice** sap, vitality.
137 **for thee** worthy of you.
140 The source for this may lie in contemporary portrait painting, which placed special emphasis on the eyes. Compare Hilliard: 'for of all the features in the face of a picture the eye showeth most life' (*The Arte of Limning*, ed. Philip Norman, *The Walpole Society*, 1 (1911–12), 24).
141 April was sacred to Venus in the Roman calendar, and an etymological connection may, as has been supposed, exist between the name of the month and the goddess's Greek name Aphrodite (*Encyclopaedia Britannica*, eleventh edn, 1910–11).
142 **marrow** sexual essence. Compare *AWW* 2.3.281: 'Spending his manly marrow in her arms'.
143 **moist hand** A sign of sensuality or fertility. Compare line 25 and *Ant.* 1.2.52–3: 'Nay, if an oily palm be not a fruitful prognostication'.
144 The note of transformation or semblance of dissolution appears to signal the mood of enchantment (with its changing guises) that Venus develops in 145ff.
146 **trip** dance with a quick light step.
147–8 For the image's recurrence much later in Shakespeare see *Temp.* 5.1.34–35: 'And ye that on the sands with printless foot / Do chase the ebbing Neptune'. If this nymph is also a sea-nymph, all

four elements are present in the stanza. 'Footing' means ambiguously 'footprint' or 'the movement of the feet'. The latter meaning, together with the casualness of 'dishevelled hair', suggests the influence of the highly valued attitude of *sprezzatura* as recommended by Castiglione: 'to use in everye thing a certaine disgracing to cover arte withall, and seeme whatsoever he doth and saith, to doe it without paine, and (as it were) not minding it' (*The Book of the Courtier*, p. 46). See also 1028n.
149–50 Compare *Ant.* 5.2.288–9: 'I am fire, and air; my other elements / I give to baser life'; and for a more precise distinction between the rarer and grosser elements see also *H5* 3.7.21–3: 'He is pure air and fire; and the dull elements of earth and water never appear in him.' Shakespeare would have known the ideas expounded in Ovid's *Metamorphoses*: 'The fire most pure and bright, / The substance of the heaven itself, because it was so light, / Did mount aloft, and set itself in highest place of all' (Golding 1.25–7).
149 **compact** composed.
150 **aspire** (1) rise, mount up, (2) aim for glory.
151–6 Venus again employs an enchanting argument (see 144n), this time based on the charm of disproportion.
152 **forceless** frail, weak.

Two strengthless doves will draw me through the sky
From morn till night, even where I list to sport me.
    Is love so light, sweet boy, and may it be   155
    That thou should think it heavy unto thee?

'Is thine own heart to thine own face affected?
Can thy right hand seize love upon thy left?
Then woo thyself, be of thyself rejected;
Steal thine own freedom, and complain on theft.   160
    Narcissus so himself himself forsook,
    And died to kiss his shadow in the brook.

'Torches are made to light, jewels to wear,
Dainties to taste, fresh beauty for the use,
Herbs for their smell, and sappy plants to bear: 165
Things growing to themselves are growth's abuse.
    Seeds spring from seeds, and beauty breedeth beauty;
    Thou wast begot, to get it is thy duty.

'Upon the earth's increase why shouldst thou feed,
Unless the earth with thy increase be fed?   170
By law of nature thou art bound to breed,
That thine may live when thou thyself art dead;

160 on theft] Q1; of theft Q4+

153 **doves** Traditionally associated with Venus, whose chariot they draw in the concluding stanza.

155 **light** Both 'without gravity' and 'unconstrained'. Venus puns on the duality of spirit and matter (see the pairing in 149–50).

156 **heavy** (1) oppressive, (2) heavy (see 155n).

157 **affected** attracted.

158 **Can . . . left** i.e. grasp love by putting one's hands together.

160 **freedom** freedom from affection. Venus anticipates Adonis's objection (as yet expressed only by looks or gestures) that love is oppression or loss of freedom.

160 **on** of.

161–2 An ominous warning, since the deities punished Narcissus with death for defying the laws of love. See supplementary note.

162 **shadow** image, reflection. The word can connote either light or darkness or combine the two, as here and in *R2* 4.1.292–3: 'The shadow of your sorrow hath destroy'd / The shadow of your face.'

163–74 Compare 129–32n. Many parallels exist between these lines and the arguments in favour of procreation in the first seventeen of Shakespeare's

Sonnets. See also *HL*, 1.223–54, and *Rom*. 1.1.215–20.

163–4 Compare *Rom*. 1.5.44–47, where torches and jewels contribute to a sense of 'Beauty too rich for use, for earth too dear'.

164 **Dainties** Sweetmeats.

164 **use** active enjoyment, drawing on the word's explicitly sexual meaning.

165 **sappy** full of sap, vitality. *OED* cites Thomas Phaer, the sixteenth-century translator of the *Aeneid*: 'Well agyd now, but sappy strength he kepes of grener yeres.'

166 Steevens (Malone) detects a reference to horticulture: 'Alluding to twinn'd cherries, apples, peaches, &c. which accidentally grow into each other'.

168 **get** beget.

170 **earth . . . fed** Venus invokes the command of the Hebrew God with its insistence on duty: 'Bring forthe frute, and multiplie, and replenish the earth' (Gen. 9.1) The effect of this is to keep serious ideas in view despite the prevailing tone of comedy.

172 **thine** your descendants.

And so in spite of death thou dost survive,
In that thy likeness still is left alive.'

By this the love-sick queen began to sweat,   175
For where they lay the shadow had forsook them,
And Titan, tirèd in the midday heat,
With burning eye did hotly overlook them,
    Wishing Adonis had his team to guide,
    So he were like him and by Venus' side.   180

And now Adonis, with a lazy sprite
And with a heavy, dark, disliking eye,
His low'ring brows o'erwhelming his fair sight
Like misty vapours when they blot the sky,
    Souring his cheeks cries, 'Fie, no more of love!   185
    The sun doth burn my face, I must remove.'

'Ay me', quoth Venus, 'young and so unkind,
What bare excuses mak'st thou to be gone!
I'll sigh celestial breath, whose gentle wind

175 to sweat Both with desire and as a result of the temperature (for the sexual meaning compare *Ham.* 3.4.92: 'In the rank sweat of an enseamed bed').

177 Titan the sun god.

177 tirèd (1) tired, weary, (2) attired. Paradoxically, the god both expresses heat (is 'attired' in it) and yet suffers its effects. Compare 814 and *HL* 1.139, 'Where by one hand light-headed Bacchus hung', in which Bacchus personifies both the grape and the feeling it induces. It is characteristic of the wit of such poetry to divide the god into aggressor and victim, making him endure the feelings he inflicts.

178 burning . . . hotly i.e. both inflicting and suffering heat. See 177n.

178 overlook look down at.

179 team Referring to the horses which in mythology drew the chariot of the sun. Perhaps 'team' has a rustic connotation, adding a touch of the Warwickshire fields.

181 sprite spirit, mind. But 'lazy sprite' implies sluggishness and draws on the psycho-physiological theory of bodily humours (blood, bile, phlegm, choler). An excess of one of these (phlegm in the case of Adonis) was supposed to cause 'unnatural' behaviour.

182 disliking disapproving.

183 low'ring glowering. The image receives more complex development in *Son.* 33.

183 fair sight handsome appearance (i.e. his features are disfigured by his frown). Wordplay on sight, as eyes or as object of the eyes (i.e. Venus), is unlikely. The poem's puns are not generally so densely packed as those of the *Sonnets*.

184 vapours clouds, mists, fog. See *OED* sv *sb* 2b, 'An exhalation rising by natural causes from the ground or from some damp place'. The parallel between the human and cosmic frames, which furnishes the whole conceit, carries the reminder that 'vapour' often connotes foulness (issuing from the depths of the earth as from the body's bowels).

185 Souring Pursing up.

186 Adonis tries to end the argument by breaking the cosmic analogy. His 'fair sight', which posed as the 'sun' of 183–4, now succumbs to the real sun. But Venus reasserts the parallel in 189ff.

187 young . . . unkind For the idea that cruelty is unnatural to youth see also *Lear* 1.1.106, 'So young, and so untender?'

188 bare (1) poor, (2) shameless.

189 celestial breath See 186n.

Shall cool the heat of this descending sun.   190
   I'll make a shadow for thee of my hairs;
   If they burn too, I'll quench them with my tears.

'The sun that shines from heaven shines but warm,
And lo I lie between that sun and thee;
The heat I have from thence doth little harm,   195
Thine eye darts forth the fire that burneth me;
   And were I not immortal, life were done
   Between this heavenly and earthly sun.

'Art thou obdurate, flinty, hard as steel?
Nay, more than flint, for stone at rain relenteth;   200
Art thou a woman's son, and canst not feel
What 'tis to love, how want of love tormenteth?
   O, had thy mother borne so hard a mind,
   She had not brought forth thee, but died unkind.

'What am I that thou shouldst contemn me this?   205
Or what great danger dwells upon my suit?
What were thy lips the worse for one poor kiss?
Speak, fair, but speak fair words, or else be mute.
   Give me one kiss, I'll give it thee again,
   And one for int'rest if thou wilt have twain.   210

'Fie, liveless picture, cold and senseless stone,
Well-painted idol, image dull and dead,

---

190 heat] heate Q1; heart Q5   **203** hard] Q1; bad Q2, 4+

190 heat . . . sun The heat descending from this sun. The sun's rays rather than the sun himself descend; otherwise, the sun would be declining and so less strong (which would contradict Venus's point). But the interchangeability of the human and the cosmic pursued thus far in the passage makes it appropriate that the sun should appear to descend as an earthly protagonist. See further the exchange of roles at 198.

196 The image has both medieval and classical antecedents, but the pointed contrast between a material (the sun) and ideal (Adonis) flame may owe something to contemporary Neoplatonism (see pp. 19–21).

197 life were done Venus refers primarily to her own life, but the absence of a possessive pronoun is telling. The scope offered by 'heavenly' and 'earthly' suns, as well as the infinite range of 'immortal', suggests that universal rather than individual life is in question.

200 at . . . relenteth is worn away by rain (with play on stone as 'stubbornness').

202 want lack.

203 hard unyielding. Venus seems to ignore the fact that Myrrha's 'wicked' mind was full of thoughts of love for her own father and that Adonis was therefore the progeny of an incestuous union (Golding 10.327ff.). But the poem by and large concentrates on Adonis as a type of youthful male beauty rather than exploring the myth of his conception.

204 unkind (1) cruel, (2) without kindred, offspring, (3) unnatural (recalling 'unkind' at 187).

205 this like this, thus.

208 speak fair speak true, speak kind.

209 give . . . again give it back to you.

210 twain two. But there would be three kisses in all, the one he will 'lend' her and the two she promises him.

Statue contenting but the eye alone,
Thing like a man, but of no woman bred!
    Thou art no man, though of a man's complexion,   215
    For men will kiss even by their own direction.'

This said, impatience chokes her pleading tongue,
And swelling passion doth provoke a pause.
Red cheeks and fiery eyes blaze forth her wrong;
Being judge in love, she cannot right her cause.   220
    And now she weeps, and now she fain would speak,
    And now her sobs do her intendments break.

Sometime she shakes her head, and then his hand,
Now gazeth she on him, now on the ground.
Sometime her arms enfold him like a band: 225
She would, he will not in her arms be bound.
    And when from thence he struggles to be gone,
    She locks her lily fingers one in one.

'Fondling', she saith, 'since I have hemmed thee here
Within the circuit of this ivory pale,   230
I'll be a park, and thou shalt be my deer:
Feed where thou wilt, on mountain or in dale;

---

213 contenting] Q1; contemning Q5   223 Sometime] Q1; Sometimes Q4+

211–16 This stanza may have been inspired by Ovid's story of Pygmalion's love for the statue he had carved (Golding 10.261ff.): it was appropriately Venus who gave the statue life in response to Pygmalion's prayers. The lines also bring out the poem's interest in 'living' art (see further 289–94.)

211 liveless lifeless.

211 senseless (1) without feeling, (2) without understanding.

215 though . . . complexion though you look like a man. Some editors, following Brown, gloss this as 'natural disposition' on the basis of the bodily humours (see 181n). But Venus more probably has surface appearance in mind.

216 even . . . direction even of their own accord or nature.

218 provoke Paradoxical, since 'provoke' causes expectations of something happening whereas what 'happens' is 'a pause'.

219 blaze forth Combining two senses (sight and sound) since 'blaze' links with the appearance of 'fiery eyes' and 'blaze forth' refers to a herald's trumpet proclamation. The synaesthesic effect bears out the contemporary Sidneian

theory of poetry as a 'speaking picture' (see *Apology*, p. 101).

220 Although as goddess of love she has authority to settle its disputes, she is powerless to decide in her own favour (compare 251).

222 intendments i.e. what she intends to say.

223–8 The comic effect of sudden shifts of movement depends on the agile use of such rhetorical tropes as syllepsis ('her head . . . his hand') and syncope ('She would . . . he will not').

228 one in one in each of his.

229 Fondling Foolish boy (here meant affectionately).

230 ivory pale i.e. her white arms as they encircle Adonis, with a pun on 'pale' as 'the fence of a deer park'.

231–40 The anatomising of a woman's body in terms of the delights of nature was a common feature of Renaissance love poetry, deriving in part from works such as Clément Marot's *Blason du Beau Tétin*. (Compare Sidney's 'What tongue can her perfections tell?' and Donne's 'Love's Progress'.)

231 deer a typical pun (Q1 'deare').

Graze on my lips, and if those hills be dry,
Stray lower, where the pleasant fountains lie.

'Within this limit is relief enough,   235
Sweet bottom-grass and high delightful plain,
Round rising hillocks, brakes obscure and rough,
To shelter thee from tempest and from rain:
    Then be my deer, since I am such a park,
    No dog shall rouse thee, though a thousand bark.'   240

At this Adonis smiles as in disdain,
That in each cheek appears a pretty dimple;
Love made those hollows, if himself were slain
He might be buried in a tomb so simple,
    Foreknowing well, if there he came to lie,   245
    Why there love lived, and there he could not die.

These lovely caves, these round enchanting pits,
Opened their mouths to swallow Venus' liking.
Being mad before, how doth she now for wits?
Struck dead at first, what needs a second striking?   250

---

234 fountains Probably 'breasts', but see 236n.

235 limit restricted area.

235 relief (1) pasturage (*OED* 2.8a), sustenance, (2) ease, protection, shelter.

236 bottom-grass i.e. grass growing in a low valley, hence luxuriant. The modern imagination (e.g. Partridge, *Shakespeare's Bawdy*) finds it hard to resist a pun on 'bottom', but *OED* provides no contemporary evidence. In fact, 'bottom' is a later, polite substitute for 'breech' or 'buttock'. Despite Partridge's further offering of 'brakes' (237) as 'pubic hair', the analogy between landscape and anatomy works less in precise detail and more generally in terms of the pleasures and convenience each affords.

237 brakes thickets.

237 obscure hidden.

239–40 Punctuation (which is as Q1) is unequal to the fluidity of the syntax: line 239 may be complete in itself, or 'since' may introduce the clauses of 240 ('since . . . *that* no dog', etc.): both senses are equally entertained.

240 No dog . . . thee Proleptic irony, since with the help of his own dogs Adonis will eventually 'rouse' or drive the game from cover only to become himself the prey – as depicted here.

242 That So that.

243–6 The conceit depends on distinguishing between love embodied and as abstract principle, with consequent play on body–spirit duality (see also 155n). The paronomasia (or nearly equivalent sound) of 'love lived' smoothes the antithesis.

243 if himself so that if he himself.

244 simple (1) innocent, (2) artless (*OED* sv *adj.* 2,3).

247 caves . . . pits dimples.

248 to . . . liking to receive Venus's admiration of them. The conceit operates not visually – which would make the effect grotesque – but by quasi-logical association, as is customary in Elizabethan poems (compare *AS* 11.11: 'In her cheek's pit thou didst thy pitfould set'). Images of 'caves' and 'pits', the lairs and traps associated with wild animals and described paradoxically as 'lovely' and 'enchanting', prefigure in an unforced manner the ultimate fate of love, and perhaps act as a reminder that the impulse towards beauty in the poem merges with that of destruction.

249 how . . . wits i.e. to be mad is to be out of one's wits.

250 Struck . . . first Having been smitten already. The image continues the ideas of 243–6: the effect of love is to deprive one of life and yet bring the feelings unbearably alive.

Poor queen of love, in thine own law forlorn,
To love a cheek that smiles at thee in scorn.

Now which way shall she turn? What shall she say?
Her words are done, her woes the more increasing;
The time is spent, her object will away,   255
And from her twining arms doth urge releasing.
  'Pity', she cries, 'some favour, some remorse!'
  Away he springs, and hasteth to his horse.

But lo, from forth a copse that neighbours by,
A breeding jennet, lusty, young, and proud,   260
Adonis' trampling courser doth espy,
And forth she rushes, snorts and neighs aloud.
  The strong-necked steed, being tied unto a tree,
  Breaketh his rein, and to her straight goes he.

Imperiously he leaps, he neighs, he bounds,   265
And now his woven girths he breaks asunder;
The bearing earth with his hard hoof he wounds,
Whose hollow womb resounds like heaven's thunder;
  The iron bit he crusheth 'tween his teeth,
  Controlling what he was controllèd with.   270

253 she say] Q1; we say Q5–6

---

251 in . . . forlorn (1) punished by your own law, (2) without benefit of your law. Such contradictory impulses and effects sustain the poetic argument throughout.

252 cheek . . . smiles Developing the conceit that depicts dimples as mouths (248), coupled probably with the notion that to turn one's cheek is a form of snub.

255 object Combining the sense of (1) Adonis as object of her desire, and (2) her intention to enjoy her desire.

257 remorse compassion, tenderness.

260 breeding jennet brood mare. A jennet is a small Spanish horse. By celebrating natural sexual instinct in its description of the horses, the poem varies and even increases its vitality without over-compromising the human protagonists and endangering decorum. Were Venus to consummate her passion for Adonis, the effect would be to upset the delicate balance which keeps them indefinitely opposed.

261 trampling Both (1) stamping with impatience, and (2) appearing energetic enough to cover the mare.

263–70 Because they conduct the narrative, these

lines possess a vigour that quite exceeds the *simile* from Marlowe that probably inspired them: 'For as a hot proud horse highly disdains / To have his head controlled, but breaks the reins, / Spits forth the ringled bit, and with his hooves / Checks the submissive ground: so he that loves, / The more he is restrained, the worse he fares' (*HL*, 2.141–5).

263 strong-necked Compare the description of Mars's 'sinewy neck' (99) and later the boar's (627). Such epithets recall their similar application elsewhere in the poem and hint at the common interest that unites them. Adonis is confronted here by an example of sexual ferocity which Venus urges him to emulate but which is in fact a threat to him.

264 straight immediately.

266 woven For strength rather than ornament.

267 bearing (1) supporting, (2) enduring (as of an insult), (3) receiving (as of an impression) (compare *H5* Prologue 26–7: 'Think, when we talk of horses, that you see them / Printing their proud hoofs i'th'receiving earth'). 'Bearing' may also imply 'procreative' (reinforced by 'womb' at 268), with the further effect of dividing sexuality into its tender and aggressive aspects – a conflict the poem constantly ponders.

His ears up-pricked, his braided hanging mane
Upon his compassed crest now stand on end;
His nostrils drink the air, and forth again
As from a furnace vapours doth he send;
    His eye which scornfully glisters like fire 275
    Shows his hot courage and his high desire.

Sometime he trots, as if he told the steps,
With gentle majesty and modest pride;
Anon he rears upright, curvets and leaps,
As who should say, 'Lo, thus my strength is tried, 280
    And this I do to captivate the eye
    Of the fair breeder that is standing by.'

What recketh he his rider's angry stir,
His flattering 'Holla' or his 'Stand, I say'?
What cares he now for curb or pricking spur, 285
For rich caparisons or trappings gay?

---

272 stand] Q1; stands Q7+   **281 this]** Q1; thus Q5+

271–2 mane . . . stand The verb's number may be the result of including 'ears' as part of its subject; but Malone (followed generally) understood 'mane' ('composed of many hairs') as plural.

272 compassed crest i.e. the tuft of hair on the top of the head which is arched like a bow. The longer hair of the mane seems to stand above this.

275 scornfully glisters This (Q1's reading) is metrically awkward and may result from the compositor's accidentally reversing the intended phrase, 'glisters scornfully'.

276 hot courage The horse shows an excess of choler ('hot') in contrast to its owner's excess of phlegm. 'Courage' connoted sexuality as well as boldness or valour, a significance which assists the paradoxically effective interchange of epithets (in place of the more expected 'high courage' and 'hot desire').

277 told counted, emphasising the ideas of precision and restraint. The Elizabethans, an equestrian nation, prided themselves on their horsemanship or 'manege', the equivalent of modern 'dressage'.

279 curvets A term from manege. Wyndham traces it from Italian *corvetta* = a curvet or bound, and *corvo* = a raven, explaining: 'The horse was made to rear and prance forward with his hind legs

together, and this action was likened to the hopping of a raven.'

280 As . . . say Like one who says.

280 tried proven.

282 fair breeder Perhaps echoing Venus's 'beauty breedeth beauty' (167) since the argument attributed to the courser repeats hers and recalls her tactics.

283 What recketh he What does he care for.

283 stir agitation.

284 'Holla' A term from manege meaning 'hold steady'. Here, 'flattering' means that the command is delivered gently.

286 caparisons (1) trappings, (2) saddle-cloth (Sp. 'caparazon'). The two phrases 'rich caparisons' and 'trappings gay' duplicate each other both pleonastically and chiastically. A pleonasm is a filling-out of descriptive detail, sometimes redundantly, though this 'superfluous speech' may not be 'misliked, for even a vice sometime being seaonably used, 'hath a pretie grace' (Puttenham, p. 257). A chiastic effect occurs when parallel phrases contrast each other in reverse order, i.e. abba, so that 'rich' corresponds with 'gay' and 'caparisons' with 'trappings'. The rhetorically embellished effect of the line may be intended to emulate the palfrey's accoutrements and contrast with the *naked* passion which the mare's unadorned form inspires in him.

He sees his love, and nothing else he sees,
For nothing else with his proud sight agrees.

Look when a painter would surpass the life
In limning out a well-proportioned steed,   290
His art with nature's workmanship at strife,
As if the dead the living should exceed –
  So did this horse excel a common one,
  In shape, in courage, colour, pace, and bone.

Round-hoofed, short-jointed, fetlocks shag and long,   295
Broad breast, full eye, small head, and nostril wide,
High crest, short ears, straight legs and passing strong,
Thin mane, thick tail, broad buttock, tender hide:
  Look what a horse should have he did not lack,
  Save a proud rider on so proud a back.   300

Sometime he scuds far off, and there he stares;
Anon he starts at stirring of a feather;
To bid the wind a base he now prepares,
And where he run or fly they know not whether;

---

293 this horse] Q1; his horse Q8, 10+   302 starts] Q1; stares Q8, 10–14   304 where] Q1

288 **proud sight** i.e. he disdains to look upon anything else. But there could be further play on sight as 'appearance' (as in 'fair sight', 183), meaning that he is a 'handsome creature' who finds a corresponding beauty only in the mare.

289–294 The allusion to the familiar art–nature topos – already hinted at in 211ff. – raises questions which are discussed more fully in the Introduction (pp. 3–5). The description may be interestingly contrasted with Venus's taunt to the 'image dull and dead' of Adonis at 211–14. Here the tone appears uncomplicated by any thought of the doubtful propriety of art's making the 'dead' appear to live and the ethical problems such practice posed for a Protestant poet or artist in his use of imagery.

289 **Look when** The frequency with which this expression occurs (see also 67, 79, 299, 529) may indicate that, quite apart from its function in introducing a comparative term, it also highlights the particularly visual nature of the poetic demonstration, perhaps in accordance with the Horatian precept, *ut pictura poesis*.

290 **limning out** Punning on (1) drawing, and (2) giving limbs to.

291 See 11n and 289–94n.

294 **courage** vitality (see 276n).

295–8 The source of this description is most likely Thomas Blundeville's *Arte of Ryding* (1565), translated from the Italian Federico Grisone's *Ordini di Cavalcare*. Comparing Shakespeare's verse rhythm with the prose of Blundeville – 'Round hoofe; pasterns short; his joints great with long feawter locks behind which is a sign of force' etc. – it may be appreciated how in its evocation of the horse's strength and power the poem's own vigorous expression dispenses with the need for explanatory or qualifying clauses (e.g. 'which is a sign of force'). Ben Jonson appears to have been inspired to make parodic use of the passage when he has Nockem the horse-courser speak in similar terms of the virtues of Mrs Littlewit (*Bartholomew Fair* 4.5.21–8).

295 **shag** shaggy, rough.

297 **passing** extremely.

301 **scuds** runs straight and fast.

303 **bid . . . base** challenge the wind to a race. *OED* sv sb [2]: 'A popular game among boys; it is played by two sides who occupy contiguous "bases" or "homes": any player running out from his "base" is chased by one of the opposite side, and, if caught, made a prisoner.'

304 **where** Probably a contracted form of 'whether' (some editors emend to 'whe'er'; see Abbott §466), since while the line appears odd none

For through his mane and tail the high wind sings,   305
Fanning the hairs, who wave like feathered wings.

He looks upon his love and neighs unto her,
She answers him as if she knew his mind;
Being proud, as females are, to see him woo her,
She puts on outward strangeness, seems unkind,   310
    Spurns at his love and scorns the heat he feels,
    Beating his kind embracements with her heels.

Then like a melancholy malcontent
He vails his tail, that like a falling plume
Cool shadow to his melting buttock lent;   315
He stamps, and bites the poor flies in his fume.
    His love, perceiving how he was enraged,
    Grew kinder, and his fury was assuaged.

His testy master goeth about to take him,
When lo the unbacked breeder, full of fear,   320
Jealous of catching, swiftly doth forsake him;
With her the horse, and left Adonis there.
    As they were mad unto the wood they hie them,
    Outstripping crows that strive to overfly them.

All swoln with chafing, down Adonis sits,   325
Banning his boist'rous and unruly beast.
And now the happy season once more fits

325 chafing] Q1; chasing Q5–8, 12, 16

of the quartos bothered to change it (see collation). The rhetorical character of Elizabethan grammar makes for a good deal of verbal replication (though Shakespeare affords no further examples of this combination), and so where we would use a word once it appears twice, albeit in varied form.

312 A clever adaptation of observable nature, since the mare responds to being covered by kicking the stallion.

313 melancholy malcontent Apart from its obvious wordplay, this expression affords amusement by likening the horse to a type fashionable in the drama of the time – a disaffected courtier suffering from an excess of black bile (the Greek meaning of 'melancholy') who 'purges' himself with satire. Shakespeare created such a figure in the person of Jaques (jakes = privy, water-closet) in *AYLI*.

314 vails . . . tail lets his tail hang.

316 fume anger.

319 testy (1) headstrong, (2) irritable. (*OED* traces its etymology to Old Fr. *'teste'* = 'head').

320 unbacked (1) unmounted, (2) uncovered (see 312n).

321 Jealous . . . catching Wary of being caught. 'Jealous' in the more modern sense may also be invoked by 'forsake' and the emotional context generally.

323 As As if.

323 mad . . . wood The phrase punningly increases the impression of madness, since the contemporary sense of 'wood' is 'out of one's mind', 'raging', as in *FQ* 1.4.34: 'Through unadvizèd rashness woxen wood'.

325 swoln . . . chafing raging with frustration.

326 Banning Cursing.

327 now . . . . fits time is again propitious.

That love-sick love by pleading may be blest;
For lovers say, the heart hath treble wrong,
When it is barred the aidance of the tongue.   330

An oven that is stopped, or river stayed,
Burneth more hotly, swelleth with more rage;
So of concealèd sorrow may be said
Free vent of words love's fire doth assuage;
But when the heart's attorney once is mute,   335
The client breaks, as desperate in his suit.

He sees her coming, and begins to glow,
Even as a dying coal revives with wind;
And with his bonnet hides his angry brow,
Looks on the dull earth with disturbèd mind,   340
Taking no notice that she is so nigh,
For all askance he holds her in his eye.

O what a sight it was wistly to view
How she came stealing to the wayward boy,
To note the fighting conflict of her hue,   345
How white and red each other did destroy:

---

328 lovesick love i.e. Venus, the incarnation of the spirit of love, also suffers from it. See 177n.

329 treble wrong A pun on 'treble' as (1) 'triple' and (2) 'treble' as in music, since 'the aidance of the tongue' (330) would take the form of a 'treble' or 'soprano' voice.

330 aidance help.

331–4 The image is commonplace, pre-Shakespearean variations abounding in Spenser, Lodge, Sidney, and Greene. Compare *Tit.* 2.4.36–7: 'Sorrow concealed, like an oven stopped, / Doth burn the heart to cinders where it is.'

333 concealèd sealed up, pent up.

335 heart's attorney tongue. Contemporary lyric poetry characteristically uses those features – tongue, lips, eyes, etc. – which enact the 'language of the heart'.

336 breaks Combining the sense of (1) bursts (see 460), and (2) is broken. The image is one of heart-break, since the 'client' for whom the tongue acts as attorney is the heart. Brown (1913) detects a pun on bankruptcy and cites *Rom.* 3.2.57: 'O, break, my heart, poor bankrout, break at once!' But the sense is differently applied: the line in *Rom.* means that the heart has nothing to sustain it, whereas here the meaning is that it is too full of emotion.

336 as as if.

337 begins to glow This image revives that of 331–4 (applied to Venus) as well as recalling 325, which describes Adonis. The poem thus maintains a consistent narrative manner while shifting attention back and forth between the two protagonists.

339 bonnet hat (see 351). It is tempting to read particular girlish overtones into the sense in which the word is applied, but it was used universally for men's headgear until 'cap' took over in about 1700 (*OED*). In Shakespeare, even undeniably manly figures wear bonnets (see *Cor.* 3.2.73).

340 disturbèd i.e. as the heavens might appear disturbed or threatening (reviving the cosmological conceit of 183–4).

342 askance . . . eye i.e. he watches her out of the corner of his eye.

343 wistly earnestly, intently. (See *Luc.* 1355 and *PP* 6.12.) Grammatically, 'wistly' is a dangling modifier qualifying 'came stealing'; but since it also forms a phrase with 'to view' it may equally relate to the onlooker (narrator/reader), sympathising with Venus's plight.

344 wayward recalcitrant, unwilling.

345–8 Compare the opening stanzas and notes, and *Luc.* 71.

But now her cheek was pale, and by and by
It flashed forth fire, as lightning from the sky.

Now was she just before him as he sat,
And like a lowly lover down she kneels; 350
With one fair hand she heaveth up his hat,
Her other tender hand his fair cheek feels:
His tend'rer cheek receives her soft hand's print,
As apt as new-fall'n snow takes any dint.

O what a war of looks was then between them, 355
Her eyes petitioners to his eyes suing!
His eyes saw her eyes as they had not seen them;
Her eyes wooed still, his eyes disdained the wooing;
And all this dumb play had his acts made plain
With tears, which chorus-like her eyes did rain. 360

Full gently now she takes him by the hand,
A lily prisoned in a gaol of snow,
Or ivory in an alablaster band:
So white a friend engirts so white a foe.

---

352 cheek] cheeke Q1; cheekes Q7–16   353 tend'rer cheek receives] tendrer cheeke, receives Q1; tender cheeks revives Q5–8, 12; tender cheeks receive Q9–11, 13+   362 gaol] Q11, 13+; gaile Q1

347 But now . . . by and by One moment . . . the next.

350 lowly humble, suppliant (contrasting with her status as a goddess).

351 heaveth pushes. The word seems too strong for the action, but a paradoxical strenuousness cum delicacy is surely intended as part of the comedy. Prince argues that 'heave' may not have conveyed the sense of effort that it does today and cites 'upheaveth' (482) and 'heaved-up' (*Luc.* 111). But the logic governing both his examples denotes either physical or emotional exertion, as do other Shakespearean usages. *OED*'s examples all support the sense of effort.

354 apt ably.

354 dint impression.

356 suing qualifying 'petitioners'.

357 as as if (see 342n).

359–60 Adonis's taciturnity and Venus's silent pleading are likened to the theatrical convention of the dumb-show, or unspoken mime of the action of the plot, which preceded the play proper. The chorus's function was both to interpret the action to the audience ('acts made plain') and, especially

in classical tragedy, give formal expression to the emotions it inspired.

359 his its (referring to the 'dumb play'); see Abbott §228.

362–4 The delicacy by which degrees of whiteness are measured contrasts with the more obvious play of red on white in 76–8 and elsewhere. The point of such refinement is probably not mere virtuosity but the wish to extend the poem's range of feeling beyond the immediately passionate, instinctual, or comic, and establish its capacity for sensitivity and pathos. The images may owe something to Ovid's description of Hermaphroditus: 'As if a man an Ivorie Image or a Lillie white / Should overlay or close with glasse that were most pure and bright' (Golding 4.438–9).

362 gaol Possibly also punning on 'gale' (Q1's spelling is 'gaile', which *OED* gives as a variant of 'gale', sv *sb* 3).

363 alablaster alabaster. 'The spelling in 16th–17th c. is almost always *alablaster*; app. due to a confusion with *arblaster* a cross-bowman, also written *alablaster*' (*OED*).

364 engirts surrounds.

This beauteous combat, wilful and unwilling,   365
Showed like two silver doves that sit a-billing.

Once more the engine of her thoughts began:
'O fairest mover on this mortal round,
Would thou wert as I am, and I a man,
My heart all whole as thine, thy heart my wound: 370
  For one sweet look thy help I would assure thee,
  Though nothing but my body's bane would cure thee.'

'Give me my hand', saith he. 'Why dost thou feel it?'
'Give me my heart', saith she, 'and thou shalt have it.
O give it me, lest thy hard heart do steel it,   375
And being steeled, soft sighs can never grave it.
  Then love's deep groans I never shall regard,
  Because Adonis' heart hath made mine hard.'

'For shame', he cries, 'let go, and let me go;
My day's delight is past, my horse is gone,   380
And 'tis your fault I am bereft him so.
I pray you hence, and leave me here alone,
  For all my mind, my thought, my busy care,
  Is how to get my palfrey from the mare.'

Thus she replies: 'Thy palfrey, as he should,   385
Welcomes the warm approach of sweet desire.

---

366 two] Q1; to Q5–6, 8, 10+

365 wilful willing (referring to Venus and perhaps also implying over-assertiveness).
367 the engine . . . thoughts her voice, tongue.
368 mover This means more than merely 'living
creature' and, as 'mortal round' implies, indicates
that Adonis is part of the celestial motion that rules
the universe (as in 'O thou eternal Mover of the
heavens' (*2H6* 3.3.19), which refers to Aristotle's
'Primum Mobile').
370 thy . . . wound i.e. where he has a heart
she has a wound. The underlying sense is 'Would
your heart were wounded as mine is', but to gloss
it thus diminishes the powerful metonymy of heart
as wound which the elliptical phrasing effects.
372 Even if your recovery (from a putative broken heart) depended on my destruction ('my body's
bane'). By clever use of conditional phrasing, Venus
depicts her love as sacrificial and therefore noble.
373–4 Adroit use of stichomythia, or alternating dialogue, in which speakers repeat each other's

lines with a defiant or challenging variation. The
device is often employed by Seneca, whose plays
were performed or read in university halls or private houses such as Southampton's.
375 steel it (1) turn it to steel, (2) steal it.
376 grave make an impression on (as in engrav-
ing).
377 regard pay sympathetic attention to.
378 heart . . . hard Whether God hardened
one's heart or whether one did it voluntarily (either
way, a place in hell being the consequence) was a
keenly argued point of contemporary, particularly
Calvinist, theology. Venus shrewdly applies the
doctrine to her own loveless condition to increase
Adonis's sense of responsibility for it – another
example of her logic of seduction. (*See Luc.* 560n.)
384 palfrey A saddle-horse normally preferred
by ladies – a hint perhaps at Adonis's over-
delicateness.

Affection is a coal that must be cooled,
Else suffered it will set the heart on fire.
  The sea hath bounds, but deep desire hath none;
  Therefore no marvel though thy horse be gone.   390

'How like a jade he stood tied to the tree,
Servilely mastered with a leathern rein;
But when he saw his love, his youth's fair fee,
He held such petty bondage in disdain,
  Throwing the base thong from his bending crest,   395
  Enfranchising his mouth, his back, his breast.

'Who sees his true-love in her naked bed,
Teaching the sheets a whiter hue than white,
But when his glutton eye so full hath fed,
His other agents aim at like delight?   400
  Who is so faint that dares not be so bold
  To touch the fire, the weather being cold?

'Let me excuse thy courser, gentle boy,
And learn of him, I heartily beseech thee,

392 Servilely] Servilly Q1   397 sees] Q1; seeks Q2–6

387 **Affection** Passion. The word had a stronger
sense than its modern connotation. (*OED* sv *sb* 3
gives a 1567 example: 'Slaves to their lustes and
affection'.)
388 **suffered** i.e. allowed to burn. The argument
uses the theory of bodily humours or the belief that
psychic health requires a corresponding physiolog-
ical balance. See 181n.
389 Compare Duke Orsino's remark, 'But [my
love] is all as hungry as the sea – And can digest
as much' (*TN* 2.4.100–1).
  390 **though** if.
391 **jade** (1) worn-out horse, (2) cheap woman.
393 **fee** due, reward.
395 **bending crest** i.e. submitting to the thong.
The line strongly echoes earlier statements of sexual assertiveness (see 104 and n).
396 **Enfranchising** Setting free. To enfranchise
here alludes to the practice of releasing a slave from
bondage – an idea prepared for by phrases like
'servilely mastered' and 'petty bondage'. This in
turn helps Venus's argument that with his physical liberty the horse achieves freedom of spirit or
self-realisation (as would Adonis if he indulged his
senses).
397–400 All one sentence, but the initial subject
'Who' (He who) changes via the construction 'But
when' to 'His agents'. The meaning is: his eyes

having fed, his other senses wish to also.
  397 **in . . . bed** naked in her bed. The word order
is a typical example of transferred epithet. The
phrase was much in use and did not always have the
erotic application that it does here; but there is no
need to explain it (as Wyndham and others do) as a
parody of Hieronymo's anxious complaint, 'What
out-cries pluck me from my naked bed' (*The Spanish Tragedy* 2.5.1). Shakespeare's and Kyd's usages
are to be understood in context: nudity as titillation in the former and as emotional desolation in
the latter.
398 **whiter . . . white** See 362–4n, and compare
Luc. 472.
399 **glutton eye** The synaesthesia (or doubling
one sense with another) of this expression plays
its part in Venus's advocacy of her passion. The
philosophy of ideal love (as propounded by Ficino)
arranged the senses in a hierarchy whereby sight
and hearing were purer or more elevated because
they could transcend the immediacy of the body as
well as being the medium of all artistic expression.
Touch, taste, and smell, by contrast, were limited in
range, bound more closely to the body, and therefore inferior. By giving the eye a belly and a palate,
Venus abolishes such disinctions and advances the
cause of physical enjoyment (as in 400).
  401 **faint** cowardly.

To take advantage on presented joy;   405
Though I were dumb, yet his proceedings teach thee.
    O learn to love; the lesson is but plain,
    And once made perfect, never lost again.'

'I know not love', quoth he, 'nor will not know it,
Unless it be a boar, and then I chase it.   410
'Tis much to borrow, and I will not owe it;
My love to love is love but to disgrace it,
    For I have heard it is a life in death,
    That laughs and weeps, and all but with a breath.

'Who wears a garment shapeless and unfinished?   415
Who plucks the bud before one leaf put forth?
If springing things be any jot diminished,
They wither in their prime, prove nothing worth;
    The colt that's backed and burdened being young,
    Loseth his pride, and never waxeth strong.   420

'You hurt my hand with wringing, let us part,
And leave this idle theme, this bootless chat;
Remove your siege from my unyielding heart,

---

405 **advantage on** advantage of.

405 **presented** (1) offered, (2) present, made present.

406 **proceedings** actions, conduct.

407–8 Love is represented as something that may be acquired by instruction, like ethics. For every aspiration there was an appropriate form of conduct (see 406n) which could be learnt from authors such as Castiglione or Stefano Guazzo (see 147–8n).

410 **Unless . . . boar** Particular narrative units may as here suggest an overall thematic preoccupation, the ferocity of impulse represented in the boar corresponding to one aspect of love (lust), the boar's inducement in Venus of fear for Adonis's safety being another (tenderness). The individual line enacts the contradictions that are to be resolved only when the narrative is complete.

411 **owe it** (1) acknowledge the debt, (2) accept the principle involved.

412 My only regard for love is to render it contemptible. The force of 'disgrace' is 'to disdain' rather than to bring shame upon by one's own improper behaviour. 'Disgracing' is the translation Hoby finds for Castiglione's famous word *sprezzatura* (see 147–8n, and p. 19) to suggest that the performer appears to disdain or make light of his own skill or excellence.

413 **For . . . heard** Perhaps a reminder that

despite his fierce denunciation of love here and in 793ff., Adonis has no personal experience of it.

414 **all . . . breath** all in the same breath.

415–20 Despite his inexperience, Adonis proves as adept as Venus in arguing from nature. The difference in outlook and opposition of feeling between the two protagonists sustains – as do the many local examples of oxymoron – the poem's main thematic vision of the irreconcilable principles embodied in love.

415 **shapeless** that has not yet received its shape. Since the analogy of the garment is to the human body in its stages of maturity, the image may contain an allusion to the Fates who would spin out individual life according to its apportioned time.

417 **springing things** things just beginning to grow.

417 **diminished** i.e. not allowed their full growth.

419 **backed** made to bear a rider.

420 **pride** strength (of character).

420 **waxeth strong** grows to maturity.

423 **Remove your siege** The convention of expressing love's passion through military or martial imagery has already been used by Venus (97–114). To introduce it again through Adonis is one of the ways in which the poem maintains its symmetry.

To love's alarms it will not ope the gate;
    Dismiss your vows, your fainèd tears, your flatt'ry,   425
    For where a heart is hard they make no batt'ry.'

'What, canst thou talk?' quoth she, 'hast thou a tongue?
O would thou hadst not, or I had no hearing.
Thy mermaid's voice hath done me double wrong;
I had my load before, now pressed with bearing: 430
    Melodious discord, heavenly tune harsh sounding,
    Ears' deep sweet music, and heart's deep sore wounding.

'Had I no eyes but ears, my ears would love
That inward beauty and invisible;
Or were I deaf, thy outward parts would move   435
Each part in me that were but sensible:
    Though neither eyes nor ears, to hear nor see,
    Yet should I be in love by touching thee.

'Say that the sense of feeling were bereft me,
And that I could not see, nor hear, nor touch,   440
And nothing but the very smell were left me,

---

432 Ears'] Eares Q1; Earths Q5+   439 feeling] Q1; reason Q9–11, 13+

424 alarms assaults, attacks.
425 Dismiss Punning on the military sense of 'disband'.
426 hard resolved. Compare Venus's reproach of his hardheartedness in 375–8.
426 batt'ry A 'battery' is a sustained assault by heavy bombardment on a military position: here it additionally connotes the effectiveness of the impact, as in *3H6* 3.1.37: 'Her sighs will make a batt'ry in his breast.'
429 mermaid's voice Venus attributes feminine guile to Adonis.
430 now pressed now I am pressed ('pressed' means 'as in a press' or 'vice', i.e. her burden has become insupportable).
431–2 Although some editors have deplored the taste for oxymoron exhibited here, it is consistent with the general symmetrical pattern of the poem, both in style and theme. The versatility of these examples is furthermore very pleasing: 431 hinges on two self-contained if similar contradictions, while 432 maintains the paradox across the entire line, the phrases 'Ears' . . . sweet' and 'heart's . . . sore' very nearly reproducing each others' sounds.

433–50 Venus develops the argument earlier hinted at in 399–400. The poignancy with which she imagines being deprived of one sense after another cunningly disguises the eagerness with which she abandons the traditionally more refined senses and indulges the coarser or more sensual organs. As Wyndham notes, the argument has much in common with the progress of Chapman's poem *Ovids Banquet of Sence* (1595). Both employ Neoplatonic logic, though Chapman's (which governs his entire poem) is the more orthodox.
434 inward beauty i.e. the voice as expression of his soul – a Neoplatonic idea. Sidney similarly employs the word 'inward' to refer to his mistress's spiritual beauty in *AS* 71.8: 'That *inward sun* in thine eyes shineth so.' See also *Apology*, p. 113.
436 that . . . sensible that experienced only sensation. Here the argument may be drawing further on contemporary literary and artistic theory (in part Neoplatonic) which considers images as having the power to 'move' (435) to virtuous action. Sidney is again the probable mediator of the idea; in his description of poetry as a 'speaking picture' (*Apology*, pp. 101, 103).
437 Though neither Though having neither.

Yet would my love to thee be still as much;
    For from the stillitory of thy face excelling
    Comes breath perfumed, that breedeth love by smelling.

'But O what banquet wert thou to the taste,   445
Being nurse and feeder of the other four.
Would they not wish the feast might ever last,
And bid Suspicion double-lock the door,
    Lest Jealousy, that sour unwelcome guest,
    Should by his stealing in disturb the feast?'   450

Once more the ruby-coloured portal opened,
Which to his speech did honey passage yield,
Like a red morn that ever yet betokened
Wrack to the seaman, tempest to the field,
    Sorrow to shepherds, woe unto the birds,   455
    Gusts and foul flaws to herdmen and to herds.

This ill presage advisedly she marketh:
Even as the wind is hushed before it raineth,
Or as the wolf doth grin before he barketh,
Or as the berry breaks before it staineth,   460
    Or like the deadly bullet of a gun,
    His meaning struck her ere his words begun.

And at his look she flatly falleth down,
For looks kill love, and love by looks reviveth.

460   staineth] Q1; straineth Q5

443 **stillitory** A still in which, for example, perfume is made or distilled. The pun on 'stillitory' (urged by 'still' at 442) registers the constancy of love's condition.

443 **face excelling** surpassingly beautiful face.

445–6 By the elastic rules of Elizabethan grammar, 'thou' (i.e. Adonis), and not 'taste', is the 'nurse and feeder'. Every sense receives life and sustenance from him, but the most intimate of them, 'taste', is accorded most. Venus characteristically inverts the senses' order of privilege as defined by the Neoplatonists (see 445n).

445 **banquet** 'Banquet' was a frequent Elizabethan name for Plato's seminal text, the *Symposium*, which in Ficino's translation and commentary of 1471 had become a point of focus for contemporary Neoplatonism. (Chapman borrows the title openly in the poem referred to in 433–50n.) Despite 'banquet's encouraging connotations, Ficino does not allow 'taste' the supremacy

it enjoys here (see Ficino, pp. 84–7).

448–9 **Suspicion . . . Jealousy** The pointed similarity between these two words in effect brings out their difference: 'Suspicion' indicates wariness, 'Jealousy' disapproval.

451–6 It is stylistically apt that the image that introduces Adonis at the point of speech should continue Venus's train of ideas on 'taste' by remarking the voluptuous quality of his mouth – while at the same time suggesting that further pleasure is not in prospect.

451 **ruby-coloured portal** red lips; 'portal' (gate, doorway) connotes richness or magnificence.

453–6 The wisdom is proverbial and as likely as not biblical (e.g. Matt. 16.2–3); but its expression is pastoral and literary (e.g. 'Sorrow to shepherds') and accords with the more courtly form of 451–2.

456 **flaws** blasts of wind.

457 **advisedly** attentively (compare *Luc.* 1527).

A smile recures the wounding of a frown: 465
But blessèd bankrupt, that by loss so thriveth!
   The silly boy, believing she is dead,
   Claps her pale cheek, till clapping makes it red,

And all amazed brake off his late intent,
For sharply he did think to reprehend her, 470
Which cunning love did wittily prevent:
Fair fall the wit that can so well defend her!
   For on the grass she lies as she were slain,
   Till his breath breatheth life in her again.

He wrings her nose, he strikes her on the cheeks, 475
He bends her fingers, holds her pulses hard,
He chafes her lips: a thousand ways he seeks
To mend the hurt that his unkindness marred.
   He kisses her, and she by her good will
   Will never rise, so he will kiss her still. 480

The night of sorrow now is turned to day:
Her two blue windows faintly she upheaveth,

---

466 loss] *This edn (conj. Walker);* love Q1

463 **flatly** (1) flat on her back, (2) without further ado. The word and the gesture it describes prepare us for a slightly farcical interlude.
465 **recures** heals.
466 i.e. the only happy bankrupt is the lover who prospers even through what ruins him, hopes rising and lowering at an instant. (For 'but' as meaning 'only' see Onions.) Walker's sensible conjecture, 'loss' for 'love' (see collation), is adopted. (The substitution of the mistaken word could have occurred as the copyist's or compositor's eye – or indeed the poet's own intention – was distracted by the two appearances of 'love' in 464.) The contradiction whereby loss promotes recovery consists with the paradoxical logic that prevails throughout.
470 **he did think** he had thought.
470 **reprehend** reprimand
471 **cunning love** Personifying Venus.
471 **wittily** cunningly, cleverly ('wittily' more or less repeats the sense of 'cunning' which it balances).
472 **Fair fall** Good luck to. The expression carries a reminder of her provident action in falling as she has (463), as well as implying what her motive is in lying beneath Adonis.
473–4 Shakespeare may have had Marlowe in mind: 'By this, sad Hero, with Love unacquainted, / Viewing Leander's face, fell down and fainted. /

He kissed her, and breathed life into her lips' (*HL* 2.1–3).
473 **as** as if.
475–8 Of course Venus would hardly submit to such treatment for very long in the real world; however, the stylistic criterion is not realism but comedy as Adonis *increases* her pain in trying to 'mend the hurt'. It is unfeasible as well as pointless to construe (as some editors have done) a more gentle sense to words such as 'wrings' (475).
478 The grammar of this phrase is not straightforward, but its meaning is clear: 'to repair the injury caused by his unkindness'. While 'hurt' can hardly be the object of 'marred', the poet seems to be thinking rather of the parallel antithesis of 'marred' and 'mend'. Compressions and intensifications of expression resulting from the shifting of alignment between words occurs more typically in Shakespeare's drama. For an example similar to the one here, see *Err.* 2.1.96–7, 'What ruins are in me that can be found / By him not ruin'd.'
479 **good will** readiness, responsiveness (implying determination as in the recurrence of 'will' in 'Will . . . rise').
480 **so . . . still** if he will continue to kiss her.
481–6 These lines offer a further example of cosmic parallelism (compare 181ff.); but they vary and enrich the effect by making use of the troubadour

Like the fair sun when in his fresh array
He cheers the morn and all the earth relieveth;
   And as the bright sun glorifies the sky,   485
   So is her face illumined with her eye,

Whose beams upon his hairless face are fixed,
As if from thence they borrowed all their shine.
Were never four such lamps together mixed,
   Had not his clouded with his brows' repine;   490
     But hers, which through the crystal tears gave light,
     Shone like the moon in water seen by night.

'O where am I?' quoth she, 'in earth or heaven?
Or in the ocean drenched, or in the fire?
   What hour is this? Or morn, or weary even?   495
   Do I delight to die, or life desire?
     But now I lived, and life was death's annoy;
     But now I died, and death was lively joy.

'O thou didst kill me, kill me once again!
Thy eyes' shrewd tutor, that hard heart of thine,   500
Hath taught them scornful tricks, and such disdain,
   That they have murd'red this poor heart of mine;
     And these mine eyes, true leaders to their queen,
     But for thy piteous lips no more had seen.

484 earth] Q1; world Q2+

aubade tradition, whereby the lady's eyes are identified with daylight so that morning cannot begin until she opens them.

482 blue windows Editors dispute whether this refers to her eyes or her eyelids, the overall meaning being either (1) she raises her eyelids to reveal her eyes, or (2) she raises her eyes towards Adonis. Both meanings are very likely intended, i.e. she opens her eyes *and* looks upwards.

482 faintly . . . upheaveth This suggests effort: compare the disputed interpretation of 'heaveth up' (351n).

487 hairless Therefore smooth and radiant (keeping up the planetary analogy). For a similar play, see *1H6* 1.1.2–3: 'Comets . . . Brandish your crystal tresses in the sky.'

488 shine As a noun (see 728).

490 repine vexation.

491–2 The couplet effects a fresh modulation of tone from comedy to tenderness.

493–8 The stanza assuredly combines the Petrarchan convention of sharp, expressive contrasts with

the gentle romance motif of wonder and discovery (for the latter compare the moment at which Viola, having just been 'in the ocean drenched', asks 'What country, friends, is this?' – *TN* 1.2.1).

497–8 The extremes of oxymora testify to the power of his kiss (479) – that banquet which 'taste' had in prospect (445ff.).

499 kill . . . again The comedy produced by the notion of repeated 'killings' restrains the tone and keeps exuberance in check. It is perhaps worth recalling that her 'death', though extreme, is induced by a kiss only, and that conditions fall somewhat short of those required for an orgasm.

500 shrewd malicious, evil.

503 leaders captains, subalterns (i.e subordinate officers enjoying a limited command). Because they are 'true' they reveal the heart ('queen') openly and sincerely – unlike Adonis's eyes, which have learnt 'scornful tricks'. The imagery reproduces the motif of the erotic battlefield previously noted (see 103–14 and 423–6nn).

504 piteous compassionate, pitying.

'Long may they kiss each other for this cure!   505
O never let their crimson liveries wear;
And as they last, their verdour still endure,
To drive infection from the dangerous year,
    That the star-gazers, having writ on death,
    May say the plague is banished by thy breath.   510

'Pure lips, sweet seals in my soft lips imprinted,
What bargains may I make still to be sealing?
To sell myself I can be well contented,
So thou wilt buy, and pay, and use good dealing.
    Which purchase if thou make, for fear of slips,   515
    Set thy seal manual on my wax-red lips.

505 Either (1) long may his lips kiss hers to cure her ailment, or (2) long may his lips kiss themselves to preserve their restorative capacity. Although at first sight (1) would naturally seem to be what Venus intends, (2) seems retrospectively to be implied, as the stanza, developing, refers exclusively to his lips.

506 crimson liveries The redness of his lips. The image of the household servant, elegantly costumed to reflect his master's status, continues the motif of the features or bodily organs as subservient to their lord or sovereign (the face, as here, or the heart in 503).

506 wear wear out.

507 verdour verdure. 'The fresh green colour characteristic of flourishing vegetation' (*OED* sv 1.1); it includes the idea of fragrant herbs used to combat contagion, while conveying an appropriate supporting sense of freshness of taste (*OED* sv 1b). Because of the seeming inconsistency of hue between 'crimson' and 'verdour', Staunton (*Athenaeum*, 14 March 1874) conjectured that the poet must have intended 'virtue'. However, the verse's improvisational wordplay constantly modifies one idea into another (as in the examples noted above – 503 and 506 – in which military officers become footmen); and in a poem of narrative length one may expect repeated shifts of direction. Furthermore, it is arguable that, although different from each other, 'crimson' and 'verdour' are both subject (as with antithesis) to a governing principle (colour).

508 dangerous year Just as beauty is given cosmic proportions in 481–93, so here Adonis's breath has the power to dispel not merely the present moment's infection but that of an entire year. The year in question is generally taken to be 1592–3, when the plague was at its most severe. Wyndham notes that the theatres were closed between July and December 1592, causing Shakespeare to apply his pen to some other activity, the result being this poem.

509 star-gazers Probably writers of almanacs.

509 writ on forecast, predicted.

510 plague See 508n.

511–16 These lines change the subordinate poetic motif from images of fertility to law and commerce, in accordance with the tactic of sustaining the main idea (the sweetness of lips) by varying the means of stating it.

511 seals By 'seal' is meant a wax impression (of a sign or signature) usually affixed to a document as authorisation. Such a seal would give Adonis ownership of Venus (see 513). Mariana's song (*MM* 4.1.1–6) similarly speaks of kisses as the seals of love. See also pp. 4–5.

512 still always (thus prolonging the kiss). The idea of sealing a bargain, along with the attendant notion of impermeability, further develops the wordplay.

514 use good dealing deal fairly.

515 slips deceptions, counterfeits (especially of coins as frequently in Elizabethan 'low-life' writers such as Nashe and Greene – see *OED* sv *sb.* 4). But the equally Elizabethan phrase, 'to give someone the slip', meaning to evade him, is also implicit.

516 seal manual signature (as in 511). Notwithstanding 'manual' he must sign with his mouth. Further, since, according to Renaissance theories of knowledge, it was characteristic of God to put his mark or signature on all things (which sages then had to interpret), Venus may well be according Adonis divine status. (The notion of lips being sealed, i.e. silent, would equally accord with the general theory of the need to interpret signs.)

'A thousand kisses buys my heart from me,
And pay them at thy leisure, one by one.
What is ten hundred touches unto thee?
Are they not quickly told and quickly gone?   520
    Say for non-payment that the debt should double,
    Is twenty hundred kisses such a trouble?'

'Fair queen', quoth he, 'if any love you owe me,
Measure my strangeness with my unripe years.
Before I know myself, seek not to know me: 525
No fisher but the ungrown fry forbears;
    The mellow plum doth fall, the green sticks fast,
    Or being early plucked, is sour to taste.

'Look the world's comforter with weary gait
His day's hot task hath ended in the west;   530
The owl (night's herald) shrieks, 'tis very late;
The sheep are gone to fold, birds to their nest,
    And coal-black clouds that shadow heaven's light
    Do summon us to part and bid good night.

'Now let me say good night, and so say you;   535
If you will say so, you shall have a kiss.'
'Good night', quoth she, and ere he says adieu,
The honey fee of parting tend'red is:

519 touches] Q1; kisses Q7+   522 hundred] Q1; thousand Q4–6   533 And] Q1; The Q5+

517–22 Using the convention of the *basia* or kissing trope, as in Catullus's 'Vivamus, mea Lesbia,
atque amemus', which Jonson translated as 'Come,
my Celia, let us prove / While we may the sports of
love.' Catullus tries to count the number of kisses
he desires but discovers that no number may be
imposed on a lover's wishes. The introduction as
in previous stanzas of a fresh idea within the same
argumentative framework (lips–kissing) constantly
varies the reader's response.
517 buys The choice of singular person for the
verb (which occurs often in Shakespeare) may be
influenced, according to Abbott (§333), by the concept of number as a collective noun. (See also 519,
which gives 'is' for 'are'.) The internal echo of
'kisses buys' may also have influenced choice stylistically, and such combinations certainly never jar.
But no coherent theory exists as to why Shakespeare treated verb number so casually. (See also
632.)

518 And Therefore, accordingly.
519 touches kisses.
523 owe possess, have ('me' is equivalent to 'for
me'). While 'owe' does not here mean 'to owe a
debt', its usage is prompted by Venus's elaborate
argument on the debts of love to which Adonis has
just listened.
524 strangeness aloofness, indifference.
526 ungrown fry small fry.
529–34 The chronographic manner of these lines
effects a break with the speaker's normal mode and
allows him to summon up to our imagination the
changes in the natural atmosphere which accompany the action. It is a way of making the protagonist his own chorus.
529 Look Look how (see 67 and 289nn).
533 shadow cover with shadow, conceal.
538 tend'red offered (but also playing on
*tender*ness).

Her arms do lend his neck a sweet embrace;
Incorporate then they seem, face grows to face; 540

Till breathless he disjoined and backward drew
The heavenly moisture, that sweet coral mouth,
Whose precious taste her thirsty lips well knew,
Whereon they surfeit, yet complain on drouth.
He with her plenty pressed, she faint with dearth, 545
Their lips together glued, fall to the earth.

Now quick desire hath caught the yielding prey,
And glutton-like she feeds, yet never filleth;
Her lips are conquerors, his lips obey,
Paying what ransom the insulter willeth, 550
Whose vulture thought doth pitch the price so high
That she will draw his lips' rich treasure dry.

And having felt the sweetness of the spoil,
With blindfold fury she begins to forage;
Her face doth reek and smoke, her blood doth boil, 555
And careless lust stirs up a desperate courage,
Planting oblivion, beating reason back,
Forgetting shame's pure blush and honour's wrack.

540 Incorporate As one body.
540 grows to grows into. This closely resembles the metamorphosis of Salmacis and Hermaphroditus as told by Ovid: 'To both them did remain / One countenance' (Golding 4.462–3).
541 disjoined broke away.
541–2 drew . . . mouth The subject of 'drew' is more likely 'he' rather than 'mouth' (in an inverted clause construction). Despite the absence of a comma after 'moisture' in Q1, 'that . . . mouth' is probably in apposition to the preceding noun phrase.
545 her plenty (1) her body's ample form, (2) her strength of desire.
545 pressed weighed down, burdened.
547–58 In these two stanzas the disturbing nature of lust is fully portrayed, the ideas anticipating those of *Lucrece*, as the military–erotic analogy finds a logical extreme in images of blood and fury. But Shakespeare soon brings the tone back to its more usual level of pathos mingling with comedy. The poem's sense of proportion (its 'decorum') affords no more than a glimpse at the more terrifying possibilities of sexual passion. (See pp. 7–8.)
547 quick desire Desire is personified as a swift-moving predator. Throughout the two following stanzas images of predatory animal instinct combine with those of military plunder or slaughter.
550 insulter assailant (a military term).
551 vulture thought rapacious desire. Since vultures feed on carrion the image supports the idea that desire destroys its object.
554 blindfold fury Venus appears to combine the image of her son, blind Cupid, and her warrior lover, Mars, especially in the battlefield description of her face, which 'doth reek and smoke' (555). Abraham Fraunce describes Mars in his lust for Venus as 'hoate raging' (see Fraunce, p. 98).
554 forage As an animal, but also as a looter (see 547n). Compare *H5* 1.2.108–10: 'Whiles his most mighty father on a hill / Stood smiling to behold his lion's whelp / Forage in blood of French nobility'.
556 careless reckless.
556 courage The word's sexual connotation (see 276n) reinforces its symmetrical balancing of 'lust'.
557–8 This couplet anticipates the condition and predicament of Tarquin (e.g. *Luc.* 197–8). Compare also *Son.* 129.
557 Planting oblivion Producing mindlessness.
558 wrack ruin.

Hot, faint, and weary with her hard embracing,
Like a wild bird being tamed with too much handling,   560
Or as the fleet-foot roe that's tired with chasing,
Or like the froward infant stilled with dandling,
  He now obeys, and now no more resisteth,
  While she takes all she can, not all she listeth.

What wax so frozen but dissolves with temp'ring,   565
And yields at last to every light impression?
Things out of hope are compassed oft with vent'ring,
Chiefly in love, whose leave exceeds commission:
  Affection faints not like a pale-faced coward,
  But then woos best when most his choice is froward.   570

When he did frown, O had she then gave over,
Such nectar from his lips she had not sucked.
Foul words and frowns must not repel a lover:
What though the rose have prickles, yet 'tis plucked.
  Were beauty under twenty locks kept fast,   575
  Yet love breaks through, and picks them all at last.

For pity now she can no more detain him;
The poor fool prays her that he may depart.
She is resolved no longer to restrain him,
Bids him farewell, and look well to her heart,   580
  The which by Cupid's bow she doth protest
  He carries thence encagèd in his breast.

'Sweet boy', she says, 'this night I'll waste in sorrow,
For my sick heart commands mine eyes to watch.

---

560 Like . . . bird As it recovers a more gentle mood, the poem maintains continuity by keeping its animal imagery (now used to renew natural sympathy) while discarding that of military conflict.
561 with chasing with being chased.
562 froward fretful, petulant.
564 listeth wants.
565 temp'ring massaging, manipulating.
566 light slight.
567 out of hope beyond hope.
567 compassed accomplished.
568 whose . . . commission which is permitted to exceed its duty: i.e. love observes no limits.
569 Affection Passion. See 387n.
570 his choice the object of his choice.
570 froward unwilling (compare 562n).

573 Foul Harsh.
575 twenty locks Possibly proverbial (*ODEP*); the specific number revives the hyperbolic enthusiasm of 522, while the idea of lock-picking receives more sombre treatment in *Luc.* 302–15.
580 look well to take good care of (governed by 'Bids').
582 encagèd Her heart is thus likened to a trapped bird or animal, the image being effected by Cupid's 'bow' (581), which indirectly evokes Adonis's role as a hunter; and this in turn is followed up in 587–8.
583 waste (1) spend, and probably (2) waste away (see 'sick heart' in 584).
584 watch keep awake. A way of expressing love's time-honoured sleeplessness.

Tell me, love's master, shall we meet tomorrow? 585
Say, shall we, shall we? Wilt thou make the match?'
    He tells her no, tomorrow he intends
    To hunt the boar with certain of his friends.

'The boar!' quoth she, whereat a sudden pale,
Like lawn being spread upon the blushing rose, 590
Usurps her cheek; she trembles at his tale,
And on his neck her yoking arms she throws.
    She sinketh down, still hanging by his neck;
    He on her belly falls, she on her back.

Now is she in the very lists of love, 595
Her champion mounted for the hot encounter.
All is imaginary she doth prove;
He will not manage her, although he mount her:
    That worse than Tantalus' is her annoy,
    To clip Elizium and to lack her joy. 600

Even so poor birds deceived with painted grapes
Do surfeit by the eye and pine the maw;

589–90 The delicacy of these lines has left its impression on later generations of poets (Prince cites Robert Herrick as one example). Malone, followed by several editors, thinks that Shakespeare may in turn have been imitating the song by H. C. (Henry Constable? Henry Chettle?): 'At the name of boare / Venus seemed dying / Deadly-colour'd pale / Roses overcast' (*EH*, 1600). Chronology is inexact, so there is no way of telling; but the phrasing of Shakespeare's heroic line is far more accomplished than that of the song.

589 pale paleness.

590 lawn A fine white and semi-transparent linen; hence the colour and substance of what it covers still shows through, though delicately.

592 yoking The careful transition from 'Usurps' (591) to 'yoking' (both words signifying seizure and possession) once more marks the successful progression of tone from delicacy to boisterousness.

594 her belly Malone [2] chastely insists on a misprint, substituting 'his' for 'her'.

595 lists i.e. as in a tournament and ready for the 'tilt'. There is perhaps an additional pun on 'lists' as 'desiring' (see 'listeth', 564n).

597 She finds that it is not to be as she imagines.

598 manage An equestrian term meaning to put a horse through its paces (see 279n).

599 Tantalus' A classic example of the extremities of desire and frustration. Various accounts exist of his legend and the reasons for his punishment in Hades, but Ovid only refers to his suffering, which was to contemplate a pool of water and a bunch of grapes which never quite came within reach (Golding 4.567–8).

599 annoy suffering.

600 clip embrace.

600 Elizium Paradise, heaven. Elizium, or Elysium, referred to the islands of the blest where, following death and after a term in Hades, those favoured by the gods were permitted to dwell. In the popular imagination – to which Venus appeals – Elizium signified a lovers' or erotic paradise. Viola assigns the Christian meaning of heaven to the word when she imagines her brother to be dead (*TN* 1.2.4).

601 deceived . . . grapes The classical source for *trompe-l'œil* is Pliny (*Natural History* 35.36); but Elizabethan references were common, and Shakespeare may have consulted Lodge's 1590 romance ('I resemble the birds that fed themselves with Zeuxis painted grapes', Lodge [2] vol. 1, *Rosalynde*, p. 80) or Greene's 1588 work *Pandosto* (Salzman, p. 187). The illusoriness of pictorial or fictional representation formed a part of the art–nature debate, and the poet as artist may be indulging in a moment of self-reflection, as in 289–94.

602 pine the maw starve the stomach.

Even so she languisheth in her mishaps,
As those poor birds that helpless berries saw.
   The warm effects which she in him finds missing   605
   She seeks to kindle with continual kissing.

But all in vain, good queen; it will not be.
She hath assayed as much as may be proved;
Her pleading hath deserved a greater fee;
She's love, she loves, and yet she is not loved.   610
   'Fie, fie', he says, 'you crush me, let me go;
   You have no reason to withhold me so.'

'Thou hadst been gone', quoth she, 'sweet boy, ere this,
But that thou told'st me thou wouldst hunt the boar.
O be advised, thou know'st not what it is   615
With javelin's point a churlish swine to gore,
   Whose tushes never sheathed he whetteth still,
   Like to a mortal butcher bent to kill.

'On his bow-back he hath a battle set
Of bristly pikes that ever threat his foes;   620
His eyes like glow-worms shine when he doth fret,
His snout digs sepulchres where'er he goes;
   Being moved, he strikes whate'er is in his way,
   And whom he strikes his crooked tushes slay.

'His brawny sides, with hairy bristles armèd,   625
Are better proof than thy spear's point can enter;
His short thick neck cannot be easily harmèd;
Being ireful, on the lion he will venter.

603 **mishaps** misfortunes.
604 **helpless** affording no relief.
605 **effects** sexual vigour (Q12 conj. 'affects' = passionate feelings).
609 **fee** recompense. The analogy is to law (e.g. 'pleading' a case).
610 An example of the comic use of *polyptoton* (i.e. ringing the changes on the forms a word may take).
612 **reason** reason in law (see 609n).
612 **withhold** detain.
617 **tushes** tusks.
618 **mortal** deadly.
618 **bent** determined; but also describing the boar's posture as he lowers his head to charge.
619 **bow-back** back arched like a bow.
619 **battle** i.e. drawn up in battle formation.

Compare Golding's description of the Calydonian boar: 'And like a front of armed Pikes set close in battell ray / The sturdie bristles on his back stood staring up alway' (8.379–80). See supplementary notes for 97–100.
621 **fret** rage.
623 **Being moved** i.e. to anger.
623 **strikes** Probably transitive; intransitive use is mostly confined to meaning 'strike up', as in music (Onions). Q1's following comma ('strikes,') very likely indicates a noun clause object (as in *Ant.* 2.1.29: 'I learn, you take things ill' – Simpson, p. 41).
626 **better proof** stronger steel. Compare *Ham.* 2.2.490: 'On Mars's armor forg'd for proof eterne'.
628 **venter** venture.

The thorny brambles and embracing bushes
As fearful of him part, through whom he rushes. 630

'Alas, he naught esteems that face of thine,
To which love's eyes pays tributary gazes;
Nor thy soft hands, sweet lips, and crystal eyne,
Whose full perfection all the world amazes;
But having thee at vantage–wondrous dread! – 635
Would root these beauties as he roots the mead.

'O let him keep his loathsome cabin still;
Beauty hath naught to do with such foul fiends.
Come not within his danger by thy will;
They that thrive well take counsel of their friends. 640
When thou didst name the boar, not to dissemble,
I feared thy fortune and my joints did tremble.

'Didst thou not mark my face? Was it not white?
Saw'st thou not signs of fear lurk in mine eye?
Grew I not faint, and fell I not down right? 645
Within my bosom whereon thou dost lie
My boding heart pants, beats, and takes no rest,
But like an earthquake shakes thee on my breast.

'For where Love reigns, disturbing Jealousy
Doth call himself affection's sentinel; 650
Gives false alarms, suggesteth mutiny,
And in a peaceful hour doth cry, 'Kill, kill!'

---

632 eyes pays] eyes paies Q1; eye pays Q7+ *(subst.)*   645 down right] Q1

632 **pays** Shakespeare often uses the singular person of the verb where the plural is expected; see also 517n and Abbott §333 for further discussion and examples.

633 **eyne** A variant of 'eyes', often used when 'eye' or 'eyes' has already occurred in the context (compare *Luc.* 643, 1229).

636 **root** tear up, raze. The simile remarks a correspondence between Adonis's beauty and that of the landscape, just as previously his features have been compared to the heavens (see 183–4).

636 **mead** meadow.

637 **cabin** cave, lair; used more figuratively at 1038.

639 **danger** power to inflict harm.

639 **by thy will** willingly.

642 **feared** feared for.

645 **down right** right down. To print as 'down-right' (i.e. 'forthwith', 'straight away') lessens the comic impact of the image of her falling, on which the context insists. From 641 to 648 Venus steps into the role of partly comic narrator.

647 **boding** i.e. full of foreboding.

648 **earthquake . . . thee** Our perception of this as comic combines with Venus's intention of it as serious. For the narrative mode see 645n.

649 **Jealousy** anxiety, fear.

650 **affection** passion.

652 **peaceful hour** i.e. when there is no cause for alarm. Note the renewed use of military images for erotic themes.

Distemp'ring gentle Love in his desire,
As air and water do abate the fire.

'This sour informer, this bate-breeding spy,   655
This canker that eats up Love's tender spring,
This carry-tale, dissentious Jealousy,
That sometime true news, sometime false doth bring,
    Knocks at my heart and whispers in mine ear
    That if I love thee, I thy death should fear.   660

'And more than so, presenteth to mine eye
The picture of an angry chafing boar,
Under whose sharp fangs on his back doth lie
An image like thyself, all stained with gore;
    Whose blood upon the fresh flowers being shed,   665
    Doth make them droop with grief and hang the head.

'What should I do, seeing thee so indeed,
That tremble at th' imagination?
The thought of it doth make my faint heart bleed,
And fear doth teach it divination: 670
    I prophesy thy death, my living sorrow,
    If thou encounter with the boar tomorrow.

'But if thou needs wilt hunt, be ruled by me:
Uncouple at the timorous flying hare,

---

655 bate-breeding] Q1; bare-breeding Q5–6   662 chafing] Q1; chasing Q5–6, 12   668 tremble] Q1; trembling Q4+

653 Distemp'ring Disturbing.
655 sour ill-tempered; the epithet connotes natural corruption as in the images that follow ('bate-breeding', 'canker', etc.).
656 spring early growth.
657 carry-tale gossip.
657 dissentious i.e. causing discord.
658 The stanza personifies jealousy in a highly classical manner, which supports Steevens's claim (1780) that this line bears marks of Virgil's description of rumour: 'tam ficti pravique tenax quam nuntia veri' ('as concerned to report false or ill news as true' – *Aen.* 4.188).
659 Knocks . . . heart (1) Seeks entry to my heart, (2) Causes my heart to beat intemperately.
662 chafing raging.
665–6 This detail may derive in altered form from Comes (*Mythologiae*, Bk 5, ch. 16), who records that it was in fact Venus who was scratched by a rose thorn as she ran to see what had become of Adonis; the ensuing drops of blood stained the

roses red, which till then had all been white. (Compare *Tit.* 2.3.200–1: 'Upon whose leaves are drops of new-shed blood / As fresh as morning dew distill'd on flowers'.)
667 seeing thee if I were to see you.
668 th'imagination the thought of it (as in 669).
670 divination power of prophecy.
671 I prophesy See 1135ff., in which Venus resumes and expands her prophecy.
672 encounter The word applies particularly to hunting; see also 676 and Golding 10.632: '*Encounter* not the kynd of beastes whom nature armed hath.'
673–8 Ovid's Venus follows her own advice as she accompanies Adonis on one of his hunts, 'Pursewing game of hurtlesse sort, as Hares made lowe before / Or stagges with lofty heades' (Golding 10.622–3).
674 Uncouple Set the hounds loose (they would be coupled together while tracking).

Or at the fox which lives by subtlety, 675
Or at the roe which no encounter dare;
    Pursue these fearful creatures o'er the downs,
    And on thy well-breathed horse keep with thy hounds.

'And when thou hast on foot the purblind hare,
Mark the poor wretch, to overshoot his troubles, 680
How he outruns the wind, and with what care
He cranks and crosses with a thousand doubles;
    The many musits through the which he goes
    Are like a labyrinth to amaze his foes.

'Sometime he runs among a flock of sheep, 685
To make the cunning hounds mistake their smell;
And sometime where earth-delving conies keep,
To stop the loud pursuers in their yell;
    And sometime sorteth with a herd of deer:
    Danger deviseth shifts, wit waits on fear. 690

'For there his smell with others being mingled,
The hot scent-snuffing hounds are driven to doubt,
Ceasing their clamorous cry till they have singled
With much ado the cold fault cleanly out.
    Then do they spend their mouths; echo replies, 695
    As if another chase were in the skies.

680 overshoot] *This edn (conj. Steevens); over-shut* Q1

678 **well-breathed** sound in wind.
679 **purblind** weak-sighted (traditionally applied to the hare).
680 **poor wretch** Venus's account of the hare's attempts to evade the kill brings out the pathos of the hunt and looks forward to the moment when, according to her prophecy (671–2), Adonis will be transformed from hunter into hunted.
680 **overshoot** lose track of (a hunting term). The activity normally applies to hounds, but it would suit the hare to lose its own scent. Q1's reading seems to be a variant spelling; Steevens emends, but Malone (hardly plausibly) suggests retaining 'overshut' as meaning 'conclude' (i.e. bring troubles to an end).
682 **cranks** winds, twists (as of a river).
682 **doubles** doublings-back.
683 **musits** holes, hideaways (from Fr. *mussette*)

684 **amaze** confuse (punning on 'maze'; cf. labyrinth')
687 **earth-delving conies** rabbits which burrow into the earth.
687 **keep** dwell.
689 **sorteth** keeps company.
690 **shifts** stratagems.
690 **waits on** attends, accompanies.
694 **cold fault** The 'fault' is the loss of scent which has gone 'cold'; it has to be distinguished from other scents ('singled out'). Grammatically, it would be expected that 'smell' rather than its lack ('fault') would recur as the object of 'singled . . . out', but here is a further example of the compression or ellipsis found at 478.
695 **spend . . . mouths** i.e. they are prodigal with their cries (denoting excessive joy).

'By this poor Wat, far off upon a hill,
Stands on his hinder-legs with list'ning ear,
To hearken if his foes pursue him still.
Anon their loud alarums he doth hear,   700
    And now his grief may be comparèd well
    To one sore sick that hears the passing bell.

'Then shalt thou see the dew-bedabbled wretch
Turn and return, indenting with the way.
Each envious briar his weary legs do scratch,   705
Each shadow makes him stop, each murmur stay;
    For misery is trodden on by many,
    And being low never relieved by any.

'Lie quietly, and hear a little more;
Nay, do not struggle, for thou shalt not rise.   710
To make thee hate the hunting of the boar,
Unlike myself thou hear'st me moralise,
    Applying this to that, and so to so,
    For love can comment upon every woe.

'Where did I leave?' 'No matter where', quoth he,   715
'Leave me, and then the story aptly ends.

---

705 do] Q1; doth Q5+   712 myself] my selfe Q1; thy selfe Q4–8, 12

697–702 See supplementary note.
697 poor Wat 'A familiar term among sports-
men for a hare; why does not appear. Perhaps for
no better reason than Philip, for a sparrow, Tom,
for a cat, and the like' (Nares, *Glossary*, 1822).
699 hearken listen attentively.
700 Anon Presently.
700 alarums warning noises. (These are strictly
sounded by the defendants to warn of an attack, but
the image attributes them to the attackers.)
701 grief wretchedness.
702 passing bell The image is prompted by
'alarums' (700), which connotes the alarum or
warning bell. The passing bell tolls for the soul
of one who has died, one peal being rung for each
year of his life. In a time of grave epidemic – under
which climate the poem is supposed to have been
written (see 508n) – those who were seriously ill
may have taken the continual sound of the bell as
a personal omen.
704 indenting zigzagging (see Golding 7.1016:
'But [the fox] doubling and *indenting* still avoydes

his enmies lips'). The word originates in law: an
indenture is a document bearing an agreement in
duplicate between two parties which is then torn
in half along a jagged (indented) line; each party
retains one half of the document (plus its comple-
mentary duplicate half), and only when all parts are
joined, in the presence of witnesses, is the agreement legal.
705 envious malicious, hurtful.
712 Unlike myself . . . moralise Venus is
referring to her reputation for lasciviousness.
713 Venus is probably alluding to the habit in
sermons of arguing by analogy.
714 A preacher, or indeed a secular moralist,
would proceed by *anatomising* or analysing his subject (malady), making each aspect of it ('*every* woe')
a part of his argument.
715–20 The stanza turns effectively on the
device of stichomythia: see 373–4n.
715 leave leave off.
716 aptly conveniently.

The night is spent.' 'Why, what of that?' quoth she.
'I am', quoth he, 'expected of my friends,
   And now 'tis dark, and going I shall fall.'
'In night', quoth she, 'desire sees best of all.'   720

'But if thou fall, O then imagine this:
The earth in love with thee thy footing trips,
And all is but to rob thee of a kiss.
Rich preys make true men thieves: so do thy lips
   Make modest Dian cloudy and forlorn,   725
   Lest she should steal a kiss and die forsworn.

'Now of this dark night I perceive the reason:
Cynthia for shame obscures her silver shine,
Till forging nature be condemned of treason
For stealing moulds from heaven that were divine;   730
   Wherein she framed thee in high heaven's despite,
   To shame the sun by day and her by night.

'And therefore hath she bribed the destinies
To cross the curious workmanship of nature,
To mingle beauty with infirmities,   735
And pure perfection with impure defeature,
   Making it subject to the tyranny
   Of mad mischances and much misery:

724 true men] Q1; rich men Q4+   738 mad] Q1; sad Q7+

718 expected of expected by.
720 Compare *HL* 1.191, 'darke night is *Cupids* day'. Marlowe's conceit explains Shakespeare's: love (Cupid) being blind, darkness is its proper element.
721–3 Compare *HL* 2.181ff., where the sea personified as Neptune grows enamoured of the swimming Leander and impedes his progress by embracing him.
722 footing feet (implying their movement).
724 true honest.
725 modest Dian Diana ('Dian' for the metre) is both the goddess of chastity and the moongoddess. Other names for her which Shakespeare uses are Cynthia (728) and Dictynna, Phoebe, and Luna (*LLL* 4.2.36–8).
726 forsworn In having betrayed her ideal of chastity.
727 dark night The phrase is placed in antithesis to 'reason', which as well as retaining its principal meaning is thus equivalent to the idea of light.
728 Cynthia . . . shame See 725 and 726nn.

728 shine As a noun; see 488.
729 forging counterfeiting.
730 moulds models, patterns (of beauty).
731 she nature.
731 in . . . despite against heaven's will.
732 her Cynthia.
733 destinies Fates; see 415n. The notion of the three Fates (Clotho, Lachesis, and Atropos) at their loom may lie behind the image of elaborate 'workmanship' in 734. Their task was to weave the thread of human life: Clotho spun the thread, Lachesis measured it, and Atropos snapped it off with her shears.
734 cross spoil, frustrate.
734 curious elaborate, finely wrought.
736 defeature disfigurement.
738 mad mischances accidents which drive the victim mad; 'mad' describes the *effect* of 'mischances' rather than their nature. See also 739 – 'burning' fevers', 'agues *pale and faint*' – personifications of disease which reflect the condition of the sufferer.

'As burning fevers, agues pale and faint,
Life-poisoning pestilence, and frenzies wood,   740
The marrow-eating sickness whose attaint
Disorder breeds by heating of the blood.
    Surfeits, imposthumes, grief, and damned despair
    Swear nature's death for framing thee so fair.

'And not the least of all these maladies   745
But in one minute's fight brings beauty under;
Both favour, savour, hue, and qualities,
Whereat th'impartial gazer late did wonder,
    Are on the sudden wasted, thawed, and done,
    As mountain snow melts with the midday sun.   750

'Therefore, despite of fruitless chastity,
Love-lacking vestals and self-loving nuns,
That on the earth would breed a scarcity
And barren dearth of daughters and of sons,
    Be prodigal: the lamp that burns by night   755
    Dries up his oil to lend the world his light.

---

746 fight] Q1; sight Q6+   748 impartial] Q1; imperial Q5+   754 dearth] Q1; death Q5–6, 8, 12

740 wood mad, frenzied; the phrase 'frenzies wood' is a pleonasm (see 286n).

741 marrow-eating sickness Prince cites the article on 'Medicine' (*Shakespeare's England*, vol. 1), pointing out that phthisis or syphilis is probably meant. There would be some irony, and no little guile, in the goddess of *venereal* pursuits blaming any consequent disease on the goddess of chastity. But Venus is also indirectly expressing a lament for the golden age, in which love was without limits or blame, as in Tasso's chorus in the *Aminta* – translated by Samuel Daniel as 'A Pastoral of Tasso' (1601). See pp. 10–12.

743 Surfeits, imposthumes 'Surfeits' are excesses, while 'imposthumes' means abscesses. Compare the list in Greene's *Planetomachia* 5.1.18–23 (1585, ed. Grosart), from which Shakespeare also drew in *Tro.* 5.1.19–23; Greene attributes all these diseases to the influence of the planet Venus (see 741n).

744 framing creating, fashioning (see 729 and 730nn).

747 favour grace, comeliness.

747 savour appetising qualities.

747 hue skinglow.

748 impartial gazer objective judge.

748 late lately.

749 wasted laid waste.

749 thawed The choice of 'thawed' is explained by the image of snow melting at 750, but its evocation of coldness (which would include purity) contrasts also with the *overheated* nature of the various diseases to which beauty is prey.

751 despite of in defiance of.

751 fruitless chastity Compare *HL* 1.317–20: 'Abandon fruitless cold Virginitie, / The gentle queene of Loves sole enemie, / Then shall you most resemble *Venus* Nun / When *Venus* sweet rites are performed and done.'

752 Love-lacking Without the instinct or capacity for love.

752 vestals Priestesses who guarded the sacred flame in the temple of Vesta; if found guilty of unchastity their fate was to be buried alive in an underground chamber – an idea which may have prompted the minatory image of 757.

755–6 Perhaps alluding to the parable of the wise and foolish virgins (Matt. 25.1–13); see also 767–8n. But the tone of erotic comedy is always present.

756 Dries up his oil Uses his sexual capacity.

'What is thy body but a swallowing grave,
Seeming to bury that posterity
Which by the rights of time thou needs must have
If thou destroy them not in dark obscurity?   760
    If so, the world will hold thee in disdain,
    Sith in thy pride so fair a hope is slain.

'So in thyself thyself art made away,
A mischief worse than civil home-bred strife,
Or theirs whose desperate hands themselves do slay,   765
Or butcher sire that reaves his son of life.
    Foul cank'ring rust the hidden treasure frets,
    But gold that's put to use more gold begets.'

'Nay then', quoth Adon, 'you will fall again
Into your idle over-handled theme.   770
The kiss I gave you is bestowed in vain,
And all in vain you strive against the stream;
    For by this black-faced night, desire's foul nurse,
    Your treatise makes me like you worse and worse.

'If love have lent you twenty thousand tongues,   775
And every tongue more moving than your own,

757–62 This argument is very similar to those put forward in some of the first seventeen *Sonnets*; see especially 3.7–8, 'Or who is he so fond will be the tomb / Of his self-love to stop posterity?'

759 rights of time payment due to time; hence 'needs must have' means that time insists on payment in terms of a new generation.

762 Sith Since.

762 in thy pride (1) as a result of your pride, (2) in your prime (including sexual vigour).

763 thyself thyself For Shakespeare's frequent use of reflexive pronouns as nouns see Abbott §20.

764–6 These lines find close echoes in Shakespeare's first civil war tetralogy; see in particular *R3* 5.5.25–6: 'The father rashly slaughter'd his own son, / The son, compell'd, been butcher to the sire'.

767–8 Compare the parable of the talents (Matt. 25.14–30) which follows that of the wise and foolish virgins (see 755–6n). The servant who does not make use of his lord's talent buries it in the earth (see 757–60). Compare also *HL* 1.232–6: 'What difference betwixt the richest mine / And basest mould but use? for both, not used, / Are of like

worth. Then treasure is abused / When misers keep it; being put to loan, / In time it will return us two for one.'

767 The line closely resembles in image and diction the personification of jealousy at 656; Venus's personal apprehensions as well as her larger impersonal arguments in favour of procreation maintain consistency with each other.

767 frets eats, rubs away.

769 fall again enter (but underlining Venus's proclivity to 'fall' in another sense).

770 over-handled obsessive. The epithet 'handled' denotes the tactile, sensual spirit of Venus's way of arguing. (In his moralistic continuation of Marlowe's poem, Chapman devises the expression 'Hero-handled' to describe Leander's body after their love-making; see *HL* 3.21.)

773 Resuming and confuting Venus's argument at 720.

775 have has (conditional mood).

775 twenty thousand Adonis's numerical hyperbole reiterates Venus's (see 522) – an example of the poem's many ways of demonstrating its stylistic principle of antithetical symmetry.

Bewitching like the wanton mermaid's songs,
Yet from mine ear the tempting tune is blown;
   For know, my heart stands armèd in mine ear,
   And will not let a false sound enter there,   780

'Lest the deceiving harmony should run
Into the quiet closure of my breast;
And then my little heart were quite undone,
In his bed-chamber to be barred of rest.
   No, lady, no, my heart longs not to groan,   785
   But soundly sleeps while now it sleeps alone.

'What have you urged that I cannot reprove?
The path is smooth that leadeth on to danger.
I hate not love but your device in love,
That lends embracements unto every stranger.   790
   You do it for increase – O strange excuse,
   When reason is the bawd to lust's abuse!

'Call it not Love, for Love to heaven is fled
Since sweating Lust on earth usurped his name,
Under whose simple semblance he hath fed   795
Upon fresh beauty, blotting it with blame;
   Which the hot tyrant stains and soon bereaves,
   As caterpillars do the tender leaves.

---

777 mermaid's] Marmaids Q1

777 **wanton mermaid** See 429, for Venus's use of 'mermaid', and 775n.

779 **heart . . . armèd . . . ear** In his turn to adopt the language of the erotic–military convention (see 103–14n), Adonis, perhaps with unconscious irony, assumes the familiar posture of the despairing lover, resisting love unconvincingly. Wyatt uses almost the same image in his sonnet, 'The longe love' (Wyatt, p. 4).

780 **false** betraying, deceitful.

782 **closure** enclosure, refuge.

783 **little heart** Adonis's choice of diminutive expression may intend to emphasise his youthful inexperience and modesty, but it also assists Venus's complaint that he shrinks from his manly obligations.

784 **barred** deprived.

786 **sleeps alone** The convention of representing the self as an area of dispute, with an imagined physical location, betrays Adonis into an inadvertently bawdy witticism.

787 **reprove** (1) prove against you, (2) reproach.

789 **device** (1) conduct, (2) ingenuity.

791 **increase** procreation.

792 **bawd** female pimp, pander.

792 **lust's abuse** abuse practised by lust.

793–4 Adonis is quite likely invoking the Platonic distinction, newly set forth by Ficino and others, between Venus Urania (or heavenly, chaste Venus) and the earthier Venus Pandemos (identified with the procreative instinct and regarded more positively than she is by Adonis). See Ficino, pp. 53–4.

795 **Under . . . semblance** i.e. assuming love's harmless appearance.

796 **blotting . . . blame** making it shameful.

797 **hot tyrant** 'sweating Lust' (794).

797 **stains** corrupts, ruins.

797 **bereaves** Combining the word's original sense of (1) 'to rob' or 'plunder' with that of (2) 'deprive of kin'. Both senses fit the use of 'tyrant', since he is one who customarily both plunders and subdues his subjects by slaughter. Sense (2) (destruction of kin) provides – in accordance with

'Love comforteth like sunshine after rain,
But Lust's effect is tempest after sun;   800
Love's gentle spring doth always fresh remain,
Lust's winter comes ere summer half be done;
    Love surfeits not, Lust like a glutton dies;
    Love is all truth, Lust full of forgèd lies.

'More I could tell, but more I dare not say;   805
The text is old, the orator too green.
Therefore in sadness now I will away;
My face is full of shame, my heart of teen;
    Mine ears that to your wanton talk attended
    Do burn themselves for having so offended.'   810

With this he breaketh from the sweet embrace
Of those fair arms which bound him to her breast,
And homeward through the dark laund runs apace;
Leaves Love upon her back, deeply distressed.
    Look how a bright star shooteth from the sky,   815
    So glides he in the night from Venus' eye,

Which after him she darts, as one on shore
Gazing upon a late embarkèd friend
Till the wild waves will have him seen no more,
Whose ridges with the meeting clouds contend;   820

the poem's logical deployment of imagery – a riposte to Venus's use of arguments for procreation and progeny to justify her desire.

804 forgèd lies The phrase is pleonastic ('lies' attracting an epithet which repeats and underlines its meaning); it may refer equally to Lust's tactic of attempting seduction by false promises or to its habit of self-delusion.

805 dare not Presumably because his modesty will not allow it (see 783n).

806 text Referring to the use of a biblical passage for a sermon; compare *MV* 3.2.77–79; 'In religion / What damned error but some sober brow / Will bless it, and approve it with a text'.

806 green (1) youthful, inexperienced, (2) tender (as of a young shoot) – see *PP* 4.2.

807 sadness sobriety, seriousness. Compare *Rom.* 1.1.199: 'Tell me in sadness, who is that you love?'; but Adonis's unhappy mood adds a dimension of sorrow.

808 teen vexation.

810 burn themselves Adonis plays on the

blushing colour of his ears but also on such scriptural lessons as, 'If thine eye *offend* thee, pluck it out' (Matt. 5.29).

812 bound bind ('bound' suggests placing a boundary round him, as at 230).

813 laund glade (an open space in a wood).

815–16 See 289n for the relevance of the phrase 'look' etc. to the poem's sense of visual effect; and also Coleridge who quotes this couplet to affirm the superiority of the poetic imagination over painting (*Biographia Literaria* 2.18; and further, *Shakespeare Criticism*, ed. Raysor (second edn, London, 1960) 1, 187–93.

816 glides . . . eye This corresponds to the continuing Renaissance belief, derived from Plato, that the eye was the source of light. See *Republic* 6.507 and *Timaeus* 45 B. The logic of the image further identifies Venus's eye as heavenly light (the light of the 'sky', 815) – another example of the poem's observation of and delight in cosmic parallels.

820 ridges crests (suggesting sharpness or warlike aggression).

So did the merciless and pitchy night
Fold in the object that did feed her sight.

Whereat amazed as one that unaware
Hath dropped a precious jewel in the flood,
Or stonished as night-wand'rers often are,   825
Their light blown out in some mistrustful wood,
    Even so confounded in the dark she lay,
    Having lost the fair discovery of her way.

And now she beats her heart, whereat it groans,
That all the neighbour caves, as seeming troubled,   830
Make verbal repetition of her moans;
Passion on passion deeply is redoubled:
    'Ay me', she cries, and twenty times, 'Woe, woe',
    And twenty echoes twenty times cry so.

She marking them begins a wailing note,   835
And sings extemporally a woeful ditty,
How love makes young men thrall, and old men dote,
How love is wise in folly, foolish witty.
    Her heavy anthem still concludes in woe,
    And still the choir of echoes answer so.   840

821 pitchy thick black.

822 Fold in Envelop.

825 stonished suddenly confused, stunned (from Lat. *ex tonare*, meaning 'to thunder').

826 mistrustful i.e. that causes mistrust, apprehension.

827 confounded confused.

828 fair discovery i.e. the light cast by Adonis which not only illumines her path through the wood but more significantly reveals the object of her desire. Prince rightly objects to Malone, Steevens and others that to interpret 'discovery' as 'discoverer' (i.e. Adonis) reduces the word's expressive range.

829–34 Ovid's story of Narcissus and Echo is generally agreed to be a source for these lines (see *Metam.* 3.495–8; Golding 3.622–3), but the word-play is Shakespearean, especially the recurrence of the number motif ('twenty times').

829 her heart her breast. But the idea that her heart *beats* is also present.

832 Passion . . . passion i.e. a series of cries, outbursts, or lamentings.

832 deeply Walker (*Critical Examination*, 1860) thinks 'doubly' was intended, and cites *Mac.* 1.2.38; 'Doubly redoubled strokes upon the foe'; White

(1865) supports with *R2* 1.3.80: 'And let thy blows, doubly redoubled,' etc. But 'deeply' conveys an appropriately internal feeling, whereas the other examples refer to external actions.

837–8 Venus's paradoxically balanced couplet, despite maintaining the style of the poem as observed throughout, draws a complaint from Brown (1913): 'The sentiment in this ditty fits neither the situation (in which Adonis has just succeeded in repulsing love) nor the character of the goddess of love. One suspects that it may be an echo of some lyric of the time.' But the couplet looks forward to her more intense prophecy at 1135–64, which is defiantly 'out of character'; the paradoxes of her 'ditty' are resumed especially at 1146 and 1152. The present lines have the generalised feeling of an interlude song – appropriate to a chronographic moment such as this one is – and indeed in the next two stanzas the poem completes its night-time action and begins a fresh section with the announcement of day-break at 853.

837 thrall captive.

839 anthem An anthem is generally a song of praise, but in Shakespeare it can carry sombre overtones. Compare *TGV* 3.1.242, 'As ending anthem of my endless dolor', and *PhT* 21ff.

Her song was tedious and outwore the night,
For lovers' hours are long, though seeming short;
If pleased themselves, others they think delight
In such like circumstance, with such like sport.
    Their copious stories, oftentimes begun, 845
    End without audience, and are never done.

For who hath she to spend the night withal
But idle sounds resembling parasites,
Like shrill-tongued tapsters answering every call,
Soothing the humour of fantastic wits? 850
    She says, ''Tis so', they answer all, ''Tis so',
    And would say after her if she said 'No.'

Lo, here the gentle lark, weary of rest,
From his moist cabinet mounts up on high,
And wakes the morning, from whose silver breast 855
The sun ariseth in his majesty;
    Who doth the world so gloriously behold,
    That cedar tops and hills seem burnished gold.

Venus salutes him with this fair good morrow:
'O thou clear god, and patron of all light, 860
From whom each lamp and shining star doth borrow
The beauteous influence that makes him bright,
    There lives a son that sucked an earthly mother
    May lend thee light, as thou dost lend to other.'

---

841 outwore both 'outlasted' and 'wore out'.

842 The sense is that though a lover's delight passes all too quickly his absorption in his love is wearisome to others.

844 circumstance description (i.e. a detailed account).

845 copious abundant (rich in words). Copiousness is a recognised and highly regarded form of style (from Lat. *copiosus* = plentiful), being practised in literature from Lyly to Milton; and indeed it serves Shakespeare on the present occasion. The pejorative use of the word in this context may additionally imply a criticism of the excesses to which the style is prone.

847 withal 'Withal' is preferred to 'with' when a sentence or clause ends emphatically. See Abbott §196 and §274.

848 parasites The 'idle sounds' refer to the 'echoes' at 840 which depend for their existence on her voice.

849 tapsters drawers of ale in a tavern.

850 fantastic wits Those whom drink has put into a strange mood or 'humour'.

853–8 Compare this account of day-break with that of the beginning of the poem. In contrast to the bustle and energy of the earlier description, these lines move in a more measured, gentle, and, above all, dignified manner as if anticipating the solemnity of the events which will follow.

854 moist dewy.

854 cabinet nest, dwelling (compare the use of 'cabin' at 637 to describe the boar's den).

857 gloriously As the following line indicates, the sun imparts his glory to the world in the act of looking on it.

860 clear light-giving.

862 influence In astrology, power or virtue was supposed to *flow* (compare Lat. *influere*) from planets to men or things.

863 son With an unmistakable pun on 'sun'.

This said, she hasteth to a myrtle grove,   865
Musing the morning is so much o'erworn
And yet she hears no tidings of her love.
She hearkens for his hounds and for his horn:
    Anon she hears them chant it lustily,
    And all in haste she coasteth to the cry.   870

And as she runs, the bushes in the way,
Some catch her by the neck, some kiss her face,
Some twine about her thigh to make her stay;
She wildly breaketh from their strict embrace,
    Like a milch doe whose swelling dugs do ache,   875
    Hasting to feed her fawn hid in some brake.

By this she hears the hounds are at a bay,
Whereat she starts like one that spies an adder
Wreathed up in fatal folds just in his way,
The fear whereof doth make him shake and shudder: 880
    Even so the timorous yelping of the hounds
    Appals her senses, and her spirit confounds.

873 twine] twined Q1; twine Q7+

863 **earthly mother** Myrrha in fact bore Adonis after being changed into a myrrh tree (*Metam.* 10.503–14; Golding 10.585–90). Either Venus or Shakespeare chooses not to dwell on the incestuous circumstances of his conception (see *Metam.* 10.530–49).

865 **myrtle grove** The myrtle was the tree most favoured by Venus, similar in status to the rose among flowers. See Comes (*Mythologiae*, fols. 123–4), who cites Virgil's seventh eclogue. A myrtle grove is accordingly an obvious place for love: Botticelli's painting of Mars and Venus (National Gallery, London) places the couple among myrtles. See further Alciati (*Emblemata*, pp. 155, 482, and 851) who discusses the myrtle's venereal and funereal meanings.

866 **Musing** Wondering that.

869 **chant it** bark (the musical connotation of 'chant' is in response to 'horn', line 868). See Abbott §266 for 'it' as indefinite object.

870 **coasteth to** runs towards, alongside. Probably from hunting: Pooler cites Turberville (*Noble Arte of Venerie*, 1576) to the effect that the term means running parallel with an animal in order to get ahead of it. 'The implication . . . is that movement is sidelong, uncertain, or groping, Here such a sense is appropriate, since Venus moves towards

the cry, her only guide, which is itself in movement' (Prince).

871–4 Compare the waves' delaying action in *HL* 2.181–91.

873 **twine** The first six editions give 'twined', thereafter 'twine' (see collation). But 'twined' is perhaps defensible either as a momentary switch from present to past tense or as an adjectival participle.

874 **strict** tight. At a secondary level, the connotations of discipline in 'strict' play against 'wildly' in the first half of the line, while *strictness* is further contradictory to the lascivious and promiscuous behaviour of the bushes.

875 **milch** feeding.

877 **By this** Now.

877 **at a bay** The phrase involves two meanings: (1) the hounds have found or cornered their quarry and are *baying* at it, and (2) the quarry is holding them *at bay*. Pooler cites Turberville: 'A great Bore . . . wil sildom keepe houndes at a Baye, unless he be forced'.

879 **Wreathed** Curled.

882 **Appals** Casts down.

882 **spirit** Monosyllabic, as often in contemporary usage.

882 **confounds** undermines.

For now she knows it is no gentle chase,
But the blunt boar, rough bear, or lion proud,
Because the cry remaineth in one place,   885
Where fearfully the dogs exclaim aloud;
  Finding their enemy to be so curst,
  They all strain court'sy who shall cope him first.

This dismal cry rings sadly in her ear,
Through which it enters to surprise her heart,   890
Who, overcome by doubt and bloodless fear,
With cold-pale weakness numbs each feeling part:
  Like soldiers when their captain once doth yield,
  They basely fly and dare not stay the field.

Thus stands she in a trembling ecstasy,   895
Till, cheering up her senses all dismayed,
She tells them 'tis a causeless fantasy
And childish error that they are afraid;
  Bids them leave quaking, bids them fear no more;
  And with that word she spied the hunted boar,   900

---

888 court'sy] curt'sie Q1   896 all dismayed] Q1; sore dismayed Q4+   899 bids] Q1; wills Q9–11, 13+

883 **gentle** safe, harmless.

884 These details recall the Ovidian Venus's fears: 'But with the sturdy Boare / And ravening woolf, and Bearewhelpes armed with ugly pawes, and eeke / The cruell Lyons which delyght in blood, and slaughter seeke / She meddled not' (Golding 10.623–6).

886 **fearfully** The apprehensiveness belongs as much to Venus as to the dogs, the transference being made easier by the echo of 880 and 881–2 (which notes the effect of 'timorous yelping').

887 **curst** vicious (often used of animals: e.g. *Ado.* 2.1.22–3, 'God sends a curst cow short horns').

888 **strain court'sy** politely defer to each other. Wordplay involves partly the antithesis of curst–court'sy ('curt'sie' Q1) and partly the double sense of 'strain', since they are straining at the leash and also *straining* to be polite. The phrase occurs in Turberville: 'I have seene Greyhounds which . . . would not refuse the Wilde Bore, nor the Wolfe, and yet they would streyne curtesie at a Foxe' (Pooler; see 870n).

888 **cope** assail, engage with.

889–94 The ideas of this stanza recall the very different use of the image by Adonis in 779–80. The two examples demonstrate the imaginative and emotional range of the military–erotic convention.

889 **dismal** fateful (Lat. *dies mala* = evil day).

889 **sadly** solemnly (see 807n).

891 **bloodless** pale. The personification of emotions such as 'bloodless fear' and 'cold-pale weakness' accords with convention (see 889–94n) and has classical antecedents: e.g. Horace's depiction of 'pallida mors' ('pallid death') – *Odes* 1.4.13.

893–4 See Wyatt's sonnet 'The long love' (and 779–80n); Bradbrook (p. 65) compares *HL* 1.119–121.

895 **ecstasy** immobility, paralysis. The word's etymology suggests that the mind or spirit 'stands forth' from the body, leaving it in a state of suspension. This meaning is often observed in literary works: e.g. John Donne's poem 'The Extasie'.

896 **cheering up** i.e. as in encouraging troops (a continuation of the simile of 893–4).

897 **causeless fantasy** baseless figment of imagination.

Whose frothy mouth bepainted all with red,
Like milk and blood being mingled both together,
A second fear through all her sinews spread,
Which madly hurries her she knows not whither.
    This way she runs, and now she will no further,   905
    But back retires to rate the boar for murther.

A thousand spleens bear her a thousand ways;
She treads the path that she untreads again.
Her more than haste is mated with delays,
Like the proceedings of a drunken brain,   910
    Full of respects, yet naught at all respecting,
    In hand with all things, naught at all effecting.

Here kennelled in a brake she finds a hound,
And asks the weary caitiff for his master;
And there another licking of his wound,   915
'Gainst venomed sores the only sovereign plaster;
    And here she meets another sadly scowling,
    To whom she speaks, and he replies with howling.

When he hath ceased his ill-resounding noise,
Another flap-mouthed mourner, black and grim,   920
Against the welkin volleys out his voice;
Another, and another, answer him,
    Clapping their proud tails to the ground below,
    Shaking their scratched ears, bleeding as they go.

Look how the world's poor people are amazèd   925
At apparitions, signs, and prodigies,

909 mated] Q1; marred Q9–11, 13+

902 This dramatic example of the contrast of red and white further indicates the variety and capacity of a single poetic idea (see 76n).
906 **rate** berate.
907 **spleens** fitful changes of mind.
909 **mated** (1) halted, checked (2) coupled.
910 **proceedings** (1) behaviour, (2) manner of walking.
911 **Full . . . respects** Looking at everything.
911 **naught . . . respecting** (1) looking at nothing, (2) having no respect (consideration) for anything.
912 **In hand** Occupied.
914 **caitiff** wretch.

916 **'Gainst** Against. *OED* recognises this as an aphetic form characteristic of verse.
916 **venomed** infected.
916 **only sovereign** uniquely efficacious. *OED* sv B *adj.* 3 gives 'Of remedies, etc.: Efficacious or potent in a superlative degree.' (See 28n.)
920 **flap-mouthed** i.e. with loose, hanging lips. The dog's gaping, 'black and grim' mouth prepares for the image of the cannon at 921.
921 **welkin** sky.
921 **volleys out** As of a cannon firing a mourning salute (see 920n).
925 **Look how** See 67 and 289nn.
925 **poor** ignorant.

Whereon with fearful eyes they long have gazèd,
Infusing them with dreadful prophecies:
    So she at these sad signs draws up her breath,
    And sighing it again exclaims on Death.   930

'Hard-favoured tyrant, ugly, meagre, lean,
Hateful divorce of love' – thus chides she Death –
'Grim-grinning ghost, earth's worm, what dost thou mean
To stifle beauty and to steal his breath,
    Who when he lived his breath and beauty set   935
    Gloss on the rose, smell to the violet?

'If he be dead – O no, it cannot be,
Seeing his beauty, thou shouldst strike at it –
O yes, it may; thou hast no eyes to see,
But hatefully at random dost thou hit: 940
    Thy mark is feeble age, but thy false dart
    Mistakes that aim and cleaves an infant's heart.

'Hadst thou but bid beware, then he had spoke,
And hearing him thy power had lost his power.
The Destinies will curse thee for this stroke: 945
They bid thee crop a weed, thou pluck'st a flower.
    Love's golden arrow at him should have fled,
    And not Death's ebon dart to strike him dead.

'Dost thou drink tears that thou provok'st such weeping?
What may a heavy groan advantage thee?   950
Why hast thou cast into eternal sleeping
Those eyes that taught all other eyes to see?

928 Infusing Imbuing (i.e. reading things into them).

930 exclaims on upbraids, denounces.

931 Hard-favoured Harsh-featured.

932 divorce terminator.

933 Grim-grinning Note the paradoxical wordplay.

933 earth's worm Perhaps simply 'earthworm', but the more likely meaning is 'the lowest creature on earth'.

935–6 Venus adapts an idea from astrology (see 862n) and likens Adonis to a superior being with the power to bestow his virtues on inferior creatures or things.

939 no eyes In personifying death Venus imag-ines the skull and its eyeless sockets.

941 mark true aim.

944 his its. 'Its' is rare in Shakespeare, the few instances coming later in his career.

945 Destinies Fates (see 733n).

947–8 Venus's complaint is made piquant by the fact that Elizabethan sonneteers were always claim-ing to have received their death wound from *love's* arrow. Prince appositely quotes *FQ* 1, Prologue iii, which asks Cupid to 'lay now thy deadly Heben bow apart'. Whitney's *Choice of Emblemes* (1586) tells the fable of love and death exchanging arrows by mistake at an inn (Malone).

952 See 935–6n.

Now Nature cares not for thy mortal vigour,
Since her best work is ruined with thy rigour.'

Here overcome, as one full of despair,   955
She vailed her eyelids, who like sluices stopped
The crystal tide that from her two cheeks fair
In the sweet channel of her bosom dropped;
But through the floodgates breaks the silver rain,
And with his strong course opens them again.   960

O how her eyes and tears did lend and borrow,
Her eye seen in the tears, tears in her eye,
Both crystals, where they viewed each other's sorrow,
Sorrow that friendly sighs sought still to dry;
But like a stormy day, now wind now rain,   965
Sighs dry her cheeks, tears make them wet again.

Variable passions throng her constant woe,
As striving who should best become her grief.
All entertained, each passion labours so
That every present sorrow seemeth chief.   970
But none is best; then join they all together,
Like many clouds consulting for foul weather.

By this, far off she hears some huntsman halloo;
A nurse's song ne'er pleased her babe so well.
The dire imagination she did follow   975

---

962 the tears] Q1; her tears Q7+   975 dire] dyre Q1; drie Q5–8, 12

---

953 **mortal vigour** deadly power (the expression is paradoxical).

954 **rigour** (1) pitilessness, (2) stiffness (as of a corpse).

956 **vailed** lowered (see 314n).

956 **who** See 87n. 'Who' for 'which' invariably accompanies personification, as Abbott (§264) demonstrates.

956 **sluices** floodgates (as in 959).

958 **channel** i.e. the cleft between her breasts. At the moment of her anguish the poem insists on Venus's physical charms, maintaining a balance between the rival appeals of eros and pathos.

960 **his . . . course** i.e. the force of *her* tears. The art of personification allows for changes of gender within image-making, thus showing the means of retaining the masculine principle, which otherwise threatens to disappear from the poem with the death of Adonis, and which is essential for its

symmetrical structure.

963 **crystals** mirrors. Wyndham (whose note has had some influence) refers the line to the magic crystals of the contemporary alchemist, John Dee, who claimed prophetic powers for them. But this is to overload the conceit, which develops naturally from the idea of 'crystal tide' (957).

967 **Variable** Swiftly changing (balancing 'constant').

967 **throng** attend, pay court to.

968 **who** See 956n.

968 **become** embellish.

969 **entertained** admitted, given audience.

969 **passion** sorrow.

970 **every . . . sorrow** each sorrow in turn.

972 **consulting for** plotting.

973 **By this** Just at this moment.

975 **Imagination** image, train of thought.

This sound of hope doth labour to expel;
   For now reviving joy bids her rejoice,
   And flatters her it is Adonis' voice.

Whereat her tears began to turn their tide,
   Being prisoned in her eye like pearls in glass; 980
   Yet sometimes falls an orient drop beside,
   Which her cheek melts as scorning it should pass
     To wash the foul face of the sluttish ground,
     Who is but drunken when she seemeth drowned.

O hard-believing Love, how strange it seems, 985
   Not to believe, and yet too credulous!
   Thy weal and woe are both of them extremes,
   Despair and hope makes thee ridiculous:
     The one doth flatter thee in thoughts unlikely,
     In likely thoughts the other kills thee quickly. 990

Now she unweaves the web that she hath wrought:
   Adonis lives, and death is not to blame.
   It was not she that called him all to nought;
   Now she adds honours to his hateful name:

994 honours] Q1; honour Q6+

977 **reviving** meaning both 'coming back' and 'bringing back' to life.
978 **flatters** falsely persuades (the word picks up the the image of sycophantic courtiers in 967–72).
979–81 Compare *HL* 1.375–6, 'And as she wept, her teares to pearle he [Cupid] turn'd / And wound them on his arme, and for her mourn'd.'
981 **an . . . drop** a tear like a pearl. Pooler cites Harrison's *Description of England* (1577); 'Pearls are called orient, because of the cleerenesse, which resembleth the colour of the cleere aire before the rising of the sun.'
982–4 The argument in these lines effectively refutes Adonis's charge that Venus merely typifies lust. The disdain registered by her *cheek* contrasts with the 'foul face' of the 'sluttish' (used for a loose woman) 'ground' – lowly in comparison with the goddess's beauty and dignity. Finally, the ground's reprehensible 'drunken' state points up by symmetry and antithesis the seriousness of Venus's truly 'drowned' (i.e. tearful) condition.

The imagery contains a possible allusion to Matt. 7.6: 'Give ye not that which is holie, to dogges, nether cast ye your pearles before swine, lest they treade them under their feete, and turning againe, all to rent you.'
985 **hard-believing** The expression seems to bring together two opposing senses as given at 986.
987 **weal** well-being.
988 **makes** See Abbott §336. There are several Shakespearean instances of an s-inflected verb having two singular nouns for its subject.
989 **unlikely** improbable. For the closeness of rhyme between 'unlikely' and 'quickly' (990) see Cercignani, p. 256.
990 **likely** probably true.
990 **quickly** Punning on the sense of 'quickly' = 'immediately' and the older and biblical sense of 'quick' = 'live' (as in 'quick and dead'), so producing a paradoxical phrase with 'kills'.
993 **all to nought** worthless (an idiomatic noun phrase).

She clepes him king of graves, and grave for kings,   995
Imperious supreme of all mortal things.

'No, no', quoth she, 'sweet Death, I did but jest;
Yet pardon me, I felt a kind of fear
When as I met the boar, that bloody beast,
Which knows no pity but is still severe.   1000
    Then, gentle shadow – truth I must confess –
    I railed on thee, fearing my love's decess.

''Tis not my fault the boar provoked my tongue;
Be wreaked on him, invisible commander.
'Tis he, foul creature, that hath done thee wrong;   1005
I did but act, he's author of thy slander.
    Grief hath two tongues, and never woman yet
    Could rule them both without ten women's wit.'

Thus hoping that Adonis is alive,
Her rash suspect she doth extenuate;   1010
And that his beauty may the better thrive,
With Death she humbly doth insinuate:
    Tells him of trophies, statues, tombs, and stories
    His victories, his triumphs, and his glories.

1013 stories] *Malone;* stories. Q1–15; stories. Q16

995 clepes calls. The word was archaic even by Shakespeare's time and was normally reserved for occasions of formal address or solemnisation (as here). Hamlet's 'They *clip* us drunkards, and with swinish phrase / Soil our addition' [i.e. titles of honour] (*Ham.* 1.4.19–20) is therefore doubly ironic.

996 supreme Accented on the first syllable.

996 mortal The context brings out ironically the darker, exact meaning of 'mortal', which usually, and paradoxically, refers to 'living' things. The sense of 'deadly', as in 'mortal butcher' (618), may also be implied.

999 When as When.

1000 still always.

1001 gentle shadow The term 'gentle' combines the honorific form of address with the meaning 'harmless' and even 'caring'. As a 'shadow' or mere reflection of reality (see 162n), death can have no effect upon life.

1002 decess decease, Q1's spelling rhymes perfectly with 'confesse' (see Cercignani, p. 168).

1004 wreaked revenged.

1004 invisible commander Death is not visible in his own person, only in what he effects or commands. The address is another flattering variant of 'gentle shadow' (1001).

1006 but act *only* act. Venus attempts (somewhat contradictorily) to plead her own passive role in the action of slandering death and the boar's active role in causing the slander – see 'provoked my tongue' (1003).

1007 two tongues Presumably one tongue accuses while the other laments.

1007–8 yet . . . wit For the likelihood that 'yet' used to sound closer to 'wit' see Cercignani, p. 68.

1010 suspect suspicion.

1010 extenuate excuse.

1011 thrive keep alive.

1012 insinuate i.e. to creep into favour by means of flattery.

1013 stories relates. It is much more likely that 'stories' is a verb rather than a noun; otherwise the couplet would be hopelessly inert. On Q1's punctuation, see 623n.

'O Jove', quoth she, 'how much a fool was I   1015
To be of such a weak and silly mind,
To wail his death who lives, and must not die
Till mutual overthrow of mortal kind.
    For he being dead, with him is beauty slain,
    And beauty dead, black chaos comes again.   1020

'Fie, fie, fond love, thou art as full of fear
As one with treasure laden, hemmed with thieves;
Trifles unwitnessèd with eye or ear
Thy coward heart with false bethinking grieves.'
    Even at this word she hears a merry horn,   1025
    Whereat she leaps that was but late forlorn.

As falcons to the lure away she flies,
The grass stoops not, she treads on it so light,
And in her haste unfortunately spies
The foul boar's conquest on her fair delight;   1030
    Which seen, her eyes, as murd'red with the view,
    Like stars ashamed of day, themselves withdrew;

1021 as] Q1; so Q4+   1031 as] Q3-11, 13+; are Q1-2

1016 silly feeble.

1018 mutual overthrow i.e. all will die when he dies. The following couplet explains why.

1019–20 Various ideas and mythological themes combine in this couplet. The Platonic notion of pure forms proceeding out of primeval chaos was available to Shakespeare in contemporary Neoplatonism, while the Ovidian account of chaos at the beginning of the *Metamorphoses* may also have bearing (see *Genetics*, pp. 49–72). But more specific to this is the mythological account of the seasonal death and rebirth of Adonis. 'Chaos' is not merely formless matter, but destruction and the opposite of the procreative principle (Adonis). Winter ('black chaos') slays Adonis in the person of the boar (see supplementary note 97–100 for the creature's other transformations); but in spring he comes back to life as the sun in his fructifying splendour. On several occasions both the poem and Venus compare Adonis with the sun (see especially 863–4 and n, and Comes, *Mythologiae*, fol. 125a).

1021 fond foolish.

1024 bethinking imaginings.

1024 grieves afflicts. Abbott (§337) accounts for the singular verb number ('Trifles' being its subject) by identifying the *effective* subject as the noun clause 'Trifles . . . ear'.

1026 leaps i.e. for joy.

1027 lure A 'lure' is strictly a bunch of feathers used to recall a hawk; the image thus implies the disappointment that awaits her.

1028 While bringing a different emphasis to the meaning, the description recalls Venus's claim for love's lightness in 151–6. Steevens (Malone) detects their source in Virgil's description of the warrior maid Camilla speeding across a cornfield without damaging the crops (*Aen.* 7.808–809). Just as possibly Shakespeare was recalling Lodge's adaptation of this in *Scillaes Metamorphosis*, 'To shoare she flitts, and swift as *Affric* wind / Her footing glides upon the yeelding grasse' (lines 601–2; Alexander, p. 50).

1029 unfortunately ill-fatedly.

1031–2 The eyes are assaulted by what they see and yet react as if responsible ('ashamed') for it – another example of the poem's continuously antithetical manner.

1032 ashamed . . . day ashamed to be seen in daylight.

Or as the snail, whose tender horns being hit,
Shrinks backward in his shelly cave with pain,
And there, all smoth'red up, in shade doth sit,   1035
Long after fearing to creep forth again;
    So at his bloody view her eyes are fled
    Into the deep-dark cabins of her head,

Where they resign their office and their light
To the disposing of her troubled brain,   1040
Who bids them still consort with ugly night
And never wound the heart with looks again;
    Who, like a king perplexèd in his throne,
    By their suggestion gives a deadly groan;

Whereat each tributary subject quakes,   1045
As when the wind imprisoned in the ground,
Struggling for passage, earth's foundation shakes,
Which with cold terror doth men's minds confound.
    This mutiny each part doth so surprise
    That from their dark beds once more leap her eyes;   1050

1035 smoth'red up, in] Q1–4, 16; smothered up in Q5–15

1033–8 Keats writing to Reynolds in 1817 praised this description, though with some confusion as to the work to which it belongs:

He has left nothing to say about nothing or any thing: for look at Snails, you know what he says about Snails, you know where he talks about 'cockled snails' – well, in one of these sonnets, he says – the chap slips into – no! I lie! this is in the Venus and Adonis; the Simile brought it to my Mind.

(*The Letters of John Keats 1814–21*, ed. Rollins, 1958, I, 189)

The 'cockled snails' are in *LLL* 4.3.334–5: 'Love's feeling is more soft and sensible / Than are the tender horns of cockled snails.'

1035 smoth'red up Concealed in a tight, suffocating manner (*OED* sv *v.* 6b gives this line as an example).

1038 cabins (1) caves, (2) eye-sockets. The image of a creature seeking its lair recalls the use of 'cabin' in 637.

1039–50 See 103–14n and 779–80n.

1041 who See 956n.

1041 still always.

1042 The poem does not forget the irony that Venus's eyes here wound her own heart – a reversal of the usual practice of wounding that of the admiring lover.

1043 Who i.e. the heart (the usage is as at 1041).

1043 perplexèd . . . throne The 'throne' is the heart's seat, while the heart is like a king who is confused as to his authority or safety.

1044 By . . . suggestion (1) At their prompting, (2) By what they show or indicate to him.

1045 tributary (1) subordinate (as one who pays tribute), but also (2) tributary as of a river or channel, thus effecting the transition to the geophysical imagery which determines 1046–8.

1046–7 The idea of the wind's seeking an exit in this way is an ancient one, and occurs in Aristotle (*Meteorology*) as well as in Pliny's *Natural History*. See also Ralegh (*Ocean to Cynthia*, lines 450–4): 'Yet as the air in deep caves under ground / Is strongly drawn when violent heat hath rent / Great clefts therein . . . Breaks out in earthquakes'.

1048 cold terror The image combines the idea both of physical cold and the chill of fear, thus keeping together the two principal metaphors in these stanzas – the military and meteorological.

1048 confound throw into confusion.

1050 beds The controlling idea unites 'beds' as 'sockets' ('dark cabins', 1038) with the sense of barrack room beds from which sentinels 'leap' at the sound of the alarum.

And being opened, threw unwilling light
Upon the wide wound that the boar had trenched
In his soft flank, whose wonted lily white
With purple tears, that his wound wept, was drenched.
    No flower was nigh, no grass, herb, leaf, or weed,   1055
    But stole his blood, and seemed with him to bleed.

This solemn sympathy poor Venus noteth;
Over one shoulder doth she hang her head;
Dumbly she passions, franticly she doteth,
She thinks he could not die, he is not dead;   1060
    Her voice is stopped, her joints forget to bow,
    Her eyes are mad that they have wept till now.

Upon his hurt she looks so steadfastly
That her sight dazzling makes the wound seem three,
And then she reprehends her mangling eye   1065
That makes more gashes where no breach should be:
    His face seems twain, each several limb is doubled,
    For oft the eye mistakes, the brain being troubled.

'My tongue cannot express my grief for one,
And yet', quoth she, 'behold two Adons dead!   1070
My sighs are blown away, my salt tears gone,

1051 light] Q1; night Q4–5; sight Q7+   1054 was] Q7–11, 13+; had Q1

1051 threw . . . light Not only do her eyes not wish to see their object, but light itself would rather not reveal it. For nature's 'sympathy' see 1055–8.

1052–3 wound . . . trenched . . . flank The sequence maintains the military–erotic parallel of 1039–50.

1052 trenched dug deep.

1054 purple bright red (see 1n).

1056 stole . . . blood His blood seems coveted by the surrounding herbage into which it seeps. The idea is perhaps a variant on that of 935–6 (see n).

1058 Possibly a familiar stage gesture (see below 1059 n and Gurr, pp. 98–102).

1059 Dumbly . . . passions Venus cannot express her suffering ('passion') in words (see 1069), and so she resorts to gesture as in a theatrical dumb-show or pageant. She also 'noteth' (perhaps as a cue) the 'solemn sympathy' performed by the unspeaking grassland (1057). In *TGV*, Julia pretends to reminisce over her performance in a Whitsun entertainment: 'For I did play a

lamentable part, / Madam, 'twas Ariadne passioning / For Theseus' perjury and unjust flight' (4.4.166–8).

1059 doteth The primary sense is that she is 'out of her wits' or 'mad', but the sense of doting on a loved one also applies.

1062 mad i.e. her eyes join in the frenzy as they realise that they now have good cause to weep.

1064 dazzling blurring, caused either by the intensity of her gaze or the brightness of the object (as in *3H6* 2.1.25: 'Dazzle mine eyes, or do I see three suns?').

1067 several separate.

1068 Note the continuity of idea with that of 1039–44.

1071–2 The feeling of grief is increased by the displacement of the less substantial elements ('sighs' and 'tears', which are the equivalents of air and water) by the fiercer and more tangible 'fire' and 'lead'. These lines and the two following them suggest a stoical resolve to die for Adonis's death.

Mine eyes are turned to fire, my heart to lead:
Heavy heart's lead melt at mine eyes' red fire –
So shall I die by drops of hot desire.

'Alas, poor world, what treasure hast thou lost?   1075
What face remains alive that's worth the viewing?
Whose tongue is music now? What canst thou boast
Of things long since, or anything ensuing?
The flowers are sweet, their colours fresh and trim,
But true sweet beauty lived and died with him.   1080

'Bonnet nor veil henceforth no creature wear:
Nor sun nor wind will ever strive to kiss you;
Having no fair to lose you need not fear –
The sun doth scorn you, and the wind doth hiss you.
But when Adonis lived, sun and sharp air   1085
Lurked like two thieves, to rob him of his fair.

'And therefore would he put his bonnet on,
Under whose brim the gaudy sun would peep;
The wind would blow it off, and being gone,
Play with his locks; then would Adonis weep;   1090
And straight, in pity of his tender years,
They both would strive who first should dry his tears.

'To see his face the lion walked along
Behind some hedge, because he would not fear him;

1072–3 An unusual instance in *Ven.* of the rhetorical device of antimetabole or chiasmus (see 286n) extending over two lines, perhaps in response to the 'doubly' dead Adonis (as well as to a climactic moment in the poem): 'eyes . . . fire . . . heart . . . lead / heart's lead . . . eyes' fire'. The figure gains in intensity by combining with an emphatic form of anadiplosis (the recurrence of words ending one line at the beginning of the next).

1073 melt i.e. may it melt.

1074 drops . . . desire True to her nature, Venus prefers death by desire rather than through the coldness of grief. As fire heats lead, the heart's grief dissolves, but so, fatally, does the heart ('by drops' carries a suggestion of torture).

1078 ensuing that may come.

1080 A recurrence of the idea of 935–6 that Adonis is the repository and source of beauty and that the universe depends on him for it.

1081–6 Compare *HL* 1.27–30: 'She ware no gloves, for neither sun nor wind / Would burne or parch her hands, but to her mind, / Or warm

or coole them, for they took delite / To play upon those hands, they were so white.'

1083–4 The lines (as 1086 makes clearer) play on the idea of the elements 'robbing' someone of his beauty: i.e. destroying it. The conceit applies characteristic logic to this figurative sense by suggesting that one person's *dispossession* of beauty must mean that another *possesses* it.

1083 fair fairness, beauty.

1084 scorn i.e. *glare* disdainfully at (possibly playing on 'scorch').

1085 sharp (1) biting, cold, (2) cunning (with the idea of theft, as in 1086).

1086 Lurked Along with the idea of conspiracy, which fits the sense of 'rob', goes the notion of 'hanging back' as if in deference to his beauty, which they dare not accost directly.

1088 gaudy (1) bright, merry, (2) full of trickery (*OED* sv *a* ^{2}).

1089 being gone i.e. the bonnet being gone.

1091 straight straight away.

To recreate himself when he hath sung, 1095
The tiger would be tame, and gently hear him;
   If he had spoke, the wolf would leave his prey,
   And never fright the silly lamb that day.

'When he beheld his shadow in the brook,
The fishes spread on it their golden gills; 1100
When he was by, the birds such pleasure took
That some would sing, some other in their bills
   Would bring him mulberries and ripe-red cherries:
   He fed them with his sight, they him with berries.

'But this foul, grim, and urchin-snouted boar, 1105
Whose downward eye still looketh for a grave,
Ne'er saw the beauteous livery that he wore:
Witness the entertainment that he gave.
   If he did see his face, why then I know
   He thought to kiss him, and hath killed him so. 1110

1095 sung] song Q1–13; sung Q14–15

1093–1104 The description of Adonis's charms strongly evokes the legend of Orpheus, whose music was supposed to tame wild beasts (Comes, *Mythologiae*, fol. 226b). It does not advance the narrative in the ordinary way but belongs to it as an ecphrasis, or moment of suspended description, in which Venus pays tribute to the memory of Adonis. (See pp. 20–21.) It would be incorrect or insufficient to say merely that its declaration is untrue; but its truth is of another kind than action and dialogue normally observe; otherwise, Venus would not have needed to warn Adonis against wild beasts such as the boar, nor indeed would the boar have slain him so straightforwardly. The commemoration, which effectively begins at 1075, closely resembles Cleopatra's remembrance of Antony (*Ant.* 5.2.76–92).

1094 fear frighten.

1095 When he sang for his own amusement.

1095 sung See collation. Q1's 'song' may have been pronounced 'sung' (see Cercignani, p. 111).

1097 If . . . spoke If he spoke.

1098 silly innocent, helpless. From the beginning of the sixteenth century the word had served as a conventional poetic epithet for harmless animals, especially sheep (see *OED adj* 1c; also see *Luc.* 167).

1099 shadow reflection (see 162).

1100 spread . . . gills i.e. the image of Adonis in the water is golden like the sun; the fish appear to fasten on and draw sustenance from it (see 935–6 and 1019–20nn).

1103 bring . . . cherries The fruit imagery is emblematic of his lips and cheeks, and the birds' action (which both recalls and redeems her judgement of 601–6) identifies him as the deity of youthful procreativity to whom offerings are made.

1104 He . . . sight Their vision of him inspired ('fed') them.

1105 urchin-snouted With a snout like a hedgehog. There is also a suggestion of deformity. *OED sv sb.* 3 cites Topsell, 'In English, a Hedgehog, or an urchine: by which name also we call a man that holdeth his Necke in his bosome.' There is an even further sense that an urchin is an 'offspring of Hell' (*OED sv sb.* 5c), which might add to the meaning of 'downward eye' (1106).

1106 downward . . . grave See 1105n.

1106 still always.

1107 beauteous livery i.e. his comeliness (compare 'crimson liveries', 506).

1108 entertainment This not only refers to the boar's cruel treatment of Adonis but also plays on the sense of entertainment as a festive and brightly costumed occasion (from 'livery', 1107).

1109 If . . . see i.e. if on the other hand the boar did see him his death was still inevitable since the animal would have rushed eagerly to kiss him so delivering the fatal wound. Venus establishes that Adonis could only have inspired admiration and not enmity in the beast (see 1093–1104n).

1110–16 The poetic idea was popularly thought to have originated with Theocritus. But see supplementary note.

"'Tis true, 'tis true, thus was Adonis slain:
He ran upon the boar with his sharp spear,
Who did not whet his teeth at him again,
But by a kiss thought to persuade him there;
    And nuzzling in his flank, the loving swine   1115
    Sheathed unaware the tusk in his soft groin.

'Had I been toothed like him, I must confess,
With kissing him I should have killed him first;
But he is dead, and never did he bless
My youth with his; the more am I accursed.'   1120
    With this she falleth in the place she stood,
    And stains her face with his congealèd blood.

She looks upon his lips, and they are pale,
She takes him by the hand, and that is cold;
She whispers in his ears a heavy tale,   1125
As if they heard the woeful words she told;
    She lifts the coffer-lids that close his eyes,
    Where lo, two lamps burnt out in darkness lies:

Two glasses where herself herself beheld
A thousand times, and now no more reflect;   1130
Their virtue lost wherein they late excelled,
And every beauty robbed of his effect.

1113 did] Q1; would Q2   1116 the tusk] Q1; his tusk Q2+

1113 **again** in turn.

1114 **there** Either an ellipsis for 'to stay there', meaning 'hold back', or as an adverb meaning 'in that way' (Abbott §70): i.e. 'He thought that a kiss was the way to persuade (disarm) him.'

1116 **unaware** unknowingly.

1117 **him** the boar.

1118 **first** beforehand. The line is sometimes taken as a sign of the destructiveness of sexuality as manifested in Venus. But her argument – which needs bearing in mind – is that the savage part of nature is charmed from its usual course by Adonis (e.g. 1096–8), and that the boar kills him by unlucky chance rather than wilfully or with malice.

1119–20 **bless . . . his** i.e. bestow his likeness on me in the form of a child. The expression resembles a prayer for blessings on a union.

1120 **accursed** The word may simply convey the feeling of having been spited by fortune (as at 1133), but it looks forward significantly to the curse which Venus is about to pronounce on *love* (1135–64), which is *herself* (see 814).

1121–2 The image recurs in *Luc.* 1774–5 at a similar moment when 'vengeance' is about to be professed.

1122 **congealèd** Accented on the first syllable. The act of congealing turns the blood to a thicker, viscid substance; Venus may be applying this ceremoniously like dye or paint.

1127 **coffer-lids** i.e. treasure-chest lids, but 'coffin' is probably also intended subliminally.

1128 **lies** For plural verb instead of singular in cases involving numbers, see Abbott §333 (also examples in 517–22).

1129 **glasses** mirrors.

1129 **herself herself** Shakespeare sometimes repeats the reflexive pronoun for emphasis, as he does here, using it once as a noun (instead of 'she herself'). The usage is appropriate in context, since the pronoun reflects *itself*, as does Venus by looking in the 'glasses' (See also 763.)

1131 **virtue** power, strength.

1132 **effect** effectiveness.

'Wonder of time', quoth she, 'this is my spite,
That thou being dead the day should yet be light.

'Since thou art dead, lo, here I prophesy,   1135
Sorrow on love hereafter shall attend;
It shall be waited on with jealousy,
Find sweet beginning, but unsavoury end;
    Ne'er settled equally, but high or low,
    That all love's pleasure shall not match his woe.   1140

'It shall be fickle, false, and full of fraud,
Bud, and be blasted, in a breathing while,
The bottom poison, and the top o'er-strawed
With sweets that shall the truest sight beguile;
    The strongest body shall it make most weak,   1145
    Strike the wise dumb, and teach the fool to speak.

'It shall be sparing, and too full of riot,
Teaching decrepit age to tread the measures;
The staring ruffian shall it keep in quiet,
Pluck down the rich, enrich the poor with treasures;   1150
    It shall be raging mad, and silly mild,
    Make the young old, the old become a child.

'It shall suspect where is no cause of fear,
It shall not fear where it should most mistrust;
It shall be merciful, and too severe,   1155
And most deceiving when it seems most just;

1144 truest] Q1; sharpest Q5+

1133 **spite** ill fortune (see 1120n).
1137 **waited . . . with** attended by.
1139 (1) Never between social equals, (2) Never at the same intensity between lovers.
1142 **in . . . while** in the space of a breath.
1143 **o'er-strawed** The image is of a pit or animal-trap, with a sizable drop ('bottom'), and whose opening ('top') is camouflaged by straw.
1144 **sweets** delights.
1144 **truest** (1) keenest, (2) most faithful.
1145 With possible reference to venereal disease (see 741n).
1146 **teach . . . speak** Venus is concerned to establish love as perverse so that even its apparently positive transformations will prove somehow unwelcome. Malone detects a reference to Boccac-

cio's story of Cimone (*Decameron* 5.1), a blockhead whom love transforms into a man of parts. Whether the allusion is deliberate or not, Boccaccio's humanist purpose is out of keeping with what Venus intends.
1147 **sparing** abstemious.
1147 **too . . . riot** excessive, given to debauch.
1148 **tread . . . measures** dance. There is a possible sexual hint in 'tread'.
1149 **staring** boldfaced, impudent.
1151 **silly** feeble.
1155 **merciful** Since none of Venus's pronouncements favours love as virtuous or happy, a state of mercy must alternate with one of severity to keep things continuously unsettled.

Perverse it shall be where it shows most toward,
Put fear to valour, courage to the coward.

'It shall be cause of war and dire events,
And set dissension 'twixt the son and sire,   1160
Subject and servile to all discontents,
As dry combustious matter is to fire.
      Sith in his prime death doth my love destroy,
      They that love best their loves shall not enjoy.'

By this the boy that by her side lay killed   1165
Was melted like a vapour from her sight,
And in his blood that on the ground lay spilled
A purple flower sprung up, check'red with white,
      Resembling well his pale cheeks and the blood
      Which in round drops upon their whiteness stood.   1170

She bows her head the new-sprung flower to smell,
Comparing it to her Adonis' breath,
And says within her bosom it shall dwell,
Since he himself is reft from her by death.
      She crops the stalk, and in the breach appears   1175
      Green-dropping sap, which she compares to tears.

'Poor flower', quoth she, 'this was thy father's guise –
Sweet issue of a more sweet-smelling sire –

1157 shows] Q1; seems Q7+   1164 loves] Q1; love Q5+   1178 sweet-smelling] Q1; sweet-swelling Q5

1157 **Perverse** Obstinate, stubborn. Compare *Rom.* 2.2.95–6, 'Or if thou thinkest I am too quickly won, / I'll frown and be perverse, and say thee nay.'

1157 **toward** compliant, easy.

1160 See 764–6n.

1161 **discontents** malcontents (*OED* sv B. *sb.* [2]); in this context the word corresponds more precisely to disaffected members of a retinue or political body. See *1H4* 5.1.74–6: 'To face the garment of rebellion / With some fine color that may please the eye / Of fickle changelings and poor *discontents*'.

1165–8 In Ovid, Venus creates the flower from the blood of Adonis by sprinkling it with nectar; Shakespeare seems less concerned to identify the flower (Ovid compares it both to a pomegranate and an anemone: Golding 10.851–63) than to display its contrasting tones of red and white,

which (as 1169–70 reminds us) have been evident throughout the poem.

1168 **purple** bright red (see 1n).

1168 **sprung** sprang.

1168 **check'red** See p. 74.

1169–70 See 1165–8n.

1171 **new-sprung flower** Along with other stylistic motives (see 1165–68n) Shakespeare may wish to imply that the flower is an entirely new creation. However, his main object is to allow Venus to speak of Adonis's regeneration or rebirth (her concern for which perhaps finally justifies her declared interest in procreation).

1172 **Adonis' breath** The comparison may be a delicate way of recalling that in Greek 'anemone' means 'wind-flower'.

1177 **guise** manner, habit.

For every little grief to wet his eyes;
To grow unto himself was his desire,　　　　　　　　　1180
　　And so 'tis thine, but know it is as good
　　To wither in my breast as in his blood.

'Here was thy father's bed, here in my breast;
Thou art the next of blood, and 'tis thy right.
Lo, in this hollow cradle take thy rest,　　　　　　　1185
My throbbing heart shall rock thee day and night;
　　There shall not be one minute in an hour
　　Wherein I will not kiss my sweet love's flower.'

Thus weary of the world away she hies,
And yokes her silver doves, by whose swift aid　　　1190
Their mistress, mounted, through the empty skies,
In her light chariot quickly is conveyed,
　　Holding their course to Paphos, where their queen
　　Means to immure herself, and not be seen.

1183 in] Q1; is Q4+　1185 Lo] Q1; Low Q5–6　1187 minute in] Q1; minute of Q7+

1180 Compare 166 where the same observation is issued accusingly, now the elegiac mood renders Adonis's wish almost acceptable ('as good', 1181).

1184 **next of blood** (1) next of kin, (2) new manifestation of his blood.

1189 **hies** hastens.

1190–4 The poem ends with a description of a character hastening sorrowfully from the scene, in reflective contrast to one hurrying eagerly into the action at its opening. Perhaps Shakespeare transposed the sequence in Ovid – where Venus's chariot has taken her almost to Cyprus when she becomes aware of Adonis's fate (Golding 10.840–3) – for the sake of symmetry. Also at the close of the poem he restores to her her full goddess's magnificence (in a stanza which has been rightly commended for its delicacy and grace) as he releases her (or almost – see 1194n) from the human dimensions that have so far bound her.

1192–3 **quickly . . . Paphos** Perhaps echoing Virgil, 'ipsa Paphum sublimis abit sedesque revisit / laeta suas' (*Aen.* 1.415–16).

1194 The syllepsis of 'Means', juxtaposing the contrasting senses of 'immure' and 'not be seen', perhaps engineers a last gentle teasing of Venus, who, despite her godliness, is subject to beauty's classic moodiness.

The Rape of Lucrece

TO THE RIGHT HONOURABLE
Henry Wriothesley, Earl of Southampton,
and Baron of Titchfield.

The love I dedicate to your Lordship is without end; whereof this pamphlet 5
without beginning is but a superfluous moiety. The warrant I have of your
honourable disposition, not the worth of my untutored lines, makes it
assured of acceptance. What I have done is yours, what I have to do is yours,
being part in all I have devoted yours. Were my worth greater, my duty would
show greater; meantime, as it is, it is bound to your Lordship, to whom I 10
wish long life still lengthened with all happiness.

Your Lordship's in all duty,
William Shakespeare.

5 **pamphlet** In Shakespeare's day 'pamphlet' could mean any form of publication including all the literary genres (*OED* sv. 1); it was often short, as the diminutive '-et' implies, and the poet may have chosen to describe his very long work in this way as a modest disclaimer, treating it as trivial or ephemeral. Interestingly, the word derives its meaning from the *Pamphilus, seu de Amore*, an amatory poem of the twelfth century, though Shakespeare probably did not have this in mind.

6 **without beginning** This may refer to the poem's beginning *in medias res* (see *Ven.* 1–6n), but again it is self-deprecatory, suggesting incompetence and unworthiness (see 'untutored lines', 4), and the poet is perhaps pretending that he does not know *how* to begin the poem.

6 **superfluous moiety** 'Moiety' commonly means trifle (from Fr. *moitié*); i.e. although only half a poem, it is still too much.

8 **What . . . yours** Meaning both this poem and *Venus and Adonis*.

8 **what . . . yours** Either Shakespeare is hoping for future preferment with no specific work in mind (for, as far as is known, these two works which were dedicated to him are all that was written for Southampton), or he means some particular project which he has yet to begin, or having started, yet to finish. It is tempting to think that he may be referring to the *Sonnets*, some of which he would already have written, while others he was still composing. But nothing more definite than hypothesis connects Southampton with them.

9–10 **my duty . . . greater** I would be asked to do something more important.

THE ARGUMENT

Lucius Tarquinius, for his excessive pride surnamed Superbus, after he had caused his own father-in-law Servius Tullius to be cruelly murdered, and, contrary to the Roman laws and customs, not requiring or staying for the people's suffrages, had possessed himself of the kingdom, went, accompanied with his sons and other noblemen 5 of Rome, to besiege Ardea. During which siege the principal men of the army meeting one evening at the tent of Sextus Tarquinius, the king's son, in their discourses after supper every one commended the virtues of his own wife; among whom Collatinus extolled the incomparable chastity of his wife Lucretia. In that pleasant humour 10 they all posted to Rome; and intending, by their secret and sudden arrival, to make trial of that which every one had before avouched, only Collatinus finds his wife, though it were late in the night, spinning amongst her maids: the other ladies were all found dancing and revelling, or in several disports. Whereupon the noblemen 15 yielded Collatinus the victory, and his wife the fame. At that time Sextus Tarquinius being inflamed with Lucrece' beauty, yet smothering his passions for the present, departed with the rest back to the camp; from whence he shortly after privily withdrew himself, and was, according to his estate, royally entertained and lodged by Lucrece at 20 Collatium. The same night he treacherously stealeth into her chamber, violently ravished her, and early in the morning speedeth away. Lucrece, in this lamentable plight, hastily dispatcheth messengers, one to Rome for her father, another to the camp for

---

The Argument 'The Argument' is generally considered to have been composed by Shakespeare, although there is nothing to prove this. Why it was written is an interesting question. Southampton and his circle would not have needed it, but the publisher may have asked Shakespeare, or perhaps someone Shakespeare approved of, to supply it for a wider audience. (See supplementary note.)

4 requiring requesting.

12 avouched boasted.

15 several disports various frivolous activities.

17–18 smothering suppressing, tightly concealing (compare *Ven.* 1035).

19 privily secretly.

21 Collatium Collatia.

21–2 stealeth . . . ravished . . . speedeth The change of tense between past and historic present maintains pace while affording stylistic variety.

23–4 dispatcheth messengers In the poem, Lucrece sends only to Collatine, while of the sources only Painter specifies messengers both to Rome and to Collatine (see headnote).

Collatine. They came, the one accompanied with Junius Brutus, the   25
other with Publius Valerius; and finding Lucrece attired in mourning
habit, demanded the cause of her sorrow. She, first taking an oath of
them for her revenge, revealed the actor and whole manner of his
dealing, and withal suddenly stabbed herself. Which done, with one
consent they all vowed to root out the whole hated family of the   30
Tarquins; and bearing the dead body to Rome, Brutus acquainted the
people with the doer and manner of the vile deed, with a bitter
invective against the tyranny of the king: wherewith the people were
so moved, that with one consent and a general acclamation the
Tarquins were all exiled, and the state government changed from   35
kings to consuls.

28 actor culprit. But the word stresses the
importance of gesture, and the phrase 'revealed . . .
dealing' suggests in addition a demonstration of
how he has behaved. In Painter Lucrece describes
Tarquin brandishing his sword and then almost
immediately draws a knife against herself.

35–6 from . . . consuls Despite this detail,
Lucrece provides no evidence that Shakespeare was
anti-monarchist.

THE RAPE OF LUCRECE

From the besiegèd Ardea all in post,
Borne by the trustless wings of false desire,
Lust-breathèd Tarquin leaves the Roman host
And to Collatium bears the lightless fire,
Which in pale embers hid lurks to aspire   5
    And girdle with embracing flames the waist
    Of Collatine's fair love, Lucrece the chaste.

Haply that name of 'chaste' unhapp'ly set
This bateless edge on his keen appetite;
When Collatine unwisely did not let   10
To praise the clear unmatchèd red and white
Which triumphed in that sky of his delight,

8 unhapp'ly] unhap'ly Q1

1–7 The stanza form is that of rhyme royal, which Chaucer used for *Troilus and Criseyde* (seven lines as opposed to the six lines or sixain of *Venus and Adonis*). The extra line perhaps serves to increase the meditative character of the stanza. The action begins, as in Shakespeare's earlier poem, *in medias res* (see *Ven.* 1–6n), while with remarkable economy the narrative announces the essential points of the theme.

1 **Ardea** Accented on the first syllable. There is possibly a pun on 'ardour', which would accord with the excitement expressed in the stanza.

1 **post** haste.

2 **trustless wings** Shakespeare quickly establishes his Roman theme by making use of characteristic classical devices such as personification, as well as thematically introducing the concept of hubris (overly bold behaviour). 'False desire' flies like 'rumor' or 'fama', and the 'trustless wings' most likely recall the fate of the hubristic Icarus whose aspirations bore him too close to the sun which melted the wax of his artificial wings.

3 **Lust-breathèd** Lust-inspired (filled with lust).

4 **lightless fire** The paradox serves as a reminder that the poem blends its Roman manner of representation (see 2n) with a typically Elizabethan style of stating conflict and antithesis.

5 **pale** Contrasting with the red glow connoted by 'fire'. The antithesis looks forward to the play on red and white in the description of Lucrece's virtuous colouring in 11–14 and 53–70.

5 **aspire** The word (from Lat. *aspirare*, meaning 'breathe towards') plays on 'Lust-breathèd' (3)

7 **Lucrece** Accented probably on the first syllable despite the iambic pattern of the line. This way the caesura falling between 'love', and 'Lucrece' gives a more emphatic, triumphal character to the phrase in which she is described. 'Lucrece' occurs thirty-four times in the poem and is invariably accented on the first syllable (see also, e.g., 512).

8 **Haply** Perhaps, by chance. Q1's spelling of 'unhap'ly' makes for smoother wordplay.

9 **bateless** insatiable. The presence of 'appetite' suggests a pun on 'bait', 'baitless' perhaps then meaning either that his appetite needs no bait or that chastity is no proper bait.

10 **let** forbear, desist.

12 **triumphed** shone in glory. The suggestion is of a processional triumph depicting, in literature or painting, an allegorised virtue (the *Trionfi* of Petrarch includes the triumph of chastity); at a secular level, a royal or noble household in a real pageant.

12 **sky** face. The cosmic conceit as well as the play on red and white recall the opening stanzas of *Ven.* (see also 53–70).

Where mortal stars, as bright as heaven's beauties,
With pure aspects did him peculiar duties.

For he the night before, in Tarquin's tent,   15
Unlocked the treasure of his happy state:
What priceless wealth the heavens had him lent
In the possession of his beauteous mate;
Reck'ning his fortune at such high proud rate
    That kings might be espousèd to more fame,   20
    But king nor peer to such a peerless dame.

O happiness enjoyed but of a few,
And if possessed, as soon decayed and done
As is the morning silver melting dew
Against the golden splendour of the sun: 25
An expired date cancelled ere well begun.
    Honour and beauty, in the owner's arms,
    Are weakly fortressed from a world of harms.

---

13 stars] Q1; star Q6–9   19 such high proud] Q1; so high a Q6+   21 peer] Q1; prince Q2+   24 morning] Q1 *(Malone 34, Yale;* mornings *the rest)*   24 melting] Q1; melted Q4   26 An . . . well] Q1; A date expir'd: and canceld ere Q6+

13 mortal stars The eyes of Lucrece, 'mortal' because they are human or earthly as opposed to 'heaven's beauties'.

14 aspects This refers (1) to the position and appearance of one planet with respect to another, as seen from the earth (figuratively Tarquin's viewpoint), and (2) to the 'pure' look of respect which Lucrece bestows on her husband.

14 peculiar i.e. for him alone; in this context 'duties' suggests attitudes of obedience.

17 lent The Elizabethan word more often means 'give' or 'bestow' rather than our meaning of 'lend'; but here it also perhaps ironically underlines that Collatine will soon lose his possession.

19 proud glorious. Here the primary meaning of 'proud' is similar to that of 'triumphed' (12n); but the line's juxtaposition of 'proud' with 'fortune' produces an ominous combination, since traditionally, both in classical and medieval concepts of tragedy, the hero falls from a high or prosperous state of fortune, often through some offence (which may be unwitting) akin to pride.

22–35 Moralising interpolations by the narrative voice are much more frequent in *Lucrece* than in *Venus and Adonis*, where the moral argument tends to be put by one or other of the protagonists.

22–5 Sarrazin (p. 161) detects an echo of Samuel Daniel's forty-second *Delia* sonnet: 'Beautie, sweet love, is like the morning dewe, / Whose short refresh upon the tender greene / Cheeres for a time but tyll the Sunne doth shew: / As straight tis gone as it had never beene.'

23 decayed wasted away; 'decay' has a specific application to states of fortune (*OED* sv v. 1b; 'to decline from prosperity or fortune').

24 morning The choice lies between this and 'morning's', which appears to be the press correction (see collation and analysis, p. 299). Rhetorically, the phrase 'morning dew' is interrupted by 'silver melting' (an example of *tmesis*). The press editor may have thought the result ungrammatical and added the apostrophe. What Shakespeare probably wrote is more euphonious and less sibilant – though in pronunciation the two versions are difficult to tell apart, and it is equally conceivable that the confusion originated in dictation.

24 silver melting Since both adjectives qualify 'dew' they are not hyphenated.

26 The general sense is that the term or period ('date') is over before it has properly started. The presence of 'cancelled', where 'expired' might seem enough, adds an effect of intensity, as it suggests that the period or lease (another meaning of 'date') does not run out naturally but is brought forcibly to a close by intervention.

Beauty itself doth of itself persuade
The eyes of men without an orator.   30
What needeth then apology be made
To set forth that which is so singular?
Or why is Collatine the publisher
   Of that rich jewel he should keep unknown
   From thievish ears, because it is his own?   35

Perchance his boast of Lucrece' sov'reignty
Suggested this proud issue of a king;
For by our ears our hearts oft tainted be.
Perchance that envy of so rich a thing,
Braving compare, disdainfully did sting   40
   His high-pitched thoughts, that meaner men should vaunt
   That golden hap which their superiors want.

But some untimely thought did instigate
His all too timeless speed, if none of those.
His honour, his affairs, his friends, his state,   45
Neglected all, with swift intent he goes
To quench the coal which in his liver glows.

31 apology] Appologie Q1 *(Malone 34, Yale;* Apologies *the rest)*   47 glows] glowes Q1; growes Q4; 8, 9

30 without . . . orator silently. The poem applies the ancient sense of 'oratory', which was to plead a cause ('persuade') in a court of law or before the senate or tribunal.

31 apology argument. In classical oratory (see 30n) the *apology* for or justification of a cause would emphasise and proclaim its merits.

32 singular unique, unrivalled. Speech in her favour is unnecessary since speeches on behalf of rivals can be of no account.

33 publisher proclaimer, reporter. The word probably includes the idea of making available for sale; 'publish' in this sense does not only mean books but also engravings and art objects (*OED* sv. b4).

35 thievish ears ears of thieves. Making the ears themselves actively and vividly thief-like is a good example of *catachresis*, a figure of speech often used by Shakespeare to dramatic purpose. Its effect depends on a word (usually a verb or adjective) being deliberately misapplied.

36 sov'reignty unique excellence (see *Ven.* 28, 916).

37 Suggested Tempted, provoked (compare

'suggestion', *Ven.* 1044n).

37 proud arrogant. Qualifying the purposefully undistinguished 'issue', 'proud' is deprived of the connotations it has when referring to Collatine at 19.

40 Braving compare Defying comparison.

40–1 disdainfully . . . thoughts i.e. his pride felt slighted. Since 'envy' is the subject of 'sting', the sense may further be that his inflated ('high-pitched') self-regard is not only made to appear mean (the effect of 'disdainfully' is that his 'thoughts' feel their disdain) but that his mind is poisoned (a connotation of 'sting' – as at *Ham.* 1.5.39; 'The serpent that did sting thy father's life').

42 hap happiness, fortune (compare 8).

42 want lack.

43 untimely inappropriate, ill-fitting.

44 timeless hasty.

46 with . . . intent intending to act swiftly.

47 liver Contemporary physiology understood the liver to be the seat of both sexual passion and anger (often described as spleen).

O rash false heat, wrapped in repentant cold,
Thy hasty spring still blasts and ne'er grows old.

When at Collatium this false lord arrivèd,   50
Well was he welcomed by the Roman dame,
Within whose face Beauty and Virtue strivèd
Which of them both should underprop her fame.
When Virtue bragged, Beauty would blush for shame;
    When Beauty boasted blushes, in despite   55
    Virtue would stain that o'er with silver white.

But Beauty, in that white entitulèd
From Venus' doves, doth challenge that fair field.
Then Virtue claims from Beauty Beauty's red,
Which Virtue gave the golden age to gild   60
Their silver cheeks, and called it then their shield;
    Teaching them thus to use it in the fight,
    When shame assailed, the red should fence the white.

48 repentant] Q1; repentance Q3–4   50 Collatium] Colatium Q1 *(Malone 34, Yale;* Colatia *the rest)*   56 o'er] Q6 +;
ore Q1; or *Malone*

48 rash . . . heat See 47n.
48 repentant cold The reference may be to the
body, which in cooling after the excitement of lust
seems to express regret. The process of aging may
also be implied: no matter how reluctant the body,
the spirit of lust is still capable of being kindled.
49 hasty quick to activate itself.
49 still always, continuously.
49 blasts withers, perishes.
53 underprop support (perhaps as a plinth to a
monument).
53 fame glory, repute.
54 Virtue bragged The paradox of Virtue's
behaving unvirtuously is characteristic of the
poem's style and ultimately has bearing on its perception of the irony of fate. Equally, balancing
Virtue in the same line, Beauty's modesty only
manages to call keener attention to itself.
55 in despite in order to frustrate (Beauty).
56 o'er A pun on 'ore' may be intended. (Q1's
'ore' is not conclusive, since that is its spelling of
'o'er' throughout.) Malone emends to 'or' – the
heraldic term for gold; but without the emendation both meanings can be more easily perceived.
57 in . . . entitulèd having a title to that white.
58 challenge claim possession of.
58 fair field Lucrece's face (with heraldic overtones – see also 'shield', 61): as well as being commended in cosmic terms, it is compared to an
earthly paradise. Campion provides a lyric version

of the same idea (see *Ven.* 65n).
60 the golden age Virtue argues that she has
added Beauty's red to her own white, making the
silver age golden and thus achieving perfection.
The golden age is a mythological paradise referred
to by successsive generations of poets in both the
classical and Renaissance periods and always means
a place of pure, unfallen happiness in which the
oppositions and contradictions which make present
life miserable, for example pleasure and virtue, are
reconciled. For the Renaissance Tasso celebrated it
in a chorus of his pastoral drama, the *Aminta (Ven.*
741n).
61 Their . . . cheeks Virtue personifies white
and red as denizens of the silver and golden ages.
61 shield protection. But the word also plays
on heraldic significance (as 64 makes clear). Pooler
cites Sidney: 'Cupid then smiles, for on his crest
there lies / Stella's faire haire; her face he makes
his shield, / Where rose gueuls are borne in silver
field' *(AS* 13.9–11).
63 i.e. shame must now be external to both red
and white, since they are now reconciled and the
duty of the one is to enclose and protect ('fence')
the other. The conceit registers an important distinction for the poem (especially with regard to
Lucrece), which is that to blush *at* shame is not
the same thing as to embody shame or to be guilty
of its operation.

This heraldry in Lucrece' face was seen,
Argued by Beauty's red and Virtue's white;   65
Of either's colour was the other queen,
Proving from world's minority their right;
Yet their ambition makes them still to fight,
    The sov'reignty of either being so great
    That oft they interchange each other's seat.   70

This silent war of lilies and of roses
Which Tarquin viewed in her fair face's field,
In their pure ranks his traitor eye encloses;
Where, lest between them both it should be killed,
The coward captive vanquishèd doth yield   75
    To those two armies, that would let him go
    Rather than triumph in so false a foe.

Now thinks he that her husband's shallow tongue,
The niggard prodigal that praised her so,
In that high task hath done her beauty wrong,   80
Which far exceeds his barren skill to show.
Therefore that praise which Collatine doth owe

---

64 heraldry See 61n.

65 Argued Expressed, demonstrated. The sense of dispute is also present as another aspect of the conceit.

67 world's minority the beginning of time.

69 sov'reignty supremacy (repeating the idea of 66). Wyndham insists that 'sov'reignty' has heraldic application, though he appears to overstate its use in his source, Guillim's *Display of Heraldrie* (1610). In context, both this word and 'ambition' signal the narrative's return to the encounter between Lucrece and Tarquin.

71 war Malone would emend to 'band' for the sake of consistency; 'pure ranks' (73) then belong to a single army. But 74 still poses problems for such a reading, as does 'two armies' (76). It is perhaps better to see the whole as a perpetually resolved conflict.

72 fair . . . field See 58n.

73 traitor eye The conceit seems to be that the eye treacherously sides with both armies in the 'war', but because of the danger (it is no match for either's purity) it surrenders to both simultaneously: 'yield' has the sense of hoping for terms. Since by the nature of the idea the warring factions are simultaneously reconciled to one another, the only practical enemy must lie outside

the 'conflict' (see 63n). The elaboration of the idea keeps the analogy of the human situation closely in mind.

73 encloses The subject of 'encloses' is most likely the noun phrase 'war . . . roses' rather than simply 'war'. This would explain the plural, 'their pure ranks', which is also an adjunct of the singular verb. Abbott (§337) would probably argue that the subject is the whole of the noun clause, extending to include 'field'.

77 triumph in triumph over.

77 false a foe cowardly an enemy (i.e. he is no real or worthy foe). But the idea of treachery is also relevant in that, like Tarquin, the eye does not disclose what lies behind its gaze.

78 shallow insufficient, inadequate.

79 niggard prodigal i.e. excessive and yet insufficient praise. The oxymoron maintains the stylistic principle apparent in, for example, the beauteous 'war' of 71.

82 doth owe needs to pay. The modern sense of 'owe' is more likely than 'possess', which is its frequent meaning in Shakespeare. Malone preferred the latter and glosses 'praise' as 'object of praise', interpreting the line as meaning Collatine's possession of Lucrece. But most subsequent editors disagree.

Enchanted Tarquin answers with surmise,
In silent wonder of still-gazing eyes.

This earthly saint, adorèd by this devil,   85
Little suspecteth the false worshipper;
For unstained thoughts do seldom dream on evil;
Birds never limed no secret bushes fear.
So guiltless she securely gives good cheer
    And reverend welcome to her princely guest,   90
    Whose inward ill no outward harm expressed;

For that he coloured with his high estate,
Hiding base sin in pleats of majesty;
That nothing in him seemed inordinate,
Save sometime too much wonder of his eye,   95
Which having all, all could not satisfy;
    But, poorly rich, so wanteth in his store,
    That cloyed with much, he pineth still for more.

But she that never coped with stranger eyes,
Could pick no meaning from their parling looks,   100
Nor read the subtle shining secrecies
Writ in the glassy margents of such books.

87 unstained thoughts] Q1; thoughts unstain'd Q6 +   88 limed] lim'd Q1; limb'd Q5–7

83 **answers** answers for him, pays. But 'responds to' is possible if Malone's reading of 82 is accepted.
83 **surmise** wonder, surprised admiration.
84 **still-gazing** i.e. never interrupting their gaze.
85–6 The sin of lust is presented in overtly Christian terms for the first time in the poem.
87 **unstained** uncorrupted.
87 **dream on** suspect.
88 **limed** caught with birdlime.
88 **secret** i.e. hiding a trap.
89 **securely** suspecting no danger.
90 **reverend** reverent, respectful.
91 **harm** danger. The balance of the line requires a word synonymous with 'ill', but the action dictates that the harm is still only potential.
92 **that** refers to 'outward harm' (91).
92 **coloured** disguised. The idea possibly involves a play on the sense of household colours (compare 476–7 and 481).
93 **pleats** plaits, folds. *Lear* (Quartos) has, 'Time shall unfold what pleated cunning hides' (1.1.280). Compare *FQ* 5.9.28.6–7: 'Whose skirts were bor-dred with bright sunny beams, / Glistring like

gold, amongst the plights enrold'.
94 **That** So that.
94 **inordinate** unusual, extraordinary.
97 **so . . . store** is so lacking in his abundance.
99 **coped with** encountered (implying a test or trial – see *Ven.* 888).
99 **stranger** i.e. of a stranger. The noun acts as an adjective.
100 **parling** speaking (perhaps including the sense of military negotiation, as in 'parley', 471).
101 **shining secrecies** The phrase is paradoxical; 'shining', in addition, plays both on the sense of the gleam in the eye and on the idea that such 'secrecies', far from being obscure, signal clearly to those who know how to interpret them.
102 **margents** margins. The margin of a book was the place for annotation and clarification of obscure meanings. Lady Capulet uses the image in recommending the face of Paris: 'And what obscur'd in this fair volume lies / Find written in the margent of his eyes' (*Rom.* 1.3.85–6). (NB The figure works by ignoring the fact that the margin is at the edge of the page whereas the eyes are in the middle of the face.) Therefore, 'glassy

She touched no unknown baits, nor feared no hooks;
    Nor could she moralise his wanton sight,
    More than his eyes were opened to the light.   105

He stories to her ears her husband's fame,
    Won in the fields of fruitful Italy;
    And decks with praises Collatine's high name,
    Made glorious by his manly chivalry,
    With bruisèd arms and wreaths of victory.   110
        Her joy with heaved-up hand she doth express,
        And wordless so greets heaven for his success.

Far from the purpose of his coming thither,
    He makes excuses for his being there.
    No cloudy show of stormy blust'ring weather   115
    Doth yet in his fair welkin once appear;
    Till sable night, mother of dread and fear,
        Upon the world dim darkness doth display,
        And in her vaulty prison stows the day.

For then is Tarquin brought unto his bed,   120
    Intending weariness with heavy sprite;

117 mother] Q1; sad source Q6+   119 stows] Q1; shuts Q6+

margents' means 'eyes which make intentions
clear'. The phrase 'of such books' may refer indirectly to the face (as does 'volume' in the *Rom.*
passage), or it may fill out pleonastically the meaning of 'margents'.
    103 touched touched on, sensed.
    104 moralise interpret morally (as of a text; see
102n).
    105 light i.e. the light of morality.
    106 stories relates (as a verb, 'stories' is used
specifically to list accomplishments – compare *Ven.*
1013). Although there is no reason to doubt Collatine's achievements, the word implies something
of implausibility in so far as Tarquin has a hidden
motive for what he does.
    110 bruisèd arms dinted armour. (Compare *R3*
1.1.5–6: 'Now are our brows bound with victorious
wreaths, / Our bruisèd arms hung up for monuments.')
    110 wreaths of victory The phrase looks back
to 107 and helps transform 'fields' and 'fruitful'
from their literal to a figurative meaning. See also
110 above n.
    111 heaved-up i.e. raised as if in salutation or
thanks. The gesture possibly belongs to the theatrical repertoire.

    116 welkin face. 'Welkin' is a poeticism for
'sky'. Having already described Lucrece's face in
terms of cosmic analogy (see especially 11–14), the
poem now applies the principle to Tarquin. In each
case the imagery carries strong moral connotations,
more emphatic than in the corresponding process
in *Ven.*
    117–19 Malone compares Daniel's *Complaint of
Rosamond*: 'Com'd was the night, mother of sleepe
and feare, / Who with her sable mantle friendly
covers / The sweet-stolne sports, of ioyfull meeting lovers' (432–4). (See Introduction, pp. 39–41.)
    118 doth display spreads out (as of a cloth or
blanket).
    119 vaulty prison The word 'vaulty', meaning
vault- or arch-like, conveys the sense of enclosed
space either high above or under the ground. The
image therefore may suggest that (1) as the vault of
the heavens darkens it becomes day's prison, or (2)
day descends underground where darkness stores
('stows') it like a blanket in a chest (see 118n).
    121 Intending Pretending.
    121 sprite spirits.

For after supper long he questionèd
With modest Lucrece, and wore out the night.
Now leaden slumber with life's strength doth fight,
    And every one to rest himself betakes,   125
    Save thieves and cares and troubled minds that wakes.

As one of which doth Tarquin lie revolving
The sundry dangers of his will's obtaining;
Yet ever to obtain his will resolving,
Though weak-built hopes persuade him to abstaining.   130
Despair to gain doth traffic oft for gaining,
    And when great treasure is the meed proposèd,
    Though death be adjunct, there's no death supposèd.

Those that much covet are with gain so fond
That what they have not, that which they possess   135
They scatter and unloose it from their bond,
And so by hoping more they have but less;
Or gaining more, the profit of excess

---

124 life's] lifes Q3–4; lives Q1   125–6 himself betakes . . . wakes] Q1 *(Malone 34, Yale;* themselves betake . . . wake *the rest)*   135 That . . . possess] Q1; That oft they have not that which they possess, Q6 +

122 questionèd conversed.

124 leaden slumber Perhaps the fact that Elizabethan coffins were of lead makes the image of 'leaden slumber' more death-like.

125–6 See collation.

127 revolving turning over in his mind.

128–9 will's obtaining . . . obtain his will The chiastic movement across the lines is characteristic of the poem's depiction of back-and-forth reasoning and unresolved moral dilemmas. Ewig (pp. 399ff.) compares 144, 401, 600–1, 660, etc.

131 doth . . . gaining often trades for gain.

132 meed reward.

133 adjunct an inseparable consequence. Compare *John* 3.3.57–8: 'Though that my death were adjunct to my act, / By heaven, I would do it.'

133 supposèd imagined beforehand, anticipated.

134 are . . . fond (1) are made foolish by what they have gained, (2) dote so much on the idea of possession.

135–6 The general sense is that in desperation to acquire what they do not have they rid themselves of ('scatter') what they *do* have, taking it out of security ('their bond'). In 'scatter' there may be the sense of bestowing liberally in the vain hope of multiple return. Maxwell notes the syntactical anacoluthon: 'Shakespeare begins as if about to

say . . . but hastens on to the final clause without expressing what comes between.' In fact the movement this produces in the syntax captures appropriately the uncontrolled eagerness and speed with which the impulse to covet operates. Malone sees a distinction between *having* and *possessing* (true having), an interpretation which is supported by Pooler who argues that the comma should follow 'have', thus neatly setting 'not that which they possess' in parenthesis. (See collation for variants in punctuation among the quartos.) Gildon (1710) traces the idea of 135 to Publius Syrus, *Tam deest Avaro quod habet, quam quod non habet* ('the miser is further from possessing what he has than what he has not').

138 profit . . . excess (1) the advantage of having more than enough (Pooler), but also (2) the advantage gained from usury (see *MV* 1.3.61–2, 'albeit I neither lend nor borrow / By giving or by taking of excess'). The sense of 'excess' as usury brings out by contrast its other sense as 'surfeit' (139); i.e. the self-indulgence made possible by the profits of usury impairs one's health (the meaning of 'griefs sustain'). In exploiting the different meanings of 'excess' the argument varies and strengthens its indictment of covetousness by expressing it through an unpopular contemporary practice.

Is but to surfeit, and such griefs sustain,
That they prove bankrupt in this poor rich gain.   140

The aim of all is but to nurse the life
With honour, wealth, and ease in waning age;
And in this aim there is such thwarting strife
That one for all or all for one we gage:
As life for honour in fell battle's rage;   145
    Honour for wealth; and oft that wealth doth cost
    The death of all, and all together lost.

So that in vent'ring ill we leave to be
The things we are for that which we expect;
And this ambitious foul infirmity,   150
In having much, torments us with defect
Of that we have: so then we do neglect
    The thing we have; and, all for want of wit,
    Make something nothing by augmenting it.

Such hazard now must doting Tarquin make,   155
Pawning his honour to obtain his lust;
And for himself himself he must forsake
Then where is truth, if there be no self-trust?
When shall he think to find a stranger just,
    When he himself himself confounds, betrays   160
    To sland'rous tongues and wretched hateful days?

147 all together] Q8–9; altogether Q1

141–2 Compare *Mac.* 5.3.24–5.
143 **thwarting** self-opposing, contradictory.
144 **one . . . all** one thing for everything.
144 **gage** pledge, wager.
145 **fell** fierce, savage.
147 **of all** of everybody. The significance of 'all' has subtly altered and grown in seriousness from its application in 144.
148 **vent'ring ill** taking an ill-advised risk (compare 'adventure').
148 **leave to be** The expected predicate of 'leave' might be 'to own' followed by 'things we have'; but 'things we are' insists that what is at stake is self-possession or selfhood, not just material having.
149 **expect** hope for.
150–4 Compare 134–7.
150 **this . . . infirmity** this foul infirmity, ambition.

151 **defect** the insufficiency.
153 **wit** intelligence, wisdom.
154 A very compact expression which may be interpreted in two separate ways: (1) what is augmented is not the 'something' but the desire to have more of it, so that the thing possessed appears to lose value and become 'nothing'; (2) the thing possessed is initially increased by risking it in a venture (see 134–7) and then finally lost.
155 **hazard** i.e. a dangerous gamble.
155 **doting** obsessed.
157 **himself himself** The emphatic use of the double reflexive pronoun (see also Abbott §20) is characteristic of early Shakespeare; compare 160 and *Ven.* 161.
160 **confounds** destroys, undermines.

Now stole upon the time the dead of night,
When heavy sleep had closed up mortal eyes;
No comfortable star did lend his light,
No noise but owls' and wolves' death-boding cries.   165
Now serves the season that they may surprise
    The silly lambs. Pure thoughts are dead and still,
    While lust and murder wakes to stain and kill.

And now this lustful lord leaped from his bed,
Throwing his mantle rudely o'er his arm,   170
Is madly tossed between desire and dread:
The one sweetly flatters, th'other feareth harm;
But honest fear, bewitched with lust's foul charm,
    Doth too too oft betake him to retire,
    Beaten away by brainsick rude desire.   175

His falchion on a flint he softly smiteth,
That from the cold stone sparks of fire do fly;
Whereat a waxen torch forthwith he lighteth,
Which must be lodestar to his lustful eye,
And to the flame thus speaks advisedly: 180
    'As from this cold flint I enforced this fire,
    So Lucrece must I force to my desire.'

162–8 Malone is the first to point out the similarity with *Mac.* 2.1.49–56:

> Now o'er the one half world
> Nature seems dead, and wicked dreams abuse
> The curtain'd sleep; witchcraft celebrates
> Pale Hecat's off'rings; and wither'd Murther,
> Alarum'd by his sentinel, the wolf,
> Whose howl's his watch, thus with his stealthy pace,
> With Tarquin's ravishing strides, towards his design
> Moves like a ghost.

163 Compare Sidney, 'When far spent night perswades each mortall eye' (*AS* 99.1). Sidney's sonnet sequence, which reflects on the troubled relationship between love, honour, and lust (though with much more sympathy for its male protagonist) may influence some of *Lucrece's* contemplative statements.
164 comfortable comfort-giving.
167 silly feeble (see *Ven.* 1098n).
167 dead and still A hendiadys emphasising depth of sleep; but 'dead' may anticipate the fate that is in store for purity.
168 wakes Abbott (§336) notes that Shakespeare

often inflects the verb in 's' when it follows two singular nouns (compare *Ven.* 988).
170 rudely roughly (see 175).
173 honest fear i.e. fearful for honesty or modesty.
173 bewitched . . . charm Lust charms away fear's opposition in this line yet removes it by force in 175, both of which expose its dual nature of pleasure and violence.
174 him himself (fear).
174 retire withdraw (as in a combat).
175 brainsick obsessive.
176 falchion A short curved sword with its blade on its convex side (from Lat. *falx* = sickle). In Shakespeare it can change its nature according to the context (for example, it is likened to a rapier in *R3* 1.2.94–6). In *Lucrece* 'falchion' allows for wordplay with 'falcon' (506, 509).
176 softly quietly (trying to make no sound). Note the paradoxical 'softly *smiteth*'.
179 lodestar pole star, guiding star.
180 advisedly (deliberately) as if having taken counsel.

Here pale with fear he doth premeditate
The dangers of his loathsome enterprise,
And in his inward mind he doth debate   185
What following sorrow may on this arise;
Then looking scornfully, he doth despise
    His naked armour of still-slaught'red lust,
    And justly thus controls his thoughts unjust.

'Fair torch, burn out thy light, and lend it not   190
To darken her whose light excelleth thine;
And die, unhallowed thoughts, before you blot
With your uncleanness that which is divine.
Offer pure incense to so pure a shrine.
    Let fair humanity abhor the deed   195
    That spots and stains love's modest snow-white weed.

'O shame to knighthood, and to shining arms.
O foul dishonour to my household's grave.
O impious act including all foul harms,
A martial man to be soft fancy's slave.   200
True valour still a true respect should have;
    Then my digression is so vile, so base,
    That it will live engraven in my face.

188 still-slaught'red] still slaughtered Q1

183 **premeditate** think about in anticipation.
The sense is of a mind not yet made up (see
'debate', 185) as opposed to a premeditated action
in the modern legal sense.
185 **inward mind** conscience, soul (as distinct
from the merely mechanical operations of the outward mind or senses; see also 1779). For the contemporary significance of 'inward' see *Ven.* 434n).
188 **still . . . lust** This probably means lust that
dies as it is satisfied. The nature of lust – to revive
perpetually only to expire as quickly – accounts
for 'still' (always). Kittredge explicates the whole
line as follows: 'His only armor in this enterprise
is lust – which is no real armor, for it is always
slain (perishes, comes to naught) when it is satisfied. The fulfilment of such desire kills the desire.'
This fits the sense better than the contrary explanation that 'still-slaught'red' means lust continually suppressed. The peculiar intensity of the line
results partly from the parallel antitheses ('naked
armour' and 'still-slaught'red') and also from the
tmesis or interruption of the expected phrase 'naked
lust' to accommodate all that goes between.
190 **thy light** Compare 4n.
195 **abhor** be horrified at. The sound of 'whore'

may be heard in the word, so punning appropriately.
196 **modest . . . weed** i.e. chastity, purity
('weed' means clothing or garment).
198 **my . . . grave** my family's reputation in posterity. Wyndham, scrutinising heraldry, declares:
'the escutcheons of ancestors were displayed on the
mortuary chapels of noble families'.
199 **impious** Accented on the first syllable.
199 **including . . . harms** i.e. the gravity of this
offence is such that it encompasses all other forms
of evil.
200 **soft fancy** infatuation ('soft' alternates with
the hardness of 'martial').
201 **a true respect** The emphasis is on how
valour is to be exercised: it should have 'a careful
regard for that which is truly valorous' (Rollins).
202 **digression** deviation, transgression.
203 **engraven . . . face** Tarquin may be exag-
gerating in accordance with his heightened sense of
guilt, but he is perhaps equally alluding to the popular idea (argued seriously in Neoplatonist philosophy) that comeliness of feature represented beauty
of soul and vice versa (see Castiglione, p. 309 and
below 1632n).

'Yea, though I die the scandal will survive,
And be an eye-sore in my golden coat.   205
Some loathsome dash the herald will contrive
To cipher me how fondly I did dote;
That my posterity, shamed with the note,
    Shall curse my bones, and hold it for no sin
    To wish that I their father had not been.   210

'What win I if I gain the thing I seek?
A dream, a breath, a froth of fleeting joy.
Who buys a minute's mirth to wail a week?
Or sells eternity to get a toy?
For one sweet grape who will the vine destroy?   215
    Or what fond beggar, but to touch the crown,
    Would with the sceptre straight be strucken down?

'If Collatinus dream of my intent,
Will he not wake, and in a desperate rage
Post hither, this vile purpose to prevent?   220
This siege that hath engirt his marriage,
This blur to youth, this sorrow to the sage,
    This dying virtue, this surviving shame,
    Whose crime will bear an ever-during blame.

'O what excuse can my invention make   225
When thou shalt charge me with so black a deed?

205 eye-sore blemish (see 206).
206 loathsome dash Wyndham cites Guillim (69n) and identifies here a reference to the practice of 'abatements': 'accidentall markes annexed to Coate-Armour, denoting some ingentleman-like, dishonorable, or disloyall demeanour, quality, or staine in the Bearer, whereby the dignity of the Coate-Armour is greatly abased'.
207 cipher i.e. represent or interpret by a sign. Compare the use of 'cipher' in 1396.
207 fondly foolishly.
207 dote act besottedly.
208 note mark, sign.
209–210 sin . . . been A reference to the fifth commandment, which speaks of honouring parents. With touches of this kind the poem subtly draws together the different threads of Christian morality, Roman custom, and Elizabethan chivalry.
212 Compare *Son.* 129.12, 'Before, a joy pro-pos'd, behind, a dream'.
214 eternity See 209–10n.
214 toy amorous fancy (compare the use of 'toy'

as a verb in *Ven.* 34 and 106).
216 fond See 207n.
217 straight immediately.
217 strucken struck. An example of proparalepsis or added syllable: Shakespeare often prefers 'struck' to 'strucken', the extra syllable being used, as here, for the metre.
220 Post See 1n.
221 engirt surrounded (compare *Ven.* 364).
222 blur blot, disgrace.
223 dying virtue Tarquin refers to his own virtue, which is in process of demise, but the conceit may also include Lucrece's virtue (under threat of death) which Collatine would be more anxious to preserve.
224 ever-during enduring, everlasting.
225 invention imagination, powers of mind. 'Invention' is used commonly to describe a poet's creative capacity.
226 thou The figure of Collatine is present in the third person throughout this contemplation so that by suddenly addressing him directly in his

Will not my tongue be mute, my frail joints shake,
Mine eyes forego their light, my false heart bleed?
The guilt being great, the fear doth still exceed;
　　And extreme fear can neither fight nor fly,   230
　　But coward-like with trembling terror die.

'Had Collatinus killed my son or sire,
Or lain in ambush to betray my life,
Or were he not my dear friend, this desire
Might have excuse to work upon his wife,   235
As in revenge or quittal of such strife;
　　But as he is my kinsman, my dear friend,
　　The shame and fault finds no excuse nor end.

'Shameful it is: ay, if the fact be known.
Hateful it is: there is no hate in loving.   240
I'll beg her love: but she is not her own.
The worst is but denial and reproving.
My will is strong, past reason's weak removing:
　　Who fears a sentence or an old man's saw
　　Shall by a painted cloth be kept in awe.'   245

239 ay, if] I, if Q1; if once Q6 +

imagination Tarquin betrays an extra degree of guilt. Prince on the other hand thinks that 'the rhetoric of the passage does not require a definite reference for "thou"'.

228 forego . . . **light** become blind (a further reference to the eye as the source of light, as in *Ven.* 816 and 1051).

229 doth . . . **exceed** is even greater.

230 extreme accented on the first syllable.

231 But But only.

231 with . . . **terror** Note that the personifications vary the intention of the phrase so that it means both 'in a spirit of terror' and 'as a companion to terror'.

234–5 this . . . **excuse** there might be some excuse to this desire. The phrasing results from the personifying of 'desire' (see 231n).

235 work upon undermine (i.e. her virtue). The connotation of siege strategy continues the ideas of 221 and 233.

236 quittal requital.

237 Compare *Mac.* 1.7.13: 'as I am his kinsman and his subject'.

238 end (1) purpose, in hendiadys with 'excuse', and (2) termination (as in the sense of 224).

239–42 This self-retort manner is typically Senecan and occurs, for example, in *R3* 5.3.182ff. and in *The Spanish Tragedy* 2.1.19–28 (Prince).

239 fact deed.

243 past . . . **removing** beyond the weak power of reason to dissuade. 'Removing' signifies the raising of a siege (see 235n). Since 'reason' argues, 'removing' may also connote the orator's attempts to 'move' or incite to virtue by persuasion.

244 sentence . . . **saw** 'Sentence' can mean judgement or merely opinion, an ambivalence which Tarquin exploits to shift the sense (with the help of parallelism) towards 'saw' (worn-out maxim).

245 painted cloth In the sixteenth century painted cloths were cheap substitutes for tapestries. Their purpose was moral instruction, and they depicted biblical or classical themes and incidents, the point of which was underlined with verbal devices or mottoes. (Compare *Tro.* 5.10.45 and *Mac.* 2.2.52; see Fairchild, p. 147.) As Tarquin suggests, their lesson was no more impressive than their workmanship. None the less, here may be the genesis of the picture Lucrece consults at 1366ff.

Thus graceless holds he disputation
'Tween frozen conscience and hot burning will,
And with good thoughts makes dispensation,
Urging the worser sense for vantage still;
Which in a moment doth confound and kill   250
    All pure effects, and doth so far proceed
    That what is vile shows like a virtuous deed.

Quoth he, 'She took me kindly by the hand,
And gazed for tidings in my eager eyes,
Fearing some hard news from the warlike band   255
Where her belovèd Collatinus lies.
O how her fear did make her colour rise!
    First red as roses that on lawn we lay,
    Then white as lawn, the roses took away.

'And how her hand, in my hand being locked,   260
Forced it to tremble with her loyal fear!
Which struck her sad, and then it faster rocked
Until her husband's welfare she did hear;
Whereat she smilèd with so sweet a cheer
    That had Narcissus seen her as she stood,   265
    Self-love had never drowned him in the flood.

---

251 effects] Q1; affects *conj. Steevens (Malone)*   260 how] Q1; now Q6+

---

246 graceless i.e. lacking or refusing divine aid.
246 holds . . . disputation disputes formally.
247 frozen conscience i.e. conscience that is by nature pure and steadfast (reintroducing the siege image of 243). The choice of 'frozen' is to be explained by the antithesis it creates with 'hot, burning' (characteristic of 'will') rather than on psychological grounds, though some editors interpret 'frozen' as 'numbed' or 'ineffective'.
248 with . . . dispensation Either (1) disregards good thoughts (*OED* sv *sb* III. 11 cites this line), or (2) finds a dispensation (i.e. licence, exemption) *in* good thoughts. The possibility of (2) depends on whether 'good thoughts' can contain anything bad (a 'worser sense') which can be exploited to ill purpose. Otherwise, as in (1), 'worser sense' is simply antithetical to 'good thoughts'.
249 for . . . still always to advantage.
250 confound destroy.
251 effects feelings. 'Effects' is akin to 'affects' (affections, passions), as in *Oth.* 1.3.263–4: 'the young affects / In me defunct'. See also *Ven.* 605.

252 Compare *Son.* 95.11 and 147.13–14.
253 kindly naturally, unselfconsciously.
254 eager This has the appearance of a transferred epithet: i.e. 'she *eagerly* gazed . . .'
255 hard news harsh news (compare *Ant.* 1.2.100: 'stiff news').
256 lies Here 'lies' combines the straightforward meaning 'dwells' with the anticipatory (proleptic) meaning 'lies dead'.
258–9 Compare *Ven.* 589–90.
259 took being taken.
261 it i.e. Tarquin's hand.
262 Which i.e. the trembling of his hand which has been induced by *her* trembling. (A similar process of mistaken signals occurs in 1352–8.)
262 struck her sad had a sad effect upon her.
262 it Lucrece's hand.
264 cheer cheerfulness.
265–6 See *Ven.* 161–2. The reference to self-love is a pertinent example of perhaps unconscious irony on Tarquin's part, since as early as 40–2 it is clear that this is one of his besetting sins.

'Why hunt I then for colour or excuses?
All orators are dumb when beauty pleadeth;
Poor wretches have remorse in poor abuses;
Love thrives not in the heart that shadows dreadeth.   270
Affection is my captain, and he leadeth;
   And when his gaudy banner is displayed,
   The coward fights and will not be dismayed.

'Then childish fear avaunt, debating die!
Respect and reason wait on wrinkled age!   275
My heart shall never countermand mine eye.
Sad pause and deep regard beseems the sage;
My part is youth, and beats these from the stage.
   Desire my pilot is, beauty my prize;
   Then who fears sinking where such treasure lies?'   280

As corn o'ergrown by weeds, so heedful fear
Is almost choked by unresisted lust.
Away he steals with open list'ning ear,
Full of foul hope, and full of fond mistrust;
Both which, as servitors to the unjust,   285
   So cross him with their opposite persuasion
   That now he vows a league, and now invasion.

Within his thought her heavenly image sits,
And in the self-same seat sits Collatine.

269 poor] poore Q1; pure Q4   282 choked] choakt Q1; cloakt Q5–8

267 **colour** pretext. For various uses of 'colour' see 92 and 476.

269 Paltry people feel sorry for their minor offences. The verb may be in the optative mood for the purpose of defiance: i.e. '*Let* poor wretches . . .'

271 **Affection** Passion (compare *Ven.* 387n).

272 **gaudy** (1) bright-coloured, (2) joyful (compare *Ven.* 1088n). 'Gaudy banner' retrospectively gives 'colour' (267) the sense of battle colours (see 476).

273 **The . . . fights** Proverbial (though *ODEP* does not give an example earlier than 1648; compare *Ven.* 1158).

274 **avaunt** be gone.

274 **debating die** let there be no more debate.

275 **Respect** Circumspection. The hendiadys occurs in inverse form in *Tro.* 2.2.49–50: 'reason and respect / Make livers pale and lustihood deject'.

275 **wait on** accompany (in the optative mood).

276 **countermand . . . eye** cancel the command given by my eye.

277 **Sad** Serious (see *Ven.* 807n).

277 **regard** caution (the word is similar in effect to 'respect' in 275).

281 **heedful** cautious.

283 **open . . . ear** Perhaps 'ear' is subliminally prompted by the image of corn in 281; in both cases corruption is a governing principle.

284 **fond mistrust** foolish wariness. The sense of this paradoxical expression is that he is concerned not to be apprehended in an enterprise in which success will mean disaster.

285 **as** as if.

285 **servitors . . . unjust** his servants or advisers in impropriety.

286 **cross him** (1) thwart him, (2) put him in two minds.

286 **opposite persuasion** conflicting advice.

287 **league** truce.

That eye which looks on her confounds his wits;   290
That eye which him beholds, as more divine,
Unto a view so false will not incline;
    But with a pure appeal seeks to the heart,
    Which once corrupted takes the worser part;

And therein heartens up his servile powers,   295
Who, flatt'red by their leader's jocund show,
Stuff up his lust, as minutes fill up hours;
And as their captain, so their pride doth grow,
Paying more slavish tribute than they owe.
    By reprobate desire thus madly led,   300
    The Roman lord marcheth to Lucrece' bed.

The locks between her chamber and his will,
Each one by him enforced retires his ward;

301 marcheth] Q1; doth march Q6 +

290 **confounds . . . wits** destroys his sense of judgement.

291 as as if.

291 more divine The eye which contemplates Collatine's image, not being clouded by lust, perceives the moral implications of the undertaking. Whether Collatine's image is represented as being superior to Lucrece's because it is free of sensual appeal is a question which is perhaps tactfully not pursued, and the poem by and large avoids it (unless Tarquin's self-excusing pleas are taken into account); but Lucrece hints at the problem of being a beautiful woman in her angry outburst at Helen as she contemplates the depiction of ruined Troy (1471–2). (See Introduction, p. 32.)

292 view . . . false i.e. the morally distorted vision which contemplating Lucrece's beauty induces (see 291n).

293 seeks to looks to (for support).

294 once corrupted already having been corrupted.

295 heartens up encourages (playing on 'heart').

295 servile powers inclinations to lust (more generally his inferior instincts). The division of feeling into an army of troops does not always provide precisely analogous terms. (See *Ven.* 1037–50 for a similar idea.)

296 Who See *Ven.* 956n and Abbott §264.

296 flatt'red encouraged.

297 Stuff up Bolster, fill out.

297 minutes . . . hours There may be a subdued or discreet touch of bawdiness to this image, in as much as the clock supplies a notorious example of indecency in *Rom.* 2.4.112–13, 'for the bawdy

hand of the dial is now upon the prick of noon': similarly, 'as minutes fill up hours' the minute hand stands upright pointing towards twelve. The image of pride's growth in the following line could be hinting at more of the same (*OED* sv *sb* [1] B. 11 defines pride as sexual excitement; see also *Son.* 151.10, 'Proud of this pride'). But the decorum of this poem ensures that such effects, while conveying the crude energy and character of lust, never betray its expression into licentiousness or titillation.

298 their captain the heart.

298 their pride resolve, strength of purpose (but see also 297n). 'They' are desire or the 'servile powers' of 295.

299 The image turns on the idea of vassals or serfs paying tribute (as an acknowledgement of their subjection) to a lord either in money or in kind. As the heart's vassal (or vassals since the noun is collective) bodily desire expresses itself to a fuller degree than the heart or mind anticipated; hence its state of unbearable excitement.

300 reprobate base, depraved.

300 madly led See 299n.

302 between . . . will This is an effective use of zeugma as the governing preposition 'between' forges a connection linking the concrete word 'chamber' and the abstract or conceptual word 'will', thus breaking the familiar closed (i.e. within a single person) relationship between will and reason and demonstrating the fearful prospect of desire in action: the 'will' is now at large as a predator.

303 enforced forced open (anticipating the forcing of Lucrece in rape).

303 retires . . . ward draws back its ward (the

But as they open, they all rate his ill,
Which drives the creeping thief to some regard.   305
The threshold grates the door to have him heard;
     Night-wand'ring weasels shriek to see him there;
     They fright him, yet he still pursues his fear.

As each unwilling portal yields him way,
Through little vents and crannies of the place   310
The wind wars with his torch to make him stay,
And blows the smoke of it into his face,
Extinguishing his conduct in this case;
     But his hot heart, which fond desire doth scorch,
     Puffs forth another wind that fires the torch.   315

And being lighted, by the light he spies
Lucretia's glove, wherein her needle sticks.
He takes it from the rushes where it lies,
And gripping it, the needle his finger pricks,
As who should say, 'This glove to wanton tricks   320
     Is not inured. Return again in haste;
     Thou seest our mistress' ornaments are chaste.'

But all these poor forbiddings could not stay him;
He in the worst sense consters their denial:

308 he still pursues his] Q1; still pursues him Q4   314 desire] Q1; delight Q4

ward accepts only the key made for that lock). But
'ward' also plays on the meaning of the watch or
guard.
   304 rate berate.
   304 ill evil intent.
   305 regard caution.
   306 grates . . . heard i.e. the threshold makes
a grating noise under the door as if to alert the
household to Tarquin's movements.
   307 Night . . . weasels The weasel, itself
a small, slyly insinuating predator, provides an
appropriate cue for Tarquin's moment of self-
reflective terror in the following line. (See supplementary note.)
   308 pursues . . . fear i.e. Tarquin is prey to his
own desire.
   311 make him stay halt his progress.
   313 conduct conductor, guide.
   313 case matter, affair.
   314 fond foolish.
   316 being lighted it being lighted.
   318 rushes Compare *Cym.* 2.2.12–14: 'Our
Tarquin thus / Did softly press the rushes ere he

waken'd / The chastity he wounded.'
   319 needle Q1's reading. Malone proposed
'neeld' (a form sometimes used by Shakespeare)
to solve a problem of metre as he saw it; but the
disyllabic form 'needle' elides smoothly enough.
Despite the occasional retention of the dialect
'neele', there is no warrant for assuming that 'needle' is pronounced other than as it is printed.
   320 As . . . say See *Ven.* 280n.
   320 glove . . . tricks The same idea occurs,
expressed more bawdily, in Middleton and Row-
ley's play, *The Changeling*, where the character De
Flores observes over Beatrice-Joanna's glove, 'She
had rather wear my pelt tann'd in a pair / Of dancing pumps than I should thrust my fingers into her
sockets here' (*NM* 1.1. 232–34). This is more to
the point than Lever's suggestion that the 'wanton
tricks' refer to 'such coquetry as dropping a glove
for a man to pick up'.
   321 inured hardened, accustomed.
   323 stay check, halt.
   324 consters construes.

The doors, the wind, the glove, that did delay him,   325
He takes for accidental things of trial;
Or as those bars which stop the hourly dial,
　　Who with a ling'ring stay his course doth let,
　　Till every minute pays the hour his debt.

'So, so', quoth he, 'these lets attend the time,   330
Like little frosts that sometime threat the spring,
To add a more rejoicing to the prime,
And give the sneapèd birds more cause to sing.
Pain pays the income of each precious thing:
　　Huge rocks, high winds, strong pirates, shelves, and sands   335
　　The merchant fears, ere rich at home he lands.'

Now is he come unto the chamber door
That shuts him from the heaven of his thought,
Which with a yielding latch, and with no more,
Hath barred him from the blessèd thing he sought.   340
So from himself impiety hath wrought,
　　That for his prey to pray he doth begin,
　　As if the heavens should countenance his sin.

But in the midst of his unfruitful prayer,
Having solicited th'eternal power   345
That his foul thoughts might compass his fair fair,
And they would stand auspicious to the hour,

---

342 prey] Q6+; pray Q1　　347 auspicious] Q1; suspicious Q4

326 accidental . . . trial 'chance happenings which test his resolution' (Prince).

327 bars divisions on the clock face.

327 stop (1) divide into minutes, (2) cause to stop or pause.

328 Who Which (i.e. the bars); Abbott §264.

328 his course i.e. the progress of the hour upon the dial.

328 let hinder.

330 attend . . . time (1) accompany time as part of its retinue (as in a royal progress), (2) sharpen anticipation.

332 prime springtime.

333 sneapèd nipped, pinched. Compare *LLL* 1.1.100–1, 'like an envious sneaping frost / That bites the first-born infants of the spring'.

334 pays pays for.

334 income revenue, maturation.

335 shelves sandbanks.

341 Impiety has made him so unlike himself. This is the most probable reading, but it has been suggested that 'impiety' personifies Tarquin, which would account for the missing object 'him'. However, the ellipsis, irregular to modern eyes, is familiar enough in Shakespeare.

341 from himself away from himself (see Abbott §158).

342 prey . . . pray Q1 gives the same spelling 'pray' for both words. Stoll (*S. St.*, 1927, p. 397) first comments on the paradoxical state of mind (see also 284n).

346 compass encompass, embrace.

346 fair fair fair fair one, fair beauty. Compare *Ven.* 1083, 1086.

347 they the heavens. Despite the singular 'eternal power' (345) which is its proper reference, 'they' reinvokes the plural antecedent 'heavens' (343). The shift between singular and plural forms of the deity in the same sequence is often practised by Shakespeare (see, for example, *R3* 1.3.217–19), and its intention may be to avoid naming God directly. Of course, stylistic decorum requires that

Even there he starts. Quoth he, 'I must deflower:
  The powers to whom I pray abhor this fact;
  How can they then assist me in the act?   350

'Then Love and Fortune be my gods, my guide!
My will is backed with resolution.
Thoughts are but dreams till their effects be tried;
The blackest sin is cleared with absolution;
Against love's fire fear's frost hath dissolution.   355
  The eye of heaven is out, and misty night
  Covers the shame that follows sweet delight.'

This said, his guilty hand plucked up the latch,
And with his knee the door he opens wide.
The dove sleeps fast that this night-owl will catch,   360
Thus treason works ere traitors be espied:
Who sees the lurking serpent steps aside,
  But she, sound sleeping, fearing no such thing,
  Lies at the mercy of his mortal sting.

Into the chamber wickedly he stalks,   365
And gazeth on her yet unstainèd bed.
The curtains being close, about he walks,
Rolling his greedy eyeballs in his head.

---

354 The blackest] Q1; Blacke Q6+

Tarquin should not seem to address himself to the Christian God, but the poem's periphrastic expression may also be influenced by an overall sense of caution with regard to theological matters.

352 backed strengthened.

352 resolution The word ends in a disyllable– 'iòn'; similarly with the rhyme words of 354 and 355, which are consequently alexandrines. Compare *Ven.* 758 and 760, and see Lewis (*English Literature*, p. 502).

353 Bush (p. 153n) cites Bacon's essay 'Of Great Place' (published in 1612): 'For good thoughts, (though God accept them) yet towards men are little better then good dreams: except they be put in Art [*sc.* Act]'.

353 effects actions. Compare its meaning in 251.

353 be tried are experienced.

354 absolution remission of sins (as performed by a priest). See 347n.

355 hath dissolution dissolves.

356 out extinguished. Compare *Mac.* 2.1.4–5.

358–9 The ideas in this couplet continue the analogy between his advance towards his victim and his anticipation of sexual pleasure.

364 mortal sting deadly lust. A play on 'sting' as 'penis' is likely, since the word originally meant 'pole' or 'staff' (*OED* sv sb. 1 and 2). Similar wordplay is apparent in *Shr.* 2.1.213–14: 'Who knows not where a wasp doth wear his sting? / In his tail.'

365 stalks i.e. approaching with the stealthy movement of a predator careful not to alarm its prey. The epithet 'wickedly' describes his intention rather than his manner of moving. Compare Chaucer's description, 'And in the nyght ful *thefely* gan he stalke' (*LGW* 1781).

367 close closed.

By their high treason is his heart misled,
    Which gives the watch-word to his hand full soon   370
    To draw the cloud that hides the silver moon.

Look as the fair and fiery-pointed sun,
Rushing from forth a cloud, bereaves our sight;
Even so, the curtain drawn, his eyes begun
To wink, being blinded with a greater light: 375
Whether it is that she reflects so bright
    That dazzleth them, or else some shame supposèd,
    But blind they are, and keep themselves enclosèd.

O had they in that darksome prison died,
Then had they seen the period of their ill;   380
Then Collatine, again by Lucrece' side,
In his clear bed might have reposèd still.
But they must ope, this blessèd league to kill,
    And holy-thoughted Lucrece to their sight
    Must sell her joy, her life, her world's delight.   385

Her lily hand her rosy cheek lies under,
Coz'ning the pillow of a lawful kiss;
Who, therefore angry, seems to part in sunder,
Swelling on either side to want his bliss;

---

370 full] Q1; too Q6+   371 the silver Q1; this silver *conj. Walker*

369 high treason The emphasis is as much on self-betrayal as on treachery towards Lucrece. Compare *Ven.* 1039–50, where the heart is depicted as a king whose safety depends on the loyal operation of his subject eyes. In *Lucrece* the eyes have already been presented with an opportunity to exercise their vision discerningly (see 288–94). As the poem develops, the theme of personal responsibility becomes gradually more prominent.

370 watch-word signal (more usually 'password').

371 draw . . . cloud draw the bed-curtains.

372 Look as See *Ven.* 67n.

372 fiery-pointed i.e. as if the sun were *darting* fire.

373 bereaves takes away. It can also mean 'deprive of life' (as in *Ven.* 797), thus bringing out the full force of 'fiery-pointed'.

375 wink close (see *Ven.* 90, 121).

375 greater light i.e. than the light of his own eyes.

376 reflects returns the light from his eyes.

376 bright brightly.

377 shame supposèd imagined shame.

378 Compare Sidney: 'In tombe of lids then buried are mine eyes, / Forst by their Lord, who is asham'd to find / Such light in sense, with such a darkned mind' (*AS* 99.12–14).

379 darksome prison Compare *Ven.* 1038.

380 period termination.

382 clear unstained (as in 366).

383 league union, marriage ('league' may be prompted by the political terms established in 369).

384 to . . . sight in exchange for their ability to see. The image of this couplet discovers, for the first time, a sacrificial aspect to Lucrece.

387 Coz'ning Cheating.

388 therefore angry This conceit occurs at the only moment of tender playfulness in the poem (though the image of 1233–4 is reminiscent), and even then it takes place under the lustful gaze of Tarquin, whom the 'angry' pillow seems to parody.

389 Swelling i.e. in anger.

389 want lack.

Between whose hills her head entombèd is,   390
    Where like a virtuous monument she lies,
    To be admired of lewd unhallowed eyes.

Without the bed her other fair hand was,
On the green coverlet, whose perfect white
Showed like an April daisy on the grass,   395
With pearly sweat resembling dew of night.
Her eyes like marigolds had sheathed their light,
    And canopied in darkness sweetly lay,
    Till they might open to adorn the day.

Her hair like golden threads played with her breath,   400
O modest wantons, wanton modesty!
Showing life's triumph in the map of death,
And death's dim look in life's mortality.
Each in her sleep themselves so beautify,
    As if between them twain there were no strife,   405
    But that life lived in death, and death in life.

Her breasts like ivory globes circled with blue,
A pair of maiden worlds unconquerèd,

---

402 Showing] Q1; Showring Q6 +

391 virtuous monument An effigy of one
whose virtues are depicted in her posture and
in inscriptions on her tomb. Compare *Oth.* 5.2.5,
where the sleeping Desdemona is likened to 'monumental alablaster'.
392 admired of wondered at by.
393–7 The gentle intrusion of these pastoral conceits reminds us that the poem takes place almost
entirely in an oppressive indoor atmosphere, and
that it is the fate of its protagonists to be deprived
of wholesome, restorative nature.
397 like marigolds A flower that was seen to
be notably responsive to sunlight. Compare *WT*
4.4.105 and *Son.* 25.6.
398 canopied in darkness Compare *Cym.*
2.2.19–22: 'The flame o' th' taper / Bows toward
her, and would under-peep her lids / To see
th'enclosed lights, now canopied / Under these
windows.'
400 golden . . . breath The epithet 'golden'
and the interplay of hair and breath, as well as
the stanza as a whole with its sharply turned paradoxes, strongly suggest the opening of Petrarch's
famous sonnet, 'Erano i capei d'oro a l'aura sparsi'
('Her golden hair was loosed to the breeze' – *rime*
90). Ovid's description of her 'flavique capilli' (*Fasti*

2.763) is also a possible influence, but the image is
not developed with the same Petrarchan attention
to paradox.
402 map picture. The lineaments of the face are
often likened to the lines and configurations drawn
on a map (compare 1712).
403 dim dark.
403 life's mortality human life ('mortality'
here means the term of life).
406 The paradoxes of this and the preceding
lines depicting the harmonious reconciliation of
normally warring elements (here life and death,
and in 401 sex and innocence) all combine to give
an impression of a paradise which is about to be
spoiled.
407–8 Compare *HL* 2.273–8: 'For though the
rising yv'rie mount he scal'd, / Which is with azure
circling lines empal'd, / Much like a globe, (a globe
may I term this, / By which love sailes to regions
full of blis,) / Yet there with *Sisyphus* he toyld in
vaine, / Till gentle parlie did the truce obtaine.'
408 maiden worlds Editors have often
expressed concern over the choice of 'maiden' in
reference to a married woman. But the theme is
changing from innocence in the strictest sense
to that of priority of possession. Lucrece is sexually

Save of their lord no bearing yoke they knew,
And him by oath they truly honourèd.   410
These worlds in Tarquin new ambition bred,
     Who like a foul usurper went about
     From this fair throne to heave the owner out.

What could he see but mightily he noted?
What did he note but strongly he desirèd?   415
What he beheld, on that he firmly doted,
And in his will his wilful eye he tirèd.
With more than admiration he admirèd
     Her azure veins, her alablaster skin,
     Her coral lips, her snow-white dimpled chin.   420

As the grim lion fawneth o'er his prey,
Sharp hunger by the conquest satisfied,
So o'er this sleeping soul doth Tarquin stay,
His rage of lust by gazing qualified;
Slacked, not suppressed; for standing by her side,   425
     His eye, which late this mutiny restrains,
     Unto a greater uproar tempts his veins;

And they, like straggling slaves for pillage fighting,
Obdurate vassals fell exploits effecting,

425 Slacked] Q2 +; Slakt Q1   429 effecting] Q1; affecting *conj. Steevens (Malone)*

virtuous or *untouched* in that, as the marriage vows have it, she has worshipped Collatine with her body ('him by oath they truly honourèd') and never 'yielded' it to an outsider. The image may owe something to Ovid, 'positis urgentur pectora palmis / Tunc primum externa pectora tacta manu' ('his outstretched hands eagerly grasped her breasts, which for the first time felt a stranger's touch' (*Fasti* 2.803–4).
416 firmly doted The expression is paradoxical, since 'doted' connotes a weak indulgence of passion.
417 will . . . wilful lust . . . lustful.
417 tirèd (1) wearied, (2) fed full. The latter is from falconry (Steevens, Malone; see *Ven.* 56n).
418 more . . . admiration Admiration or 'wonder' belongs to an innocent eye, but Tarquin brings to his gaze the addition of lust.
419 alablaster skin Alablaster (modern alabaster) is a semi-transparent gypsum which was still used for monuments in the sixteenth century; its smoothness when sculpted made it an appropriate epithet to describe a young woman's skin. See 391n and *Ven.* 363n.

421 fawneth o'er dotes on, smiles tenderly over. The verb makes up an antithetical figure with '*grim* lion'.
422 Sharp hunger See *Ven.* 55n.
423 stay pause, hesitate.
424 qualified tempered, softened.
425 Slacked 'Slakt' (Q1); the word combines both 'slackened' and 'slaked'.
426 late lately, a moment ago.
428–48 The military–erotic motif which runs through this assault-and-battery passage has already been noted in *Ven.* 889–98 and 1039–1050. It is characteristic of the sixteenth-century sonnet; but what may be different or innovative is the involvement of *two* protagonists – or their bodies – in the figure, since at 439 onwards the device transfers itself from Tarquin to Lucrece.
428 straggling slaves i.e. the lowest members of an army, barely subject to discipline. 'Pillage' establishes the baseness of motive.
429 Obdurate Unfeeling; as 'vassals' they are too low in the social order to have acquired a civilised sensibility.
429 fell harsh, cruel.

In bloody death and ravishment delighting,   430
Nor children's tears nor mothers' groans respecting,
Swell in their pride, the onset still expecting.
    Anon his beating heart, alarum striking,
    Gives the hot charge and bids them do their liking.

His drumming heart cheers up his burning eye,   435
His eye commends the leading to his hand;
His hand, as proud of such a dignity,
Smoking with pride, marched on to make his stand
On her bare breast, the heart of all her land;
    Whose ranks of blue veins, as his hand did scale,   440
    Left their round turrets destitute and pale.

They, must'ring to the quiet cabinet
Where their dear governess and lady lies,
Do tell her she is dreadfully beset,
And fright her with confusion of their cries.   445
She, much amazed, breaks ope her locked-up eyes,
    Who, peeping forth this tumult to behold,
    Are by his flaming torch dimmed and controlled.

Imagine her as one in dead of night
From forth dull sleep by dreadful fancy waking,   450

---

439 breast] Q1; breasts Q6+

431 respecting considering, showing concern for.

432 Swell . . . pride See 297n.

433 alarum striking i.e. the signal for attack, as in *Ven.* 700.

435–7 The use of anadiplosis (repetition of a word at the beginning of the next line) increases the tempo in this part of the stanza.

435 cheers up encourages; compare 'heartens up' (295).

436 commends . . . leading entrusts the leadership.

437 as as if.

438 Smoking with pride This combines the idea of a proud army advancing under the smoke of battle with that of the heat of sexual excitement (see 297n, and *Oth.* 3.3.404: 'As salt as wolves in pride').

439 heart A pointed contrast is made between her 'heart', meaning citadel, fortress, and his 'heart' (435), which means invading lust.

442 quiet cabinet Probably 'her mind' (*Ven.* 1039–42 distinguishes between 'heart' and 'brain'). But 'heart' is also a possible reading, since the meaning distinguishes between the surface area ('the heart of all her land') which her veins have just abandoned and the inner place to which they withdraw. The 'cabinet' should not be confused with her bedchamber, since the veins' 'governess' dwells within the body, whether as soul, heart, or mind.

444 beset besieged.

446 locked-up The image continues the conceit of the body as a fortress.

448 dimmed extinguished, closed.

448 controlled overpowered.

449–50 Compare Livy 1.58: 'Cum pavida ex somno mulier nullam opem, prope mortem imminentem videret' ('The gentlewoman sore afraid, being newly awaked oute of her sleepe, and seeing imminent death, could not tell what to do' – Painter's translation, Bullough, 1, 197).

450 by . . . fancy by an imaginary terror.

That thinks she hath beheld some ghastly sprite,
Whose grim aspect sets every joint a-shaking:
What terror 'tis! but she in worser taking,
　　From sleep disturbèd, heedfully doth view
　　The sight which makes supposèd terror true.　　455

Wrapped and confounded in a thousand fears,
Like to a new-killed bird she trembling lies.
She dares not look; yet winking there appears
Quick-shifting antics, ugly in her eyes.
Such shadows are the weak brain's forgeries,　　460
　　Who, angry that the eyes fly from their lights,
　　In darkness daunts them with more dreadful sights.

His hand that yet remains upon her breast –
Rude ram to batter such an ivory wall –
May feel her heart (poor citizen) distressed,　　465
Wounding itself to death, rise up and fall,
Beating her bulk, that his hand shakes withal.
　　This moves in him more rage and lesser pity,
　　To make the breach and enter this sweet city.

First like a trumpet doth his tongue begin　　470
To sound a parley to his heartless foe,
Who o'er the white sheet peers her whiter chin,
The reason of this rash alarm to know,

455 true] trew Q1; rue Q6+　　472 Who] Q1; When Q4

451 **ghastly sprite** ghostly spirit.
453 **taking** (1) apprehension, (mis)taking, (2) agitation; compare *Lear* 3.4.59–60: 'Bless thee from whirlwinds, star-blasting, and taking.'
454 **heedfully** cautiously.
455 **supposèd** imagined.
456 **confounded** confused.
458 **winking** her eyes being closed.
459 **Quick-shifting** Quickly changing.
459 **antics** grotesque images. Antics were formal representations in a play or pageant – hence 'Quick-shifting', which brings the sense of a rapid succession of stage effects and elusiveness of impressions. See *LLL* 5.1.111–12: 'delightful ostentation, or show, or pageant, or antic'.
460 **shadows** images. A 'shadow' can be the reflection of a solid object (as in *Ven.* 162), but here the emphasis is on distortion and insubstantiality.
461 **from their lights** from their stations (the eyes are seen as the guardians of light).

464 **ram** battering ram.
466 **Wounding . . . death** i.e. the heart seems to be hurling itself against the 'walls' of the body in its agitation.
467 **bulk** A 'bulk' may be a part of a building which juts out, as in the stall-like structure in front of a shop (see *Cor.* 2.1.210–11: 'stalls, bulks, windows / Are smother'd up'). Since his hand is specifically on her breast, this meaning fits the terms of the body-building analogy more precisely than glossing 'bulk' simply as 'body'.
467 **shakes withal** shakes with (i.e. her heaving breast causes his hand to shake).
469 **make the breach** make a breach in the wall.
471 **parley** discussion of terms.
471 **heartless** lacking courage.
472 **peers** (1) lets peep out, (2) lets appear.
473 **rash** sudden.

Which he by dumb demeanour seeks to show;
But she with vehement prayers urgeth still   475
Under what colour he commits this ill.

Thus he replies: 'The colour in thy face,
That even for anger makes the lily pale
And the red rose blush at her own disgrace,
Shall plead for me and tell my loving tale.   480
Under that colour am I come to scale
    Thy never-conquered fort. The fault is thine,
    For those thine eyes betray thee unto mine.

'Thus I forestall thee, if thou mean to chide:
Thy beauty hath ensnared thee to this night,   485
Where thou with patience must my will abide,
My will that marks thee for my earth's delight,
Which I to conquer sought with all my might;
    But as reproof and reason beat it dead,
    By thy bright beauty was it newly bred.   490

'I see what crosses my attempt will bring,
I know what thorns the growing rose defends,
I think the honey guarded with a sting,
All this beforehand counsel comprehends.
But Will is deaf, and hears no heedful friends;   495
    Only he hath an eye to gaze on Beauty,
    And dotes on what he looks, 'gainst law or duty.

487 marks] markes Q1; makes Q4   492 what] Q1; that Q4

474 by . . . demeanour by silent expression.
475 vehement earnest, beseeching.
476 colour (1) pretext, (2) military colour, banner (as in the military imagery of 471–2; see also 481).
478–9 The conceits adopt the love poetry convention of endowing flowers with personal emotions as a tribute to the beloved; but the choice of feelings carefully matches the theme, since anger and shame are precisely what Lucrece is destined to experience.
480 loving tale tale of love.
482–3 The . . . mine, i.e. the beauty of her eyes has made him lust for her.
486 will lust.
487 marks thee singles you out.
487 earth's delight Tarquin chooses paradise on earth, deliberately forgoing his chance of heaven.

488 Which i.e. his will.
489 reproof censure, shame.
490 bright beauty Lucrece is compared to the sun and its power of fructification (see *Ven.* 1020n; and below 1837n)
490 newly anew.
491 crosses (1) obstacles, (2) misfortunes.
492 defends A plural verb inflected in '-s'; choice is possibly determined by the noun phrase 'what thorns' (see Abbott §333 and §337).
493 think . . . guarded realise . . . is guarded.
494 counsel thought, deliberation (as in taking legal counsel).
495 heedful i.e. counselling caution.
496 Only . . . hath He has only.
497 what . . . looks what he looks on; for the ellipsis see Abbott (§394), who remarks that in relative clauses the preposition is often not repeated.

'I have debated even in my soul
What wrong, what shame, what sorrow I shall breed;
But nothing can affection's course control   500
Or stop the headlong fury of his speed.
I know repentant tears ensue the deed,
    Reproach, disdain, and deadly enmity;
    Yet strive I to embrace mine infamy.'

This said, he shakes aloft his Roman blade,   505
Which, like a falcon tow'ring in the skies,
Coucheth the fowl below with his wings' shade,
Whose crooked beak threats if he mount he dies:
So under his insulting falchion lies
    Harmless Lucretia, marking what he tells   510
    With trembling fear, as fowl hear falcons' bells.

'Lucrece', quoth he, 'this night I must enjoy thee.
If thou deny, then force must work my way;
For in thy bed I purpose to destroy thee.
That done, some worthless slave of thine I'll slay,   515
To kill thine honour with thy life's decay;
    And in thy dead arms do I mean to place him,
    Swearing I slew him, seeing thee embrace him.

---

506 falcon] Faulcon Q1   509 falchion] Fauchion Q1–6

500–1 Compare Sidney (*AS* 21.5–6); 'That Plato I read for nought, but if he tame / Such coltish gyres', which refers to *Phaedrus* 254.

500 affection passion (see *Ven.* 387n).

505 Roman blade The epithet perhaps serves to emphasise his betrayal of character and nobility since he lends the sword to an ignoble purpose.

506 falcon With a play on falchion (509); the quarto reading is 'Faulcon / Fauchion'.

507 Coucheth Makes lie close.

508 crooked curved (like a sword).

508 threats threatens.

508 if that if.

509 insulting (1) insolent, (2) threatening (compare *Ven.* 550n and *3H6* 1.3.12–14: 'So looks the pent-up lion o'er the wretch / That trembles under his devouring paws, / And so he walks, *insulting* o'er his prey').

510 Harmless (1) Innocent, (2) Helpless.

510 tells says.

513 work my way achieve my aim.

514 purpose propose (i.e. threaten).

514 destroy thee i.e. he threatens to kill her if she resists. This rather than to rape or violate is the meaning of 'destroy'. (See 'dead arms', 517).

515 slave . . . thine Chaucer has Tarquin refer to a servant of Lucrece's, whereas Painter's Tarquin refers to one of his own. Shakespeare's phrase 'worthless slave of *thine*' perhaps underlines Tarquin's threat to bring dishonour on her entire household, the derisory 'slave' emphasising the infamy his accusation, if believed, would accord her. It would in addition seem more plausible for a lady to be accused of exercising familiarity with a member of her own retinue rather than with the servant of an unexpected visitor. Although as a nobleman Tarquin would not normally travel without company, 'The Argument' indicates that he has come in secret and alone.

516 decay death.

'So thy surviving husband shall remain
The scornful mark of every open eye;   520
Thy kinsmen hang their heads at this disdain,
Thy issue blurred with nameless bastardy;
And thou, the author of their obloquy,
    Shalt have thy trespass cited up in rhymes
    And sung by children in succeeding times.   525

'But if thou yield, I rest thy secret friend;
The fault unknown is as a thought unacted.
A little harm done to a great good end
For lawful policy remains enacted.
The poisonous simple sometime is compacted   530
    In a pure compound; being so applied,
    His venom in effect is purified.

'Then, for thy husband and thy children's sake,
Tender my suit. Bequeath not to their lot
The shame that from them no device can take,   535
The blemish that will never be forgot;
Worse than a slavish wipe, or birth-hour's blot;

---

530 sometime] Q1; sometimes Q4, 7+

520 mark object.
521 disdain disgrace.
522 blurred (1) sullied, blotted (see 222), (2) made obscure (in the sense of losing social caste). Tarquin means by his threat that the 'discovery' of Lucrece in adulterous circumstances would cast doubt on the legitimacy of her living children.
522 nameless Having no legal right to a name.
523 obloquy calumny.
524 cited up in made a subject of.
526 rest remain.
526 secret friend (1) friend who shares your secret, (2) lover.
528–9 Tarquin seems to argue not merely that the end justifies the means (which is the sense of 528 and of *MV* 4.1.216: 'To do a great right, do a little wrong') but that once a morally dubious action has proved its effectiveness it becomes ratified as legislation.
530 poisonous simple The choice of 'poisonous' contradicts the definition of 'simple' as 'a herb with medicinal properties', but the sense (which repeats that of 528–9) is clear enough: in combination with other elements its noxious properties become good (532); 'simple' (single)

plays antithetically on 'compound', which becomes 'pure' as it is put together ('compacted').
532 in effect in its effect.
534 Tender Grant.
535 device contrivance, means (possibly heraldic; see 537n and Tarquin's earlier speculations at 204–10).
537 slavish wipe This probably means a scar or mark sustained by a low-class person; 'slavish' is more likely to be figurative than literal (compare the force of 'slave' in 515), and so if 'branding' is meant by 'wipe' it probably implies the punishment inflicted on a felon (with appropriate connotations of contumely). However, Malone's reading of 'wipe' as 'the brand with which slaves were marked' would apply to the 'rogues, vagabonds, and sturdy beggars' of both Edward VI's and Elizabeth's reigns, since in an effort to limit vagrancy such persons were branded on the shoulder with an 'R' and handed over as bondmen to anybody who was prepared to take them (see under 'Charity', *Enc. Brit.*, eleventh edn, 1910–11, V, 879a).
537 birth . . . blot unsightly birthmark. Wyndham unconvincingly interprets it as an heraldic mark of illegitimacy.

For marks descried in men's nativity
Are nature's faults, not their own infamy.'

Here with a cockatrice' dead-killing eye 540
He rouseth up himself, and makes a pause;
While she, the picture of pure piety,
Like a white hind under the gripe's sharp claws,
Pleads, in a wilderness where are no laws,
To the rough beast that knows no gentle right, 545
Nor aught obeys but his foul appetite.

But when a black-faced cloud the world doth threat,
In his dim mist th'aspiring mountains hiding,
From earth's dark womb some gentle gust doth get,
Which blow these pitchy vapours from their biding, 550
Hind'ring their present fall by this dividing;
So his unhallowed haste her words delays,
And moody Pluto winks while Orpheus plays.

Yet, foul night-waking cat, he doth but dally,
While in his hold-fast foot the weak mouse panteth; 555

---

543 under] Q1; beneath Q6+

538 descried discovered.
540 cockatrice . . . eye The cockatrice or basilisk is a mythical creature whose stare is deadly. It was supposedly hatched from the egg of a cock, and heraldry gives it a cock's head, wings, claws, and the barbed tail of a serpent. (The verb 'rouseth up' in 541 may equally describe the action of a cock with its hackles raised or a snake about to strike.) Cockatrice was also an Elizabethan term for a prostitute, and the sexual slant must not be forgotten here. The invocation of a mythical being to convey the frightening power of lust emphasises that Tarquin is transformed from his normal condition into something strange and unrecognisable.
543 white hind Petrarch made the hind a symbol of purity in his sonnet 'Una candida cerva' (*rime* 190), which Wyatt translated as 'Whoso list to hunt I know where is an hind.'
543 gripe griffin. The choice of creature is probably determined by wordplay, i.e. sharp *grip*ping claws. Some editors prefer to interpret 'gripe' as 'eagle' or 'vulture'; but the latter does not prey on living animals, and the mythical griffin is at home here with the cockatrice.
544 wilderness The presence of mythical creatures gives a special sense to 'wilderness'; compare the account of the woman and the dragon in Rev. 12.1–6.

545 rough beast See 544n.
545 gentle noble (see 569).
548 aspiring high-aiming.
549 See *Ven.* 1046–7n.
549 doth get is born.
550 blow The form is possibly subjunctive, used indefinitely after the relative (see Abbott §367); see also 'lie', 1342.
550 pitchy thick-black.
551 present fall immediate descent.
551 by . . . dividing by separating them from their target ('the world').
552 delays Another case of inflected '-s' with a plural subject; see Abbott §333.
553 moody (1) angry, (2) melancholic (see 1602). Orpheus charmed Pluto (the god of the pagan hell) with the music he played on his lyre, and as a reward he was allowed to take his wife Eurydice back with him to the world of the living on condition that he did not turn and look at her during the journey. He failed to comply with this requirement and so lost her once more; Pluto's boon turned out to be a mere stay of execution, which is its relevance here.
554 night . . . cat See 307n.
555 hold-fast i.e. that grips firmly.

Her sad behaviour feeds his vulture folly,
A swallowing gulf that even in plenty wanteth.
His ear her prayers admits, but his heart granteth
    No penetrable entrance to her plaining:
    Tears harden lust, though marble wear with raining.   560

Her pity-pleading eyes are sadly fixed
In the remorseless wrinkles of his face;
Her modest eloquence with sighs is mixed,
Which to her oratory adds more grace.
She puts the period often from his place,   565
    And midst the sentence so her accent breaks
    That twice she doth begin ere once she speaks.

She conjures him by high almighty Jove,
By knighthood, gentry, and sweet friendship's oath,
By her untimely tears, her husband's love,   570
By holy human law and common troth,
By heaven and earth, and all the power of both,
    That to his borrowed bed he make retire,
    And stoop to honour, not to foul desire.

Quoth she, 'Reward not hospitality   575
With such black payment as thou hast pretended;
Mud not the fountain that gave drink to thee;
Mar not the thing that cannot be amended.

556 **sad** serious, sober (in antithesis with 'folly').
556 **vulture folly** devouring madness (of lust). Compare *MM* 2.2.173–4: 'Dost thou desire her foully for those things / That make her good?'
557 **wanteth** lacks sustenance.
559 **penetrable entrance** A pleonastic phrase which has caused some bother. Maxwell (citing Franz §124) notes correctly that in Shakespeare '-able' words are often active (conversely see 645, 'uncontrollèd'), and accordingly glosses 'entrance' as 'act of entering' (which *penetrates*) rather than 'entrance which may be penetrated'. But either reading sufficiently serves the sense.
560 **harden lust** make lust more determined. The expression may with the help of 'heart' (558) be prompted by the theological idea of hardening one's heart (compare *Ven.* 378n).
561 **sadly** See 556n.
562 **In** On.
562 **remorseless wrinkles** pitiless frown; 'wrinkles' further connotes age and unregenerate sin, just as 'pity' is associated with the unblemished

condition of a 'naked, new-born babe' (*Mac.* 1.7.21).
565 **period** full stop (point at which a pause is expected).
566 **accent** speech.
568 **conjures** implores.
569 **gentry** nobility.
570 **untimely** inopportune (having no good cause).
571 **holy . . . troth** i.e. the marriage vows.
573 **make retire** withdraw (the expression is also military and applies the imagery of 295ff.).
574 **stoop** submit. 'Stoop to honour' is paradoxical. Note also the antithesis of 'honour' and 'foul desire' produced by syllepsis.
576 **pretended** offered.
577 Compare *Tit.* 5.2.170: 'Here stands the spring whom you have stained with mud.' The expression is proverbial (see *ODEP*, p. 189 and Tilley D345). In its stricter appeal to morality, *Lucrece* generally makes greater use of proverbial wisdom than does *Venus and Adonis*.

End thy ill aim before thy shoot be ended.
He is no woodman that doth bend his bow 580
To strike a poor unseasonable doe.

'My husband is thy friend: for his sake spare me;
Thyself art mighty: for thine own sake leave me;
Myself a weakling: do not then ensnare me;
Thou look'st not like deceit: do not deceive me. 585
My sighs like whirlwinds labour hence to heave thee.
  If ever man were moved with woman's moans,
  Be movèd with my tears, my sighs, my groans;

'All which together, like a troubled ocean,
Beat at thy rocky and wrack-threat'ning heart, 590
To soften it with their continual motion;
For stones dissolved to water do convert.
  O, if no harder than a stone thou art,
  Melt at my tears and be compassionate!
  Soft pity enters at an iron gate. 595

'In Tarquin's likeness I did entertain thee.
Hast thou put on his shape to do him shame?
To all the host of heaven I complain me.
Thou wrong'st his honour, wound'st his princely name.
Thou art not what thou seem'st; and if the same, 600

579 **End . . . ended** i.e. put down your bow before you shoot and hit the target. The sentence is thus constructed for the effect of epanalepsis (the same word at each end of the phrase).
579 **ill** mistaken.
579 **shoot** act of shooting. Malone ingeniously prefers 'suit' and argues that the text is wrong; he backs down slightly under pressure from Steevens (Malone²) but still insists on a play on words. An echo is possible, but more likely at a subliminal rather than intentional level.
580 **woodman** huntsman.
581 **unseasonable** i.e. not in season (compare 'untimely', 570).
583 **mighty** socially powerful, high-ranking.
585 **look'st . . . deceit** Ironic, because deceit ('deception') never resembles itself.
586 **heave** Compare 413.
588 Again an ironic plea, since it is conventionally erotic love, not chastity, that speaks in this fashion.

589–95 These lines have distinct though separate echoes of Matt. 7. For 589–92, see Matt. 7.25: 'And the raine fell, and the floodes came, and the windes blewe, and beat upon that house, and it fell not: for it was grounded on a rock'; and for 595 (more obliquely), Matt. 7.13: 'Enter in at the streicte gate: for it is the wide gate, and broade way that leadeth to destruction' (Geneva). If the echoes are conscious, then at least one of them is ironic, since the heart of Tarquin is quite the opposite of that of the wise man of the parable. (Compare *Ven.* 983–4n).
592 See 560, 959 and *Ven.* 200.
597 **thou** Possibly an evil spirit which is impersonating Tarquin.
598 **host of heaven** Maxwell remarks the recurrence of the phrase at *Ham.* 1.5.92. The following lines also anticipate Hamlet's disgust at dissimulation and the dishonouring of office.
600 **if the same** if you are what you seem.

Thou seem'st not what thou art, a god, a king;
For kings like gods should govern everything.

'How will thy shame be seeded in thine age
When thus thy vices bud before thy spring?
If in thy hope thou dar'st do such outrage,   605
What dar'st thou not when once thou art a king?
O be rememb'red, no outrageous thing
    From vassal actors can be wiped away;
    Then kings' misdeeds cannot be hid in clay.

'This deed will make thee only loved for fear,   610
But happy monarchs still are feared for love.
With foul offenders thou perforce must bear,
When they in thee the like offences prove.
If but for fear of this, thy will remove;
    For princes are the glass, the school, the book,   615
    Where subjects' eyes do learn, do read, do look.

'And wilt thou be the school where Lust shall learn?
Must he in thee read lectures of such shame?
Wilt thou be glass wherein it shall discern
Authority for sin, warrant for blame,   620

603 seeded] Q1; feeded Q6–7   613 like] Q1; light Q4

601 Tilley M898 lists several examples in Shake-speare and contemporary drama which stress merciful rule as a divine characteristic of kings (see *Tit.* 1.1.117–18: 'Wilt thou draw near the nature of the gods? / Draw near them then in being merciful').
602 govern everything i.e. including unruly impulses.
603 be seeded be full-grown, proliferate.
605 hope expectation (of authority, kingship); compare *Mac.* 1.7.35–6: 'Was the hope drunk / Wherein you dressed yourself?'
606 Compare Malcolm's threat of wickedness: *Mac.* 4.3.77–84 and 91–100.
607 be rememb'red be mindful, remember well.
608 vassal actors slaves who do a deed. Possibly 'vassal' is a subliminal prompt for 'clay' (i.e. 'vessel'), as in Isa. 64.8: 'we are the clay, and thou our potter'. Certainly 'clay' means 'body' or 'span of human life', and the significance of 'cannot . . . clay' is the same as in *JC* 3.2.75–6: 'The evil that men do . . .'
610–16 Shrewd Machiavellian caution (e.g. being 'loved for fear') modulates into an appeal to the

ideal of the philosopher prince (especially in the final couplet), with which Lucrece tries to persuade Tarquin.
611 still always.
611 feared for love Presumably this means that the love such monarchs receive from their subjects makes them all the more feared by anybody thinking of usurping their position. Otherwise, it must mean either that the subjects fear for their safety because they love them, or – if a parallel between the king and God is implied (see 601) – they fear to prove unworthy of such a lovable ruler. Even in the paradoxical terms consistently employed by the poem it makes no sense for a subject to fear a monarch simply because he loves him.
613 prove experience.
614 will remove See 243n.
615–16 Compare *2H4* 2.3.31–2: 'He was the mark and glass, copy and book / That fashioned others.'
618 lectures i.e. lessons that are read (Lat. *lectus* noun participle, 'reading').
620 blame blameworthy behaviour.

To privilege dishonour in thy name?
Thou back'st reproach against long-living laud,
And mak'st fair reputation but a bawd.

'Hast thou command? By him that gave it thee,
From a pure heart command thy rebel will;   625
Draw not thy sword to guard iniquity,
For it was lent thee all that brood to kill.
Thy princely office how canst thou fulfil,
    When patterned by thy fault foul Sin may say
    He learned to sin, and thou didst teach the way?   630

'Think but how vile a spectacle it were
To view thy present trespass in another.
Men's faults do seldom to themselves appear;
Their own transgressions partially they smother.
This guilt would seem death-worthy in thy brother.   635
    O how are they wrapped in with infamies
    That from their own misdeeds askance their eyes!

'To thee, to thee, my heaved-up hands appeal,
Not to seducing lust, thy rash relier.
I sue for exiled majesty's repeal;   640
Let him return, and flatt'ring thoughts retire.
His true respect will prison false desire,

---

630 to sin] Q1; no sin Q4   639 seducing] Q1; reducing Q4   639 relier] Q1; reply Q6 +

622 **back'st** (1) support, (2) bet on.
622 **long-living laud** enduring praise.
624 **command** power of command (including self-control).
624 **him . . . it** i.e. God (for the periphrasis see 347n).
625 **pure heart . . . rebel will** If 'will' equals 'lust' (as in 486) then the line is neatly antithetical.
627 **all . . . brood** i.e. 'iniquity'. The image expresses vividly the idea of multitudes of sins being hatched by the act of lustful procreation. Shakespeare may be recalling Spenser's evocation of *Errour's* 'scattred brood' (*FQ* 1.1.25).
629 **patterned . . . fault** following your bad example.
634 **partially** i.e. in partiality to themselves.
634 **smother** conceal (see *Ven.* 1035n).
636 **wrapped . . . infamies** enveloped or submerged in notorious deeds. The line has something of Macbeth's 'I am in blood / Stepped in so far'

(*Mac.* 3.4.135–6).
637 **askance** avert. Abbott (p. 5) quotes this example to show how 'almost any part of speech can be used as any other part of speech' (compare the usage of 'askance' in *Ven.* 342).
638 **heaved-up** lifted in supplication (compare 111). Again, the gesture is probably recognisably theatrical (see *Ven.* 1059n).
639 **rash relier** i.e. 'lust which you rashly rely on' (Prince). Schmidt, less plausibly, suggests 'Lust which confides too rashly in thy present disposition and does not foresee its necessary change'.
640 **sue** plead.
640 **repeal** recall.
641 **flatt'ring** i.e. false, sycophantic.
641 **retire** withdraw (in the military sense).
642 **true respect** (1) true authority, (2) concern for truth (see 201n).
642 **prison** imprison.

And wipe the dim mist from thy doting eyne,
That thou shalt see thy state, and pity mine.'

'Have done', quoth he, 'my uncontrollèd tide   645
Turns not, but swells the higher by this let.
Small lights are soon blown out; huge fires abide,
And with the wind in greater fury fret.
The petty streams that pay a daily debt
    To their salt sovereign with their fresh falls' haste,   650
    Add to his flow, but alter not his taste.'

'Thou art', quoth she, 'a sea, a sovereign king,
And lo, there falls into thy boundless flood
Black lust, dishonour, shame, misgoverning,
Who seek to stain the ocean of thy blood.   655
If all these petty ills shall change thy good,
    Thy sea within a puddle's womb is hearsèd,
    And not the puddle in thy sea dispersèd.

'So shall these slaves be king, and thou their slave;
Thou nobly base, they basely dignified;   660
Thou their fair life, and they thy fouler grave;
Thou loathèd in their shame, they in thy pride.
The lesser thing should not the greater hide:
    The cedar stoops not to the base shrub's foot,
    But low shrubs wither at the cedar's root.   665

---

649 petty] Q1; pretty Q6 +

645 **uncontrollèd** uncontrollable.
646 **let** impediment, obstacle (see 328n).
648 **fret** rage.
650 **their . . . sovereign** the sea. Tarquin means that attempts to buy off lust with energetic demonstrations of innocence ('fresh falls' haste') only quicken its 'flow' (determination) without changing its nature ('taste'). There is a play on 'salt' as (1) tax, tribute (with the further effect of 'tributary', as in *Ven.* 1045), and (2) lust (compare *Ant.* 2.1.20–1: 'But all the charms of love, / *Salt* Cleopatra, soften thy wan'd lip').
652 **a sea . . . king** In this stanza Lucrece appropriates and redeploys Tarquin's argument at 649–51. Note her careful recuperation of 'falls' (653) and 'petty' (656) for her own rhetorical purpose.
656 **good** goodness, nobility.
657 **puddle's womb** i.e. the tiny centre of a puddle.
657 **hearsèd** enclosed (as in a coffin – producing an antithetical tomb–womb effect with 'womb'.

Compare *Son.* 86.3–4: 'That did my ripe thoughts in my brain inhearse / Making their tomb the womb wherein they grew').
659 **these slaves** i.e. 'the petty ills' of 656.
662 **their shame** shame which really belongs to them.
662 **they . . . pride** while they enjoy your majesty. This is another example of verb ellipsis (Abbott §395): the antithetical structure requires that the missing verb be understood as the opposite and not the repetition of 'loathèd'.
664 **cedar . . . foot** Clearly proverbial (Tilley C208), and possibly, according to Maxwell, going back to the description of the wisdom of Solomon in 1 Kings 4.33: 'And he spake of trees, from the cedar tre that is in Lebanon, even unto hyssope that springeth out of the wall'; Geneva glosses this as 'from the hiest to the lowest'.

'So let thy thoughts, low vassals to thy state' –
'No more', quoth he. 'By heaven, I will not hear thee!
Yield to my love; if not, enforcèd hate,
Instead of love's coy touch, shall rudely tear thee.
That done, despitefully I mean to bear thee   670
    Unto the base bed of some rascal groom,
    To be thy partner in this shameful doom.'

This said, he sets his foot upon the light,
For light and lust are deadly enemies;
Shame folded up in blind concealing night,   675
When most unseen, then most doth tyrannise.
The wolf hath seized his prey, the poor lamb cries,
    Till with her own white fleece her voice controlled
    Entombs her outcry in her lips' sweet fold.

For with the nightly linen that she wears   680
He pens her piteous clamours in her head,
Cooling his hot face in the chastest tears
That ever modest eyes with sorrow shed.
O that prone lust should stain so pure a bed!
    The spots whereof could weeping purify,   685
    Her tears should drop on them perpetually.

But she hath lost a dearer thing than life,
And he hath won what he would lose again.
This forcèd league doth force a further strife;
This momentary joy breeds months of pain;   690
This hot desire converts to cold disdain:

680 nightly] nightlie Q1; mighty Q6–7   684 prone] Q1; proud Q4; fowle Q6 +

668 enforcèd enforcing (an example of the past participle used actively).
669 coy modest.
670 despitefully maliciously.
671 rascal low-born, ill-bred. Words such as 'villain', 'slave', 'rascal', 'churl' are used to equate petty criminality with low social status.
672 doom (1) fate, (2) judgement (in addition, the 'shameful' circumstances of her death will find her guilty of immodesty).
678 controlled overcome, stifled (see 448n). The meaning is that her voice, being gagged, prevents *itself* from crying out.
679 fold A play is likely on (1) the shape of her

lips, and (2) sheep-fold (continued in 'pens', 681).
680 nightly linen Eithier 'bedclothes' or 'smock'. The main point of the phrase, which has occasioned much speculation, is that it supports the analogy of Tarquin and Lucrece to a wolf and lamb ('white fleece' may initially be prompted by 'white sheet', 472, though it may also refer to a smock). See supplementary note.
684 prone (1) eager, (2) prostrate, face downwards.
689 forcèd league union enforced by rape; 'league' is used for 'marriage' in 383.
690–1 Compare *Son.* 129.

Pure Chastity is rifled of her store,
And Lust the thief far poorer than before.

Look as the full-fed hound or gorgèd hawk,
Unapt for tender smell or speedy flight,   695
Make slow pursuit, or altogether balk
The prey wherein by nature they delight,
So surfeit-taking Tarquin fares this night:
    His taste delicious, in digestion souring,
    Devours his will that lived by foul devouring.   700

O deeper sin than bottomless conceit
Can comprehend in still imagination!
Drunken Desire must vomit his receipt
Ere he can see his own abomination.
While Lust is in his pride, no exclamation   705
    Can curb his heat or rein his rash desire,
    Till like a jade Self-will himself doth tire.

And then with lank and lean discoloured cheek,
With heavy eye, knit brow, and strengthless pace,
Feeble Desire, all recreant, poor and meek,   710
Like to a bankrupt beggar wails his case.
The flesh being proud, Desire doth fight with Grace,
    For there it revels, and when that decays,
    The guilty rebel for remission prays.

692 **store** possession (i.e. chastity is deprived of itself).

694 **Look as** Just as.

695 **tender smell** i.e. the delicate operation of finding the scent of the game.

696 **balk** let go (intentionally).

698 **surfeit-taking** indulging pleasure to excess.

699–700 The elliptical nature of the sentence – partly the result of the epanalepsis of 700 (see 579n) – makes it difficult to account for the relation of its parts grammatically; but the sense is that delicious taste gives way to unpleasantness of digestion, which in turn quite removes, or consumes, his lustful appetite ('will'), which had lived for its own horrible satisfaction.

701 **bottomless conceit** unfathomable depth of imagining. 'Bottomless' perhaps suggests the infernal nature of such an imagination.

702 **in still imagination** in imagination alone.

703 **his receipt** what it has consumed.

704 **abomination** disgusting nature.

705 **Lust . . . pride** See 297n ('heat', at 706, is particularly apposite).

705 **exclamation** outcry.

706 **rash** headstrong.

707 **jade** (1) worn-out horse, (2) loose woman.

707 **Self-will** the urge to indulge one's lust.

708–711 These lines strike a medieval or Spenserian note in their personification of lust's aftermath as wastage (or moral and physical bankruptcy as at 711).

708 **lank and lean** A common hendiadys for 'shrunken' or 'withered' (*OED* sv A. *adj.* 1a cites Dekker (1603): 'In the lean arms of lank necessity').

710 **recreant** resigned, cowardly.

712 **flesh . . . proud** i.e. being in full vigour, perhaps with implications of penile arousal: see 297n (and 705).

712 **Grace** See 246n.

713 **there** in the flesh.

713 **that** the flesh.

713 **decays** dies, falls.

714 **remission** forgiveness, release from sin or cancellation of the debt of sin, thus playing on 'bankrupt').

So fares it with this fault-full lord of Rome, 715
Who this accomplishment so hotly chasèd;
For now against himself he sounds this doom,
That through the length of times he stands disgracèd.
Besides, his soul's fair temple is defacèd,
 To whose weak ruins muster troops of cares, 720
 To ask the spotted princess how she fares.

She says her subjects with foul insurrection
Have battered down her consecrated wall,
And by their mortal fault brought in subjection
Her immortality, and made her thrall 725
To living death and pain perpetual;
 Which in her prescience she controllèd still,
 But her foresight could not forestall their will.

Ev'n in this thought through the dark night he stealeth,
A captive victor that hath lost in gain; 730
Bearing away the wound that nothing healeth,
The scar that will despite of cure remain;
 Leaving his spoil perplexed in greater pain.

---

715 fault-full faultful, sinful. Q1's spelling conveys more graphically than the modern 'faultful' the impression of someone's being burdened with sin.

716 accomplishment aim (i.e. the thing he wished to accomplish).

717 sounds . . . doom 'proclaims this judgment (as with a trumpet)' (Prince).

719–23 The imagery corresponds to that at 439–48 which depicts Lucrece as under siege: a further essential point of correspondence is that Tarquin's temple is depicted as female, as if in the self-assault that takes place morally with the rape Tarquin violates his own inner Lucrece.

719 soul's . . . temple innermost soul. The distinction between soul and innermost soul is not an empty one, since the mind, sometimes referred to as the soul, was the foremost of *six* senses in contemporary Neoplatonist philosophy. The 'fair temple', which is closest to God, reflects the meditative part of the soul as compared to its perceiving or apprehending part, which is counted as one of the senses. (Lever finds a Pauline echo in 'Know ye not that ye are the temple of God, and that the spirit of God dwelleth in you?' – 1 Cor. 3.16.)

721 the . . . princess the defiled soul.

722 her subjects i.e. the will – or that part of the mind or soul which is inclined to lust. This is a more precise distinction than 'bodily senses' (see 719n for the mind as one of the senses).

723 consecrated wall i.e. the wall of the temple (the image of rape – see 464 – superimposes itself on that of rebellion).

724 mortal deadly (sinful).

727–8 The difference between the soul, which has foreknowledge ('prescience') of danger, and the will (which has not) makes the soul superior and dominant overall, but not sufficiently to prevent the will's mutiny. The distinction borrows from the theological concept of God's foreknowledge of man's will to fall, with the difference that God could prevent such a fall if he chose but prefers to allow man to act freely.

729 in this thought i.e. the consciousness of his action and its moral consequences.

730 Possibly an echo of Ovid, *Fasti* 2.811: 'Quid victor gaudes? haec te victoria perdet' ('Why rejoice, victor? This conquest is your ruin'); see also 688.

733 his spoil The violated Lucrece, who resembles the 'spotted princess' at 721; see 719–23n.

733 perplexed (1) i.e. deeply disturbed in mind, (2) enmeshed (Lat. 'woven').

She bears the load of lust he left behind,
And he the burden of a guilty mind.   735

He like a thievish dog creeps sadly thence;
She like a wearied lamb lies panting there.
He scowls, and hates himself for his offence;
She, desperate, with her nails her flesh doth tear.
He faintly flies, sweating with guilty fear;   740
     She stays, exclaiming on the direful night;
     He runs, and chides his vanished loathed delight.

He thence departs a heavy convertite;
She there remains a hopeless castaway.
He in his speed looks for the morning light;   745
She prays she never may behold the day:
'For day', quoth she, 'night's scapes doth open lay,
     And my true eyes have never practised how
     To cloak offences with a cunning brow.

'They think not but that every eye can see   750
The same disgrace which they themselves behold;
And therefore would they still in darkness be,
To have their unseen sin remain untold;
For they their guilt with weeping will unfold,

---

752 be] Q1; lie Q6+

734 **load . . . lust** The phrase signifies not only
the physical violation but the weight of guilt associated with it (although the following line states that
he takes his guilt away with him, Lucrece's subsequent state of mind suggests that he has imparted
some of it to her – see 744n).

739 Possibly in anger at her own beauty, which
has 'betrayed' her; see 1471–2.

740 **faintly** i.e. fainting with fear.

741 **exclaiming on** crying out against (see
705n).

742 **vanished . . . delight** Again, an echo of
Son. 129.

743 **heavy convertite** sad penitent, 'convertite'
here means one seeking reform from sin rather than
a convert to a religious way of life.

744 **castaway** lost soul (one who is damned).
See 1 Cor. 9.27: 'But I keep under my body, and
bring it into subjection: lest that by any means,
when I have preached to others, I myself should
be a castaway' (*AV*). Prince finds a 1563 source

in the second book of *Homilies, Passion II*, 419.
The condition of the castaway belongs more properly to Tarquin, but the burden of guilt is, antithetically, being transferred from him to Lucrece.
The degree of her own culpability, as well as the
question whether her eventual suicide is morally
justifiable, are matters which are debated not just
within the poem but also by continuing theological
tradition (see Introduction, pp. 23–4).

747 **scapes** transgressions (probably sexual).
Bush, in 'Notes on Shakespeare's classical mythology', (*PQ* 6 (1927), 301) notes a resemblance to *FQ*
(1590), 3.4.59.1: 'For Daye discovers all dishonest
wayes,'

748 **true eyes** i.e. eyes which can only reflect
truth.

749 **offences** as in 747n.

749 **brow** expression.

753 **untold** unrevealed.

754 **unfold** express (as by narration).

And grave, like water that doth eat in steel,   755
Upon my cheeks what helpless shame I feel.'

Here she exclaims against repose and rest,
And bids her eyes hereafter still be blind.
She wakes her heart by beating on her breast,
And bids it leap from thence, where it may find   760
Some purer chest to close so pure a mind.
    Frantic with grief thus breathes she forth her spite
    Against the unseen secrecy of night:

'O comfort-killing Night, image of hell,
Dim register and notary of shame,   765
Black stage for tragedies and murders fell,
Vast sin-concealing chaos, nurse of blame,
Blind muffled bawd, dark harbour for defame!
    Grim cave of death, whisp'ring conspirator
    With close-tongued treason and the ravisher!   770

'O hateful, vaporous and foggy Night,
Since thou art guilty of my cureless crime,

---

755 grave engrave (i.e. her tears which are not with shame will act like a corrosive on her cheeks).

755 water . . . steel i.e. aquafortis (nitric acid).

757 exclaims against accuses (see 741n).

758 still always.

761 chest (1) breast, (2) coffer, casket. 'Purer' refers to the fact that her breast is now part of a violated and corrupted body, but it may imply that, in her view, her breast is innately unfitted to be a receptacle for her heart (see 739n).

761 so . . . mind i.e. the heart (understood in its spiritual aspect). 'Heart', 'mind', and 'soul' are often interchangeable (see 442n).

762 spite vexation. Compare *Ven.* 1133; *OED* cites Sidney's *Arcadia*: 'She ioyned the vexation for her friend, with the spite to see her selfe as she thought rebelliously detained.'

763 secrecy secretiveness, attitude of conspiracy (see 769).

764–70 Bush (p. 153) notes the resemblance to *FQ* 3.4.55ff. Compare also *Mac.* 3.2.46–53.

765 Dim register Night's darkness provides an image of faded ('dim') records.

765 notary recorder.

766 Black . . . tragedies 'Black stage' is probably best explained as being supplementary to 'tragedies', the governing term in the image that contains them both. However, Malone assumes a reference to stage props: 'In our author's time, I believe, the stage was hung with black when

tragedies were performed.' Several editors have followed him, citing *1H6* 1.1.1: 'Hung be the heavens with black, yield day to night.' But this is a line of *verbal* scene-setting which may have little to do with actual practice, just as in *H5* the Prologue acknowledges that more can be realised by the cooperative imagination than the theatre can perform. Besides, the speaker in *1H6* is asking for effects beyond the scope of even an ideal production, i.e. that the sky should blacken and day become night in acknowledgement of the degree of sorrow in the world: the statement is optative rather than directorial or descriptive.

766 fell cruel.

767 sin-concealing . . . nurse of blame Note the antithesis: Night is accused both of hiding sin and yet fostering scandal.

767 chaos shapelessness, disorder. Compare *Rom.* 1.2.179: 'Misshapen chaos of well-seeming forms'. The figure works so that, as chaos precedes creation, the 'sin' that is concealed will be brought forth and *nursed* as 'blame' (calumny).

768 Blind . . . bawd The figure expresses the idea of a pander or go-between who furtively conceals her actions. See Onions for 'blind' meaning concealed or obscure.

770 close-tongued (1) speaking in whispers, cautiously (2) keeping mum.

771 vaporous misty, but perhaps with its secondary meaning of 'vain' or 'insubstantial'.

Muster thy mists to meet the eastern light,
Make war against proportioned course of time:
Or if thou wilt permit the sun to climb   775
    His wonted height, yet ere he go to bed,
    Knit poisonous clouds about his golden head.

'With rotten damps ravish the morning air;
Let their exhaled unwholesome breaths make sick
The life of purity, the supreme fair,   780
Ere he arrive his weary noontide prick;
And let thy musty vapours march so thick
    That in their smoky ranks his smoth'red light
    May set at noon and make perpetual night.

'Were Tarquin Night, as he is but Night's child,   785
The silver-shining queen he would distain;
Her twinkling handmaids too, by him defiled,
Through Night's black bosom should not peep again.
So should I have co-partners in my pain;
    And fellowship in woe doth woe assuage,   790
    As palmers' chat makes short their pilgrimage;

778 rotten] Q1; rotting Q4   782 musty] Q1; misty Q3+   783 ranks] rankes Q1; rackes Q4   786 distain] distaine Q1;
disdaine Q6+   791 palmers' . . . makes] Palmers chat makes Q1; palmers that make Q4, 9; palmers that makers Q6–7;
palmers that makes Q8

774 proportioned . . . time time's regular
progress (which Lucrece wants to halt). The idea
of time's 'proportioned course' is Pythagorean, and
proposes God as a geometer who brought order out
of shapelessness:

being as it was, inconstant, wandering, disorderly, and
unperfect, our ancients were wont to call it infinit, that
is to say undetermined and unfinished: for the forme and
figure is the terme or end of everything that is formed
and shapen; the want whereof made itselfe to be shapeless and disfigured: but after that numbers and proportions came to be imprinted upon the rude and formelesse
matter.'
                    (Plutarch, *Morals*, trans. Philemon Holland,
                    1603; in Heninger, pp. 206–7)

Compare also *Ven.* 120n.
    778 rotten damps vapours (see 771).
    779 exhaled . . . breaths 'Vapours' (see 778n)
were supposed to arise in an unhealthy stomach.
    780 i.e. the sun.
    780 supreme Accented on the first syllable.
    780 fair See 346n.
    781 arrive arrive at.
    781 prick i.e. the mark on the clock or sundial.
Compare *3H6* 1.4.33–4: 'Now Phaëton hath tum-

bled from his car / And made an evening at the
noontide prick.' Lucrece's tone is obviously remote
from the bawdy latent in 297 (see n), though her
disgust with sexuality seems to allow the poem to
play speculatively, through her, on the connection
between 'prick' and 'ravish'.
    785 Night's child i.e. favoured by Night in his
furtive behaviour (perhaps also echoing the ideas
latent in 767).
    786 The . . . queen The moon.
    786 distain defile ('silver' attracts '-stain').
    787 twinkling handmaids The stars; for the
stars as 'Diana's waiting-women' see *Tro.* 5.2.91.
    788 Night's . . . bosom This compound image
of mammary darkness facilitates a dual sense of the
stars as both eyes and nipples.
    790 Proverbial; see *ODEP* C571, which also gives
Lyly: 'In miserie Euphues it is a great comfort to
have a companion' (1579).
    791 palmers' . . . pilgrimage Those who had
been on a pilgrimage to the Holy Land returned
bearing a palm leaf. The casual anachronism indicates that Shakespeare places the requirements of
theme (in this case comfort in misery) over those
of historical accuracy.

'Where now I have no one to blush with me,
To cross their arms and hang their heads with mine,
To mask their brows and hide their infamy;
But I alone, alone must sit and pine,   795
Seasoning the earth with showers of silver brine,
    Mingling my talk with tears, my grief with groans,
    Poor wasting monuments of lasting moans.

'O Night, thou furnace of foul reeking smoke,
Let not the jealous Day behold that face   800
Which underneath thy black all-hiding cloak
Immodestly lies martyred with disgrace.
Keep still possession of thy gloomy place,
    That all the faults which in thy reign are made
    May likewise be sepulch'red in thy shade.   805

'Make me not object to the tell-tale Day:
The light will show, charactered in my brow,
The story of sweet chastity's decay,
The impious breach of holy wedlock vow.

807 will show] Q1; shall show Q5+   807 my brow] Q1; thy brow Q5   809 breach] Q1; breath Q4

793 Contemporary directions for players (to which this seems to allude) sometimes recommend the same gestures for grief as for love-melancholy:

The other parts of action, is in ye gesture, wch must be various, as required; as in a sorrowfull parte, ye head must hang downe . . . in an amorous, closed eies, hanging down lookes, & crossed armes.
(from the Preface to *The Cyprian Conqueror* (1633); in Gurr, second edn, 1980, p. 99)

794 mask . . . brows The 'brow' denotes the entire expression (as in 749) and not merely the forehead. The theme is disgrace and subterfuge, the face vainly trying to conceal the truth; the image is therefore unlikely to suggest the idea of a hat being pulled over the forehead as a sign of *grief* (see *Mac.* 4.3.208), which some editors favour on the assumption that it is a theatrical gesture (see 793n).

796 See *LC* 17.

798 wasting monuments decaying monuments (paradoxical); 'monuments' further seems a diminutive of the long-vowelled 'moans', i.e. 'moans' endure longer.

799 O Night See Chaucer, *TC* 3.1429–42 and *FQ* 3.4.55–9 (Bush, p. 153). The apostrophes to

Night, Opportunity (876ff.), and Time (925ff.) follow the classical and medieval pattern which is based on oratory (see Bush, pp. 153–4): a speaker (as Lucrece here) may permit himself digressions which embellish or otherwise add substance to the main theme. In English verse the practice occurs often within the complaint genre, to which *Lucrece* belongs (see Introduction, p. 38); but Venus, when in a plaintive mood, speaks similarly as she exclaims on Death (see *Ven.* 931ff.).

800 jealous watchful.

801 all-hiding cloak Compare *Mac.* 1.5.53: 'Nor heaven peep through the blanket of the dark'.

802 martyred Q1 'martired'; possibly a portmanteau of 'marred' and 'attired' (or 'tired'), which would give 'Immodestly' the sense of improper dress ('cloak' contributing), and so make an effective rather than redundant pleonasm out of the addition of 'Immodestly' and 'disgrace'.

805 sepulch'red Accent on second syllable.

806 object object of view.

807 charactered engraven, written. Accent on the second syllable.

808 decay ruin, perishing ('sweet' perhaps suggests the withering of a flower).

Yea, the illiterate, that know not how   810
   To cipher what is writ in learnèd books,
   Will quote my loathsome trespass in my looks.

'The nurse to still her child will tell my story,
And fright her crying babe with Tarquin's name.
The orator to deck his oratory   815
Will couple my reproach to Tarquin's shame.
Feast-finding minstrels, tuning my defame,
   Will tie the hearers to attend each line,
   How Tarquin wrongèd me, I Collatine.

'Let my good name, that senseless reputation,   820
For Collatine's dear love be kept unspotted.
If that be made a theme for disputation,
The branches of another root are rotted,
And undeserved reproach to him allotted,
   That is as clear from this attaint of mine   825
   As I ere this was pure to Collatine.

'O unseen shame, invisible disgrace!
O unfelt sore, crest-wounding private scar!
Reproach is stamped in Collatinus' face,
And Tarquin's eye may read the mot afar,   830
How he in peace is wounded, not in war.

811 **cipher** read (continuing the theme of 'charactered').

812 **quote** note, mark (from ME, meaning 'mark with numbers'; compare Lat. 'quot' = 'how many'); 'quote' is kin to 'cipher' in its sense of interpreting signs, whether letters or numbers.

812 **trespass** See 524 and 632.

815 **deck** decorate, embellish.

816 **reproach** disgrace.

817 **Feast-finding** i.e. itinerant minstrels who turn up at or are hired for a feast. The expression may carry the extra implication that they find a large audience for their tale.

817 **tuning . . . defame** singing the story of my infamy.

818 **tie** compel ('tie' is from the instrumental strings implicit in 'tuning').

820 **senseless reputation** reputation for being without sensual (or lustful) inclination. It is possible, but unlikely from the tone, that Lucrece is further playing on 'senseless' to mean that there is no foundation to her 'good name'.

822 **made . . . disputation** brought into question.

823 **another root** i.e. Collatine's lineage. The image is partly supplied by 'disputation' (formerly a speech made by a public orator): 'disputations' were divided into members (or 'branches').

824 **reproach** shame, disgrace (see 816n).

825 **attaint . . . mine** (1) disgrace, conviction (of a crime), (2) infection. The possessive 'of mine' may suggest that Lucrece feels complicity in the offence committed against her (see 734n).

828 **unfelt sore** i.e. a wound which Collatine is unaware of (the phrase is an oxymoron as is 'private scar').

828 **crest-wounding** i.e. injuring the family crest or honour (as depicted in heraldry). Although the idea is strictly of an indiscernible shame borne by the crest, the latter's transformation into the palpable shame of the horns of cuckoldry is also suggested.

829 **Reproach** Disgrace.

830 **mot** motto, device, word (perhaps punning on 'mote' as 'blemish').

830 **afar** However distant, Tarquin will always know the truth about Collatine's shame.

831 **he** Collatine.

Alas, how many bear such shameful blows,
Which not themselves but he that gives them knows!

'If, Collatine, thine honour lay in me,
From me by strong assault it is bereft;   835
My honey lost, and I a drone-like bee,
Have no perfection of my summer left,
But robbed and ransacked by injurious theft.
    In thy weak hive a wand'ring wasp hath crept,
    And sucked the honey which thy chaste bee kept.   840

'Yet am I guilty of thy honour's wrack;
Yet for thy honour did I entertain him.
Coming from thee, I could not put him back,
For it had been dishonour to disdain him.
Besides, of weariness he did complain him,   845
    And talked of virtue: O unlooked-for evil,
    When virtue is profaned in such a devil!

'Why should the worm intrude the maiden bud?
Or hateful cuckoos hatch in sparrows' nests?
Or toads infect fair founts with venom mud?   850
Or tyrant folly lurk in gentle breasts?
Or kings be breakers of their own behests?
    But no perfection is so absolute
    That some impurity doth not pollute.

'The agèd man that coffers up his gold   855
Is plagued with cramps and gouts and painful fits,

---

836 drone-like worthless. The drone is male, and its function is to impregnate the queen-bee; but Lucrece obviously identifies with its proverbial worthlessness (see Dent D612.1).

837 perfection i.e. the honey which has been stored (or chastity which has been preserved); Lucrece describes chastity as 'sweet' (808).

837 my summer (1) my personal glory, (2) my prime time. Compare the relationship of 'perfection' to 'summer' with that of 'summer' to 'flower' at *Son.* 94.9.

839 weak poorly protected.

841–42 See 239–42n.

841 wrack destruction.

842 entertain him receive him with hospitality.

843 put . . . back refuse him entry.

844 disdain slight.

846 unlooked-for unexpected.

847 profaned violated, desecrated.

848 intrude enter forcibly (*OED* sv *v.* 5, citing this example).

850 See 577.

851 folly wantonness (compare 556). Onions records various contexts which define 'folly' as lewd behaviour (e.g. *Wiv.* 2.2.244, 3.2.35; *Tro.* 5.2.18; *MM* 3.1.90; *Oth.* 5.2.132).

851 gentle nobly born (presuming a virtuous nature), see 545n; 'gentle breasts' antithetically implies the 'tyrant''s hard-heartedness (as in *TN* 5.1.124: 'Live you the marble-breasted tyrant still').

853 absolute complete.

855 coffers . . . gold Baldwin (*Genetics*, p. 135) detects a verbal echo of the Geneva commentary on Luke 12.15:

Christ condemneth the arrogancie of the riche worldelings, who as thogh they had God locked up in their coffres & barnes, set their whole felicitie in their goods, not considering that God gave the life and also can take it away when he will.

855 coffers Places in a coffer or chest

And scarce hath eyes his treasure to behold;
But like still-pining Tantalus he sits,
And useless barns the harvest of his wits,
    Having no other pleasure of his gain   860
    But torment that it cannot cure his pain.

'So then he hath it when he cannot use it,
And leaves it to be mastered by his young,
Who in their pride do presently abuse it.
Their father was too weak, and they too strong   865
To hold their cursèd-blessèd fortune long.
    The sweets we wish for turn to loathèd sours
    Even in the moment that we call them ours.

'Unruly blasts wait on the tender spring;
Unwholesome weeds take root with precious flowers;   870
The adder hisses where the sweet birds sing;
What virtue breeds iniquity devours.
We have no good that we can say is ours,
    But ill-annexèd Opportunity
    Or kills his life or else his quality.   875

'O Opportunity, thy guilt is great:
'Tis thou that execut'st the traitor's treason;

---

859 barns] Q1 barnes; bannes Q6+

('coffers' may be a submerged prompt for 'cough', thus preparing for the line that follows).

858 still-pining always starving.

858 Tantalus See *Ven.* 599n. Erasmus identifies Tantalus as a miser (*Adages*), quoting Horace, *Sat.* 1.1.68ff., in illustration (Baldwin, *Genetics*, pp. 134–5). Baldwin also cites Sidney, 'And damning their own selves to *Tantal's* smart, / Wealth breeding want, more blist, more wretched grow' (*AS* 24.3–4).

859 barns stores. 'Barns' acts as a verb like 'coffers' (see also Geneva quotation under 855n).

859 wits mental powers (used for acquisition). Compare its recurrence at *LC* 161.

862–6 Just as the reference to Tantalus at 858 derives ultimately from Horace's satires, so these lines may owe something to the Roman poet's famous warning to his friend Posthumus about the futility of preserving wealth (*Odes* 2.14, especially lines 25–8).

864 pride (1) prime, youthful vigour, (2) arrogance.

864 presently immediately.

865 strong i.e. headstrong.

867–8 A further echo of *Son.* 129.

867 sours sourings (the only example in Shakespeare of 'sour' as a noun).

869 Compare *Son.* 18.3.

870–1 Compare *Mac.* 1.5.65–6: 'look like th'innocent flower / But be the serpent under it'.

872 An antithetical statement which gains in intensity from the juxtaposition of 'breeds' with 'iniquity', especially since 'iniquity' and 'breed' (or 'brood') are normally associated (as at 626–7).

874 ill-annexèd added to ill effect.

875 Or Either.

875 his . . . his its . . . its.

875 quality nature.

876–924 See 799n; *John* 2.1.574–98 has a similar speech on 'commodity' (Prince).

877 execut'st performs (intensified by the additional idea that traitors are executed *for* treason).

Thou sets the wolf where he the lamb may get;
Whoever plots the sin, thou point'st the season.
'Tis thou that spurn'st at right, at law, at reason;   880
    And in thy shady cell, where none may spy him,
    Sits Sin, to seize the souls that wander by him.

'Thou makest the vestal violate her oath;
Thou blowest the fire when temperance is thawed;
Thou smother'st honesty, thou murth'rest troth;   885
Thou foul abettor, thou notorious bawd!
Thou plantest scandal, and displacest laud:
    Thou ravisher, thou traitor, thou false thief,
    Thy honey turns to gall, thy joy to grief.

'Thy secret pleasure turns to open shame,   890
Thy private feasting to a public fast,
Thy smoothing titles to a ragged name,
Thy sug'red tongue to bitter wormwood taste;
Thy violent vanities can never last.
    How comes it then, vile Opportunity,   895
    Being so bad, such numbers seek for thee?

'When wilt thou be the humble suppliant's friend,
And bring him where his suit may be obtainèd?

879 point'st] poinst Q1; points Q5+; 'point'st *Malone²*   881–2 him . . . him] Q1; her . . . her Q6+   892 smoothing]
Q1; smothering Q6+

878 **sets** The form is preferred to 'set'st' by all
the quartos up to 1632 (the choice is probably for
euphony). See 879n.
879 **point'st** appoints. Q1 has 'poinst' (again
probably for euphony); see Abbott §340. In this
stanza Shakespeare has produced a number of
vocatives with enforced dental endings which he
has chosen to regulate differently: presumably he
retains the full form of 'execut'st' (877) because it
combines appropriately with the sharply alliterated
'traitor's treason'.
879 **season** time which is ripe for action.
881–2 Compare the description of the fiend in
Mammon's cave (*FQ* 2.7.26.5–9).
883–9 The sexual licence associated with opportunity is proverbial: see Tilley O70 and Dent, who
quotes Lyly: 'Opportunity will mate and winn the
coyest she yᵗ is' (*Euphues and his England*, 1580).
883 **vestal . . . oath** See *Ven.* 752n.
884 **blowest the fire** inflame passion. Since the
function of the vestal virgin was to keep the flame
of chastity always alight, the effect of 'fire' here is
to bring out retrospectively and vividly the con-

trasting connotations of 883.
885 **smother'st honesty** The play on 'flame/
fire' continues, since 'honesty' is chastity (as in
Wiv. 4.2.105 and *Oth.* 3.3.384), which resumes the
meaning of 883, and 'smother'st' has the effect of
extinguishing, as in putting out a flame.
885 **troth** truth, fidelity. The archaic form incorporates the sense of 'pledging loyalty' as well as
giving a purer rhyme.
887 **laud** reputation, praiseworthiness (see
622n). *OED sv sb.* 1c cites Gascoigne: 'And by the
lawde of his pretence / His lewdnesse was acquit'
(*Complaynt of Philomene*, 1576).
889 **honey . . . gall** See Tilley H556.
891 **feasting . . . fast** It is tempting with
Kökeritz (167) to regard the two words as homo-
phones, thus making for more interesting wordplay;
but Cercignani (p. 93) is sceptical.
892 **smoothing** flattering (perhaps 'smoothing'
because they trip smoothly off the tongue – note
'sug'red tongue', 893).
894 **vanities** (1) vainglories, futile pursuits,

When wilt thou sort an hour great strifes to end?
Or free that soul which wretchedness hath chainèd?   900
Give physic to the sick, ease to the painèd?
  The poor, lame, blind, halt, creep, cry out for thee,
  But they ne'er meet with Opportunity.

'The patient dies while the physician sleeps;
The orphan pines while the oppressor feeds;   905
Justice is feasting while the widow weeps;
Advice is sporting while infection breeds.
Thou grant'st no time for charitable deeds:
  Wrath, envy, treason, rape, and murder's rages,
  Thy heinous hours wait on them as their pages.   910

'When Truth and Virtue have to do with thee,
A thousand crosses keep them from thy aid:
They buy thy help, but Sin ne'er gives a fee;
He gratis comes, and thou art well apaid,
As well to hear as grant what he hath said.   915
  My Collatine would else have come to me
  When Tarquin did, but he was stayed by thee.

'Guilty thou art of murder and of theft,
Guilty of perjury and subornation,

---

909 murder's rages] murthers rages Q1; murther rages Q6+

(2) empty delights (Malone compares *Rom.* 2.6.9:
'These violent delights have violent ends').
  899 sort appoint.
  902 halt A verb, corresponding to the substantive 'lame'; the line is an example of *correlative* verse.
  905 pines goes hungry.
  905 oppressor The word probably connotes a tyrant confiscating the goods that belong to the children of those whom he has executed (see *Ven.* 797n).
  906 Justice . . . feasting As above, suggesting the wrongful sequestering of goods.
  907 Advice . . . sporting Medical help (including opinion) is idle. Steevens (Malone) proposes a connection with contemporary plague conditions (see *Ven.* 508n).
  908 charitable deeds The reference to 'good works' may indeed conceal a further scepticism, since such undertakings as the corporal acts of mercy had long been regarded as self-serving and lacking in spiritual integrity, having declined to the order of an unspontaneous programme (for

which 'time' would be grudgingly and irregularly set aside). But Shakespeare may equally be touching on the crisis brought about by the failure of public charity (as a result both of the declining administrative power of the municipalities and of the decadence and dissolution of religious houses), the effects of which were evident both before and during much of Elizabeth's reign and eventually necessitated the Poor Law of 1601. As with 907, the indictment, while timeless, may carry specific point.
  909 This line and the stanza as a whole record all of the deadly sins: sloth in 904 and 907, gluttony and covetousness in 905 and 906; 'treason' is the offence of pride (for which Satan fell).
  910 heinous hateful (specifically denoting crimes or criminals).
  912 crosses obstacles (see 491n).
  914 gratis freely (without paying).
  914 apaid (1) paid, (2) satisfied.
  917 stayed prevented.
  919 subornation inducement to perjury.

Guilty of treason, forgery, and shift,   920
Guilty of incest, that abomination:
An accessary by thine inclination
    To all sins past and all that are to come,
    From the creation to the general doom.

'Misshapen Time, copesmate of ugly Night,   925
Swift subtle post, carrier of grisly care,
Eater of youth, false slave to false delight,
Base watch of woes, sin's pack-horse, virtue's snare;
Thou nursest all, and murd'rest all that are:
    O hear me then, injurious shifting Time,   930
    Be guilty of my death, since of my crime.

'Why hath thy servant Opportunity
Betrayed the hours thou gav'st me to repose?
Cancelled my fortunes and enchainèd me
To endless date of never-ending woes?   935
Time's office is to fine the hate of foes,
    To eat up errors by opinion bred,
    Not spend the dowry of a lawful bed.

'Time's glory is to calm contending kings,
To unmask falsehood and bring truth to light,   940

---

920 shift trickery, evasion (hence 'shifty').

922 accessary A three-syllable word, accented on the first.

922 by . . . inclination by your nature.

924 general doom Last Judgement. The idea of this line introduces the apostrophe to time in 925.

925–96 See 799n, and Ovid, *Tristia* 4.6.1ff. (Bush, p. 153).

925 copesmate companion, accomplice.

926 subtle (1) imperceptible, (2) cunning, treacherous (Onions).

926 post messenger.

926 carrier . . . care i.e. time causes aging by heaping up responsibilities.

926 grisly frightful, ghastly.

927 Eater . . . youth See Ovid, *Metam.* 15.234

928 watch . . . woes Either (1) a watch face divided by woes (drawing on the sense of 'misshapen'), or (2) a watchman calling out woefully.

928 sin's pack-horse sin's drudge (time as labour entered human experience as a result of the Fall).

928 virtue's snare i.e. experience eventually

brings innocence ('virtue') to an end.

930 shifting (1) mutable, (2) treacherous (see 920n).

931 my crime Lucrece again appears to assume complicity in the offence which has been committed against her (see 825n).

934 fortunes i.e. the happiness leased by destiny.

935 date duration (possibly with a pun on 'debt').

936 fine (1) bring an end to (compare 939; the verb 'fine' comes from the expression 'in fine', meaning 'in conclusion'), (2) punish, penalise (see 943; also the financial echo in 'spend', 938). Malone's suggestion of 'refine' (i.e. soften) is possible (see 'calm', 939).

937 Truth is traditionally time's daughter (*ODEP*, Tilley T580) and stands revealed when error, resulting from false opinion or gossip, is buried.

938 spend use up wastefully (in the sense, via 'dowry', of being destructive to marriage).

940 See 937n.

To stamp the seal of time in agèd things,
To wake the morn and sentinel the night,
To wrong the wronger till he render right,
  To ruinate proud buildings with thy hours,
  And smear with dust their glitt'ring golden towers;   945

'To fill with worm-holes stately monuments,
To feed oblivion with decay of things,
To blot old books and alter their contents,
To pluck the quills from ancient ravens' wings,
To dry the old oak's sap, and cherish springs,   950
  To spoil antiquities of hammered steel,
  And turn the giddy round of Fortune's wheel;

'To show the beldame daughters of her daughter,
To make the child a man, the man a child,
To slay the tiger that doth live by slaughter,   955
To tame the unicorn and lion wild,
To mock the subtle in themselves beguiled,
  To cheer the ploughman with increaseful crops,
  And waste huge stones with little water-drops.

941 Probably meaning to give age a venerable aspect.

942 sentinel stand watch over.

943 The paronomastic interplay throughout the line constantly modifies the shape of the word 'wrong' until it culminates in its opposite meaning. Malone's fine effort at interpretation should not go unregarded: 'To *punish* by the compunctious visiting of conscience the person who has done an injury to another, till he has made compensation'.

944–5 The idea possibly derives from Horace, *Odes* 1.4.13–14: 'Pallida Mors aequo pulsat pede pauperum tabernas / regumque turris' (Pale death tramples down equally the lodgings of the poor and the towers of kings). See also *Son.* 55.1–4 for close verbal echoes.

944 ruinate thoroughly ruin (the extra syllable makes the action emphatic).

948 alter . . . contents This could mean simply that the effects of time have obscured the contents of the page; or it may refer to the creation of a palimpsest: i.e. a manuscript in which the original words have been written over to form new and different ones.

949 ancient . . . wings The idea of writing in 948 leads on to 'quills' (which were taken from large birds, most often geese) and hence to 'ravens',

which, like the crow, were considered to be long-lived (*PhT* 17).

950 cherish springs i.e. nourish new streams. The idea works in antithesis to 'dry . . . sap' and introduces the variant motif of time's replacing and renewing as well as eroding and destroying. Some eighteenth-century editors, attempting to make the line consistent with the idea of mere ravage as in the preceding examples, emend 'cherish' to 'tarish' (wither) or even 'perish' (Johnson); in the same tradition Taylor emends to 'blemish'. Pooler suggests that 'springs' may mean young oaks (see *Ven.* 656n).

951 hammered steel i.e. particularly resistant.

953 beldame grandmother, elderly woman (the word also means ancestress).

954 man a child i.e. reduce to senility.

956 See Job 39.12–15 for the unicorn's stubbornness, and *FQ* 2.5.10 for the traditionally fierce encounter of the lion and the unicorn.

957 subtle treacherous (see 926n)

957 in . . . beguiled i.e. their treachery proves their own undoing.

958 increaseful fruitful (probably biblical, as in Prov. 3.9).

959 Compare 560, 592, and *Ven.* 200.

'Why work'st thou mischief in thy pilgrimage,   960
Unless thou couldst return to make amends?
One poor retiring minute in an age
Would purchase thee a thousand thousand friends,
Lending him wit that to bad debtors lends.
    O this dread night, wouldst thou one hour come back,   965
    I could prevent this storm and shun thy wrack.

'Thou ceaseless lackey to eternity,
With some mischance cross Tarquin in his flight;
Devise extremes beyond extremity,
To make him curse this cursèd crimeful night;   970
Let ghastly shadows his lewd eyes affright,
    And the dire thought of his committed evil
    Shape every bush a hideous shapeless devil.

'Disturb his hours of rest with restless trances;
Afflict him in his bed with bedrid groans;   975
Let there bechance him pitiful mischances
To make him moan, but pity not his moans.
Stone him with hard'ned hearts harder than stones,
    And let mild women to him lose their mildness,
    Wilder to him than tigers in their wildness.   980

'Let him have time to tear his curlèd hair,
Let him have time against himself to rave,

---

975 bedrid] bedred Q1

960 pilgrimage i.e. time's journey to eternity.
962 poor . . . minute i.e. the restoration of a single minute in which to undo the 'mischief' which has previously occurred in *that minute* (compare 965–6). 'Retire' means 'return' or 'go back' (see *Ven.* 906).
964 wit foresight. The sense is that by equipping 'him' with the judgement not to lend to 'bad debtors', time will prevent him from making the mistake he *has* already made and so enlist him as one of the 'thousand thousand friends'. The request is for time's instruction in avoiding mistakes, not for its teaching by experience.
966 prevent anticipate.
966 shun thy wrack avoid your shipwreck (meaning either the night's own destruction, which includes Lucrece, or the night's destruction of her).
967 ceaseless lackey untiring servant ('lackey' has overtones of contempt); 'ceaseless' also plays on time's incessant progress.
968 cross thwart (see 491, 912, and *Ven.* 734).

971–80 Compare *R3* 1.3.216–26 and 5.3.118ff.
971 ghastly shadows ghostly images.
971 lewd vile, wicked (the range of meaning is greater than that specified in 'lustful').
973 See *MND* 5.1.22.
975 bedrid bedridden (implying a sickness which confines him to bed).
976 pitiful wretched, sad.
978 hard'ned hearts i.e. the hearts of cruel women (as the following line makes clearer). The curse has a biblical echo, as in the story of the Pharaoh whose hardness of heart returns vengefully upon him as various pestilences, including hail (Exod. 9.13–25). See *Ven.* 378n.
979 to him confronted with him.
980 See *3H6* 1.4.137: 'O tiger's heart wrapp'd in a woman's hide!'
981 tear . . . hair Ironic because the hair would have been painfully curled by hot irons (see Ovid, *Amores* 1.14.23–30, and – for evidence that men

Let him have time of Time's help to despair,
Let him have time to live a loathèd slave,
Let him have time a beggar's orts to crave,   985
    And time to see one that by alms doth live
    Disdain to him disdainèd scraps to give.

'Let him have time to see his friends his foes,
And merry fools to mock at him resort;
Let him have time to mark how slow time goes   990
In time of sorrow, and how swift and short
His time of folly and his time of sport;
    And ever let his unrecalling crime
    Have time to wail th'abusing of his time.

'O Time, thou tutor both to good and bad,   995
Teach me to curse him that thou taught'st this ill.
At his own shadow let the thief run mad,
Himself himself seek every hour to kill:
Such wretched hands such wretched blood should spill,
    For who so base would such an office have   1000
    As sland'rous deathsman to so base a slave?

'The baser is he, coming from a king,
To shame his hope with deeds degenerate;
The mightier man, the mightier is the thing
That makes him honoured or begets him hate;   1005
For greatest scandal waits on greatest state.
    The moon being clouded presently is missed,
    But little stars may hide them when they list.

'The crow may bathe his coal-black wings in mire,
And unperceived fly with the filth away;   1010

also subjected their hair to this treatment –
Petrarch, *Letters*, p. 93).

984 slave i.e. a contemptible person, not necessarily a slave by condition.

985 orts scraps (as in 987).

986 one . . . live a beggar.

987 disdainèd scraps An echo of the parable of the rich man and Lazarus (Luke 16. 19–31).

992 folly . . . sport Both words signify 'wantonness' (see 851n).

993 unrecalling irrevocable (see Abbott §372 for '-ing' as a passive participle ending).

996 that to whom.

998 Himself himself See 157 and *Ven.* 161n.

1001 sland'rous deathsman The office of hangman or executioner ('deathsman') carried an ill

('sland'rous') reputation. See *Per.* 4.6.128 and 176 for the contemptuous expression 'common hangman'. ('Sland'rous' performs passively: i.e. attracting slander rather than causing it.)

1003 his hope i.e. what is expected of him (see 605n).

1005 begets him acquires, produces for him; 'begets' carries on the idea of birth and lineage (present also in 'deeds degenerate'). Elyot (*Governour* 2.4) warns against dishonouring one's ancestry by acting ignobly.

1007–8 Compare *Son.* 33 and *Son.* 94.13–14.

1007 presently immediately.

1008 when . . . list whenever they please.

1009–12 See 1007–8n and again *Son.* 94.

But if the like the snow-white swan desire,
The stain upon his silver down will stay.
Poor grooms are sightless night, kings glorious day;
    Gnats are unnoted wheresoe'er they fly,
    But eagles gazed upon with every eye.   1015

'Out idle words, servants to shallow fools,
Unprofitable sounds, weak arbitrators;
Busy yourselves in skill-contending schools,
Debate where leisure serves with dull debators;
To trembling clients be you mediators: 1020
    For me, I force not argument a straw,
    Since that my case is past the help of law.

'In vain I rail at Opportunity,
At Time, at Tarquin, and uncheerful Night;
In vain I cavil with mine infamy,   1025
In vain I spurn at my confirmed despite;
This helpless smoke of words doth me no right.
    The remedy indeed to do me good
    Is to let forth my foul defilèd blood.

'Poor hand, why quiver'st thou at this decree?   1030
Honour thyself to rid me of this shame;

1016 Out] Q1; Our Q5+   **1024** uncheerful] unchearfull Q1; unsearchfull Q5+

1013–14 Compare *Tit.* 4.4.81–5.

1013 sightless invisible (implying they are unnoticed, of no account).

1016–20 Forensic rhetoric as practised in Greek and Roman law provided the model for much of poetic eloquence from classical times through to the Renaissance. This poem is an example of it, a fact which colours Lucrece's denunciation with irony. The apparently irreconcilable division between fine language and effective action, which so troubles Lucrece, posed a problem equally for the poet-critic of the late sixteenth century, and it is one which Sidney's *Apology for Poetry* in particular tries to solve: 'For, as Aristotle saith, it is not *gnosis* but *praxis* must be the fruit' (*Apology*, p. 112).

1017 arbitrators judges chosen in law to decide between the claims of rival parties.

1018 skill-contending schools i.e. universities or law schools.

1019 dull debators i.e. those whose speeches take a long time and therefore require much 'leisure'.

1020 trembling Perhaps with uncertainty or

through fear of the outcome. Lucrece, by contrast, is resolute, as 1028–9 shows.

1021 force . . . straw attribute no importance to argument.

1024 uncheerful i.e. affording no cheer.

1026 confirmed despite i.e. shame against which there is no appeal ('confirmed' carries the sense of 'confirming a sentence or judgement', as in the legal argument at 1020).

1027 helpless unhelpful.

1027 smoke . . . words Compare *LLL* 3.1.63, 'Sweet smoke of rhetoric'.

1027 doth . . . right secures no justice for me.

1029 Lucrece's suicide threat refers to the medical practice of leeching or bloodletting, the theory being that contamination or fever or any *corruption* may be 'bled away'.

1030 decree judicial decision (see 1026n).

1031 Lucrece's plea that suicide in such circumstances is a defensible (honourable) action has historically engendered much discussion, beginning at least with St Augustine, who categorically deplored her justification (see Introduction, p. 23).

For if I die, my honour lives in thee;
But if I live, thou liv'st in my defame.
Since thou couldst not defend thy loyal dame,
        And wast afeard to scratch her wicked foe,   1035
        Kill both thyself and her for yielding so.'

This said, from her betumbled couch she starteth,
To find some desp'rate instrument of death;
But this no slaughterhouse no tool imparteth
To make more vent for passage of her breath,   1040
Which thronging through her lips so vanisheth
        As smoke from Ætna that in air consumes,
        Or that which from dischargèd cannon fumes.

'In vain', quoth she, 'I live, and seek in vain
Some happy mean to end a hapless life.   1045
I feared by Tarquin's falchion to be slain,
Yet for the self-same purpose seek a knife.
But when I feared I was a loyal wife:
        So am I now – O no, that cannot be;
        Of that true type hath Tarquin rifled me.   1050

'O that is gone for which I sought to live,
And therefore now I need not fear to die.
To clear this spot by death, at least I give

1039 no slaughterhouse] Q5; no slaughter house Q1; no-slaughter house Q3–4

1033 liv'st . . . defame The hand as part of
her body will participate in her blame if she survives. The distinction between soul or conscience
and body is imprecise, as the imagery of the poem
shows throughout; but it remains Lucrece's position that her *moral* person is indistinguishable from
her physical one, and that any violation of the latter
must be reflected in the former. According to her
logic, then, although she has suffered the offence
passively, it becomes *active* in her conscience, and
she is therefore culpable for as long as she remains
alive.
    1037 betumbled disordered; this may act partly
as a transferred epithet meaning that Lucrece is
equally 'betumbled' (see *Ven.* 397 and *Ham.* 4.5.62:
'Quoth she, "before you tumbled me"').
    1038 desp'rate Without heed; another example
of transferred epithet – the meaning applies not to
the instrument but rather to the one who uses it,
recklessly seeking her own life.

    1039 no slaughterhouse i.e. this place not
being a slaughterhouse (the figure is litotes, as in
'no bad thing'). The punctuation is as Q+, though
Lever argues that the phrase should be in apposition, i.e. 'this, no slaughterhouse'.
    1039 imparteth furnishes, provides.
    1041 thronging As often, a singular noun
('breath') is rendered plural by its collective nature
(recurrent actions of breathing) so that it lends
itself figuratively to the idea of the citizens or sol-
diery who make up the body's population (compare
426–46).
    1042 consumes consumes itself, vanishes.
    1045 mean means.
    1045 hapless ill-fated; a similar play is at 8.
    1050 true type proper designation ('type'
means mark or symbol).
    1050 rifled plundered, dispossessed (i.e. of the
quality or character symbolised by 'type').
    1053 spot visible mark of corruption.

A badge of fame to slander's livery,
A dying life to living infamy.   1055
    Poor helpless help, the treasure stol'n away,
    To burn the guiltless casket where it lay.

'Well, well, dear Collatine, thou shalt not know
The stainèd taste of violated troth;
I will not wrong thy true affection so   1060
To flatter thee with an infringèd oath.
    This bastard graff shall never come to growth:
    He shall not boast, who did thy stock pollute,
    That thou art doting father of his fruit.

'Nor shall he smile at thee in secret thought,   1065
Nor laugh with his companions at thy state;
But thou shalt know thy int'rest was not bought
Basely with gold, but stol'n from forth thy gate.
    For me, I am the mistress of my fate,
    And with my trespass never will dispense,   1070
    Till life to death acquit my forced offence.

'I will not poison thee with my attaint,
Nor fold my fault in cleanly-coined excuses;

1054 badge . . . fame Lucrece's remark adopts the idea of 1053 and seeks to impose a *pure* spot, signifying blameless reputation ('fame') on a costume that is entirely stained ('slander's livery'). A badge is loosely a mark or emblem (compare 'type'). Malone (who has been generally followed) identifies it with the arms of a master worn on his servants' livery.

1055 living infamy Paradoxical (balancing 'dying life'); 'infamy' means the death of reputation.

1056 helpless help help that is no help (and therefore 'poor').

1057 guiltless Punning on 'guilt' and 'gilt'.

1057 lay The verb appears to envisage a past action. Shakespeare sometimes switches tense, as he does mood (Abbott §367), apparently for fluency of expression.

1061 flatter thee lie to you.

1062–4 Lucrece nowhere else suggests that she might be pregnant, nor do the sources hint at it. But the thought belongs to the recurrent idea of lineage and inheritance since cuckoldry threatens as much as anything the prospect of an illegitimate heir.

1062 graff i.e. a shoot grafted onto another stem. Steevens (Malone) cites *Wisd. of Sol.* 4.3: 'the bastard plates shal take no depe roote' (see also Baldwin, *Genetics*, p. 138).

1067 int'rest property, claim (perhaps with a play on interest as 'growth', as in 1062).

1070 trespass transgression (with sexual overtones, as in 524, 632, 812).

1070 dispense i.e. pardon ('dispense with' is equivalent to 'give a dispensation for').

1071 life . . . death A contraction for 'passing from life to death'.

1071 acquit cancel. 'Acquit' has the sense of being discharged from a debt rather than being found not guilty of an offence. As we have seen, Lucrece cannot rid herself of a sense of guilt even as she insists that her offence was 'forced' on her.

1072 attaint See 825n.

1073 fold fold up, hide.

1073 cleanly-coined i.e. forged but made to appear genuine. *OED* (sv *v.* 3) gives 1561 as the date by which 'to coin' had acquired the meaning of counterfeiting money.

My sable ground of sin I will not paint,
To hide the truth of this false night's abuses.   1075
My tongue shall utter all; mine eyes, like sluices,
  As from a mountain spring that feeds a dale,
  Shall gush pure streams to purge my impure tale.'

By this, lamenting Philomel had ended
The well-tuned warble of her nightly sorrow,   1080
And solemn night with slow sad gait descended
To ugly hell, when lo, the blushing morrow
Lends light to all fair eyes that light will borrow;
  But cloudy Lucrece shames herself to see,
  And therefore still in night would cloist'red be.   1085

Revealing day through every cranny spies,
And seems to point her out where she sits weeping;
To whom she sobbing speaks: 'O eye of eyes,
Why pry'st thou through my window? Leave thy peeping,
Mock with thy tickling beams eyes that are sleeping;   1090
  Brand not my forehead with thy piercing light,
  For day hath nought to do what's done by night.'

Thus cavils she with every thing she sees.
True grief is fond and testy as a child,
Who wayward once, his mood with nought agrees.   1095
Old woes, not infant sorrows, bear them mild:

1074 sable ground black background (as in heraldic depiction or in painting generally); Lucrece refuses to disguise ('paint') the *sombre reality* of her situation.

1076 sluices floodgates (i.e. for regulating the flow of tears). Compare *Ven.* 956.

1078 gush pour forth.

1079 By this By this time.

1079 Philomel The nightingale. Philomel was raped by her brother-in-law, Tereus, and afterwards transformed into a nightingale by the gods (see *Metam.* 6.424–676 and *PP* 20.14n; compare also *Tit.* 2.4.38 and 4.1.52, where the myth of Philomel strongly shapes perception of the rape of Lavinia). Lucrece is accordingly identified with the nightingale and ends her complaint just as the bird finishes its song.

1080 well-tuned harmonious.

1082 blushing i.e. suffused with red. The morning is innocent of the shameful connotations of 'blushing', but it perhaps blushes on behalf of Lucrece, who, as 'cloudy' (sorrowful), is represented as a fellow heavenly element.

1084 shames is ashamed.

1085 still always.

1085 cloist'red sheltered (as in a religious house). Retreat to a nunnery was a conventional form of female penance.

1088 O . . . eyes The sun's light, but implying in a secondary sense God's judging eye (compare 356–7).

1089–90 Lucrece self-defensively tries to depict the sunlight as prurient or mischievous.

1090 tickling (1) irritating, (2) sexually arousing (see 1089–90n).

1091 See 807.

1092 to do to do with; for the contraction see Abbott §200.

1094 fond foolish.

1094 testy irritable.

1095 wayward once having once become difficult.

1096 bear them bear themselves.

Continuance tames the one; the other wild,
  Like an unpractised swimmer plunging still,
  With too much labour drowns for want of skill.

So she, deep drenchèd in a sea of care,   1100
Holds disputation with each thing she views,
And to herself all sorrow doth compare;
No object but her passion's strength renews,
And as one shifts another straight ensues.
  Sometime her grief is dumb and hath no words;   1105
  Sometime 'tis mad and too much talk affords.

The little birds that tune their morning's joy
Make her moans mad with their sweet melody;
For mirth doth search the bottom of annoy;
Sad souls are slain in merry company;   1110
Grief best is pleased with grief's society;
  True sorrow then is feelingly sufficed
  When with like semblance it is sympathised.

'Tis double death to drown in ken of shore;
He ten times pines that pines beholding food;   1115
To see the salve doth make the wound ache more;
Great grief grieves most at that would do it good;

1097 **Continuance** i.e. habituation to them.
1097 **the one** i.e. the 'old woes'.
1098 **plunging still** always diving beneath the surface.
1099 **drowns** The meaning is that the sufferer is overcome by 'wild' sorrows (see the continuation of the figure in 1100) rather than that the sorrows destroy themselves, though the logic of the sentence suggests the latter. 'Old woes' and 'infant sorrows' are personifications of both long-term and incipient suffering.
1101 **Holds disputation** Debates (see 246 and 822).
1103 **No object but** Each thing she sees.
1103 **passion** suffering.
1104 **shifts** changes, gives way.
1104 **straight** immediately.
1105 **her grief is dumb** This again identifies Lucrece with Philomel (1079n): after the rape Tereus cut out her tongue to prevent her from telling her sister – his wife – Procne. (See also 1128–34.)
1106 **too . . . talk** Perhaps alluding to Procne, who was eventually transformed into a twittering, garrulous swallow (compare 'garrir Procne': Petrarch, *rime* 310.3).

1108 **moans** sorrow ('moans', connoting sound, *dis*harmoniously fits the controlling idea of melody).
1109 **doth . . . bottom** sounds the depths (i.e. exposes and aggravates the wound).
1109 **annoy** sorrow.
1111 See 790n.
1112 **feelingly sufficed** i.e. its feelings are satisfied.
1113 'When it is brought into association with similar suffering' (Kittredge). The line has almost a surplus of words since the sense of 'like' is repeated in the 'sym-' of 'sympathised', and the latter word and 'semblance' only marginally extend each other's meanings, existing rather for decorative symmetry. Exact paraphrase is therefore impossible, though Kittredge's elegant formulation is as good as any.
1114 **ken** sight.
1115 **pines** starves (see 905n).
1116 **salve** remedy, ointment.
1117 **that would** that which would (see Abbott §244).

Deep woes roll forward like a gentle flood,
   Who, being stopped, the bounding banks o'erflows;
   Grief dallied with nor law nor limit knows.   1120

'You mocking birds', quoth she, 'your tunes entomb
Within your hollow-swelling feathered breasts,
And in my hearing be you mute and dumb;
My restless discord loves no stops nor rests.
A woeful hostess brooks not merry guests: 1125
   Relish your nimble notes to pleasing ears;
   Distress likes dumps when time is kept with tears.

'Come Philomel, that sing'st of ravishment,
Make thy sad grove in my dishevelled hair.
As the dank earth weeps at thy languishment,   1130
So I at each sad strain will strain a tear,
And with deep groans the diapason bear;
   For burden-wise I'll hum on Tarquin still,
   While thou on Tereus descants better skill.

'And whiles against a thorn thou bear'st thy part,   1135
   To keep thy sharp woes waking, wretched I,

1123 mute and] Q1; ever Q6+   1129 grove] Q1; grone Q5

1119 Who See Abbott §264.

1120 dallied trifled. 'Dallied' possibly plays on 'delayed' (see 'stopped': 1119).

1122 hollow (1) hollow, (2) insincere (playing on 'mocking'). There may be a further antithesis between 'hollow' (concave) and 'swelling' (convex).

1124 rests i.e. silent intervals in music (therefore punning on 'restless' and 'discord').

1126 Relish Sing, warble. As a noun 'relish' is a special musical term which suggests the effect of trilling or warbling: *OED* sv *sb.*² cites Castiglione: 'A musition, if in singing he rolle out but a plain note ending in a double relise with a swete tune' (Castiglione, p. 49).

1126 pleasing i.e. ears which are pleased (see 993n).

1127 dumps A dump is 'a mournful or plaintive melody or song' (*OED sb.*¹ 3); compare *TGV* 3.2.83–4: 'to their instruments / Tune a deploring dump'. The more familiar sense of dumps has always been present – *ODEP* cites *Shr.* 2.1.284, 'Why, how now, daughter Katherine, in your dumps?'

1128 ravishment rape.

1129 dishevelled Lucrece's hair is dishevelled partly as a result of the rape and also as a sign of her general distress.

1131 strain . . . strain Punning on (1) melody, and (2) wring out.

1132 with . . . bear Lucrece will accompany the nightingale's song in a lower register. *OED* sv *sb.* 1c cites this line and defines 'diapason' as 'an air or bass sounding in exact concord'.

1133 burden-wise The 'burden' is the undersong (normally for bass voice) or accompaniment. Fr. *bourdon* means 'a humming tone' – hence 'hum . . . Tarquin'.

1134 descants i.e. 'to sing with a small, yet pleasant and shrill voice as birds doe' (Onions, quoting Minsheu, *The Guide into Tongues*, 1617). The musical theme presumably inclines Shakespeare to prefer the euphonious 'descants' to 'descant'st' (see Abbott §340).

1134 better skill with better skill (for the omission of the preposition see Abbott §202).

1135 against a thorn The nightingale was thought to sing by night and to keep awake by pressing its breast against a thorn (*ODEP* illustrates with an anonymous lyric of 1510); the thorn's sharpness came to be identified with the pain ('sharp woes') of sorrow.

1135 thou . . . part (1) you sing your part, (2) you bear up.

To imitate thee well, against my heart
Will fix a sharp knife to affright mine eye,
Who if it wink shall thereon fall and die.
   These means, as frets upon an instrument, 1140
   Shall tune our heart-strings to true languishment.

'And for, poor bird, thou sing'st not in the day,
As shaming any eye should thee behold,
Some dark deep desert, seated from the way,
That knows not parching heat nor freezing cold, 1145
Will we find out; and there we will unfold
   To creatures stern sad tunes to change their kinds:
   Since men prove beasts, let beasts bear gentle minds.'

As the poor frighted deer that stands at gaze,
Wildly determining which way to fly, 1150
Or one encompassed with a winding maze
That cannot tread the way out readily,
So with herself is she in mutiny,
   To live or die which of the twain were better,
   When life is shamed and death reproach's debtor. 1155

'To kill myself', quoth she, 'alack, what were it,
But with my body my poor soul's pollution?

1141 true] Q1; give Q4

1139 Who Probably referring to 'heart' (1137); for 'who' instead of 'which' see 1119n.

1139 wink closes (as in 375).

1140 frets Punning on 'to fret' (meaning 'chafe' or 'vex'): 'frets' are ridges which regulate the strings on an instrument such as the lute.

1143 As shaming As if ashamed.

1144–5 The imagery in these lines seems to draw upon two Petrarchan examples: 'deep desert' implies an unfrequented or deserted valley, as in Petrarch's poem, 'Solo et pensoso i più deserti campi / vo mesurando' (*rime* 35.1–2); and the antithetical 'parching heat nor freezing cold' repeats such formulae as Surrey's 'Set me whereas the sonne doth perche the grene, / Or whear his beames may not dissolve the ise', which is a translation of Petrarch's *rime* 145.

1147–8 The lines allude to the power of Orpheus to charm wild beasts with his music (see *Ven.* 1093–8n).

1147 sad tunes 'Sad' tends to mean 'serious' as much as 'melancholic', and so 'sad tunes' may convey the sense of a serious or solemn appeal in

music to the beasts' moral nature (see 1147n below on 'kinds').

1147 kinds natures.

1148 gentle well-nurtured.

1149 at gaze both watching and not watching (as if transfixed); *OED sv sb.* 3b applies the expression specifically to deer.

1150 determining considering.

1151 encompassed with enclosed by, hedged in by.

1152 readily promptly, quickly.

1155 life is shamed to live is shameful.

1155 death . . . debtor i.e. to take one's life incurs reproach.

1157 with my body with my body's pollution. Lucrece means that suicide would morally compromise ('pollute') her soul along with her already violated body. Pooler remarks that 'it is not a Roman thought'; Christian doctrine is naturally uppermost in Shakespeare's mind, but it should also be recognised that among ancient writers Cicero, for example, opposed suicide on the grounds that it was contrary to God's will (see Introduction, p. 36, n).

They that lose half with greater patience bear it
Than they whose whole is swallowed in confusion.
That mother tries a merciless conclusion,   1160
    Who, having two sweet babes, when death takes one,
    Will slay the other, and be nurse to none.

'My body or my soul, which was the dearer,
When the one pure, the other made divine?
Whose love of either to myself was nearer,   1165
When both were kept for heaven and Collatine?
Ay me, the bark pilled from the lofty pine,
    His leaves will wither and his sap decay;
    So must my soul, her bark being pilled away.

'Her house is sacked, her quiet interrupted,   1170
Her mansion batt'red by the enemy;
Her sacred temple spotted, spoiled, corrupted,
Grossly engirt with daring infamy.
Then let it not be called impiety,
    If in this blemished fort I make some hole,   1175
    Through which I may convey this troubled soul.

'Yet die I will not, till my Collatine
Have heard the cause of my untimely death,
That he may vow, in that sad hour of mine,
    Revenge on him that made me stop my breath.   1180

1159 confusion ruin, destruction (as in *Mac.* 2.3.66, 'Confusion now hath made his masterpiece').

1160 conclusion experiment. Compare *Ant.* 5.2.355–6: 'She hath pursu'd conclusions infinite / Of easy ways to die.'

1164 other . . . divine i.e. the soul was made worthy of heaven by the body's purity.

1165 Whose . . . either i.e. which of the two did I love more (for 'Whose' following an irrational antecedent, see Abbott §264).

1167–9 Lucrece introduces a new aspect to the argument: that the defilement of her body is already tantamount to its destruction and hence that of her soul, which remains pure only so long as the body is unsullied (see 1164). This prepares for her resolved statement in favour of suicide at 1174–6.

1167 pilled peeled.

1170–3 Compare 722–8.

1173 Grossly (1) coarsely, lewdly, (2) as by a large military force. 'Grossly' interplays with 'infamy'.

1173 engirt encircled, besieged (see 221n).

1173 daring audacious (brazen). But in this collocation with 'infamy' 'daring' retains something of its positive meaning, producing an oxymoron such as 'courageous notoriety' (the phrase exemplifies Shakespeare's recurrent use of paradoxical expressions to bring out in its various aspects the central predicament of his theme).

1175 blemished fort The military image enables Lucrece to argue that any wound she inflicts upon her body can make no difference to the injuries already received. The language of metaphor in this instance gives all actions, whatever their degree or quality, the same significance.

1178 Have Either 'shall have' or 'may have'.

1180 stop my breath kill myself (see *Oth.* 5.2.202); the expression may also recall Tarquin's forcibly silencing her protests (if 'breath' is understood as speech) during the rape (see 678–81).

My stainèd blood to Tarquin I'll bequeath,
    Which by him tainted shall for him be spent,
    And as his due writ in my testament.

'My honour I'll bequeath unto the knife
    That wounds my body so dishonourèd.   1185
'Tis honour to deprive dishonoured life;
    The one will live, the other being dead.
So of shame's ashes shall my fame be bred,
    For in my death I murder shameful scorn;
    My shame so dead, mine honour is new born.   1190

'Dear lord of that dear jewel I have lost,
    What legacy shall I bequeath to thee?
My resolution, love, shall be thy boast,
    By whose example thou revenged mayst be.
How Tarquin must be used, read it in me: 1195
    Myself thy friend will kill myself thy foe,
    And for my sake serve thou false Tarquin so.

'This brief abridgement of my will I make:
    My soul and body to the skies and ground;
My resolution, husband, do thou take;   1200
    Mine honour be the knife's that makes my wound;
    My shame be his that did my fame confound;
    And all my fame that lives disbursèd be
      To those that live and think no shame of me.

1182 for him] Q1 *(Malone 34, 886 and Sion;* by him *the rest)*

1181–1204 The bequest or testament is a traditional literary motif (see List of abbreviations: Perrow), e.g. Nashe, *Summer's Last Will and Testament* and Villon's *Testaments* (Prince).
1182 **spent** (1) paid out (as a legacy), (2) shed.
1186 **deprive** take away, remove.
1187 **The one** i.e. 'honour'.
1188–90 Lucrece invokes the idea of the phoenix, which sets itself alight and is reborn from its own ashes. To be perfectly consistent 'shame' would have to renew itself, not produce something else, but Lucrece exploits the similar sounding 'shame' and 'fame' to effect their transmutation; in addition the phoenix is 'famed' for its capacity to regenerate itself in this way.
1189 **shameful scorn** i.e. the shameful reputation which she anticipates for herself:

'scorn' requires an object or means of self-embodiment which after her death Lucrece will not provide.
1195 **used** dealt with.
1196 **Myself . . . myself** See Abbott §20.
1198 **abridgement** compressed account (Lucrece briefly resumes the argument of 1181 – 97).
1199 **My . . . body** i.e. My . . . body I commend. Pooler notes Shakespeare's will: 'I commend my soul into the hands of God . . . and my body to the earth.'
1202 **confound** destroy.
1203 **disbursèd be** be distributed in payment ('fame', as often with personifications, is treated as a collective noun with plural effect (see 627n).

'Thou, Collatine, shalt oversee this will.   1205
How was I overseen that thou shalt see it!
My blood shall wash the slander of mine ill;
My life's foul deed, my life's fair end shall free it.
Faint not, faint heart, but stoutly say "So be it."
    Yield to my hand; my hand shall conquer thee;   1210
    Thou dead, both die, and both shall victors be.'

This plot of death when sadly she had laid,
And wiped the brinish pearl from her bright eyes,
With untuned tongue she hoarsely calls her maid,
Whose swift obedience to her mistress hies;   1215
For fleet-winged duty with thought's feathers flies.
    Poor Lucrece' cheeks unto her maid seem so
    As winter meads when sun doth melt their snow.

Her mistress she doth give demure good-morrow
With soft slow tongue, true mark of modesty,   1220
And sorts a sad look to her lady's sorrow
(For why her face wore sorrow's livery),
But durst not ask of her audaciously
    Why her two suns were cloud-eclipsèd so,
    Nor why her fair cheeks over-washed with woe.   1225

But as the earth doth weep, the sun being set,
Each flower moist'ned like a melting eye,
Even so the maid with swelling drops 'gan wet
Her circled eyne, enforced by sympathy
Of those fair suns set in her mistress' sky,   1230

1205 oversee superintend (either as an executor or as one appointed to ensure that the executors behave impartially).

1206 overseen mistaken.

1206 that . . . it that (as a result of my mistake) you shall see the will.

1207 slander infamy.

1208 free it free, absolve (see Abbott §417).

1212 plot design.

1212 laid completed, worked out.

1213 brinish pearl shiny salt-tears (compare 1231, and LC 17–18).

1214 untuned hoarse, rasping (the epithet recalls the nightingale's song of consolation at 1128–48).

1215 Whose swift obedience . . . hies Who hastens . . . in swift obedience. The expression exemplifies the poem's manner of personifying and energising abstractions (note the examples at 1216).

1216 with thought's feathers as fast as thought.

1218 meads meadows.

1221 sorts adapts, suits.

1222 For why Because.

1222 sorrow's livery an expression suitable to sorrow. Since Lucrece, the lady, personifies sorrow in this figure, it is appropriate that a member of her household should wear a 'costume' identifying her as one of sorrow's servants.

1223 audaciously presumptuously, impudently (OED sv adv. 2); compare 'daring' (1173n).

1224–32 Compare the contrasting cosmic imagery at 12–14.

1229 circled eyne eyes made round with tearfulness.

Who in a salt-waved ocean quench their light,
Which makes the maid weep like the dewy night.

A pretty while these pretty creatures stand,
Like ivory conduits coral cisterns filling.
One justly weeps, the other takes in hand   1235
No cause but company of her drops spilling:
Their gentle sex to weep are often willing,
    Grieving themselves to guess at others' smarts,
    And then they drown their eyes or break their hearts.

For men have marble, women waxen minds,   1240
And therefore are they formed as marble will.
The weak oppressed, th'impression of strange kinds
Is formed in them by force, by fraud, or skill.
Then call them not the authors of their ill,
    No more than wax shall be accounted evil   1245
    Wherein is stamped the semblance of a devil.

Their smoothness, like a goodly champaign plain,
Lays open all the little worms that creep;
In men, as in a rough-grown grove, remain
Cave-keeping evils that obscurely sleep.   1250
    Through crystal walls each little mote will peep.

1247 like a goodly] Q1; like a Q6–8; like unto a Q9   1248 that creep] Q1; to creep Q4

1231 salt-waved i.e. the salt of her tears.
1233–9 This is a characteristic Elizabethan passage in that intense grief is registered, and to some degree assuaged, by delicacy and refinement – most usually through female protagonists. Although some commentators dismiss such stanzas as precious, and precocious, apprentice work, both their manner and underlying principles recur in the mature tragic dramas (see, for example, the description of Cordelia in *Lear* 4.3.10–32; and Introduction, p. 30).
1233 A pretty while A little while (suggesting the extension through time of a beautiful, essentially spatial tableau).
1234 ivory conduits Probably fountains in the form of statues (see *Rom.* 3.5.129: 'How now, a conduit, girl? What, still in tears?'). For all its posed quality (see 1233–9n) and its statement of sorrow, the line conveys a potent image of fertility, and may derive its assurance from the biblical evocation of female loveliness as a fountain in Prov. 5.15–18.
1234 coral cisterns i.e. the eyes which are red from weeping and, like cisterns, fill with tears.

1235 justly i.e. from a just motive or 'cause'.
1235 takes in hand undertakes, entertains.
1238 to guess at as they have an understanding of.
1241 they women.
1241 will wills it.
1242 weak oppressed weak being oppressed.
1242 strange kinds foreign natures.
1244 authors responsible agents.
1244 ill In the sense both of evil apparently done by them and evil to which they are subjected.
1247 smoothness i.e. of face (implying clarity of expression).
1247 champaign open, level.
1249 rough-grown grove Playing on the image of the male beard.
1250 Cave-keeping evils Evils which lurk in caves.
1250 obscurely unobtrusively.
1250 sleep lie low.
1251 mote speck, blemish. The idea may echo the argument of the gospels against judging hastily, 'Judge not, that ye be not judged' (Matt. 7.1),

Though men can cover crimes with bold stern looks,
Poor women's faces are their own faults' books.

No man inveigh against the withered flower,
But chide rough winter that the flower hath killed;   1255
Not that devoured, but that which doth devour,
Is worthy blame. O let it not be hild
Poor women's faults that they are so fulfilled
      With men's abuses: those proud lords to blame
      Make weak-made women tenants to their shame.   1260

The precedent whereof in Lucrece view,
Assailed by night with circumstances strong
Of present death, and shame that might ensue
By that her death, to do her husband wrong.
Such danger to resistance did belong   1265
      That dying fear through all her body spread;
      And who cannot abuse a body dead?

By this, mild patience bid fair Lucrece speak
To the poor counterfeit of her complaining:
'My girl', quoth she, 'on what occasion break   1270
Those tears from thee that down thy cheeks are raining?
If thou dost weep for grief of my sustaining,

1254 inveigh] Q1; inveighs Q2 +   1255 chide] Q1; chides Q4, 8–9

which is followed by the example: 'And why seest
thou the mote, that is in thy brother's eye, and per-
ceivest not the beame that is in thine owne eye?'
(Matt. 7.3).
    1253 Compare Lucrece's statement at 749.
    1254 No man Let no man.
    1255 Echoed in *Son.* 18.3.
    1257 hild held.
    1258 fulfilled filled full.
    1259 to blame who are to blame (see Abbott
§246 for the omission of the relative; also 'that
devoured', 1256).
    1260 tenants Just as women are filled with
men's abuse of them (1258), so in turn they are
made to *occupy* the shame that men are true own-
ers of.
    1261 See Daniel, *Rosamond* 407, 'These presi-
dents presented to my view' (Sprague, p. 52).
    1261 precedent example, proof (*Ven.* 26n).
    1262 with . . . strong with a powerful likeli-
hood.
    1263 present immediate.
    1266 dying fear paralysing fear. The image

appears to register the influence of Chaucer,
according to whom she faints away ('in a swogh
she lay': see *LGW* 1814–18). The line is notice-
ably at odds with the sense of 677–83, in which
Tarquin stifles her lively protests. But the contradiction may be resolved if we take account of the
different themes the poem chooses to accentuate at
different moments: the first account highlights the
savagery of male violence in the image of the wolf
attacking the lamb, whereas here emphasis falls on
the passive nature of women (1240–43); it is appropriate, therefore, that one set of images should
depict a creature struggling, however helplessly, for
its life, while the other registers the impression of
'a body dead' (1267).
    1268 mild patience A personification of the
maid's demeanour.
    1268 bid bade.
    1269 poor counterfeit pale image, likeness
(perhaps anticipating 1366ff.).
    1270 on . . . occasion for what reason.
    1272 of my sustaining sustained by me.

Know, gentle wench, it small avails my mood;
If tears could help, mine own would do me good.

'But tell me, girl, when went' – and there she stayed   1275
Till after a deep groan – 'Tarquin from hence?'
'Madam, ere I was up', replied the maid,
'The more to blame my sluggard negligence.
Yet with the fault I thus far can dispense:
Myself was stirring ere the break of day,   1280
And ere I rose was Tarquin gone away.

'But lady, if your maid may be so bold,
She would request to know your heaviness.'
'O peace', quoth Lucrece: 'if it should be told,
The repetition cannot make it less;   1285
For more it is than I can well express,
And that deep torture may be called a hell
When more is felt than one hath power to tell.

'Go get me hither paper, ink, and pen;
Yet save that labour, for I have them here.   1290
What should I say? One of my husband's men
Bid thou be ready, by and by, to bear
A letter to my lord, my love, my dear.
Bid him with speed prepare to carry it;
The cause craves haste, and it will soon be writ.'   1295

Her maid is gone, and she prepares to write,
First hovering o'er the paper with her quill.
Conceit and grief an eager combat fight;
What wit sets down is blotted straight with will;

1299 straight] Q1; still Q3 +

1273 **small** little.
1275 **stayed** hesitated.
1278 **to blame** i.e. the more his early rising cast blame on her negligence (exposing the maid was the last thing Tarquin had in mind).
1279 **with . . . dispense** I can partly excuse my negligence (see 1070n).
1280 **Myself** See 1195n.
1283 **know** know the reason for, understand.
1283 **heaviness** low spirits, sorrow.
1285 **repetition** recital ('repetition' and 'less' combine in a mournful joke).
1287–8 As often, the poem adapts the conventional expression of love poetry, though to

marked effect: it is typically the lover who complains of the 'deep torture' of his condition and laments his inability to give effective utterance to it. While restricting herself to the sometimes obsessive-seeming, repetitive vocabulary of the sonnet speaker, about whom it is often easy to be sceptical, Lucrece finds a dimension which is undeniably tragic.
1292 **by and by** before long.
1298 **Conceit** Style (in poetry, 'conceit' normally means a well-turned image or idea).
1299 **What . . . will** i.e. her stylistic expression is spoilt by and inadequate to the force of her emotion: 'blotted' means erased in the dual sense

This is too curious-good, this blunt and ill: 1300
    Much like a press of people at a door,
    Throng her inventions, which shall go before.

At last she thus begins: 'Thou worthy lord
Of that unworthy wife that greeteth thee,
Health to thy person. Next, vouchsafe t'afford   1305
(If ever, love, thy Lucrece thou wilt see)
Some present speed to come and visit me.
    So I commend me, from our house in grief;
    My woes are tedious, though my words are brief.'

Here folds she up the tenure of her woe,   1310
Her certain sorrow writ uncertainly.
By this short schedule Collatine may know
Her grief, but not her grief's true quality.
She dares not thereof make discovery,
    Lest he should hold it her own gross abuse,   1315
    Ere she with blood had stained her stained excuse.

Besides the life and feeling of her passion
She hoards, to spend when he is by to hear her;
When sighs and groans and tears may grace the fashion
Of her disgrace, the better so to clear her   1320
From that suspicion which the world might bear her.

1310 tenure] Q1; tenor Q6 +

of both spoiling and censuring. 'Wit', akin to 'conceit', means stylistic intelligence and inventiveness and may additionally carry the sense of moral perceptiveness. The Elizabethan period in general observes a strict opposition between wit and will, though the latter has normally a more vicious connotation than that of Lucrece's will here; compare 486, and note Sidney's formulation: 'our erected wit maketh us know what perfection is, and yet our infected will keepeth us from reaching unto it' (*Apology*, p. 101).

1300 too curious-good over-elaborate.

1300 blunt and ill i.e. style is overcome by emotion (see 1299n).

1302 inventions attempts at writing.

1302 which . . . before 'striving which shall enter first' (Prince). For a general note on ellipses see Abbott §382.

1305 Health . . . person She perhaps specifies his bodily health only since he is in other respects poorly off.

1305 vouchsafe condescend.

1306 wilt The verb combines the sense of 'be willing' with the future sense of will (i.e. will be in time to).

1307 present immediate.

1309 tedious unending. 'Tedious' is placed with calculated irony, since it would normally accompany 'words' to mean excessive (as at *Ven.* 841: 'her song was tedious'), but so positioned it renews the more serious sense of 'wearisome'.

1310 tenure (1) transcript, copy (a legal term), but also possibly (2) tenor, as in tenor part (i.e. the 'certain sorrow' to which she has previously given voice). 'Tenure' is often the Elizabethan spelling of 'tenor'.

1312 schedule summary, letter (see *LC* 43).

1316 stained . . . excuse coloured (improved the appearance of) (1) her account of why she was stained (corrupted, violated), or (2) her unsatisfactory excuse.

1317 life . . . passion Perhaps alluding to the theory of dramatic representation. See below 1324–7n.

1321 suspicion Something stronger than mere suspicion is implied – perhaps disgrace, or blame

To shun this blot she would not blot the letter
With words, till action might become them better.

To see sad sights moves more than hear them told,
For then the eye interprets to the ear   1325
The heavy motion that it doth behold,
When every part a part of woe doth bear.
'Tis but a part of sorrow that we hear:
    Deep sounds make lesser noise than shallow fords,
    And sorrow ebbs, being blown with wind of words.   1330

Her letter now is sealed, and on it writ,
'At Ardea to my lord with more than haste.'
The post attends, and she delivers it,
Charging the sour-faced groom to hie as fast
As lagging fowls before the northern blast;   1335
    Speed more than speed but dull and slow she deems:
    Extremity still urgeth such extremes.

The homely villain cur'sies to her low,
And blushing on her, with a steadfast eye,

1335 blast] Q1 *(all copies except Malone 34, 886, and Sion, which have* blasts*)*

('suspicion' often carries the sense of there being grounds for suspicion, as in *Rom.* 5.3.187).

1322 this blot this disgrace (see 1321n).

1322 blot the letter mark the letter (compare the wordplay with that of 1299).

1324–7 The immediate inspiration for this may well again be Sidney, who chooses the depiction of Lucrece to exemplify the painter's ability to make a direct and moving appeal with his 'speaking picture': 'the constant though lamenting look of Lucretia, when she punished in herself another's fault' (*Apology*, p. 102). Malone traces the classical argument for the superiority of visual representation to Horace (*Art of Poetry* 18off.). (Such arguments distinguish between the power of poetic language to *visualise* effects and the more ordinary capacity of non-poetic, non-dramatic writing and speech.)

1326 heavy motion sad expression (recombining 'sad' and 'moves', 1324); also antithetical, since heaviness opposes movement. Malone further spots a reference to dumb- or puppet-shows (e.g. *Bartholomew Fair* 5.1.6: 'O the motions, that I . . . have given light to'; and 5.4.107: 'I'll *interpret* to thee').

1327 every part every feature, limb.

1327 part . . . bear plays a part of woe.

1328 We only hear a part, not the whole, of sorrow ('part' signifies portion).

1329 Proverbial (Tilley w130). 'Deep sounds' are so deep as not to be heard (with a pun on (1) sounding the depths, and (2) making a great noise.)

1330 blown i.e driven out to sea. The idea is that sorrow loses its impact the more it is expressed by words.

1332 Compare the opening line of the poem.

1333 post messenger.

1334 sour-faced groom The description simply means that he is rough mannered or uncultivated, not that he is disrespectful (see 1345–6); but Lucrece, who was formerly an innocent reader of facial expressions (see 99–105), now finds herself anxiously interpreting the least glance as a sign that her shame has been detected (see below 1352–8, and p. 31).

1337 Extremity Acute distress.

1338 homely villain plain-mannered servant (O.Fr *villein* = peasant); see 1334n.

1338 cur'sies . . . low bows extravagantly (see *TN* 2.5.61). Again the exaggeration of his behaviour merely reveals his awkwardness, though for one in Lucrece's agony of mind it will seem like mockery.

1339 steadfast (1) fixed, (2) loyal (Lucrece finds his stare accusing when it is merely devoted).

Receives the scroll without or yea or no,   1340
And forth with bashful innocence doth hie.
But they whose guilt within their bosoms lie
   Imagine every eye beholds their blame;
   For Lucrece thought he blushed to see her shame,

When, silly groom, God wot, it was defect   1345
Of spirit, life and bold audacity.
Such harmless creatures have a true respect
To talk in deeds, while others saucily
Promise more speed, but do it leisurely.
   Even so this pattern of the worn-out age   1350
   Pawned honest looks, but laid no words to gage.

His kindled duty kindled her mistrust,
That two red fires in both their faces blazèd;
She thought he blushed, as knowing Tarquin's lust,
And blushing with him, wistly on him gazèd;   1355
Her earnest eye did make him more amazèd;
   The more she saw the blood his cheeks replenish,
   The more she thought he spied in her some blemish.

But long she thinks till he return again,
And yet the duteous vassal scarce is gone.   1360
The weary time she cannot entertain,
For now 'tis stale to sigh, to weep and groan:
So woe hath wearied woe, moan tirèd moan,
   That she her plaints a little while doth stay,
   Pausing for means to mourn some newer way.   1365

1341 hie] Q1; lie Q5–7; flie Q8–9   1350 this . . . the] Q1 *(all copies except BM C.21.c.45, Folger–Devonshire, Huntington,*
and Kravs, which have the . . . this)   1361 weary] Q1; very Q4

1342 **lie** An example of the indefinite use of the
subjunctive after a relative pronoun (see Abbott
§367).

1345 **silly** simple, harmless.

1345 **God wot** Parodying the uncouth protestations such a figure would make.

1347 **true respect** proper concern, aim (compare the use of this expression at 201).

1348 **talk in deeds** i.e. actions speak louder than
words.

1348 **saucily** presumptuously.

1350 **pattern** example; see 629n.

1350 **worn-out age** i.e. the age of innocence
now long past (compare *AYLI* 2.3.56–7).

1351 **Pawned** Pledged (i.e. his face expressed
his good faith better than words – which he did
not speak); 'laid . . . to gage' means deposit as
security.

1352 **kindled . . . kindled** earnest . . . sparked.

1355 **wistly** earnestly (compare *Ven.* 343).

1359 **But . . . thinks** She thinks time passes
slowly; she grows impatient (see *Rom.* 4.5.41, 'Have
I thought long to see this morning's face'). 'But' has
an emphatic function and is equivalent to 'how'.

1361 **entertain** bear.

1362 **stale** ineffectual, wearisome.

1364 **plaints** lamentings.

1364 **stay** allay, discontinue.

At last she calls to mind where hangs a piece
Of skilful painting, made for Priam's Troy,
Before the which is drawn the power of Greece,
For Helen's rape the city to destroy,
Threat'ning cloud-kissing Ilion with annoy;   1370
   Which the conceited painter drew so proud
   As heaven, it seemed, to kiss the turrets bowed.

A thousand lamentable objects there,
In scorn of nature, art gave liveless life;
Many a dry drop seemed a weeping tear,   1375
Shed for the slaught'red husband by the wife;
The red blood reeked, to show the painter's strife;
   And dying eyes gleamed forth their ashy lights,
   Like dying coals burnt out in tedious nights.

There might you see the labouring pioneer   1380
Begrimed with sweat and smearèd all with dust;
And from the towers of Troy there would appear
The very eyes of men through loop-holes thrust,

1375 dry] Q1; dire Q5 +

1366–1568 Lucrece's contemplation of the siege and destruction of Troy has called forth a great deal of admiration as well as much debate (see Rollins, pp. 224–8). The passage can be defined as an ecphrasis or scene-within-a-scene, in which Shakespeare not only gives Lucrece's grief an epic dimension but allows himself a moment of expansiveness as he passes in review one of the seminal episodes of classical literary mythology (see pp. 31–2). The inspiration is indeed more likely to be literary than pictorial (see 1422–8n, and in particular *Aen.* 1.453–93, where Aeneas contemplates similar images of the Fall of Troy). Consequently, there seems little point in speculating whether 'a piece of skilful painting' means a tapestry or some other form of representation. See supplementary note.

1367 **made for** representing.

1368 **drawn** assembled.

1370 **cloud-kissing Ilion** 'Ilion' is another name for Troy (and derives from Ilos, the name of the son of Tros). The epithet 'cloud-kissing' suggests the height and majesty of the buildings which are about to be destroyed, and the line as a whole implies perhaps that the gods are prepared to see the city suffer for its lofty aspirations (see 1371–2). There may also be a hint in 'cloud-kissing' at the intermingling of human and divine in the sexual

realm, Helen herself having been engendered by Jove's visitation to her mother, Leda, in the form of a swan, while on another occasion he copulated with Danae disguised as a shower of golden rain.

1370 **annoy** grief, injury.

1371 **conceited** imaginative, ingenious.

1374 For the art–nature *topos*, see *Ven.* 289–94n. The capacity of visual representation to render details lifelike appears to have been its greatest appeal for Shakespeare.

1374 **liveless** lifeless (see *Ven.* 211).

1375 **dry . . . tear** The antithesis of 'dry' and 'weeping' demonstrates how effectively the art–nature interplay lends itself to the poem's governing principle of paradox (similarly the description of the horse at *Ven.* 292: 'As if the *dead* the *living* should exceed').

1377 **reeked** smoked with heat; the image has sacrificial overtones (see also 'slaught'red'): compare *Cym.* 1.2.2: 'the violence of action hath made you reek as a sacrifice'; and *JC* 3.1.158.

1377 **strife** skill in emulation (see *Ven.* 291).

1379 **tedious** never-ending, wearisome (see 1309n).

1380 **labouring pioneer** sapper (whose function is to dig trenches).

Gazing upon the Greeks with little lust.
Such sweet observance in this work was had   1385
That one might see those far-off eyes look sad.

In great commanders grace and majesty
You might behold, triumphing in their faces;
In youth, quick bearing and dexterity;
And here and there the painter interlaces   1390
Pale cowards marching on with trembling paces,
    Which heartless peasants did so well resemble
    That one would swear he saw them quake and tremble.

In Ajax and Ulysses, O what art
Of physiognomy might one behold!   1395
The face of either ciphered either's heart;
Their face their manners most expressly told:
In Ajax' eyes blunt rage and rigour rolled;
    But the mild glance that sly Ulysses lent
    Showed deep regard and smiling government.   1400

There pleading might you see grave Nestor stand,
As 'twere encouraging the Greeks to fight,
Making such sober action with his hand
That it beguiled attention, charmed the sight.
In speech it seemed his beard, all silver white,   1405
    Wagged up and down, and from his lips did fly
    Thin winding breath, which purled up to the sky.

1399 sly] slie Q1; she Q4, 7–9

1384 **lust** pleasure, **delight**.
1385 **sweet observance** delightful attention to detail. The observer's 'sweet' view or impression contrasts with the 'sad' gaze of the 'far-off eyes'.
1388 **triumphing** showing gloriously (see 12n).
1390 **interlaces** intermixes, interweaves.
1392 **heartless** terrified (see 471). 'Peasants', being of base condition, are not expected to have courage, which is a property of 'gentle' or noble state.
1394–1407 Bullough (1, 181) notes that the descriptions of Ajax, Ulysses, and Nestor all derive from *Metam.* 13; 'sly Ulysses' is Golding's recurrent phrase.
1396 **ciphered** interpreted, expressed (see 207 and 811n, and 'told', 1397).
1396 **either's** his own.
1397 **manners** moral bearing, character.

1398 **rigour** (1) severity, (2) stubbornness.
1399 **sly** cunning, subtle (see *3H6* 3.2.189, 'Deceive more slily than Ulysses could').
1399 **lent** courteously bestowed (see *JC* 3.2.73).
1400 **deep regard** (1) respect for his interlocutor, (2) circumspection.
1400 **smiling government** (1) friendly leadership, (2) 'serene self-control' (Prince).
1401 **pleading** exhorting (as an orator); see *3H6* 3.2.188, 'I'll play the orator as well as Nestor.' The name 'grave Nestor' is synonymous with sage counsel.
1403 **sober** temperate, restrained (contrasting with 'beguiled' and 'charmed'). Compare *Ham.* 3.2.4–8.
1406 **Wagged . . . down** The effect is slightly comical though the intention is rather to demonstrate art's power of drawing to the life (see 1374n).

About him were a press of gaping faces,
Which seemed to swallow up his sound advice,
All jointly list'ning, but with several graces,   1410
As if some mermaid did their ears entice,
Some high, some low, the painter was so nice;
    The scalps of many, almost hid behind,
    To jump up higher seemed, to mock the mind.

Here one man's hand leaned on another's head,   1415
His nose being shadowed by his neighbour's ear;
Here one being thronged bears back, all boll'n and red;
Another smothered seems to pelt and swear;
And in their rage such signs of rage they bear
    As, but for loss of Nestor's golden words,   1420
    It seemed they would debate with angry swords.

For much imaginary work was there:
Conceit deceitful, so compact, so kind,
That for Achilles' image stood his spear,
Gripped in an armèd hand; himself behind   1425

1407 purled (1) curled (usually as of a stream). Malone compares Drayton: 'Whose streame an easie breath doth seeme to blowe; / Which on the sparkling gravell runs in purles, / As though the waves had been of silver curles' (*Mortimeriados* (1596), 2364–6). Other senses are (2) woven or embroidered (which may be suggested by the texture of the beard which is described in the same motion), and (3) the impression of silvery brilliance (created by the beard's description) may further prompt a pun on 'pearled'.

1409 sound Punning on (1) sensible, and (2) auditory (effecting the synaesthesia of 'swallowing' sound).

1410 several graces differing postures or attitudes.

1411 mermaid See *Ven.* 429n.

1412 nice meticulous, precise.

1414 mock . . . mind Referring to the amazement induced in the spectator by subtle perspective.

1416 shadowed hidden.

1417 thronged crowded, jostled.

1417 bears back pushes back.

1417 boll'n swollen ('Her leannesse made her joynts bolne big, and kneepannes for to swell', Golding 8.1003 – Prince).

1418 smothered overwhelmed by the crush.

1418 pelt shout in anger.

1420 As As if.

1420 but . . . loss except for not wanting to lose.

1421 debate do battle (from the idea of oratory at 1401–7). The '*angry* swords' further suggest an argumentative mood.

1422–8 Gombrich (pp. 176–7) convincingly traces these details to Philostratus' *Imagines* 1.4 (Loeb edn, pp. 16–17). (Hulse (*S. Sur.* 31, 16–17) records the appearance of five Latin translations of Philostratus between 1517 and 1550, and one in French in 1578.) The evidence supports the argument that Shakespeare derives his art appreciation from literary sources (see 1366–1568n).

1422 imaginary work work of the imagination – implying that such work will be completed in 'the eye of mind' (compare the confident appeal to the audience's 'imaginary forces' at *H5* Prologue 18).

1423 Conceit deceitful Beguiling invention (paraphrase loses the effect of the words' pointed resemblance of each other). For 'conceit' see 1298n.

1423 compact solid (as if possessing substance).

1423 kind natural, lifelike.

1424 A famous instance of metonymy: Achilles' spear was legendary and would stand as sufficient emblem for him (see also *2H6* 5.1.100). Metonymy here (and synecdoche at 1427–8) shows Shakespeare's exploiting visual representation for its corresponding literary tropes.

Was left unseen, save to the eye of mind:
A hand, a foot, a face, a leg, a head
Stood for the whole to be imaginèd.

And from the walls of strong-besiegèd Troy,
When their brave hope, bold Hector, marched to field,   1430
Stood many Trojan mothers, sharing joy
To see their youthful sons bright weapons wield;
And to their hope they such odd action yield
    That through their light joy seemèd to appear
    (Like bright things stained) a kind of heavy fear.   1435

And from the strond of Dardan where they fought
To Simois' reedy banks the red blood ran,
Whose waves to imitate the battle sought
With swelling ridges; and their ranks began
To break upon the gallèd shore, and than   1440
    Retire again, till meeting greater ranks
    They join, and shoot their foam at Simois' banks.

To this well-painted piece is Lucrece come,
To find a face where all distress is stelled.
Many she sees where cares have carvèd some,   1445
But none where all distress and dolour dwelled;
Till she despairing Hecuba beheld,

1426 **eye of mind** See 1422n.
1429–32 This may owe something to North's Plutarch, where (in the 'Life of Marcus Brutus') Porcia finds relief by gazing upon a 'tablet' which depicts Hector taking leave of his wife and son (see Sarrazin, pp. 422ff.; also 1443–4 below).
1429 **strong-besiegèd** heavily besieged.
1433 i.e. they express their hopes strangely (because they fear the worst, as at 1435). 'And' has the force of 'but' or 'even if' (Onions); 'action' means gesture. (It is unhelpful to take 'hope' as referring to 'Hector' at 1430.)
1434 **light** light-hearted, cheerful
1435 **bright . . . stained** i.e. the cheerful faces are none the less darkened with anxiety. Shakespeare seems to be borrowing the painter's chiaroscuro manner of contrasting light and dark for this impression.
1435 **heavy** oppressive (in contrast to 'light').
1436 **strond of Dardan** 'Strond' (strand, shore) is sometimes used by Shakespeare for its heroic or mythological connotations (e.g. *MV* 1.1.171, *Shr.* 1.1.170, *2H4* 1.1.62). Lee informs us that 'Dard-ania was a name of Troas, the country of which

Troy was the chief city. The district was bounded by the sea, though Troy itself was an inland city on the river Simois.'
1437 **Simois** 'A river which flows from Mount Ida, and joins the river Scamander in the plain of Troy' (Feuillerat). The susurrant movement of its syllables may hint at reeds swaying.
1439 **ridges** crests (see *Ven.* 820n).
1440 **gallèd** worn (see *H5* 3.1.12). *OED* sv *v.* 5 gives a 1548 instance of 'gall' meaning 'harass or annoy in warfare'.
1440 **than** then.
1444 **stelled** delineated, portrayed. (*OED* sv *v.* 3 quotes Haydocke's 1598 translation of Giampaolo Lomazzo's *Trattato*: 'Before you begin to Stell, delineat and tricke out the proportion of a man, you ought to know his true quantity and stature.') See *Son.* 24.1–2, which gives the variant past participle form 'steeld'; see also the wordplay at *Ven.* 375–6.
1445 **where . . . some** some of whom have been 'carvèd' with sorrows; 'carvèd' means both 'engraved' and 'inflicted'.
1447 **despairing Hecuba** As with Nestor and

Staring on Priam's wounds with her old eyes,
Which bleeding under Pyrrhus' proud foot lies.

In her the painter had anatomised   1450
Time's ruin, beauty's rack, and grim care's reign;
Her cheeks with chops and wrinkles were disguised;
Of what she was no semblance did remain.
Her blue blood changed to black in every vein,
    Wanting the spring that those shrunk pipes had fed,   1455
    Showed life imprisoned in a body dead.

On this sad shadow Lucrece spends her eyes,
And shapes her sorrow to the beldam's woes,
Who nothing wants to answer her but cries,
And bitter words to ban her cruel foes: 1460
The painter was no god to lend her those;
    And therefore Lucrece swears he did her wrong,
    To give her so much grief and not a tongue.

'Poor instrument', quoth she, 'without a sound,
I'll tune thy woes with my lamenting tongue,   1465
And drop sweet balm in Priam's painted wound,
And rail on Pyrrhus that hath done him wrong,
And with my tears quench Troy that burns so long,
    And with my knife scratch out the angry eyes
    Of all the Greeks that are thine enemies.   1470

1451 reign] raign Q1; raine Q4

sagacity (1401n), the name of Hecuba is synonymous with sorrow and lamentation (see *Ham.* 2.2.505–18).

1449 Which Who (therefore referring to Priam); see 1139 n and Abbott §265.

1449 under . . . foot Bush (p. 150n) points to Marlowe's *Dido:* 'Treading upon his breast' (537; Brooke, p. 406) – a detail which is not in Virgil.

1450 anatomised dissected, laid open. Borrowed from medical practice, the concept of anatomy had expanded to mean the comprehensive analysis of different kinds of topic.

1451 rack wreckage, ruin.

1452 chops cracks (compare *Son.* 62.10: 'Beated and chopp'd with tann'd antiquity').

1454 blue blood noble blood.

1455 Wanting Lacking.

1455 spring Playing on 'spring' as source (of water) and as springtime or youth.

1455 pipes veins.

1457 shadow image, likeness.

1457 spends her eyes (1) pours forth tears, (2) gazes fixedly.

1458 beldam aged woman (also spelt 'beldame'; see 953n).

1459 wants needs (see 1455).

1460 ban curse (see *Ven.* 326).

1461 lend grant. Shakespeare may have in mind some precise mythological occasion, as when Venus granted Pygmalion's prayer and turned his statue of Galatea into a real woman (see *Ven.* 213n).

1464 instrument A musical instrument is intended (see 1465). (The idea is reminiscent of 1079–80 and 1105.)

1465 tune . . . tongue sing sorrowfully of your woes.

1466 sweet balm The 'balm' is her tears, which are 'sweet' because tender ('sweet' also means soothing).

1467 rail on cry out accusingly at.

1469 scratch out The idea is possibly ironic, since the artist may make incisions with a palette

'Show me the strumpet that began this stir,
That with my nails her beauty I may tear.
Thy heat of lust, fond Paris, did incur
This load of wrath that burning Troy doth bear.
Thy eye kindled the fire that burneth here,   1475
    And here in Troy, for trespass of thine eye,
    The sire, the son, the dame, and daughter die.

'Why should the private pleasure of some one
Become the public plague of many moe?
Let sin, alone committed, light alone   1480
Upon his head that hath transgressèd so;
Let guiltless souls be freed from guilty woe:
    For one's offence why should so many fall,
    To plague a private sin in general?

'Lo, here weeps Hecuba, here Priam dies,   1485
Here manly Hector faints, here Troilus sounds;
Here friend by friend in bloody channel lies,
And friend to friend gives unadvisèd wounds;
And one man's lust these many lives confounds.
    Had doting Priam checked his son's desire,   1490
    Troy had been bright with fame, and not with fire.'

Here feelingly she weeps Troy's painted woes,
For sorrow, like a heavy hanging bell,

1486 sounds] Q1

knife or similar sharp instrument: i.e. putting in
the eyes in the manner in which Lucrece threatens
to take them out.
   1471 stir tumult, disturbance (see *Ven.* 283).
   1473 fond doting.
   1476 trespass For the specific sense of sexual
transgression that the word carries in the poem see
524, 632, 812, and 1070.
   1478 private personal, selfish. while indict-
ing Paris's self-indulgence, Lucrece simultaneously
comments on Tarquin's very different sort of 'private' (i.e. secretive) rape.
   1479 moe more (this form is used often of quantity or number).
   1481 transgressèd See 1476n.
   1482 guilty woe the sorrow of true guilt.
Lucrece reverts to the argument that an involuntary
or compelled offence is not culpable (see Introduction, p. 26).
   1483 As well as the Trojan story, Lucrece may
have in mind the shame that will infect Collatine's

lineage as a result of the rape (see 827–33).
   1484 To make one person's offence infect everybody. 'To plague' means 'to make a plague of'.
   1486 sounds swoons, faints (both with love-
sickness, and as a result of his wounds; the point
is that the action is effeminate and unnatural, like
the fainting of 'manly Hector').
   1487 channel gutter. Most editors interpret the
action as taking place within the city, though there
is an echo of 1436–42. The picture appears to
describe the sequence of events leading up to the
destruction of Troy, showing Priam, for example,
now living and now dead, all of which may indicate
its literary rather than pictorial nature. However, it
is not unusual for canvases or tapestries to narrate
actions. (See 1366–1568n).
   1488 unadvisèd unintended.
   1489 confounds destroys.
   1490 doting Priam 'Doting' is also used to
describe lustful feeling (see 155n), which, like
fatherly affection, is not subject to rational control.

Once set on ringing, with his own weight goes;
Then little strength rings out the doleful knell: 1495
So Lucrece, set a-work, sad tales doth tell
   To pencilled pensiveness and coloured sorrow;
   She lends them words, and she their looks doth borrow.

She throws her eyes about the painting round,
And who she finds forlorn she doth lament.   1500
At last she sees a wretched image bound,
That piteous looks to Phrygian shepherds lent:
   His face, though full of cares, yet showed content;
   Onward to Troy with the blunt swains he goes,
   So mild that patience seemed to scorn his woes.   1505

In him the painter laboured with his skill
To hide deceit, and give the harmless show
An humble gait, calm looks, eyes wailing still,
A brow unbent that seemed to welcome woe,
Cheeks neither red nor pale, but mingled so   1510

1499 painting] Q1; painted Q3+   1507 deceit] Q1; conceipt Q4

Lucrece's observation suggests her despair at male passion in general.

1494 on ringing ringing, a-ringing (see Abbott §180).

1496 a-work to work (Abbott §24).

1497 pencilled pensiveness painted sorrow (for the use of 'pencil' to mean paint-brush, see Castiglione, p. 49).

1497 coloured depicted, painted.

1498 i.e. Lucrece speaks for the silent figures in the painting, who in exchange teach her how to look sorrowful.

1499 about . . . round all round the painting.

1501 wretched . . . bound figure of a bound prisoner.

1502 Who made the Trojan shepherds look with pity. 'Phrygian', which connotes fierceness, contrasts with 'piteous': for the force of the epithet, see E. K.'s 'Glosse' to Spenser's October Eclogue:

when as Timotheus the great Musitian playd the Phrygian melodie, it is said, that [Alexander] was distraught with such unwonted fury, that streight way rising from the table in great rage, he caused himself to be armed, as ready to goe to warre (for that musick is very war like).
(*SMP*, p. 101)

1504 blunt swains See 1502n.

1505 patience i.e. his patience. Patience, embodied in Sinon, seems to scorn its woes.

Maxwell prefers to interpret patience as external: 'so mild that Patience did not seem to regard his woes as sufficient to be worth exercising herself upon'. This requires referring 'his' to Sinon, but *his* still represented the genitive of *it* in Shakespeare's time (Abbott §228).

1507 hide deceit Since 'deceit' is itself a form of concealment, the painter's objective artistry ironically corresponds with the guilty motives of his subject.

1507 harmless show An ironic observation similar to the one above: as a mere picture ('show'), the figure of Sinon can do no harm, so from one point of view there is no need for disguise. But this is a further example of 'imaginary work' (1422) in which the painter's own 'conceit deceitful' (1423) again proves indistinguishable from the image of deception that he creates, the spectator being required to understand and complete the artist's intentions.

1508 eyes wailing i.e. the impression of rearfulness is so forceful that the spectator seems to hear the cries of anguish. The detail may seem at odds with 'calm looks', but as always the effect is paradoxical ('*though* full of cares, *yet* showed content', 1503).

1509 brow unbent face that is not cast down (stoically cheerful). 'Brow' means the whole face and not merely the forehead (see 749n).

That blushing red no guilty instance gave,
Nor ashy pale the fear that false hearts have.

But like a constant and confirmèd devil,
He entertained a show so seeming just,
And therein so ensconced his secret evil,   1515
That jealousy itself could not mistrust
False creeping craft and perjury should thrust
    Into so bright a day such black-faced storms,
    Or blot with hell-born sin such saint-like forms.

The well-skilled workman this mild image drew   1520
For perjured Sinon, whose enchanting story
The credulous old Priam after slew;
Whose words like wildfire burnt the shining glory
Of rich-built Ilion, that the skies were sorry;
    And little stars shot from their fixèd places,   1525
    When their glass fell wherein they viewed their faces.

This picture she advisedly perused,
And chid the painter for his wondrous skill,
Saying some shape in Sinon's was abused:

1519 hell-born] Q1; hell-borne Q2+

1511 **guilty instance** sign of guilt (Onions).

1513 **constant . . . devil** Again the phrase is paradoxical, since devilry typically lays siege to virtues such as constancy.

1513 **confirmèd** Perhaps suggesting, along contemporary theological lines, damnation through habitual sin.

1514 **entertained a show** sustained an appearance.

1515 **ensconced** sheltered. To 'ensconce' is 'to shelter behind or within a "sconce", earthwork, or fortification' (Onions). The military dimension perhaps recalls Sinon's manoeuvre in getting the wooden horse lodged within the walls.

1516 **jealousy** suspicion (see *Ven.* 649).

1516 **mistrust** suspect that.

1518–19 Images of cosmic physiognomy are previously at 11–14, 775–7, and 1224–32.

1521 **enchanting** beguiling.

1523 **like wildfire** Wildfire is 'gunpowder rolled up and set on fire' (Onions), and so has a specific military meaning; the phrase 'like wildfire' also means 'spreading with immense rapidity' (*OED*, citing this line). Shakespeare probably had his eye on Marlowe: 'And after him his band of

Mirmidons, / With balles of wilde fire in their murdering pawes, / Which made the funerall flame that burnt faire *Troy*' (*Dido* 511–13).

1524 **rich-built Ilion** See Marlowe again: 'Viewing the fire wherewith rich Ilion burnt' (*Dido*, 1.559).

1525–6 A further example of cosmic parallelism or physiognomy (see 1518–19n). Universal compassion or empathy ('the skies were sorry') is emphasised rather than Tillyardian hierarchy (though 'fixèd places' gives some support to such a view). The special kind of pathos sought by the imagery is found in such tender details as the 'little stars' being depicted as innocent beauties gazing into a mirror – an impression which, for its delicacy, recalls the images at 1226–39. Such effects disregard the heroic line that the story of Troy naturally assumes, with the result that they appear to Malone to be inconsistent: 'Why Troy, however beautiful or magnificent, should be called the mirrour in which the fixed stars beheld themselves, I do not see.'

1527 **advisedly** thoughtfully, carefully.

1529 **some . . . abused** i.e. it was an insult to depict the model as if his form ('shape') was Sinon's.

So fair a form lodged not a mind so ill.   1530
And still on him she gazed, and gazing still,
　　Such signs of truth in his plain face she spied,
　　That she concludes the picture was belied.

'It cannot be', quoth she, 'that so much guile' –
She would have said – 'can lurk in such a look.'   1535
But Tarquin's shape came in her mind the while,
And from her tongue 'can lurk' from 'cannot' took.
'It cannot be' she in that sense forsook,
　　And turned it thus: 'It cannot be, I find,
　　But such a face should bear a wicked mind.   1540

'For even as subtle Sinon here is painted,
So sober-sad, so weary, and so mild
(As if with grief or travail he had fainted),
To me came Tarquin armèd to beguild
With outward honesty, but yet defiled   1545
　　With inward vice. As Priam him did cherish,
　　So did I Tarquin; so my Troy did perish.

'Look, look how list'ning Priam wets his eyes,
To see those borrowed tears that Sinon sheds.
Priam, why art thou old, and yet not wise?   1550
For every tear he falls a Trojan bleeds;
His eye drops fire, no water thence proceeds;
　　Those round clear pearls of his that move thy pity
　　Are balls of quenchless fire to burn thy city.

1530 Neoplatonism gave special currency to the idea that the outer form reflects the inner spirit, and that beauty of appearance indicates purity of mind (see Castiglione, p. 309).

1532 **plain** open, honest.

1533 **was belied** told a lie (i.e. the 'truth' in Sinon's face contradicted the statement of the picture as a whole).

1539 **turned** twisted.

1540 **But** But that. The effect of 'It cannot be . . . But' is 'It cannot be otherwise but'.

1541 **subtle** treacherous (see 957n).

1542 **sober-sad** quietly serious.

1543 **travail** excessive labour.

1544 **beguild** beguile (Cercignani, p. 256, spells 'beguild'; compare *Ven.* 873, where Q1 has 'twin'd' – apparently for 'twine'). Wyndham plausibly sees

a pun on 'gild' (as at 60).

1546 **cherish** entertain (a guest) with kindness (Onions); see *1H4* 3.3.172.

1547 **my . . . perish** See 428–41 and 463–9, where the prelude to the rape is likened to the siege and invasion of a city.

1549 **borrowed** (1) assumed, false, (2) bestowed by the painter. Shakespeare may in part be continuing his observations on the nature of art to depict something which is both real and unreal simultaneously.

1549 **sheds** Probably pronounced to rhyme with 'bleeds'; see *Son.* 34.13, which has 'sheeds' (Cercignani, p. 82).

1551 **he falls** Sinon lets fall.

1554 **balls . . . fire** i.e. wildfire (see 1523n); 'quenchles fire' occurs at *Dido* 481 (Lee).

'Such devils steal effects from lightless hell;   1555
For Sinon in his fire doth quake with cold,
And in that cold hot burning fire doth dwell;
These contraries such unity do hold
Only to flatter fools and make them bold;
    So Priam's trust false Sinon's tears doth flatter   1560
    That he finds means to burn his Troy with water.'

Here, all enraged, such passion her assails,
That patience is quite beaten from her breast;
She tears the senseless Sinon with her nails,
Comparing him to that unhappy guest   1565
Whose deed hath made herself herself detest.
    At last she smilingly with this gives o'er:
    'Fool, fool!' quoth she, 'his wounds will not be sore.'

Thus ebbs and flows the current of her sorrow,
And time doth weary time with her complaining.   1570
She looks for night, and then she longs for morrow,
And both she thinks too long with her remaining.
Short time seems long in sorrow's sharp sustaining:
    Though woe be heavy, yet it seldom sleeps,
    And they that watch see time how slow it creeps;   1575

Which all this time hath overslipped her thought
That she with painted images hath spent,
Being from the feeling of her own grief brought
By deep surmise of others' detriment,

1555 **effects** appearances (Onions).

1555 **lightless hell** See 4n. The contrarieties observed here (see 1556–7) resemble Tarquin's contradictory lustfulness, in which he seeks what he also shirks (as at 308).

1558 i.e. such opposites are contained in each other.

1560 **So** In the same way (by 'fools' at 1559 is meant such figures as Sinon and Tarquin).

1560 **doth flatter** See Abbott §334.

1564 **senseless** i.e. being without sensation (see 820n and *Ven.* 211).

1565 **unhappy** i.e. bearing misfortune.

1566 **herself herself** See Abbott §20.

1568 **wounds . . . sore** The difference between representation and reality, as observed in the painting, is used to comment on the equally frustrat-ing dimension of time, which places deeds beyond recovery. Lucrece contemplates in the unassailable Sinon of art the futility of attempting to influence or affect the action to which she has been an unwilling party.

1570 **time . . . time** Reproducing in its phrasing the ebb and flow of the constantly reiterated 'current'.

1572 **thinks . . . long** See 1359n.

1573 **in . . . sustaining** when sorrow has painfully to be endured.

1574 **heavy** (1) oppressive, (2) drowsy.

1576 **Which** i.e. woe.

1576 **overslipped** passed unnoticed by (Onions).

1579 **surmise** contemplation.

Losing her woes in shows of discontent. 1580
    It easeth some, though none it ever curèd,
    To think their dolour others have endurèd,

But now the mindful messenger come back
Brings home his lord and other company,
Who finds his Lucrece clad in mourning black, 1585
And round about her tear-distainèd eye
Blue circles streamed, like rainbows in the sky:
    These water-galls in her dim element
    Foretell new storms to those already spent.

Which when her sad-beholding husband saw, 1590
Amazedly in her sad face he stares:
Her eyes, though sod in tears, looked red and raw,
Her lively colour killed with deadly cares.
He hath no power to ask her how she fares;
    Both stood like old acquaintance in a trance, 1595
    Met far from home, wond'ring each other's chance.

At last he takes her by the bloodless hand,
And thus begins: 'What uncouth ill event
Hath thee befall'n, that thou dost trembling stand?
Sweet love, what spite hath thy fair colour spent? 1600
Why art thou thus attired in discontent?
    Unmask, dear dear, this moody heaviness,
    And tell thy grief, that we may give redress.'

1583 come back] come back, Q1; comes back, Q3+   **1595** Both] Q1; But Q6+

1580 shows representations (perhaps with wordplay in that the sound of 'woes' is absorbed by that of 'shows').

1581–2 Compare 1111–13.

1583 mindful conscientious.

1586 tear-distainèd i.e. stained with tears.

1588 water-galls A water-gall is 'a secondary or imperfectly formed rainbow' (*OED*, citing this line).

1588 dim element dark or overcast sky (of her face); see 12.

1590 sad-beholding earnestly looking ('sad' in this phrase plays against its meaning in 1591; see 1610n).

1592 sod boiled, scalded (Onions); antithetical to 'raw'.

1593 lively . . . deadly Maintaining the antithesis noted at 1592.

1596 wond'ring . . . chance speculating on each other's fortunes.

1598 uncouth strange, unknown, barbarous (*Tit.* 2.3.211: 'I am surprised with an uncouth fear').

1600 spent extinguished, emptied. Herford suggests the influence of the Italian 'spento' (put out, extinguished); equally 'spite' seems to convey the sense of 'spietà' (pitilessness).

1602 Unmask (1) Put off (playing on 'attired'), (2) explain.

1602 moody heaviness feeling of oppression (compare 1574).

1603 tell thy grief (1) explain what has made you sad, (2) express your sorrow (in order to find relief from it, as at *Mac.* 4.3.209: 'Give sorrow words').

Three times with sighs she gives her sorrow fire,
Ere once she can discharge one word of woe.   1605
At length addressed to answer his desire,
She modestly prepares to let them know
Her honour is tane prisoner by the foe;
    While Collatine and his consorted lords
    With sad attention long to hear her words.   1610

And now this pale swan in her wat'ry nest
Begins the sad dirge of her certain ending:
'Few words', quoth she, 'shall fit the trespass best,
Where no excuse can give the fault amending.
In me moe woes than words are now depending,   1615
    And my laments would be drawn out too long
    To tell them all with one poor tirèd tongue.

'Then be this all the task it hath to say:
Dear husband, in the interest of thy bed
A stranger came, and on that pillow lay   1620
Where thou wast wont to rest thy weary head;
And what wrong else may be imaginèd
    By foul enforcement might be done to me,
    From that, alas, thy Lucrece is not free.

'For in the dreadful dead of dark midnight,   1625
With shining falchion in my chamber came

1604 **Three times** Apparently from *Fasti* 2.823: 'Ter conata loqui: ter destitit' (Three times she tried to speak, and three times was silent).

1604 **gives . . . fire** attempts to express her sorrow. The image is of applying a lighted taper to a cannon in order to 'discharge' it.

1606 **addressed** addressing herself, prepared.

1607 **modestly prepares** i.e. she looks for a chaste way of recounting an unchaste action.

1609 **consorted** associated, leagued (in a military sense, partly prompted by the idea of 1608).

1610 **sad** serious, earnest. (In a context of grief, 'sad' alternates delicately between its more familiar meaning 'sorrowful' and its frequent Elizabethan meaning of 'serious' or 'solemn').

1611–12 Referring to the legend that the swan sings shortly before its death: see *MV* 3.2.44–5, *Oth.* 5.2.247–8, *PhT* 15.

1611 **in . . . nest** amidst her tears.

1612 **certain ending** sure death.

1613 **shall . . . best** will be best suited to describe the offence. 'Trespass', as elsewhere in the poem, specifically connotes sin or sexual transgression (see 524).

1614 **give . . . amending** pardon or correct the offence.

1615 **moe** a variant of 'more' used here for its echoing effect with 'woes' (see also 1479).

1615 **depending** (1) impending (requiring expression), (2) hanging (like clouds) – see *Rom.* 3.1.119.

1619 **in . . . of** usurping, acquiring possession of. 'Interest' here means right or title (Onions).

1623 **enforcement** constraint, violation (Onions).

1624 See 734n.

1626 **falchion** See 176n.

A creeping creature with a flaming light,
And softly cried, "Awake, thou Roman dame,
And entertain my love; else lasting shame
    On thee and thine this night I will inflict,   1630
    If thou my love's desire do contradict.

'"For some hard-favoured groom of thine", quoth he,
"Unless thou yoke thy liking to my will,
I'll murder straight, and then I'll slaughter thee,
And swear I found you where you did fulfil   1635
The loathsome act of lust, and so did kill
    The lechers in their deed: this act will be
    My fame, and thy perpetual infamy."

'With this I did begin to start and cry;
And then against my heart he set his sword,   1640
Swearing, unless I took all patiently,
I should not live to speak another word.
So should my shame still rest upon record,
    And never be forgot in mighty Rome
    Th'adulterate death of Lucrece and her groom.   1645

'Mine enemy was strong, my poor self weak,
And far the weaker with so strong a fear.
My bloody judge forbod my tongue to speak;
No rightful plea might plead for justice there.
His scarlet lust came evidence to swear   1650

1644 Rome] Q3 +; Roome Q1

1627 creeping creature Recalling 365; a contrast is offered between the 'creeping creature', which connotes a figure moving in darkness, and the 'flaming light' he holds.

1629 entertain submit to, endure.

1631 love's desire lust (rendered euphemistically): the subtle increase of force registered between 'love' (1629) and 'love's desire' aptly reflects the process of self-justification and hardening of will in Tarquin.

1631 contradict withstand.

1632 hard-favoured coarse-featured (see *Ven.* 133). Tarquin's actual words are 'worthless slave' (see 515), which emphasise a groom's low station rather than his physiognomy. But Lucrece may have chosen 'hard-favoured' as a sign of crude physicality, since for her the essential dishonour is lust itself, which, throughout this stanza, directs her recall of what was said. Tarquin, who, by contrast, seeks in pursuing lust to disguise its reality,

tries to frighten her with the threat of something closer to social dishonour.

1633 yoke submit.

1634 slaughter Perhaps with sacrificial connotations (see 1376n), but the symmetrical balance of 'murder'–'slaughter' is sufficient explanation.

1635 fulfil perform, consummate.

1639 start be alarmed.

1641 patiently submissively.

1645 adulterate adulterous.

1647 See 1266n.

1648 bloody bloodthirsty (playing on the colour of the judge's robes, as at 1650).

1648 forbod forbade.

1650 scarlet lust Scarlet is traditionally the colour of (1) reprehensible passion (as in the expression 'scarlet woman'), and (2) the judge's robes.

1650 evidence to swear to give evidence (presumably of the senses as opposed to reason).

That my poor beauty had purloined his eyes;
And when the judge is robbed, the prisoner dies.

'O teach me how to make mine own excuse,
Or (at the least) this refuge let me find:
Though my gross blood be stained with this abuse,   1655
Immaculate and spotless is my mind;
That was not forced, that never was inclined
    To accessary yieldings, but still pure
    Doth in her poisoned closet yet endure.'

Lo, here the hopeless merchant of this loss,   1660
With head declined, and voice dammed up with woe,
With sad set eyes, and wreathèd arms across,
From lips new waxen pale begins to blow
The grief away that stops his answer so.
    But, wretched as he is, he strives in vain;   1665
    What he breathes out his breath drinks up again.

As through an arch the violent roaring tide
Outruns the eye that doth behold his haste,
Yet in the eddy boundeth in his pride
Back to the strait that forced him on so fast,   1670

1661 declined] Q1; inclined Q2+   1662 wreathèd] *conj. Walker;* wretched Q1

1651 **poor** (1) innocuous, (2) impoverished (the second sense allows for a play on the idea that a poor man is a likely 'purloiner').

1652 **judge is robbed** The property of a judge is judgement, which according to this conceit is what he is robbed of – to the disadvantage of those who appear before him.

1655–6 Possibly from Livy 1.58: 'ceterum corpus est tantum violatum, animus insons' (while the rest of my body has been greatly violated, my mind is innocent).

1655 **gross blood** Either (1) referring to the material nature of blood and its inescapable impurity, or (2) conceding by transferred epithet that her blood will have been corrupted by this *gross* abuse.

1657–8 **inclined . . . yieldings** disposed to yield or grant access (the phrase is pleonastic).

1659 **poisoned closet** corrupted body.

1659 **endure** survive, hold out.

1660 **hopeless . . . loss** The conceit depicts Collatine as a merchant who has entrusted his precious ship to the perilous seas of his own foolish boasting (at 15–21). The image anticipates the condition of

Antonio in *The Merchant of Venice.*

1662 **set** fixed, staring.

1662 **wreathèd . . . across** For the gesture, see 793n. Walker's sharp-eyed emendation of 'wretched' to 'wreathèd' has been adopted, despite the consistency of the quartos, which all follow Q1's 'wretched'. Walker supports his case by citing examples of formal postures of love-melancholy (including *LLL* 4.3.133 and Beaumont and Fletcher's *Faithful Shepherdess* 3.1.105–6) in which the phrase 'wreathed arms' recurs. The present scene depicts precisely such a tableau of grief as the formula recommends. In printing or reading 'wretched' the compositor may have been distracted by its appearance at 1665.

1663 **new waxen** newly grown.

1666 A description of the violent swallowings occasioned by grief mingled with anger. The idea is continued over the following stanza.

1667–70 Spurgeon (pp. 96–9) interestingly and charmingly relates this simile to her observation of the river at Stratford-Upon-Avon.

1669 **boundeth in** draws in, restrains.

1669 **pride** force, exuberance.

In rage sent out, recalled in rage, being past;
   Even so his sighs, his sorrows, make a saw,
   To push grief on, and back the same grief draw.

Which speechless woe of his poor she attendeth,
And his untimely frenzy thus awaketh: 1675
'Dear lord, thy sorrow to my sorrow lendeth
Another power; no flood by raining slaketh.
My woe too sensible thy passion maketh
   More feeling-painful. Let it then suffice
   To drown one woe, one pair of weeping eyes.   1680

'And for my sake, when I might charm thee so,
For she that was thy Lucrece, now attend me:
Be suddenly revengèd on my foe,
Thine, mine, his own; suppose thou dost defend me
From what is past. The help that thou shalt lend me   1685
   Comes all too late, yet let the traitor die;
   For sparing justice feeds iniquity.

'But ere I name him, you fair lords', quoth she,
Speaking to those that came with Collatine,
'Shall plight your honourable faiths to me,   1690
With swift pursuit to venge this wrong of mine;
   For 'tis a meritorious fair design

1680 one woe, one] Q3+; on woe, one Q1

1671 **being past** having gone out (and now ready to return).
1672 **make a saw** perform a back-and-forth sawing motion.
1674 **attendeth** observes.
1675 **his . . . awaketh** brings him out of his inopportune madness.
1677 **Another** Further.
1677 **slaketh** diminishes (see 425n).
1678 **sensible** keenly felt.
1678 **passion** suffering.
1679 **feeling-painful** sensitive of its pain.
1680 **one woe** Q1 has 'on woe' (see collation and Sisson, 1.209). Pooler cites, tentatively in support of Q1 (which he does not follow), the pun 'on' / 'one' at *TGV* 2.1.1–2. Rather, the similarity of pronunciation may have accounted for the error.
1681–94 The source is probably Livy or Painter: 'But if you be men give me your handes and trouth, that the adulterer may not escape unrevenged . . .' (Bullough, 1, 198; also Ewig, p. 22, and Baldwin, *Genetics*, pp. 148–9).
1681 **when** if.

1681 **charm** It is perhaps curious that Lucrece should use this word, given her newly found experience of the destructiveness of female charm (whether practised deliberately or not); but she is casting herself in the role of a lady who asks her knight to perform a service (see 1692–4). Her appeal to chivalry is an attempt to reassert the selflessness of its ideal and its subjugation of all unworthy passions (in particular lust).
1682 **she** See Abbott §211 for an explanation why 'she' is used rather than 'her'.
1683 **suddenly** immediately.
1684 **suppose** think that, imagine.
1684 **defend me** defend my reputation, exonerate me.
1687 See *MM* 2.1.283–4 and Tilley P50; 'sparing' (stinting on) is antithetical to 'feeds'.
1691 **venge** avenge.
1692–4 See 1681n. Malone objects to the anachronism: 'Here one of the laws of chivalry is somewhat prematurely introduced'; but the concepts of knighthood and chivalry are present in the poem at least as early as 197.

To chase injustice with revengeful arms:
Knights by their oaths should right poor ladies' harms.'

At this request, with noble disposition   1695
Each present lord began to promise aid,
As bound in knighthood to her imposition,
Longing to hear the hateful foe bewrayed.
But she, that yet her sad task hath not said,
  The protestation stops. 'O speak', quoth she,   1700
  'How may this forcèd stain be wiped from me?

'What is the quality of my offence,
Being constrained with dreadful circumstance?
May my pure mind with the foul act dispense,
My low-declinèd honour to advance?   1705
May any terms acquit me from this chance?
  The poisoned fountain clears itself again;
  And why not I from this compellèd stain?'

With this they all at once began to say,
Her body's stain her mind untainted clears;   1710
While with a joyless smile she turns away
The face, that map which deep impression bears
Of hard misfortune, carved in it with tears.
  'No, no', quoth she, 'no dame hereafter living
  By my excuse shall claim excuse's giving.'   1715

Here with a sigh as if her heart would break,
She throws forth Tarquin's name: 'He, he', she says,
But more than 'he' her poor tongue could not speak;

1710 her mind Q1; the mind Q5 *(Trinity College)*, Q6–9   1712 The face, that] Q1; Her face, that *conj. Walker;* That
face, the *conj. Kinnear*   1713 in it] *Capell MS;* it in Q1

1697 **her imposition** the task she has imposed.
1698 **bewrayed** revealed.
1699 **sad** solemn.
1699 **said** revealed.
1700 **protestation** i.e. general vow of service.
1702 **quality** nature.
1703 See 1262n.
1704 **with . . . dispense** pardon the foul act (i.e. Lucrece asks if purity of conscience does not sufficiently exonerate her). See 1070n; the construction is always 'dispense with' (Onions).
1706 **terms** arguments.
1706 **chance** i.e. circumstance beyond her control (the 'forced offence' of 1071).
1707 Compare the argument at 577.

1708 **compellèd stain** See 1706n.
1712 **map** See 402n. A navigator's map would represent particular areas of danger ('hard' – i.e. harsh – 'misfortune' perhaps corresponds to the idea of places of recorded disaster); a relief map with its raised contours would likewise correspond to wrinkles or haggard features.
1713 **carved** Corresponding to the action of water on the shore-line.
1714–15 Livy 1.58 again appears to be the prominent source: 'nec ulla deinde impudica Lucretiae exemplo vivet'; or in Painter's version: 'for no unchast or ill woman shall hereafter impute no dishonest act to Lucrece' (Bullough, I, 198).

Till after many accents and delays,
Untimely breathings, sick and short assays,   1720
  She utters this: 'He, he, fair lords, 'tis he,
  That guides this hand to give this wound to me.'

Even here she sheathèd in her harmless breast
A harmful knife, that thence her soul unsheathèd:
That blow did bail it from the deep unrest   1725
Of that polluted prison where it breathèd.
Her contrite sighs unto the clouds bequeathèd
  Her wingèd sprite, and through her wounds doth fly
  Life's lasting date from cancelled destiny.

Stone-still, astonished with this deadly deed,   1730
Stood Collatine and all his lordly crew;
Till Lucrece' father, that beholds her bleed,
Himself on her self-slaught'red body threw;
And from the purple fountain Brutus drew
  The murd'rous knife, and as it left the place,   1735
  Her blood, in poor revenge, held it in chase;

And bubbling from her breast, it doth divide
In two slow rivers, that the crimson blood

1721 lords] Q1; lord Q5 +

1719 **accents** vocal sounds, attempts to speak.
1720 **Untimely** Irregular.
1720 **sick** distempered, disordered.
1720 **assays** efforts. In all this Shakespeare is following the guidelines for convincing displays of distress as laid down by such writers on oratory as Quintilian. While Lucrece's agitation is natural, she 'performs' according to a recognisable style, which in 1594 was probably still influential in the theatre (see Gurr, pp. 95–101).
1723 **harmless** innocent.
1725 **bail it** buy its release.
1726 **polluted prison** See 1659.
1727 **contrite sighs** Lucrece's soul can be received in heaven, freed of its polluted earthly body.
1729 **Life's . . . date** Everlasting life.
1729 **from . . . destiny** A condensed phrase which principally means that she has escaped from the damnation that she had feared was her lot (see her argument at 934–5), which, as Lever points out, is now reversed or redeemed. A secondary meaning is that she has cancelled her allotted span of life (by suicide), but so far as spiritual life is concerned ('wingèd sprite') her action does not, according to

the poem, condemn her.
1730–6 In contrast to *Fasti* 2.835ff., where both husband and father fall on Lucrece's body, Shakespeare seems to aim at a stylistic division of the action into three separate aspects: Collatine's motionless horror, Lucretius's prostrate grief, and Brutus's political initiative.
1730 **astonished** The pun on 'Stone-still' is obvious enough, though it may have been prompted by *FQ* 2.6.31.9 (Lever, Maxwell).
1733 **self-slaught'red** With this phrase compare the reflection on suicide at *Ham.* 1.2.131–2.
1734–6 Compare the action of Marcus Brutus at *JC* 3.2.176–80.
1734 **purple fountain** Here 'purple' may be likened to blue to denote Lucrece's nobility (see 1454n, and below, 1738); it traditionally signifies a bright (mainly though not exclusively red) colour (see *Ven.* 1n), and is used in Latin epic poetry for the colour (*purpureus*) of blood shed in battle.
1736 **poor revenge** an inadequate attempt at revenge.
1736 **held . . . chase** chased after it.
1738 **that** so that.

Circles her body in on every side,
Who like a late-sacked island vastly stood   1740
Bare and unpeopled in this fearful flood.
   Some of her blood still pure and red remained,
   And some looked black, and that false Tarquin stained.

About the mourning and congealèd face
Of that black blood a wat'ry rigol goes,   1745
Which seems to weep upon the tainted place;
And ever since, as pitying Lucrece' woes,
Corrupted blood some watery token shows,
   And blood untainted still doth red abide,
   Blushing at that which is so putrified.   1750

'Daughter, dear daughter', old Lucretius cries,
'That life was mine which thou hast here deprivèd.
If in the child the father's image lies,
Where shall I live now Lucrece is unlivèd?
Thou wast not to this end from me derivèd: 1755
   If children predecease progenitors,
   We are their offspring, and they none of ours.

'Poor broken glass, I often did behold
In thy sweet semblance my old age new born;
But now that fair fresh mirror, dim and old,   1760

1743 stained] Q1; sham'd Q5 *(Huntington)*

1739 **Circles . . . in** encircles, encloses (siege-like).
1740 **Who** Which (Abbott §264).
1740 **vastly** (1) in desolation, (2) far and wide.
1741 **Bare** Denuded (continuing the simile of the 'late-sacked island'). But 'naked' may be a secondary sense of the word, for while Lucrece should realistically be imagined as clothed (Chaucer even makes a point of her falling with modest attention to her dress, *LGW* 1857–60), Shakespeare may be influenced in his choice of epithet (as in his simile) by iconographic considerations: in the many Renaissance portraits Lucrece is depicted as nude at the moment of suicide.
1743 **stained** i.e. accused.
1745 **wat'ry rigol** Referring to the separation in blood of the serum (a watery liquid) from the clot. A 'rigol' is a circle (meaning crown in *2H4* 4.5.36). Feuillerat argues the connection (*OED* in support) with the Fr. *rigole* (channel, rivulet); and Gildon's

linking of it with mirth (*rigolo, rigoler*) may not be so 'queer' as Rollins supposes, given the strongly paradoxical tendency of the poem's phrasing. But if intentional, such wordplay is here very much muted.
1747–50 'Like the death of Adonis, Lucrece's death is said to bring about a new metamorphosis. The watery serum of *Corrupted* blood weeps for her woes; the red *untainted* blood blushes at the corruption suffered' (Lever).
1747 **as** as if.
1752 **deprivèd** taken away (see 1186n).
1754 **unlivèd** without life, dispossessed of life.
1757 **they . . . ours** There is perhaps a hint of his disowning her in this idea, though logically it follows from 'we . . . offspring'. Prince compares *Rom.* 5.3.214–15.
1758–9 Compare *Son.* 3.9.–10: 'Thou art thy mother's glass, and she in thee / Calls back the lovely April of her prime.'

Shows me a bare-boned death by time outworn.
O from thy cheeks my image thou hast torn,
  And shivered all the beauty of my glass,
  That I no more can see what once I was.

'O time, cease thou thy course and last no longer,   1765
If they surcease to be that should survive.
Shall rotten death make conquest of the stronger,
And leave the falt'ring feeble souls alive?
The old bees die, the young possess their hive.
  Then live, sweet Lucrece, live again and see   1770
  Thy father die, and not thy father thee.'

By this, starts Collatine as from a dream,
And bids Lucretius give his sorrow place;
And then in key-cold Lucrece' bleeding stream
He falls, and bathes the pale fear in his face,   1775
And counterfeits to die with her a space;
  Till manly shame bids him possess his breath,
  And live to be revengèd on her death.

The deep vexation of his inward soul
Hath served a dumb arrest upon his tongue;   1780
Who, mad that sorrow should his use control,
Or keep him from heart-easing words so long,
Begins to talk; but through his lips do throng

1762 thy cheeks] Q1; my cheeks Q4+   **1765** last] Q1; hast Q4+   **1766** they] Q1; thou Q4+   **1781** mad] Q1; made Q2+

1761 Shows . . . death The image plays on the idea of a death's-head or *memento mori*, and naturalism yields to metaphor as the elderly Lucretius *reads*, in a way that applies to him personally, the ravages of time and ageing in Lucrece's features rather than observing the actual appearance of a recently dead young woman.

1763 shivered shattered (a 'shiver' is a splinter or fragment). The connotation of coldness as in 'bare-boned' is also present.

1763 glass mirror (as at 1760).

1766 surcease cease ('surcease' is an alternative, earlier form of 'cease', used for its symmetry and antithesis with 'survive'; compare the example at *Mac.* 1.7.4: 'surcease, success').

1767 rotten i.e. rotted away, weak (in contrast to 'stronger').

1769 Compare 836–40.

1774 key-cold . . . bleeding Merging two contrasting ideas: (1) the coldness of death (Tilley K23, *R*3.1.2.5: 'Poor key-cold figure of a holy king'), and (2) the application of cold metal in an attempt to stanch bleeding. This latter practice probably led to the proverbial observation of (1).

1776 counterfeits imitates. The Elizabethan meaning is rather that of representation or emulation than our idea of fake (see 1269).

1780 Hath . . . arrest Has made him speechless; the force of 'dumb arrest' is proleptic in that the effect of dumbness is anticipated in the action of 'arresting'.

1781 Who Which (see 1740n).

1781 mad furious.

1781 control inhibit.

Weak words, so thick come in his poor heart's aid
That no man could distinguish what he said.   1785

Yet sometime 'Tarquin' was pronouncèd plain,
But through his teeth, as if the name he tore.
This windy tempest, till it blow up rain,
Held back his sorrow's tide, to make it more.
At last it rains, and busy winds give o'er;   1790
    Then son and father weep with equal strife
    Who should weep most, for daughter or for wife.

The one doth call her his, the other his;
Yet neither may possess the claim they lay.
The father says, 'She's mine.' 'O mine she is',   1795
Replies her husband: 'do not take away
My sorrow's interest; let no mourner say
    He weeps for her, for she was only mine,
    And only must be wailed by Collatine.'

'O', quoth Lucretius, 'I did give that life   1800
Which she too early and too late hath spilled.'
'Woe, woe', quoth Collatine, 'she was my wife;
I owed her, and 'tis mine that she hath killed.'
'My daughter' and 'my wife' with clamours filled
    The dispersed air, who, holding Lucrece' life,   1805
    Answered their cries, 'my daughter' and 'my wife'.

Brutus, who plucked the knife from Lucrece' side,
Seeing such emulation in their woe,
Began to clothe his wit in state and pride,

1784 so thick come arriving so thick and fast (i.e. hurriedly and confusingly).

1787 as . . . tore A naturalistic touch: 'Tarquin' spoken through clenched teeth may sound like the word 'tearing'.

1788 blow up rain cause rain (tears).

1790 A popular idea.

1791 strife competition (see 1377n and *Ven.* 291n).

1797 sorrow's interest entitlement to sorrow (or claim that sorrow exerts); see 1619n.

1801 too late i.e. too late to have done her any good (therefore needlessly). Some editors suggest that 'too late' means 'too recently' (on the basis of *3H6* 2.5.93–94).

1803 owed owned (see *Ven.* 411).

1804–5 filled . . . air i.e. their cries were dis-

persed in the air; for the construction see Abbott §419a.

1805 who which (see 1740n).

1805 holding . . . life See 1727–8.

1806 i.e. the air now possesses her spirit and therefore can say '*my* daughter' etc.

1807–17 For this interpretation of Brutus, as well as the question of Shakespeare's use of sources, see Introduction, pp. 35–6).

1808 emulation rivalry.

1809 Began to give a proper and worthy demonstration of his intelligence. Until now his wit has been naked and foolish, but by decking it out in an attractive manner he makes it an object of admiration.

1809 state dignity (the sense of 'statecraft' is perhaps also present).

Burying in Lucrece' wound his folly's show.   1810
He with the Romans was esteemèd so
　As silly jeering idiots are with kings,
　For sportive words and utt'ring foolish things.

But now he throws that shallow habit by,
Wherein deep policy did him disguise,   1815
And armed his long-hid wits advisedly,
To check the tears in Collatinus' eyes.
'Thou wrongèd lord of Rome', quoth he, 'arise;
　Let my unsounded self, supposed a fool,
　Now set thy long-experienced wit to school.   1820

'Why, Collatine, is woe the cure for woe?
Do wounds help wounds, or grief help grievous deeds?
Is it revenge to give thyself a blow
For his foul act by whom thy fair wife bleeds?
Such childish humour from weak minds proceeds.   1825
　Thy wretched wife mistook the matter so,
　To slay herself that should have slain her foe.

'Courageous Roman, do not steep thy heart
In such relenting dew of lamentations;
But kneel with me and help to bear thy part   1830
To rouse our Roman gods with invocations
That they will suffer these abominations

1815 deep] Q1; the Q6+   1829 relenting] Q1; lamenting Q6+

1810 folly's show appearance – or disguise – of foolishness.

1812 silly foolish, ineffectual (see 'silly lambs', 167); Q1's spelling of 'seelie' possibly connotes the word's etymological meaning, 'innocent'.

1812 jeering jesting.

1813 sportive i.e. uttered in jest (similarly with 'foolish').

1814 habit (1) manner, (2) costume (see 1809).

1815 deep policy carefully planned strategy. 'Deep' is antithetical to 'shallow', and 'disguise' continues the clothing conceit begun at 1809. The overall meaning is that his earlier foolishness had been according to plan.

1816 advisedly carefully, deliberately (see 180 and 1527).

1819 unsounded untried, unplumbed (the idea of 'sounding depth' may be prompted by the earlier

play on 'deep' and 'shallow').

1821–34 The comparison to Livy (1.59) is again made by Ewig (p. 23) and Baldwin (*Genetics*, pp. 149–52), who further discusses a sixteenth-century edition of Ovid.

1821 Why Come now! (Pooler notes the similar use of 'why' to denote exasperation at *MV* 2.5.6).

1822 grievous harmful (playing on 'grief').

1824 by whom by which (unless Tarquin is understood as the antecedent, in which case 'by whom' stands; but 'who' is often used for 'which', as the poem frequently shows).

1825, 1829 See Painter: 'they should cease from teares and other childish lamentacions' (Bullough, I, 199).

1825 humour disposition of mind.

1829 relenting i.e. with softening or melting effect (used actively).

(Since Rome herself in them doth stand disgracèd)
By our strong arms from forth her fair streets chasèd.

'Now by the Capitol that we adore,   1835
And by this chaste blood so unjustly stainèd,
By heaven's fair sun that breeds the fat earth's store,
By all our country rights in Rome maintainèd,
And by chaste Lucrece' soul that late complainèd
    Her wrongs to us, and by this bloody knife,   1840
    We will revenge the death of this true wife.'

This said, he struck his hand upon his breast,
And kissed the fatal knife to end his vow;
And to his protestation urged the rest,
Who, wond'ring at him, did his words allow;   1845
    Then jointly to the ground their knees they bow,
    And that deep vow which Brutus made before
    He doth again repeat, and that they swore.

When they had sworn to this advisèd doom,
They did conclude to bear dead Lucrece thence,   1850

1838 rights] Q1; rites Q3+

1834 chasèd to be chased (an example of ellipsis, for which see Abbott §382 and ff.).

1835–48 For the details, again see Painter (Bullough, I, 198–9).

1835 Capitol . . . adore Such passionate regard for the symbol of the Capitol is an emphasis more particular to Shakespeare than his sources, and may indicate his search for a Roman equivalent to Elizabethan reverence of the Crown. This point may be set against suspicions that the theme of the expulsion of the Tarquins, the Roman monarchy, drew forth the covert republican in Shakespeare (see Introduction, p. 32).

1836 Ewig (p. 23) again compares Livy 1.59, but the intervening Painter may have been enough: '"I swear by the chast bloud of this body here dead"' (Bullough, I, 198).

1837 A curious line in its context: Shakespeare may be giving Brutus an oath based appropriately on pagan worship, but there is a sense in which 'heaven's fair sun' is emblematic of Lucrece (compare *Ven.* 860–2, where Adonis is described as the 'patron of all light'). The 'fat earth' is both the plentiful earth ('store' = abundance) and also

perhaps the *gross* earth (a sense recorded by Onions), the produce of which can only grow through the redemptive power of the heavenly sun. 'This Neoplatonic emphasis (Venus Pandemos) fits another of Lucrece's aspirations, since she wishes to leave behind her an example of chastity which she hopes will have some influence in worldly affairs (see, for example, 1714–15).

1838 country   rights provincial   claims, entitlements; Q3 introduces 'rites' (a possible secondary sense).

1838 maintainèd upheld, recognised.

1839 that who (i.e. Lucrece); see 1740n.

1839 complainèd complained of.

1842–8 The source again principally seems to be Livy; Ewig (p. 23) notes that nothing of this appears in Chaucer or Ovid. For similarities of diction see Painter (Bullough, I, 199); also note *Tit.* 4.1.89–91.

1844 protestation oath, vow (see 1700).

1845 wond'ring marvelling.

1845 allow approve, accept.

1846 jointly No doubt an involuntary pun.

1847 deep heartfelt.

1849 advisèd doom considered judgement.

To show her bleeding body thorough Rome,
And so to publish Tarquin's foul offence;
Which being done with speedy diligence,
    The Romans plausibly did give consent
    To Tarquin's everlasting banishment.   1855

1852 **publish** make public, evident (note the echo of 33).

1854 **plausibly** with applause, acclamation (see 'The Argument' 34–5; also Abbott §3 on active and passive adjectival forms).

1855 **everlasting** perpetual (possibly with spiritual overtones).

THE PHOENIX AND THE TURTLE

Let the bird of loudest lay,
On the sole Arabian tree,
Herald sad and trumpet be,
To whose sound chaste wings obey.

But thou, shrieking harbinger, 5
Foul precurrer of the fiend,
Augur of the fever's end,
To this troop come thou not near.

From this session interdict
Every fowl of tyrant wing, 10
Save the eagle, feath'red king:
Keep the obsequy so strict.

Let the priest in surplice white,
That defunctive music can,

---

1 bird . . . lay Opinion is divided over whether this is the phoenix or another bird, e.g. the cock or Chaucer's 'crane, the geaunt, with his trompes sound' (*The Parlement of Foules*, 344). For the phoenix, Dronke, *Orbis Litterarum* 23 (1968), 208, notes that Lactantius in *De Ave Phoenice* commends it for its wonderful, matchless voice, though volume seems not to be one of its properties. There is no compelling reason for urging identification, since the line contents itself with the expressive alliteration dependent on periphrasis.

2 See Florio's *Italian Dictionary* (1598): '*Rasin*, a tree in Arabia, whereof there is but one found, and upon it the Phenix sits'; and Shakespeare, 'Now I will believe / That there are unicorns; that in Arabia / There is one tree, the phoenix' throne, one phoenix / At this hour reigning there' (*Temp.* 3.3.21–4).

3 trumpet trumpeter (metonymically).

4 obey The use of the verb with the preposition 'to' is recorded in Spenser: 'Lo! now the hevens obey to me alone' (*FQ* 3.2.35).

4 chaste wings See 3n. The use of metonymy, synecdoche, and periphrasis frees the poem from depicting the birds merely as creatures and allows it to concentrate on those qualities or essences which they represent.

5 shrieking harbinger Often identified as the
240

screech-owl; but see 1n and 4 below n.

6 precurrer precursor (*OED* gives only this example of its usage; under 'precurrent' it cites John Hume's *The Jewes deliverance out of Babylon* (1628): 'The precurrent signes of the day of Iudgment').

6 fiend devil.

7 Augur Soothsayer, Prophet (in ancient Rome). The augur predicted the course of events from the flights of birds or by studying their entrails (details which may have prompted the pattern of association). The poem chooses to stress the negative character of the office.

7 fever's end The course the fever will take, for good or ill.

9 session sitting (usually of a court or parliament – perhaps echoing Chaucer's poem).

9 interdict keep away by decree.

10 tyrant wing It is not enough to gloss this merely as 'bird of prey' since 'tyrant' carries further emblematic resonance (compare 'chaste wings', 4n).

12 strict exclusive.

13 surplice white i.e. referring to the swan's down.

14 can i.e. to be skilled or versed in. 'Defunctive music' is funeral music. The swan is also the bird of Apollo, the god of music. See 15n.

Be the death-divining swan,   15
Lest the requiem lack his right.

And thou treble-dated crow,
That thy sable gender mak'st
With the breath thou giv'st and tak'st,
'Mongst our mourners shalt thou go.   20

Here the anthem doth commence:
Love and constancy is dead;
Phoenix and the turtle fled
In a mutual flame from hence.

So they loved, as love in twain   25
Had the essence but in one:
Two distincts, division none;
Number there in love was slain.

Hearts remote, yet not asunder;
Distance, and no space was seen   30
'Twixt this turtle and his queen:
But in them it were a wonder.

---

15 death-divining The swan is supposed to sing melodiously as it senses its imminent death (see *Luc.* 1611–12) and for this reason is preferred to the 'shrieking harbinger' of line 5.

16 his right Either (1) its (the requiem's) right (see Abbot §228), or (2) its (the swan's) right. (1). is more likely. Also, 'right' most probably plays on the sense of 'rite' (see *Luc.* 1838n).

17 treble-dated long-lived. The expression is formulaic: 'date' means extent or limit of (see *Luc.* 26, 935, and 1729), giving the meaning here of three times the ordinary span.

18 sable gender black offspring ('sable' is a carefully chosen poeticism); 'gender' = thing engendered.

19 Shakespeare may be voicing a popular belief: 'They (ravens) are said to conceive and to lay their eggs at the bill. The young become black on the seventh day' (from the *Hortus Sanitatis*, in Seager, *Natural History* (Rollins, p. 326)).

19 giv'st . . . tak'st The phrase suggests an exchange of lovers' vows.

21 anthem song of praise.

22 is The singular may signify the theme of resolved dualism (two hearts in one); but Abbott (§336) notes the frequency of sing. usage when two

or more nouns precede the verb.

23 fled are fled, having fled. The compact verb forms contribute to the gnomic, lapidary character of the poem.

25 as that, as a result that; 'love' is a noun.

25 in twain in two.

26 essence irreducible. or indivisible nature (see 'single nature' in 39). Critics have discussed the scholastic character of 25–48: Cunningham defines 'essence' as the intellectual soul and interprets the indivisible love of the phoenix and turtle as analogous to relationships within the Trinity (see Cunningham, pp. 266, 273–6).

27 Ridley further observes the scholastic terms: '"distinction" implies a verbal, "division" a real difference'.

28 'Number' may be 'slain' as an enemy because it poses a threat to indivisible love.

29 remote apart.

30 Distance . . . seen Distance was seen and yet not seen.

31 his queen This expression has given rise to speculation that the 'queen' is Elizabeth and the turtle Essex (see pp. 42–3).

32 But Except.

32 were would be, would have been.

So between them love did shine,
That the turtle saw his right
Flaming in the phoenix' sight; 35
Either was the other's mine.

Property was thus appalled
That the self was not the same;
Single nature's double name
Neither two nor one was called. 40

Reason, in itself confounded,
Saw division grow together,
To themselves yet either neither,
Simple were so well compounded:

That it cried, How true a twain 45
Seemeth this concordant one!
Love hath reason, reason none,
If what parts can so remain.

Whereupon it made this threne
To the phoenix and the dove, 50

---

34 right due, possession.

35 (1) Glowing in his vision of the phoenix, and (2) Glowing for the phoenix to see. The word 'sight' means both appearance (see *Ven.* 183n) and eyesight.

36 mine (1) possession (the possessive pronoun used as a noun), (2) 'rich source of wealth' (Schmidt). Despite the reluctance of some editors, the latitude of wit in the stanza makes (2) possible. John Constable further detects wordplay on 'mine' as a variant of 'mien' (appearance). See *N&Q* NS, 36 no. 3 (1989), 327.

37 Property Selfhood, Self-ownership. Cunningham (p. 275) adduces further scholastic terms such as *proprium* and *alienum:* 'what is proper to the one, but not to the other'.

37 appalled weakened, enfeebled (O. Fr. appalir = 'grow pale').

38 That the self was not itself (but involved another).

39 Single nature indivisible essence (see 26n).

39 double name Perhaps referring to the 'Two distincts' (27), or to the two-in-one phoenix and turtle.

41 in itself in essence, thoroughly.

41 confounded overthrown, destroyed (see *Ven.* 1048, *Luc.* 250).

42 division . . . together things separate become one.

43 Each in himself was nothing without the other. Paraphrase does little justice to the gnomic wittiness of the line.

44 'Simples' (see *Luc.* 530n) normally form a compound; but this compound is so well unified as to appear a simple.

45 true a twain Maxwell notes wordplay on 'true': (1) how *faithful* a pair they are, (2) how *truly* one seems to be two.

46 concordant one i.e. agreeing with itself (a further resolved paradox since concord requires the agreement of two parties).

47 Since love has taken over reason, reason is dispossessed of itself ('has none' = has no reason). This exercise in logic is one familiar in Socratic dialogues (and was taken up earnestly by contemporary Neoplatonists).

48 In defiance of reason, what 'parts' (divides) none the less continues to form a unity. Also implied is togetherness in spite of separation and distance (as in 30). The line demonstrates the fulfilment of logic through paradox – consistent with the ideal of Neoplatonic love poetry (compare Donne's 'A Valediction: Forbidding Mourning').

49 Apart from the need for fluency of narrative transition, there seems little significance in the fact that it is Reason who sings the threne. The unidentified imperative narrator of 1–20 modulates into the quieter anthem-speaking voice of 21–44;

Co-supremes and stars of love,
As chorus to their tragic scene.

THRENOS

Beauty, truth, and rarity,
Grace in all simplicity,
Here enclosed, in cinders lie.   55

Death is now the phoenix' nest,
And the turtle's loyal breast
To eternity doth rest.

Leaving no posterity,
'Twas not their infirmity,   60
It was married chastity.

Truth may seem, but cannot be;
Beauty brag, but 'tis not she;
Truth and beauty buried be.

To this urn let those repair   65
That are either true or fair;
For these dead birds sigh a prayer.

Reason then declares its surprised admiration for the love of the pair, and it is appropriately this tone which continues to the end. However, Lewis (p. 509) and Middleton Murry both ascribe importance to 'Reason's deliberate homage to a higher power' (Murry, p. 25).

49 threne (1) threnody, lament, (2) epitaph.

51 Co-supremes Joint rulers ('supremes' is accented on the first syllable).

51 stars presiding deities. Fate is also evoked by 'stars', in keeping with astrological notions of fortune (compare *Rom.* line 7: 'star-crossed'). As supreme examples of love, they must also submit to its 'tragic' laws.

52 scene drama, performance (*OED* sv *sb* 3; *H5*, Prologue 4: 'And monarchs to behold the swelling scene').

THRENOS Threnody (see 49n).

53 truth fidelity.

55 enclosed, Prince seems right to retain Q's comma: the qualities named are enclosed in each other and only incidentally in the cinders.

56 One version of the phoenix legend is that it will renew itself from its ashes; but this does not account for the turtle. The tenor of the poem is rather that the two birds will find themselves mutually renewed in 'eternity' (58).

58 (1) finds repose in eternity, (2) endures eternally.

59 posterity, Q's comma is preferable to later emendations to a colon; the three lines of the tercet stand in equal relationship.

60 i.e. their childlessness was not the result of physical incapacity.

61 married chastity A married couple may enjoy conjugal relations without blame; but the point of these words is to deny even that. Donne's Neoplatonism (see 48n) is again relevant:

But we by a love, so much refin'd,
  That our selves know not what it is,
Inter-assured of the mind,
  Care lesse, eyes, lips, and hands to misse.
            ('A Valediction', 17–20)

62 seem . . . be i.e. only a semblance of truth remains.

63 Whoever boasts she is beauty is an impostor. This and the line above strike a further Platonic note by arguing that what is now perceived on earth as truth or beauty merely reflects the ideal.

66 either . . . or Expressed as alternatives, perhaps because the two qualities can no longer be combined in a single person.

The Passionate Pilgrim

THE PASSIONATE PILGRIM

I

When my love swears that she is made of truth,
I do believe her, though I know she lies,
That she might think me some untutored youth,

1.0 *Copy-text O1*

1.0 See *Son.* 138:
When my loue sweares that she is made of truth,
I do beleeve her though I know she lyes,
That she might thinke me some vntuterd youth,
Vnlearned in the worlds false subtilties.
Thus vainely thinking that she thinkes me young,
Although she knowes my dayes are past the best,
Simply I credit her false speaking tongue,
On both sides thus is simple truth supprest:
But wherefore sayes she not she is vniust?
And wherefore say not I that I am old?
O loues best habit is in seeming trust,
And age in loue, loues not t'haue yeares told.
　　Therefore I lye with her, and she with me,
　　And in our faults by lyes we flattered be.

(1609 text)

(I have in the main concentrated on those points which intersect with the 1609 *Sonnets* text; for a fuller annotation of *Son.* 138 and *Son.* 144, refer to Kerrigan and particularly Booth.) Francis Meres's reference to his 'sugred Sonets' in 1598 makes it clear that some of Shakespeare's sonnets were circulating in manuscript prior to the appearance in print of two of them in the *PP*.

Discussion has turned on whether the version here is earlier than that of the 1609 publication or a mis-reporting of it. Prince, for example, favours the latter, but Maxwell argues for 1609 as a revision. The main argument Maxwell cites in favour of its being an earlier version of the 1609 text is that of vocabulary, in particular the use of 'forgeries' in 1.4, a word which has only one pre-Shakespearean recorded usage. (Maxwell adds as typically Shakespearean 'unskilful' (4) and 'outfacing' (8), while admitting that they are common enough at the time.) But it would help his case more if the 1609 text had reproduced 'forgeries', since such evidence loses strength if the example is not preserved.

The argument for memorial contamination is twofold: (1) some of the readings make poor sense

in the *PP* version (see especially 1.8), (2) they present a simpler, less interesting version of the theme and reduce the imaginative wordplay of 1609. The pivotal line, 'But wherefore says my love that she is young', looks, as Booth points out, as if it has been provided by someone writing down the poem from memory. The fear of ageing and loss of sexual attractiveness are the poem's twin themes, but they preoccupy the lover rather than his mistress, who in the 1609 version is accused of dishonesty or infidelity (the precise contemporary inflection of 'vniust', 1.9, 1609) towards him, not of trying to appear younger than she is. Growing old is conventionally what women fear, and so it would be natural for a memorial transcriber to assume that the mistress is as worried by this as the speaker; the result not only confuses the issue but reduces its complexity.

It is unlikely that a poetic mind moving along such well-worn grooves would discover in developing the poem the more original idea of male anxiety in the face of female self-possession. At the level of creativity exemplified by the 1609 text, authorial revision more likely progresses from complication to lucidity of expression rather than from the commonplace to the imaginative. Booth further observes that 1.8, 'Outfacing faults in love with love's ill rest', has, at least in its second half, the characteristic of a line written by someone who has forgotten everything about it except that it rhymes with 'best'. Equally, 'Outfacing faults in love', which feels more original, may simply be responding to the double bluff of '*I* smiling credit *her* false-speaking tongue' (i.e. the remembered line prompts a plausible invention to stand in for the unremembered follow-up line). The same goes for the lame repetition of the 'young' / 'tongue' rhyme (1.5, 7 and 9, 11); the phrase 'soothing tongue' looks like a filler prompted by 'told' in the correctly remembered 1.12.

Unskilful in the world's false forgeries.

Thus vainly thinking that she thinks me young,   5

Although I know my years be past the best,

I smiling credit her false-speaking tongue,

Outfacing faults in love with love's ill rest.

But wherefore says my love that she is young?

And wherefore say not I that I am old?   10

O, love's best habit's in a soothing tongue,

And age in love loves not to have years told.

  Therefore I'll lie with love, and love with me,

  Since that our faults in love thus smothered be.

                                    2

Two loves I have, of comfort and despair,

That like two spirits do suggest me still;

1.11 habit's in] 01; habite is 02–3   1.11 soothing tongue] 01–3; smoothinge tongue *FO MS 2071.7*   **2.0** *Copy-text 01*

All this argues strongly for a contaminated text in *PP*, and not an earlier draft. It also suggests to us something about careful control kept on a manuscript sequence. Even if they were circulating, they did not do so freely, and the two *PP* sonnets are the only ones that appear to have got into print, in any form, before the 1609 publication.

    1.4 forgeries An interesting variant of 1609's 'subtilties', in that by emphasising something falsely made it develops the hint in 1 ('made of truth') as well as looking forward to 1.9. But in concentrating on the cosmetic art of 'truth' it perhaps loses something of the complexity of 'subtilties' and presents no real defence against the argument that it results from memorial contamination.

    1.8 See 1.0. The most radical departure from *Son.* 138, as well as being a difficult line to gloss. (The seeming echo of 'ill wresting' from *Son.* 140 gives rise to further but unfortunately fruitless speculation that the *PP* transcriber had access to more than these two sonnets.) *OED* variously defines 'outface' as to stare out of countenance or brazen out. The sense then would be as follows: so desperate is his love for her (his state of 'ill rest' or lover's anxiety) that he is willing to confront her obvious defects and none the less accept them. This is somewhat bolder than merely to overlook her faults, since it means that the faults themselves put him, not her, on the defensive by challenging him to recognise them for what they are, which forces him into the false posture of asserting that they are not faults. Such a meaning accords with the hopelessness of 'love's ill rest' and makes her

victim ironically her champion. Something like this happens in the relationship between the poet and the young man in *Son.* 95 and 96, which again raises the possibility that the transcriber is bringing his knowledge or memory of other Shakespearean sonnets he has somehow seen to bear on his reconstruction of this one.

    1.9 my . . . young See 1.0.

    1.11 habit (1) manner, practice, (2) costume (this reading fits the poem's interest in appearances).

    1.12 told (1) divulged, (2) reckoned up.

    2.0 Compare *Son.* 144:

Two loves I haue of comfort and dispaire,
Which like two spirits do sugiest me still,
The better angell is a man right faire:
The worser spirit a woman collour'd il.
To win me soone to hell, my femall evill,
Tempteth my better angel from my sight,
And would corrupt my saint to be a divel:
Wooing his purity with her fowle pride.
And whether that my angel be turn'd finde,
Suspect I may yet not directly tell,
But being both from me both to each friend,
I gesse one angel in an others hel.
  Yet this shal I nere know but liue in doubt,
  Till my bad angel fire my good one out.
                    (1609 text)

PP's version is much closer to the 1609 printing than is poem 1, and notwithstanding two interesting variants (see 2.6 and 2.8nn) probably represents a good memorial transcription.

    2.2 suggest incite, encourage. See *Ven.* 651 and *Luc.* 37.

My better angel is a man right fair,
My worser spirit a woman coloured ill.
To win me soon to hell, my female evil   5
Tempteth my better angel from my side,
And would corrupt my saint to be a devil,
Wooing his purity with her fair pride.
And whether that my angel be turned fiend,
Suspect I may, yet not directly tell: 10
For being both to me, both to each, friend,
I guess one angel in another's hell.
    The truth I shall not know, but live in doubt,
    Till my bad angel fire my good one out.

3

Did not the heavenly rhetoric of thine eye,
'Gainst whom the world could not hold argument,
Persuade my heart to this false perjury?
Vows for thee broke deserve not punishment.
A woman I forswore; but I will prove,   5
Thou being a goddess, I forswore not thee:
My vow was earthly, thou a heavenly love;
Thy grace being gained cures all disgrace in me.

2.11 me, both to] me; both, to 01   3.0 *Copy-text 01*

2.6 side *PP*'s reading accords with the generally accepted emendation of the 1609 Quarto's 'sight'. The recurrence of 'better angell' (see 2.3) may have inadvertently drawn the printer's eye to 'right' in the above line. Compare *Oth.* 5.2.208.

2.8 fair Some editors prefer *PP*'s reading, but 1609's 'fowle' accords with the fiercely antithetical balance of the whole sonnet.

2.10 directly precisely.

2.11 both to me i.e. both friends of mine. The parallel phrases here lack *Son.* 144's interesting play of contrasts whereby 'both *from* me both to each friend' means that they are friends to each other through their common friendship with him *and* that they are currently enjoying each other's company away from him. See collation for 01's pointing.

2.12 hell A sexual allusion: see *Decameron*, Third Day, Tenth Story, where the friar talks the girl into allowing him to 'put the devil in hell'.

2.14 fire . . . out A similar allusion to that of 2.12, this time to syphilis. Lee and Pooler note Everard Guilpin's epigram: 'I told *Chrestina* I would lie with her / When she with an old phrase doth me advise / To keepe my selfe from water and from fier / And she would keepe me from betwixt her thighs. / That there is water I doe make no doubt / But Il'e be loth (wench) to be fired out' (See *Skialetheia* (1598), ed. D. Allen Carroll (1973), p. 50). The expression 'to fire out' applied more simply to the practice of driving animals from their lair (as in *Lear* 5.3.22–3), but lent itself as an image of moral anger (the *Lear* example speaks of 'a brand from heaven'). In this instance the threatened scourge is of a hellish nature.

3.0 See *LLL* 4.3.58–71 (Longaville's sonnet to Maria); also poems 5 and 16, which reproduce the sonnet of Don Armado and Dumaine's song. The *PP* versions may have been taken from the play's 1598 quarto or, as Lee first suggested, from extracted copies circulating privately.

3.2 whom For this usage see Abbott §264 (and *Ven.* 87n).

My vow was breath, and breath a vapour is;
Then thou, fair sun, that on this earth doth shine,   10
Exhal'st this vapour vow. In thee it is:
If broken then, it is no fault of mine.
    If by me broke, what fool is not so wise
    To break an oath, to win a paradise?

4

Sweet Cytherea, sitting by a brook,
With young Adonis, lovely, fresh, and green,
Did court the lad with many a lovely look,
Such looks as none could look but beauty's queen.
She told him stories to delight his ear;   5
She showed him favours to allure his eye;
To win his heart, she touched him here and there –
Touches so soft still conquer chastity.
But whether unripe years did want conceit,
Or he refused to take her figured proffer,   10

3.11 Exhal'st] Exhalst *LLL;* Exhalt 01; Exhale 02–3   3.14 break] 01–3; loose *LLL*   4.0 *Copy-text 01*   4.1 Sweet]
01–3; ffaire *FO MS 1.8*   4.5 ear] eare *FO MSS 1.8, 2071.7;* eares 01–3   4.8 soft] 01–3; sought *FO MS 2071.7*   4.10
refused] 01–3; did scorne *FO MS 1.8*   4.10 her] 02–3; his 01

3.11 Exhal'st Draw up (from the earth into the
atmosphere). See collation for *PP* variants. There
are various ways of accounting for the changes
between the source and the octavos: 01's compositor may have dropped an 's' which the proofreader
did not pick up, or he may have read 'Exhalt' as
'Exalt', which the context supports – though if he
was any sort of Latinist he would not have expected
an 'h' in the middle of the word. The copyist of
02 saw the mistake, but in emending he kept the
imperative form of 01 (*LLL*'s form is indicative).
Another possibility is that the intention in 02 was to
emend 'Exhalt' to 'Exhald' (i.e. Exhal'd), but that
the final 'd' was misread as 'e' by the compositor
(see Riverside).

3.11 In thee it is The vow is now in you.

4.0 For other versions see FO MSS 1.8 and
2071.7 (in which the poem is initialled 'W. S.' in
a later hand – probably that of J. P Collier (see
Adams, p. cix)). Bartholomew Griffin is a candidate
for authorship since his sequence *Fidessa* (1596)
contains a version of poem 11. In addition, poems 6
and 9 turn on the Venus–Adonis story and are written in a similar ebullient style. Malone thinks that
this and the others are 'essays of the author when

he first conceived the idea of writing a poem on the
subject of Venus and Adonis'; but they are much
more likely to represent other poets' responses to
the vogue of Venus and Adonis temporarily established by the success of the narrative poem (see
p. 57). So close in feeling and style are poems 4,
6, 9 and 11 that there is good reason to suppose
Griffin wrote them all.

4.1 Cytherea Another name for Venus. Shakespeare does not use the appellation in *Ven.*, nor
does Ovid in his account of Venus and Adonis
in *Metam.*; but it figures prominently in the *Art
of Love*, being used three times, twice invoking
through the goddess the spirit of wantonness. The
author of *PP* 4, 6, 9, and 11 no doubt consulted the
love treatise, the tone of which he emulates more
than that of the epic poem. (See also headnote to
poem 11.)

4.3 lovely amorous (playing against the meaning
of 'lovely' in 4.2).

4.9 conceit understanding.

4.10 take (1) accept, (2) understand.

4.10 figured proffer i.e. offer of herself by sign
or implication.

The tender nibbler would not touch the bait,
But smile and jest at every gentle offer.
   Then fell she on her back, fair queen, and toward,
   He rose and ran away, ah, fool too forward.

5

If love make me forsworn, how shall I swear to love?
O never faith could hold, if not to beauty vowed.
Though to myself forsworn, to thee I'll constant prove;
Those thoughts to me like oaks, to thee like osiers bowed.
Study his bias leaves, and makes his book thine eyes,   5
Where all those pleasures live that art can comprehend.
If knowledge be the mark, to know thee shall suffice:
Well-learnèd is that tongue that well can thee commend,
All ignorant that soul that sees thee without wonder;
Which is to me some praise, that I thy parts admire.   10
Thine eye Jove's lightning seems, thy voice his dreadful
   thunder,
Which, not to anger bent, is music and sweet fire.
   Celestial as thou art, O do not love that wrong,
   To sing heaven's praise with such an earthly tongue.   15

6

Scarce had the sun dried up the dewy morn,
And scarce the herd gone to the hedge for shade,

4.11–12 touch . . . smile . . . jest] 01–3; take . . . blusht . . . smild *FO MS 1.8*   4.13 queen] 01–3; *omitted FO MS 1.8*   4.14 rose] 01–3; blusht *FO MS 1.8*   5.0 *Copy-text 01*   5.2 O] 01–3; Ah *LLL*   5.3 constant] 01–3; faithfull *LLL*   5.4 like oaks] like Okes 01–3; were Okes *LLL*   5.6 can] 01–3; would *LLL*   5.11 Thine] 02–3; Thin 01; Thy *LLL*   5.11 seems] 01–3; beares *LLL*   5.13 do not love that] 01–3; pardon love this *LLL*   5.14 To sing] 01–3; That singes *LLL*   6.0 *Copy-text 02*

4.13 Compare *Ven.* 41 ('Backward she pushed him, as she would be thrust') and 814 ('Leaves Love upon her back, deeply distressed'). Both of these are memorable lines which would inspire imitators or parodists to miniature efforts of just the kind represented here.

4.13 **toward** compliant, submissive.

4.14 Compare *Ven.* 811–13.

4.14 **forward** obstinate, unwilling.

5.0 Compare *LLL* 4.2.105–18, and see headnote to poem 3 (3.0).

5.4 i.e. my strong resolutions submit to you (*LLL*'s reading is slightly clearer).

5.5 **Study . . . leaves** The student abandons his natural inclination ('bias' is a bowling term).

5.10 **Which . . . praise** i.e. it is to my credit, etc.

5.13 **do . . . wrong** See collation; *LLL*'s reading gives a better sense.

6.0 A version in FO MS 2071.7. Compare *Shr.* Induction 2, 49–51: 'Dost thou love pictures? We will fetch thee straight / Adonis painted by a running brook, / And Cytherea all in sedges hid'. Sightings have also been taken, through and beyond Venus, of Ovid's story of Salmacis and Hermaphroditus (Golding 4.418ff.), which

When Cytherea, all in love forlorn,
A longing tarriance for Adonis made
Under an osier growing by a brook,   5
A brook where Adon used to cool his spleen.
Hot was the day, she hotter that did look
For his approach, that often there had been.
Anon he comes, and throws his mantle by,
And stood stark naked on the brook's green brim: 10
The sun looked on the world with glorious eye,
Yet not so wistly as this queen on him.
    He spying her, bounced in whereas he stood;
    'O Jove', quoth she, 'why was not I a flood!'

7

Fair is my love, but not so fair as fickle,
Mild as a dove, but neither true nor trusty,
Brighter than glass, and yet as glass is brittle,
Softer than wax, and yet as iron rusty;

6.12 this] 02–3; the FO MS 2071.7   **7.0** Copy-text 02

provides a verbal echo for 6.4. Spenser observes the detail of Adonis bathing under Venus's slyly watchful eye: 'And whilest he bath'd, with her two crafty spyes / She secretly would search each daintie lim' (FQ 3.1.36.5–6); but the dramatic context is different in that Adonis immerses himself as Venus's 'paramoure' in a fountain to which she leads him. The Spenserian effect is one of loving tenderness, whereas the whimsical sensuality of PP bears a closer resemblance to Ovid's Amores 1.5, as translated by Marlowe (see lines 9–10n and 14n). The use of the sun as onlooker and the combination of heat and lust which his image furnishes echo the opening section of Venus and Adonis. Again, as with PP 4, the sonnet appears to be a jocular response to the more boisterous details of the longer poem.

6.4 tarriance waiting (see Golding 4.430: 'Scarce could she tarience make').

6.6 spleen Probably irritability caused by heat. Some commentators point to the sexual significance of 'spleen', but that seems inappropriate for Adonis; as Kittredge argues, 'here spleen is literal – not figurative'.

6.9–10 Compare Golding 4.424–6: 'he tooke so great delight / In coolenesse of the pleasant spring,

that streight he stripped quite / His garments from his tender skin'; and the bawdier Marlowe, Ovid's Elegies 1.5.17–18: 'Starke naked as she stood before mine eye / Not one wen in her body could I spie.'

6.12 wistly longingly (compare Ven. 343).

6.13 whereas where.

6.14 Compare Marlowe's similar last-line protestation: 'Iove send me more such after-noones as this' (Ovid's Elegies 1.5.26).

7.0 The sole other version is in FO MS 2071.7. The poem echoes the theme of female untrustworthiness in PP 1 (or Son. 138), as well as resembling the musing bitterness of A Lover's Complaint. Its rhyme-scheme, which seems to be of an earlier period (compare the eighteen-line sonnets of Thomas Watson's Passionate Centurie of Love (1582)), makes it much slacker in feeling than Shakespeare's Sonnets, though its feminine rhymes, in common with those of LC, give it a feeling of hardly sustainable dejection.

7.3 brittle The rhyme suggests 'brickle', which would be acceptable, as in FQ 4.10.39.9, 'But being faire and brickle, likest glasse did seeme', or Wyatt, 'Alas, not of steill but of brickell glasse' (Wyatt, p. 24).

A lily pale, with damask dye to grace her, 5
None fairer, nor none falser to deface her.

Her lips to mine how often hath she joinèd,
Between each kiss her oaths of true love swearing;
How many tales to please me hath she coinèd,
Dreading my love, the loss whereof still fearing. 10
    Yet in the midst of all her pure protestings,
    Her faith, her oaths, her tears, and all were jestings.

She burnt with love, as straw with fire flameth,
She burnt out love, as soon as straw out-burneth;
She framed the love, and yet she foiled the framing; 15
She bade love last, and yet she fell a-turning.
    Was this a lover, or a lecher whether?
    Bad in the best, though excellent in neither.

8

If music and sweet poetry agree,
As they must needs, the sister and the brother,
Then must the love be great 'twixt thee and me,
Because thou lov'st the one, and I the other.
Dowland to thee is dear, whose heavenly touch 5
Upon the lute doth ravish human sense;
Spenser to me, whose deep conceit is such
As passing all conceit needs no defence.
Thou lov'st to hear the sweet melodious sound

7.10 whereof] 02; thereof 03   7.11 midst] 03; mids 02

7.5–6 i.e. her complexion, which is that of a lily's paleness graced with the red of damask, ensures that none is fairer; but to her discredit, neither is there anybody more false. (Prince observes that the Elizabethan use of 'damask' for rosy complexions derives from the mingled colour of the damask rose; see *OED* entry under 'Damask rose'.)

7.6 **deface her** (1) spoil her complexion, (2) discredit her.

7.9 **coinèd** invented (conveying the idea of false coinage as in *Luc.* 1073).

7.10 **Dreading** Being anxious about (Onions).

7.14 **out-burneth** burns out.

7.15 **framed** (1) fashioned, made, (2) made a setting for (as in a portrait miniature), suggesting that her intention appeared to be to preserve her love.

7.15 **foiled** spoiled, rendered worthless. The presence in 'foiled' of 'foil' (i.e. a setting, as in *LC* 153–4: 'which remained the foil / Of this false jewel') strengthens the antithetical effect.

7.17 **whether** which of the two. Compare 14.8 and *Ven.* 304.

8.0 This and *PP* 20 are by Richard Barnfield and were printed by Jaggard's brother in 1598 in the collection *Poems: In divers humors* (see p. 54, n). The sonnet is mainly interesting for its contemporary references, either veiled or explicit. The poem is addressed *To his friend Maister R. L.*, whom Grosart identifies as Richard Linche, author of *Diella* (1596), an identification which Harry Morris doubts (see *Richard Barnfield: Colin's Child* (1963), pp. 112–13).

8.7–8 **conceit . . . conceit** meaning . . . power of invention.

That Phoebus' lute, the queen of music, makes;   10
And I in deep delight am chiefly drowned
When as himself to singing he betakes.
    One god is god of both, as poets feign;
    One knight loves both, and both in thee remain.

9

Fair was the morn when the fair queen of love,

. . . .

Paler for sorrow than her milk-white dove,
For Adon's sake, a youngster proud and wild,
Her stand she takes upon a steep-up hill.   5
Anon Adonis comes with horn and hounds;
She, silly queen, with more than love's good will,
Forbade the boy he should not pass those grounds.
'Once', quoth she, 'did I see a fair sweet youth
Here in these brakes deep-wounded with a boar,   10
Deep in the thigh, a spectacle of ruth.
See, in my thigh', quoth she, 'here was the sore.'
    She showèd hers, he saw more wounds than one,
    And blushing fled, and left her all alone.

10

Sweet rose, fair flower, untimely plucked, soon vaded,
Plucked in the bud, and vaded in the spring;

10.0 *Copy-text 02*

8.10 Phoebus' lute i.e. the moon. The analogy works on the principle of Pythagorean planetary harmony, or the music of the spheres: Phoebus, the sun-god (and also the god of music and poetry), imparts his genius to and through his sister Diana, the goddess of the moon and therefore 'queen of music'.

8.13 feign relate in fiction (Onions).

8.14 One knight This seems to be a personal reference. Grosart identifies the knight as Sir George Carey, to whom Dowland dedicated his first book of airs (1597) and to whose wife Spenser had dedicated *Muiopotmos* (1590).

9.0 No other version has been discovered, but see headnote to poem 4 (4.0).

9.2 A line omitted (first noted by Malone).

9.5 steep-up steeply rising (compare, *Son.* 7.5).

9.8 pass . . . grounds i.e. descend to the low-lying areas (such as the 'brakes' of 9.10). Venus's

argument for territorial advantage recalls *Ven.* 229–40, and, as in *PP* 4, 6, and 9, is probably inspired by its ribald possibilities.

9.10 brakes thickets. Probably understood as a euphemism for pubic hair as the sense shifts into a bawdier strain (see 9.8n).

9.12–13 A well-worn piece of ribaldry, traceable at least to Rabelais (Fourth Bk, ch. 47).

10.0 No other version has been discovered.

10.1 vaded faded. The word occurs four times in *PP* and once additionally as 'vadeth' (all the examples being confined to poems 10 and 13). Established Shakespearean usage is limited to one occurrence (in *Son.* 54.14, where alliteration seems to justify it: 'When that shall vade, by verse distils your truth'; and to vary the effect of 'fade' at the end of line 10). This does not necessarily

Bright orient pearl, alack too timely shaded,
Fair creature, killed too soon by death's sharp sting:
Like a green plum that hangs upon a tree,   5
And falls through wind before the fall should be.

I weep for thee, and yet no cause I have,
For why thou lefts me nothing in thy will.
And yet thou lefts me more than I did crave,
For why I cravèd nothing of thee still.   10
O yes, dear friend, I pardon crave of thee:
Thy discontent thou didst bequeath to me.

11

Venus, with Adonis sitting by her,
Under a myrtle shade began to woo him;

10.8 why] why: 02; why; 03   **10.10 why]** why: 02–3   **11.0** *Copy-text 02*   **11.1** Venus, with] 02–3; Venus, and yong *Griffin;* Venus & young *FO MS 1.8;* Venus & *FO MS 2071.7*

tell against Shakespeare's authorship of either of these poems, since we still have to reckon with the printer's intervention (for example, the First Folio, which is of course also printed by Jaggard, sometimes emends the quartos' 'fade' to 'vade', as in *R2* 1.2.20). However, the distinction is perhaps something more than a mere variation in spelling since 'vade' carries a sense of positive and final departure (from its Lat. root *vadere* – to go), and the concentration of examples in *PP* would indicate that the printer is not casually substituting 'v' for 'f' each time. Allowing for the veil that printing ineluctably imposes between such speculation and what the author intended, there is perhaps a case for arguing that the persistence of 'vade' in these examples betrays a non-Shakespearean poetic habit.

10.3 Bright orient pearl See *OED* 'orient' sv *sb*. 2b 'Pearl of orient': 'a pearl from the Indian seas, as distinguished from those of less beauty found in European mussels; hence, a brilliant or precious pearl'.

10.3 timely early.

10.8 For why Because (see Abbott §75).

10.9 lefts i.e. 'left'st', which is more awkward to pronounce (see Abbott §340 and *Luc.* 878–79n).

10.10 still always.

10.11 pardon crave i.e. excuse me for I am mistaken.

11.0 A version of the poem exists in Bartholomew Griffin's *Fidessa* (1596) – see 4.0. Of the four Venus–Adonis sonnets in *PP* (4, 6, 9, 11) this is the only one in which the name 'Venus' occurs, which has given rise to speculation that the

'Cytherea' sonnets in particular (4 and 6) may be by a different author. But the four sonnets are so alike in tone, temper, and theme that the mere difference of name, epecially given the periphrastic habit of such poetry, hardly provides substance for such a claim. (For example, Shakespeare never calls Mars as such in *Venus and Adonis*.) Indeed, periphrastic variation provides a good argument for supposing that the four sonnets form part of a series by the same poet, who is keen to avoid the monotony of always using the same name. (But see 4.1n.) Adonis, for whom mythology has fewer onomastic resources, is variously 'Adon', 'the lad', and 'the youngster'. The difference between poem 11 and the others is that it mingles conventional male frustration more freely with female (which may otherwise form a counterpart to homoerotic passion), and accords more easily with a sonnet sequence in which the lover goes through the traditional moves of hopeless courtship. The final couplet here is also the only one in which the poet directly intervenes with an observation about his own lady. But against those who dispute Griffin's authorship of all four sonnets – on the grounds that the other three were not included in *Fidesse* and furthermore do not fit its character – it can be argued that this one was made to fit by recasting the final couplet; it is easy to imagine a different ending and resolution.

11.2 a myrtle shade Myrtles traditionally form the bower of Venus and are depicted in Renaissance artistic representations of the love of Venus and Mars (e.g. Botticelli's painting in the National Gallery, London).

She told the youngling how god Mars did try her,
And as he fell to her, she fell to him.
'Even thus', quoth she, 'the warlike god embraced me',   5
And then she clipped Adonis in her arms;
'Even thus', quoth she, 'the warlike god unlaced me',
As if the boy should use like loving charms;
'Even thus', quoth she, 'he seizèd on my lips',
And with her lips on his did act the seizure;   10
And as she fetchèd breath, away he skips,
And would not take her meaning nor her pleasure.
　Ah, that I had my lady at this bay,
　To kiss and clip me till I run away.

12

Crabbèd age and youth cannot live together:
Youth is full of pleasure, age is full of care;

11.3 god] 02–3; great *FO MS 1.8*   11.4 she fell] 02–3; so fell she *Griffin; FO MS 1.8*   11.5 warlike] 02–3; wanton *Griffin*   11.6 clipped] 02–3; clasp'd *Griffin;* tooke *FO MS 1.8*   11.7 Even] 02–3; & *FO MS 2071.7*   11.7 warlike] 02–3; lusty *FO MS 1.8*   11.9–12] 02–3; But he a wayward boy refusde her offer, / And ran away, the beautious Queene neglecting; / shewing both folly to abuse her proffer, / And all his sex of cowardise detecting. *Griffin*   11.9 Even] 02–3; then *FO MS 2071.7*   11.11 And] 02–3; But *FO MS 1.8*   11.11 fetchèd] 02–3; tooke hir *FO MS 1.8*   11.13 Ah . . . this] 02–3; Oh . . . that *Griffin, FO MS 1.8*   11.13 lady] 02–3; mistress *Griffin, FO MSS*   11.14 kiss . . . me] 02–3; clipp & kiss hir *FO MS 1.8*   11.14 run] 02–3; ranne *Griffin, FO MS 1.8*   12.0 *Copy-text 02*   12.2 pleasance] 02–3; pleasure *Deloney*

11.3 **try her** test her resistance.

11.4 **fell . . . fell** A play on contrasting and conflicting meanings: (1) set about, assault, (2) succumb. It is appropriate that the idea of assault should accompany the naming of Mars, the fierce and even *fell* god of war.

11.6 **clipped** embraced, clasped (Griffin).

11.10 **act . . . seizure** (1) enact Mars's seizing of her, (2) took Adonis captive (playing on the military sense).

11.13 **at this bay** See *Ven.* 877n. Here the meaning is that he holds his lady at bay (possibly thinking of Actaeon hunted by his own hounds, except that his punishment is kissing); as Pooler observes, the poet identifies with Adonis as the prey but possesses the eagerness of the hunter.

12.0 This is also the first stanza of a poem called 'A maiden's choice twixt age and youth', which was printed in Thomas Deloney's *Garland of Good Will*. No edition of the *Garland* survives earlier than 1631; however, Thomas Nashe referred to the poem in 1596 (Nashe, McKerrow, III, 84), and the Stationers' Register of 1591 records 'A pleasant newe ballad Called the Maydens choyce' (both F. O.).

Mann, in his edition of Deloney, and *STC* assume that this is the same poem as appears in the *Garland*). But certainly the poem was around at least as early as Nashe's reference. Mann prints the entire poem, while Rollins (pp. 548–9) gives the remaining four stanzas each of twenty lines, which means that the *PP* version condensed the first stanza and elongated the lines, giving it the appearance of a sonnet. Whether Jaggard merely printed this version as he found it or tampered with it to make it more like a 'Shakespearean' sonnet is open to conjecture, but it is a fair bet that he saw the advantage of rearranging it. While Venus does not appear by name in the shortened version, she is made into a court of recurrent appeal in the *Garland* poem (e.g. 'Here I do wait / for my only treasure / *Venus* sugred bait / fancies dainty sweet'), and in line 80 the desired lover is compared to Adonis, all of which perhaps supports the argument that the putative common-place book contained the poem because of its association with the theme of Venus (see pp. 56–8).

12.1 **Crabbèd** Harsh, sour.

12.2 **pleasance** light-heartedness.

Youth like summer morn, age like winter weather;
Youth like summer brave, age like winter bare.
Youth is full of sport, age's breath is short,   5
    Youth is nimble, age is lame;
Youth is hot and bold, age is weak and cold,
    Youth is wild, and age is tame.
Age, I do abhor thee, youth, I do adore thee:
    O, my love, my love is young!   10
Age, I do defy thee. O sweet shepherd, hie thee,
    For methinks thou stays too long.

13

Beauty is but a vain and doubtful good,
A shining gloss that vadeth suddenly,
A flower that dies when first it 'gins to bud,
A brittle glass that's broken presently:
    A doubtful good, a gloss, a glass, a flower,   5
    Lost, vaded, broken, dead within an hour.

And as goods lost are seld or never found,
As vaded gloss no rubbing will refresh,
As flowers dead lie withered on the ground,
As broken glass no cement can redress:
    So beauty blemished once, for ever lost,   10
    In spite of physic, painting, pain and cost.

12.3 summer . . . winter] 02–3; summers . . . winters *Deloney*   12.4] 02–3; *omitted Deloney*   12.12 stays] 02–3; stay'st *Deloney*

12.4 **brave** of impressive appearance (Prince gives 'finely dressed' which contrasts neatly with 'bare').

12.6 **Youth . . . nimble** Compare *Ven.* 146–8.

12.6 **age . . . lame** Compare *Ven.* 134 ('crookèd').

12.7 **Youth . . . hot . . . bold** Compare *Ven.* 149.

12.7 **age . . . cold** Compare *Ven.* 150 ('gross to sink').

12.11 **hie thee** hurry (as in *Ven.* 3).

12.12 **thou stays** you linger (easier to pronounce than 'stay'st'; compare the form 'lefts' in 10.8 and 10.9).

13.0 No other version of the poem has been found. Compare *PP* 10. The mid-eighteenth century saw a flurry of interest, the poem being twice printed in the *Gentleman's Magazine* (1750 and 1760) and again in a miscellany of 1765, each time with the title 'Beauty's Value'. The miscellany version claims, of course without substantiation, to be 'from a very correct Manuscript of William Shakespear, in a private Hand' (Rollins, p. 292).

13.2 **vadeth** fadeth, fades (see 10.1).

13.4 **presently** instantly.

13.7 **seld** seldom.

13.8 **gloss** glossiness, polish.

13.10 **cement** Accent on first syllable (text is 'symant').

13.12 **physic** medicine.

13.12 **pain** labour.

14

Good night, good rest: ah, neither be my share.
She bade good night, that kept my rest away,
And daffed me to a cabin hanged with care,
To descant on the doubts of my decay.
   'Farewell', quoth she, 'and come again tomorrow.'   5
   Fare well I could not, for I supped with sorrow.

Yet at my parting sweetly did she smile,
In scorn or friendship nill I conster whether:
'T may be she joyed to jest at my exile,
'T may be again to make me wander thither: 10
   'Wander', a word for shadows like myself,
   As take the pain, but cannot pluck the pelf.

Lord, how mine eyes throw gazes to the east!
My heart doth charge the watch; the morning rise

14.0 *Copy-text* 02   14.3 care] 02; eare 03

14.0 Not found elsewhere. Authorship uncertain. Malone, followed by some editors, assumes it to be two separate poems, the second beginning at line 13. He seems to have made nothing of the presence in 02 of a catchword 'Lord' at the foot of the page containing the first two stanzas; it occurs uniquely at this point in 02. The printer may have found it unnecessary to use the device for the previous poems, each of which is printed on a single page, and introduced the catchword here to remind himself that in the case of *PP* 14 the poem particularly requires the matching of different sheets. Oddly, it is not used for any of the succeeding poems, despite their length. 03 drops the catchword here and uses them only for the material incorporated from Heywood.

14.3 **daffed me** dismissed me, thrust me aside.

14.3 **cabin** Indicating not only a dark, enclosed space but also a brooding state of mind (as in *Luc.* 442).

14.3 **hanged** adorned.

14.4 **descant on** enlarge upon. The musical sense is pertinent (compare Lucrece's address to the nightingale: *Luc.* 1134).

14.4 **doubts** apprehensions, fears.

14.4 **decay** death, ruin. Compare *R3* 4.4.409: 'Death, desolation, ruin, and decay'.

14.8 **nill . . . whether** I will not conjecture which (for the construction compare *Ven.* 304 and *PP* 7.17).

14.12 **As** Such as.

14.14–16 Punctuation is substantially as 02 except that the semi-colon following 'watch' strengthens the effect, to the modern eye, of 02's comma. (Depending on sense and phrasing, the Elizabethan comma may have the same period effect as a modern semi-colon or colon.) However they are read, these three lines do not make easy sense, and some editors have conjectured emending them. But 'charge the watch' may be taken to mean that his eyes (see line 13, which prompts the image of this line) receive a commission or injunction from his heart to keep a watch or look-out for morning's arrival; morning as it rises stirs his other senses into life, 'each moving sense', the subject of 'daring' (16), sharing his apprehension that his eyes will fail to report the arrival of day (and perhaps her?). The overall trope is similar to that which governs *Luc.* 426–45, and enacts a similar anxiety: waiting for the approach of something or someone whose precise point of arrival is unsure. Malone proposes instead a stop or period after 'rest' and a comma after 'eyes' (16), making 'I' (17) the subject of 'daring'. Pooler incorporates Malone's conjecture, though uneasily, and in his notes (1927) conjectures that 'the watch' may be an error for 'the*m* watch', i.e.: 'My heart doth charge them watch the morning rise, / Doth cite each moving sense from idle rest, / Not daring trust the office of mine eyes'. Malone and Pooler both attempt to solve the problem of grammatical identity, which they perceive to be caused by the

Doth cite each moving sense from idle rest, 15
Not daring trust the office of mine eyes.
　While Philomela sits and sings, I sit and mark,
　And wish her lays were tunèd like the lark.

For she doth welcome daylight with her ditty,
And drives away dark-dreaming night: 20
The night so packed, I post unto my pretty;
Heart hath his hope, and eyes their wishèd sight:
　Sorrow changed to solace, and solace mixed with sorrow;
　For why she sighed, and bade me come tomorrow.

Were I with her, the night would post too soon, 25
But now are minutes added to the hours;
To spite me now, each minute seems a moon;
Yet not for me, shine sun to succour flowers!
　Pack night, peep day; good day, of night now borrow;
　Short night, tonight, and length thyself tomorrow. 30

14.27 a moon] *Steevens conj.*; an houre 02–3

transfer of subject from clause to clause. But the domino effect of constantly changing the subject of the sentence accords with the character of mounting tension or eagerness which the trope produces.

14.15 cite stir up, summon.

14.15 moving sense living sense, animated sense. The use of 'moving' humanises or personifies 'sense'. The authority for this is perhaps the still available medieval notion that bodies move because they have souls or spirits which desire motion. Kepler in *Mysterium cosmagraphicum* (1597) explains that planets had 'moving souls' (see *Ven.* 368n).

14.17 Philomela i.e. the nightingale.

14.17 sits and The line has a surplus of syllables, and Cambridge thinks that these two are the redundant ones: the compositor may have inadvertently doubled the letters. But there is something attractive and successful about the symmetry, and the lightness of the four-syllable 'Philomela'

means that the line does not feel burdened. (See 14.20n)

14.20 Two syllables appear to be missing. But just as its lightness makes line 17's alexandrine negotiable, so the heavy alliterative stress of this line compensates for its brevity. Editors variously propose pentameter solutions such as introducing 'daylight' before 'drives' (Prince) or, less plausibly, splitting 'dark dreaming' with yet another adjective (Maxwell).

14.21 packed sent off.

14.21 post hasten.

14.24 For why Because (see 10.8 and 10.10).

14.27 moon month (see collation).

14.28 Yet If.

14.29 Pack Be off with you (see 14.21n).

14.30 i.e. 'Be short, tonight, and be longer tomorrow.' He is addressing the night, asking it to end soon so that he can see the girl. He offers night a longer sojourn when it (and, with any luck, she) returns tomorrow.

SONNETS TO SUNDRY NOTES OF MUSIC

15

It was a lording's daughter, the fairest one of three,
That likèd of her master as well as well might be,
Till looking on an Englishman, the fairest that eye could see,
    Her fancy fell a-turning.
Long was the combat doubtful, that love with love did fight,   5
To leave the master loveless, or kill the gallant knight;
To put in practice either, alas, it was a spite
    Unto the silly damsel!
But one must be refusèd; more mickle was the pain,
That nothing could be usèd, to turn them both to gain,   10
For of the two the trusty knight was wounded with disdain:
    Alas, she could not help it!
Thus art with arms contending was victor of the day,

15.0 *Copy-text* o2 *(Arranged in twenty lines in* o3*)*   15.3 that] o2; *omitted* o3

15.0 No other version of this poem appears, but it derives from a popular medieval tradition of amorous contest between a cleric and a knight. For an account see Neilson, pp. 31ff. Though medieval, the motif sustained itself well into Shakespeare's time; for example, Chapman published a poem in a similar vein, though in a quite different metre of narrative quatrains, in the volume containing his *Ovids Banquet of Sence* (1595), which he called 'The Amorous Contention of Phillis and Flora'. This is a translation of a Latin poem from around 1400. As Neilson points out (pp. 32–3), such contentions usually took place between ladies who debated the respective merits of the two groups of suitors. The clerics held sway in the earliest, thirteenth-century examples, because they sang the praises of women in a devoted fashion and did not betray them, as knights were likely to do, in talking of their conquests. The present example abides by this rule, though with evident reluctance. The fact that tradition declares the cleric (or scholar) to have enlisted voluntarily in Venus's service may serve as a link between the theme of the poem and the Venus motif discernible in the early part of the *PP* miscellany. Knights, by contrast, feel themselves pressed into service, rather like Mars, against their own better interests. Despite its membership of elevated medieval court-of-love circles, such poetry passed easily into oral tradition. The jaunty, catchy rhythm suggests a children's song or even a nursery-rhyme (note 'lullaby' in line 15).

15.1 lording little lord. The usage is appropriate for a child's song (see 15.0), and the metre similarly determines the form. Its depreciation is tender rather than sardonic, but it is worth quoting Puttenham (in Pooler) on *meiosis*: 'Also such terms are used to be given in derision and for a kind of contempt, as when we say Lording for Lord.'

15.2 master tutor (see 15.0).

15.3 Englishman The patriotic appellation increases sympathy for the knight and justifies the girl's indecisiveness (she would *never* feel this way for a Frenchman). Andreas Capellanus in *De Amore* (2.8) describes a British knight in search of King Arthur's court who performs valiant deeds in the service of love. In codifying the rules of conduct for knights in love, authors such as Capellanus appear to have mediated the passage of Arthur's British heroes into poems or songs like this one, strengthening knightly claims to those virtues originally supposed to belong exclusively to the clerics (see 15.0).

15.5 doubtful uncertain.

15.8 silly weak, helpless.

15.9 more mickle the greater.

15.10 nothing . . . usèd no means could be employed.

Which by a gift of learning did bear the maid away;
Then lullaby, the learned man hath got the lady gay;   15
    For now my song is ended.

16

On a day (alack the day)
Love, whose month was ever May,
Spied a blossom passing fair,
Playing in the wanton air.
Through the velvet leaves the wind   5
All unseen gan passage find,
That the lover, sick to death,
Wished himself the heavens' breath:
'Air', quoth he, 'thy cheeks may blow;
Air, would I might triumph so!   10
But, alas, my hand hath sworn
Ne'er to pluck thee from thy thorn:
Vow, alack, for youth unmeet,
Youth so apt to pluck a sweet.

16.0 *Copy-text* o1 *(Entitled* The Passionate Sheepheards Song *in EH)* 16.2 was] o1–3; is *LLL* 16.6 gan] o1–3; can *LLL* 16.7 lover] o1–3; Sheepheard *EH* 16.8 Wished] o1–3; Wish *LLL* 16.11 alas . . . hath] o1–3; alacke . . . is *LLL* 16.12 pluck] plucke o2–3; pruck o1 16.12 thorn] *EH*; throne o1–3, *LLL* 16.13 alack] alacke o2–3; allcke o1 16.14 *Two additional lines in LLL:* Do not call it sinne in me, / That I am forsworne for thee

16.0 This is Dumaine's 'sonnet' (see *LLL* 4.3.99–118). There is another version in *Englands Helicon*, where of the four *PP* poems found in that volume (five if you count the last stanza of poem 19 separately) it is the only one attributed to Shakespeare.

16.2 **Love** i.e. the lover (in whom the spirit of love is personified).

16.3 **passing** extremely, more than.

16.4 **wanton** The word can, depending on context, convey any tone from innocent mischief (as here) to lasciviousness. (Compare the paradoxical play in *Luc.* 401.)

16.5–6 The image uses the conventional idea of the lover's envying the innocent intimacy which some indifferent creature or object (a lap-dog, comb, or the breeze in this instance) enjoys with the beloved. He wishes he could do what the wind does, equally imperceptibly and without disturbance (the 'velvet leaves' correspond to the girl's velvet costume). Compare *Rom.* 2.2.24–5: 'O that I were a

glove upon that hand, / That I might touch that cheek!'

16.7 **That** So that.

16.8 See 16.5–6n.

16.9 **cheeks . . . blow** i.e. like a trumpeter sounding a triumphant note.

16.12 **thee** i.e. the blossom of line 10.

16.12 **thorn** See collation.

16.14 Prince suggests plausibly that the two lines that follow in *LLL* ('Do not call it sin in me / That I am forsworn for thee') are omitted here because they refer to the play's dramatic situation (Dumaine, like the other members of the King's court, breaks his platonic vow not to fall in love). It would be absurd of 'love' to speak of forswearing itself by loving. (By contrast, the vow of 16.11–12 merely promises not to use force in love.)

16.14 **sweet** sweetmeat; 'sweet' may also imply the property of perfume, as in *Son.* 99.2, 15.

Thou for whom Jove would swear   15
Juno but an Ethiope were,
And deny himself for Jove,
Turning mortal for thy love.'

17

My flocks feed not, my ewes breed not,
My rams speed not, all is amiss;
Love is dying, faith's defying,
Heart's denying, causer of this.
All my merry jigs are quite forgot,   5
All my lady's love is lost, God wot:
Where her faith was firmly fixed in love,
There a nay is placed without remove.
One silly cross wrought all my loss,
O frowning fortune, cursèd fickle dame!   10

16.18 thy] 01–3, *LLL;* my *EH*   17.0 *Copy-text 01 (Entitled* The unknowne Sheepheards complaint *in EH)*   17.1 flocks feed . . . breed] 01–3; flocke feedes . . . breeds *HAR MS*   17.2 speed . . . amiss] 01–3; speedes not in their blis *HAR MS*   17.3 Love is dying] 01–3; Love is denying *EH*   17.3 faith's defying] Faithes defieng 01; Faith is defying *EH*   17.4 Heart's denying] harts denieng 01; Harts denying 03; Harts nenying 02; Harts renying *EH*   17.5 my] 01–3; our *Weelkes*   17.5 quite] 01–3; cleane *HAR MS*   17.6 lady's love is] 01–3; layes of love are *HAR MS*   17.7 her] 01–3; my *HAR MS;* our *Weelkes*   17.8 a nay is] 01–3; annoyes are *HAR MS;* annoy is *Weelkes*   17.9 One silly] 01–3; our seely *Weelkes*   17.9 cross . . . my] 01–3; poore crosse hath wrought me this *HAR MS*   17.10 frowning . . . cursèd fickle] 01–3; fickle . . . cruel cursèd *HAR MS*

16.16 **Ethiope** i.e. a woman of darker complexion. The distinction is not so much racial as a means of measuring women against a Petrarchan ideal of fair skin and light-coloured hair. Compare *TGV* 2.6.25–6: 'And Silvia (witness, heaven, that made her fair) / Shows Julia but a swarthy Ethiope.'

16.17 **for Jove** as Jove.

16.18 A witty compliment, since it was often Jove's way to turn himself into an earthly creature (a swan or a bull) in pursuit of an amorous exploit.

17.0 Authorship remains unestablished. The poem first appeared in Thomas Weelkes's *Madrigals* (1597), and again in *Englands Helicon* (1600). See also the version in BM Harleian MS 6910, *EH*'s version follows that of *PP* (see collation) and attributes the poem to 'Ignoto'. Lee (1905, 1907) and Grosart both claim the poem for Richard Barnfield on the grounds that in *EH* it is followed by a poem identifiably by Barnfield (poem 20 in *PP*)

which carries the title 'Another of the same Sheepheards'. But, as we see above, the *EH* compiler can only give his 'shepheard's' identity as 'Ignoto' (the title being emphatically 'The unknowne Sheepheards complaint') and presumably knows nothing about Barnfield. As Rollins (p. 552) makes clear, *EH*'s compiler took the three poems that he printed together (corresponding to *PP* 16, 17, and 20) all from *PP*, and knew only that what he calls 'The Passionate Sheepheards Song' was from *LLL* (hence the attribution to Shakespeare). For good measure, *EH* assigns 'As it fell upon a day' (*PP* 20) also to 'Ignoto'.

17.2 **speed** prosper.

17.3 **defying** Punning on its own composition, 'de-fying', i.e. 'unfaithing'; hence the paradoxical idea of faith (loyalty) being defiant (disloyal).

17.4 **Heart's denying** i.e. she is denying her heart to him (see 11.6–8).

17.9 **One . . . cross** A foolish or feeble blunder.

For now I see inconstancy
More in women than in men remain.

In black mourn I, all fears scorn I,
Love hath forlorn me, living in thrall;
Heart is bleeding, all help needing, 15
O cruel speeding, fraughted with gall.
My shepherd's pipe can sound no deal,
My wether's bell rings doleful knell;
My curtal dog that wont to have played
Plays not at all, but seems afraid: 20
　　With sighs so deep procures to weep,
　　In howling wise, to see my doleful plight.
　　How sighs resound through heartless ground,
　　Like a thousand vanquished men in bloody fight.

Clear wells spring not, sweet birds sing not, 25
Green plants bring not forth their dye;
Herds stands weeping, flocks all sleeping,
Nymphs back peeping fearfully.
All our pleasure known to us poor swains,
All our merry meetings on the plains, 30

17.11 For . . . see] 01–3; Now you may see that *HAR MS*　17.12] 01–3; In women more than I myselfe have found *HAR MS*　17.12 men remain] 01–3; many men to be *Weelkes*　17.13 fears] 01–3; feare *Weelkes*　17.14 Love . . . living] 01–3; lo how forlorn I, live *HAR MS*　17.15 help] 01–3; helpes *HAR MS*　17.16 cruel] 01–3; cursed *HAR MS*　17.16 fraughted] 01–3; fraught *HAR MS, Weelkes*　17.17 can] 01–3; will *HAR MS, Weelkes*　17.18 rings] 01–3; ringe a *HAR MS*　17.19 curtal] curtaile 01–3; curtail'd *HAR MS*　17.19 that wont to] 01–3; wch would *HAR MS*　17.20 at] 01–2; *omitted* 03　17.20 afraid] 01–3; dismayd *HAR MS*　17.21 With . . . procures] 01–3; My sights so deepe, doth cause him *HAR MS;* My . . . procures *Weelkes*　17.22 In . . . wise] 01–3; With . . . noise *HAR MS, Weelkes*　17.22 see . . . doleful] 01–3; wayle . . . woefull *HAR MS*　17.23] 01–3; My shrikes resoundes, throughe Arcadia groundes *HAR MS*　17.23 How] 01–3; harke how *Weelkes*　17.23 heartless] 01–3; harcklesse *Weelkes*　17.24 a] 01–3; *omitted HAR MS*　17.24 thousand . . . bloody] 01–3; thousandes . . . deadly *HAR MS*　17.26] 01–3; Lowde bells ring not, cherefully *Weelkes*　17.26 plants] 01–3; palmes *HAR MS*　17.26 their dye] 01–3; yor dye *HAR MS*　17.27 stands] 01–3; stand *Weelkes, EH*　17.27 flocks all] 01–3; ecchoes *HAR MS*　17.28 back peeping] *EH;* blacke peeping 01–3; looke peeping *HAR MS;* back creeping *Weelkes*　17.28 fearfully] 01–3; pittyfully *HAR MS*　17.29 our pleasure] 01–3; the pleasures *HAR MS;* our pleasures *Weelkes*　17.30 meetings] 01–3; meeting *EH*

17.11 inconstancy fickleness (as in line 10). It is likely that his 'cross' (line 9) is a minor transgression which ought not to have produced this revulsion in her. Whatever it was, he evidently feels less culpable than she is.

17.16 speeding See 17.2n.

17.16 fraughted (1) laden, (2) checked, frustrated.

17.17 no deal not at all.

17.19 curtal i.e. with a docked tail.

17.21 With sighs Maxwell prefers Weelkes's 'My sighs'; but 02's sense is sound enough if we read 'procures' as manages or contrives (following Steevens, 1780).

17.23 heartless ground the abject, or stricken landscape (line 24 makes the meaning clearer; see also *Luc.* 471).

All our evening sport from us is fled,
All our love is lost, for love is dead.
Farewell, sweet love, thy like ne'er was
For a sweet content, the cause of all my woe.
Poor Corydon must live alone: 35
Other help for him I see that there is none.

18

When as thine eye hath chose the dame,
And stalled the deer that thou shouldst strike,

17.31 sport . . . is] 01–3; sportes . . . are *EH, HAR MS, Weelkes*   17.31 us] 01–3; greenes *HAR MS*   17.32 our love is] 01–3; alas is *HAR MS;* our loves are *Weelkes*   17.32 for love] 01–3; now Dolus *HAR MS*   17.33–36] *omitted HAR MS*   17.33 love] 01–3; lasse *Weelkes*   17.34 woe] 01–3; moane *EH*   17.36 see . . . is] 01–3; know ther's *Weelkes*   18.0 *Copy-text 01*   18.1 When as] 01–3; when y^t *FO MSS*   18.2 shouldst] 01–3; woudst *FO MSS*

17.35 **Corydon** The name of a lovesick shepherd who complains in a similar fashion in Virgil's second Eclogue.

18.0 This is one of the most interesting poems in *PP* from a textual and editorial point of view. It exists elsewhere only in two manuscript versions, both in the Folger Library: FO MS 1.112 and 2071.7 (NB: Folger reclassified its call numbers in the 1950s, and recent editors such as Wells–Taylor use the new system. This edition retains the old call numbers to facilitate reference to Rollins and Adams, whose work remains indispensable. Folger has a cross-reference card file so that readers may consult the original manuscripts using either system of call numbers.) FO MS 1.112 is a miscellany in several hands which is 'approximately contemporary with the publication of *PP*' (Adams, pp. liv–lv). Some of the poems are anonymous, others attributed to such figures as the Earl of Oxford, Sidney, Dyer, Vavasor, and John Bentley. FO MS 2071.7 is a common-place book compiled later (1630–40) by one Joseph Hall. It was later owned by J. P. Collier, who probably affixed 'W. S.' to some of the poems, including this one (Adams, pp. lviii–lix). The tone of the poem oddly mixes the voices of courtliness and irreverence, as if Chaunticleer had strayed into 'The Knight's Tale'. This perhaps accounts for its failure to find a printing other than in *PP*, sonnet decorum generally keeping well clear of it. On the other hand, the poem no doubt enjoyed a wide oral reputation, and there are likely to have been many manuscript versions in addition to those that have survived. There appears also to be some connection between the poem and canto xlvii of *Willobie his Avisa* (see supplementary note).

Despite the view of Wells–Taylor that the Folger manuscripts represent an alternative textual tradition to that of *PP*, all three probably derive from the same stem since they join and part company in equal measure. For example, instead of 01's 'fancy (partyall might)' (line 4) the Folger versions have 'fancye parcyall like' (1.112) and 'partiall fancie like' (2071.7): while it shares the same words as 2071.7, 1.112's phrasing is that of *PP*. Also 1.112 reflects a long 'e' in its pronunciation of 'heade' (rhymed with 'unwayde' – i.e. 'restless' (*OED* sv *adj.* 2) – lines 5–6) whereas 2071.7 reproduces *PP*'s shorter 'head' – 'unwed'. Again, the Folger manuscripts appear to differ significantly from *PP* in 18.12 where for *PP*'s 'And set her person forth to sale', 1.112 has (substantially) 'and set thy person forth to sell', a switch of identity which 2071.1 takes even further with '& set thy body forth to sell'. But even as the manuscript versions affect a change from lady to lover as subject, 1.112 more closely resembles *PP* in the restraint of 'person' as compared with 2071.7's 'body'. It is also possible that as the only (though hastily) printed version, *PP* opposes itself here to the entire manuscript tradition in introducing a note of male modesty.

But perhaps the most significant point to make about the manuscripts is that they support the primacy of 01 (see Textual Analysis) by following its stanza order in lines 13–24 (see collation); they differ from it (and from 02–3) in the order of the two penultimate stanzas, but the octavos seem to be right in their choice of the properly climactic 'Think women still to strive', etc., as the final resounding statement before the 'recantation' of the close.

Let reason rule things worthy blame,
As well as fancy, partial might;
   Take counsel of some wiser head,   5
   Neither too young nor yet unwed.

And when thou com'st thy tale to tell,
Smooth not thy tongue with filèd talk,
Lest she some subtle practice smell –
A cripple soon can find a halt –   10
   But plainly say thou lov'st her well,
   And set her person forth to sale.

And to her will frame all thy ways;
Spare not to spend, and chiefly there

18.4 fancy, partial might] fancy (parcyall might) 01–3; fancye parcyall like *FO MS 1.112*; parciall fancie like *FO MS 2071.7*   18.5 Take] 01–3; Aske *FO MS 201.7*   18.5 wiser] 01–3; other *FO MSS*   18.6 too young] 01–3; unwise *FO MSS*   18.6 unwed] 01–3; unwayde *FO MS 1.112*   18.8 Smooth] 01–3; whet *FO MSS*   18.10 find] 01–3; spie *FO MS 2071.7*   18.11 say] 01–3; *omitted FO MS 2071.7*   18.12 her . . . sale] 01–3; thy . . . sell *FO MS 1.112*; thy body foorth to sell *FO MS 2071.7*   18.13–24] *This is the order in 01 and FO MSS; 13–24 follow 25–36 in 02–3*   18.13 And to] 01–3; unto *FO MS 2071.7*

18.1–2 Pooler detects an Ovidian reference: 'Scit bene venator cervis ubi retia tendat . . . Tu quoque, materiam longo qui quaeris amori / Ante frequens quo sit disce puella loco' ('Well knows the hunter where to spread his nets for the stag . . . you too, who seek the object of a lasting passion learn first what places the maidens haunt': *Art of Love* 1.45–50; Loeb translation).

18.2 stalled 'To stall' means 'to bring (a hunted animal) to a stand' (*OED* sv *v.*[1] 10, citing this example).

18.3 things . . . blame passionate enterprises ('reason' antithetically indicates the subject of the periphrasis).

18.4 fancy, partial might 01's reading (substantially) seems to be that 'fancy' (imagination) has a limited or distorting effect compared with 'reason'; 'partial' plays on (1) prejudicial, (2) reduced.

18.6 nor yet unwed Perhaps the best that can be said for the line is that it is weak, since what it does is merely to restate the first half in the second. The words 'nor yet unwed' mean 'married', i.e. 'mature'. The phrase may fill out a poorly remembered line: FO MS 1.112's 'unwayde' (see 18.0) establishes disagreement among the variants and hints at more interesting possibilities.

18.8 filèd polished (compare Wyatt, 'There was never file half so well filed', p. 15).

18.10 i.e. it takes one to know one (the element of cynicism with regard to women enters at this point

with an overall unbalancing effect – see 18.0). See *ODEP* c828 and Dent H60.

18.10 halt limp.

18.12 i.e. extol her charms (with yourself as prospective buyer). This meaning of 'sale' is more discreet or deferential than either of the manuscripts' (see collation and 18.0), though it shortly leads to difficulties (see 14–16n). *PP* may be rephrasing the line in an attempt at modesty which is impossible to sustain.

18.13–24 The order as found in 01 and FO MSS (see collation and p. 295).

18.14–16 These lines should be considered along with the corresponding stanza of canto xlvii of *Willobie his Avisa* (see supplementary note). There seems to be a double play, (1) on persuasive eloquence ('ringing . . . ear'), and (2) on gift-giving ('spend', line 14, can take either meaning: spend money or spend praises). The meaning of 'desert' (15) depends on how 'ringing' is interpreted: the idea of coins jingling is crude but in keeping with the tone of the poem as a whole and, significantly perhaps, close to the letter of *Willobie*, though markedly at odds with its attempt to maintain a delicate spirit. This would give 'desert' the sense of 'wealth'. But 'desert' as 'worthiness' is also conceivable if we think of eloquence rather than money: i.e. the lover is encouraged to pursue his suit by means of flattery, etc. However, this reading confronts the difficulty that the lover appears to

Where thy desert may merit praise,   15
By ringing in thy lady's ear:
   The strongest castle, tower and town,
   The golden bullet beats it down.

Serve always with assurèd trust,
And in thy suit be humble true;   20
Unless thy lady prove unjust,
Press never thou to choose anew:
   When time shall serve, be thou not slack
   To proffer, though she put thee back.

What though her frowning brows be bent,   25
Her cloudy looks will calm ere night,
And then too late she will repent
That thus dissembled her delight;
   And twice desire, ere it be day,
   That which with scorn she put away.   30

18.15 desert . . . merit] 01–3; expences . . . sounde thy *FO MS 1.112;* expence . . . sound thy *FO MS 2071.7*   **18.16** By] 01–3; & still be *FO MS 2071.7*   **18.16** in thy lady's] 01–3; allwayes in her *FO MS 1.112;* in in her *FO MS 2071.7*   **18.17** castle, tower] 01–3; towres fort *FO MS 2071.7*   **18.17** and] 01–3; or *FO MSS*   **18.18** beats it] 01–3; hathe beat *FO MS 1.112;* beateth *FO MS 2071.7*   **18.20** humblel 01–3; ever *FO MSS 2071.7*   **18.21** Unless] 01–3; untill *FO MS 2071.7*   **18.22** Press] 01–3; seeke *FO MS 1.112*   **18.22** choose] 01–3; change *FO MSS*   **18.22** anew] 01–3; for newe *FO MS 2071.7*   **18.23** shall . . . be thou] 01–3; dothe . . . then be *FO MS 1.112;* doth . . . thee be *FO MS 2071.7*   **18.24** thee] 01–3; it 03, *FO MSS*   **18.25** though . . . frowning] 01–3; if shee frowne wᵗʰ *FO MS 2071.7*   **18.26** calm ere] calme yer 01–3; cleare ere *FO MS 1.112;* calme at *FO MS 2071.7*   **18.27** And . . . will] 01–3; And she perhappes will sone *FO MS 1.112;* when yᵗ perhaps shee will *FO MS 2071.7*   **18.28** thus] 01–3; she *FO MS 1.112;* so *FO MS 2071.7*   **18.29** twice] 01–3; thrice *FO MS 2071.7*   **18.29** ere it] 01–3; it ere *FO MS 2071.7*   **18.30** which with] 01–3; wᵗʰ suche *FO MSS*

be advised to sing his own praises in 15–16 (on this point we recall the disagreements between *PP* and the manuscripts over line 12). We can stretch the expression to mean that his eloquence about *her* persuades her of his worth, etc., but that is to appeal to subtlety where simplicity will do. It appears rather that the poet is playing on the forms of eloquence merely to reveal that money is the best persuader.

18.18 golden bullet (1) smooth and well-aimed eloquence, (2) financial inducement (see 18.14–16n).

18.19 assurèd i.e. giving assurance, reliable.

18.21 unjust untrue, unfaithful (compare *Son.* 138.9).

18.24 proffer put yourself forward.

18.24 put . . . back resist you.

18.25 What though Although.

18.26 The play on physiognomy (i.e. the face as the heavens, as in *Luc.* 11–14) facilitates the comparison with real night-time, which antithetically deepens as her expression clears.

18.28 dissembled . . . delight hid or masked her desire (looking back to line 26); 'delight' means 'what she would delight in'.

18.29 twice desire i.e. she will require a repetition of sexual enjoyment.

18.30 put away denied herself, rejected.

What though she strive to try her strength,
And ban and brawl, and say thee nay,
Her feeble force will yield at length,
When craft hath taught her thus to say:
   'Had women been so strong as men,   35
   In faith, you had not had it then.'

The wiles and guiles that women work,
Dissembled with an outward show,
The tricks and toys that in them lurk,
The cock that treads them shall not know.   40
   Have you not heard it said full oft,
   A woman's nay doth stand for nought?

Think women still to strive with men
To sin, and never for to saint:
There is no heaven, be holy then   45
When time with age shall them attaint.
   Were kisses all the joys in bed,
   One woman would another wed.

18.31 though . . . her] 01–3; if . . . thy *FO MS 2071.7*   18.32 ban] 01–3; chide *FO MS 1.112*   18.32 say] 01–3; sweare *FO MS 2071.7*   18.34 When] 01–3; & *FO MSS*   18.34 hath taught] 01–3; will cause *FO MS 2071.7*   18.35 so] 01–3; as *FO MSS*   18.36 In faith] 01–3; by cock *FO MS 2071.7*   18.37–42] *These lines follow* 01*'s line 48 in FO MS*   18.37] 01–3; A thousand wiles in wantons lurkes *FO MS 2071.7*   18.37 women work] 01–3; in them lurkes *FO MS 1.112*   18.39 that . . . lurk] 01–3; & meanes to woorke *FO MS 1.112*; he meane to worke *FO MS 2071.7*   18.40 shall] 01–3; doth *FO MS 2071.7*   18.41 it] 01–3; that *FO MS 1.112*   18.43 still to strive] 01–3; love to matche *FO MS 1.112*; seeke to match *FO MS 2071.7*   18.44] 01–3; and not to live soe like a sainte *FO MS 1.112*; to live in sinne & not to saint *FO MS 2071.7*   18.45 There] 01–3; here *FO MSS*   18.45 be holy then] *FO MS 2071.7*; (by holy then) 01–3; they holye then *FO MS 1.112*   18.46 When . . . them] 01–3; beginne when age dothe them *FO MS 1.112*; till time shall thee wth age *FO MS 2071.7*   18.47 kisses] 01–3; kyssinge *FO MSS*

18.32 ban scold, perhaps 'curse', as in *Ven.* 326.

18.32 brawl shout. The term is from dance music (see *LLL* 3.1.8–9: 'Master, will you win your love with a French brawl?').

18.37 work make use of.

18.39 toys whims, fancies.

18.40 The crude explicitness ('treads' describes the male role in copulation, as in Chaucer's *NPT*: 'He feathered Pertelote twenty time / And trad hire eke as ofte' – *CT* 3177–8) marks the transition from courtliness to bawdy (until now the poem has maintained a form of tonal ambivalence, as in, for example, 18.14–16) – evidence perhaps of a courtly original acquiring characteristics of parody (see 18.0 and supplementary note).

18.42 nought Probably punning on 'nothing' as

a word for the vulva (see *Son.* 20.12 and Booth, pp. 164–5).

18.43–6 A tricky passage in the octavos, edited with the help of FO MS 2071.7, which provides 'be holy then' for *PP*'s unworkable 'by holy then', though it may be that 'by' is simply a variant of 'be' (for otherwise *PP* makes better sense than either Folger version). The meaning may be construed: 'Remember that women always try to outdo men in the pursuit of sexual pleasure ('sin'), but never in chastity. There is nothing pure about them ('There' is emphatic and means 'in them', as in *Lear* 4.6.127: 'there's hell, there's darkness'), so start looking for holiness when age has taken away their physical appeal.'

But soft, enough – too much, I fear –
Lest that my mistress hear my song;   50
She will not stick to round me on th'ear,
To teach my tongue to be so long.
        Yet will she blush, here be it said,
        To hear her secrets so bewrayed.

19

Live with me and be my love,
And we will all the pleasures prove
That hills and valleys, dales and fields,
And all the craggy mountains yield.   5

There will we sit upon the rocks,
And see the shepherds feed their flocks,
By shallow rivers, by whose falls
Melodious birds sing madrigals.

There will I make thee a bed of roses,   10
With a thousand fragrant posies,

18.49 But soft] 01–3; Nowe hoe *FO MS 1.112;* ho now *FO MS 2071.7*   18.49 too much, I fear] 01–3; & more I feare *FO MS 2071.7*   18.50 Lest . . . mistress] 01–3; for if my ladye *FO MS 1.112;* for if my m^{rs} *FO MS 2071.7*   18.50 hear my] 01–3; heare this *FO MS 1.112;* hard this *FO MS 2071.7*   18.51 She will] 01–3; she would *FO MS 2071.7*   18.51 round me on th'ear] round me on th'are 01–2; round me on th'ere 03; ringe my eare *FO MS 1.112;* warme my eare *FO MS 2071.7*   18.53 will] 01–3; would *FO MSS*   18.53 blush] 01–3; blushe *FO MS 1.112;* smile *FO MS 2071.7*   18.54 so] 01–3; thus *FO MSS*   19.0 *Copy-text* 02 *(Entitled* The passionate Sheepheard to his love *in EH and attributed to Christopher Marlowe. The poem here represents stanzas 1, 2, 3, and 5 of Marlowe's poem. 'Love's Answer' is the first stanza of what is called* The Nimphs reply to the Sheepheard *in EH (by 'Ignoto' but generally attributed to Ralegh).)*   19.1 Live] 02–3; Come live *EH*   19.3] 02–3; That Vallies, groves, hills, and fieldes *EH*   19.4 And . . . craggy] 02–3; Woods, or steepie *EH*   19.4 mountains] 02–3; mountaine *EH*   19.4 yield] 02–3; yeeldes *EH*   19.5 There will we] 2–3; And we will *EH*   19.6 And see] 02–3; Seeing *EH*   19.7–8 falls . . . madrigals] 02, *EH;* tales . . . madrigales 03   19.7 by] 02–3; to *EH*   19.8 sing] 02–3; sings *EH*   19.9 There will I] 02–3; And I will *EH*   19.9 a bed] 02–3; beds *EH*   19.10 With . . . posies] 02–3; And . . . poesies *EH*

18.51 stick hesitate (as in 'stick at nothing').

18.51 round . . . ear (1) reproach me, (2) box my ears? FO MS 1.112 has 'ring my ear' (which recalls line 16), while MS 2071.7 reads 'warme my eare'. The octavo version appears to conflate this sense with that of *sotto voce* remonstrance. 'Round in' as distinct from 'round on' originally meant whisper, then later acquired the sense of 'taking privately to task' (*OED* sv *v²* 3). This is the meaning Johnson distinguishes; but 'round . . . on' is more forceful, particularly as expressed here. Though *OED* does not provide any example of 'round' as a verb meaning 'strike' or 'hit', it does supply such senses to its noun and adjectival forms (sv *sb¹* and *a* III.10).

18.54 bewrayed betrayed, broadcast.

19.0 A fuller version attributed to Christopher Marlowe will be found in *EH;* *PP*'s final stanza ('Love's Answer') begins a new poem in *EH* called 'The Nimphs reply'. *EH* does not attribute this poem, but Walton in his *Compleat Angler* (1655) assigned it to Ralegh (for the arguments see Rollins, pp. 554–5).

19.7–10 See Sir Hugh Evans's song in *Wiv.* 3.1.17ff.

19.8 madrigals Songs associated with pastoral (the Italian 'madrigale' is thought to derive from 'mandria' = sheepfold).

A cap of flowers, and a kirtle
Embroidered all with leaves of myrtle;

A belt of straw and ivy buds,
With coral clasps and amber studs:
And if these pleasures may thee move,   15
Then live with me and be my love.

Love's Answer

If that the world and love were young,
And truth in every shepherd's tongue,
These pretty pleasures might me move   20
To live with thee and be thy love.

                                    20

As it fell upon a day
In the merry month of May,
Sitting in a pleasant shade
Which a grove of myrtles made,
Beasts did leap and birds did sing,   5
Trees did grow and plants did spring;
Everything did banish moan,
Save the nightingale alone:
She, poor bird, as all forlorn,
Leaned her breast up-till a thorn,   10
And there sung the dolefull'st ditty,
That to hear it was great pity.
'Fie, fie, fie', now would she cry,
'Tereu, Tereu', by and by;
That to hear her so complain,   15

19.16 Then] 02–3; Come *EH*   **19.17** that] 02–3; all *EH*   **19.20** thy] 02, *EH*; my 03   **20.0** *Copy-text 02 (Entitled* An Ode *in Barnfield,* Another of the same Sheepheards *in EH)*   **20.10** up-till] 02–3; against *EH*

20.0 By Richard Barnfield, first appearing in his *Poems: In divers humors* (1598) (see also 8.0, 17.0). *EH* has a shorter version which omits lines 27–56. The Shakespearean connection, such as it is, lies perhaps in the resemblance of lines 8–30 to Lucrece's lament to the nightingale (1128–48). This rare moment of lyrical outpouring in the narrative poem may have given Barnfield his theme, or, equally possibly, whoever compiled Jaggard's miscellany may have been struck by the similarity between the two.

    20.10 up-till against.

    20.14 Tereu The sound made by the nightingale. Tereus is also the name of the king who raped his sister-in-law Philomela. Lucrece alludes to the myth in the lines cited in the headnote and addresses the nightingale by her name (1128). Ovid provided the Elizabethans with the fullest account of the story (see *Metam.* 6.455–674).

Scarce I could from tears refrain,
For her griefs so lively shown
Made me think upon mine own.
Ah, thought I, thou mourn'st in vain,
None takes pity on thy pain.   20
Senseless trees, they cannot hear thee,
Ruthless bears, they will not cheer thee;
King Pandion, he is dead,
All thy friends are lapped in lead;
All thy fellow birds do sing,   25
Careless of thy sorrowing.
Whilst as fickle fortune smiled,
Thou and I were both beguiled.
Every one that flatters thee
Is no friend in misery.   30
Words are easy, like the wind;
Faithful friends are hard to find.
Every man will be thy friend
Whilst thou hast wherewith to spend;
But if store of crowns be scant,   35
No man will supply thy want.
If that one be prodigal,
Bountiful they will him call,
And with such-like flattering:
'Pity but he were a king!'   40
If he be addict to vice,
Quickly him they will entice;
If to women he be bent,
They have at commandement.
But if fortune once do frown,   45
Then farewell his great renown;
They that fawned on him before
Use his company no more.

20.22 bears] Beares 02–3; beasts *EH*   20.27–56] 02–3; *omitted EH, which concludes, following line 26,* Even so poore bird like thee, / None a-live will pitty mee.

20.21 Senseless Insensible, unfeeling.
20.23 Pandion The father of Philomela.
20.24 lapped in lead Burial in lead coffins was more prevalent in the Middle Ages than latterly, which may indicate that the song draws upon long-established lyric antecedents. (The reference, for example, to 'fickle fortune' (27) shows the survival of a commonplace medieval idea.)
20.40 Pity . . . were What a pity he isn't.
20.41 addict addicted. See Abbott §342.
20.44 They have They have women.
20.44 commandement This form is as common as 'commandment' and seems chosen here to assist scansion.

He that is thy friend indeed,
He will help thee in thy need: 50
If thou sorrow, he will weep;
If thou wake, he cannot sleep:
Thus of every grief in heart
He with thee doth bear a part.
These are certain signs to know   55
Faithful friend from flatt'ring foe.

20.52 **wake** i.e. cannot sleep.

A Lover's Complaint

A LOVER'S COMPLAINT

From off a hill whose concave womb reworded
A plaintful story from a sist'ring vale,
My spirits t'attend this double voice accorded,
And down I laid to list the sad-tuned tale,
Ere long espied a fickle maid full pale,   5
Tearing of papers, breaking rings atwain,
Storming her world with sorrow's wind and rain.

Upon her head a platted hive of straw,
Which fortified her visage from the sun,
Whereon the thought might think sometime it saw   10
The carcass of a beauty spent and done:

---

7 sorrow's wind] *Gildon*[2]*;* sorrowes, wind Q

Title In the sixteenth century, 'lover', in the erotic sense, more often than not denoted a woman; see *OED* examples. Shakespeare applies the term to Venus (*Ven.* 573; see also *AYLI* 3.4.43 and *MM* 1.4.40). Nicholas Breton, in *The Arbor of Amorous Devices* (1597), includes several short lyrics under the title 'A Lover's Complaint' or variants thereof. In these the poet himself is the speaker, though the apparatus of tearful wailing is a distinct feature. One lyric is entitled 'A Ladies complaint for the losse of her Love', spoken for her knight-servitor whom 'most cruell death hath slain'. See Breton, 1, d.

1 reworded repeated, echoed.

2 plaintful i.e. full of complaint. The word evokes the complaint genre (see p. 62).

2 sist'ring neighbouring (influenced by the female connotations of 'womb' as well as perhaps anticipating the sex of the sufferer).

3 accorded put themselves in a sympathetic mood.

5 fickle A difficult and troubling reading. Hudson[2] (1881) suggests 'fitful' or 'uneasy', which certainly seems right for the context. However, all Shakespeare's other uses of 'fickle' denote 'capricious' as do *OED* entries without exception. All we know of the maid initially is that she is in a dreadful state; the implicit culpability of 'fickle' = 'capricious' seems unwarranted (but see Kerrigan). I suggest either that this is an unnoted use of 'fickle' to mean 'fitful', 'agitated', *or* that 'fitful' was the word

intended and that it was mistranscribed or wrongly set up. The familiar collocation 'fickle maid' would be a natural (misleading) influence.

6 atwain in two.

7 Storming . . . world i.e. raging tearfully. Just as the hill and vale of 1–2 can be personified, so conversely may human emotions acquire cosmic attributes.

8 hive hat. Straw hats were shaped like beehives. Apart from the establishment of pastoral detail, in itself fictitious, the wearing of such a hat may give no sure clue to its owner's status. Kerrigan, however, sees it as a sign of social lowliness.

9 fortified protected.

10 thought . . . think The doubling of the concept of 'thought' increases the sense of uncertain perception. For the phrase, compare *MV* 1.1.36–7: 'Shall I have the thought / To think on this?'

11 carcass body, corpse. The image and the lines that follow reach beyond merely physical impressions and raise the trickier question whether she has grown old in fact (which would be difficult to reconcile with her appearance as a maid given in 5) or whether it is the extinction of her beauty which makes her age prematurely (see below, 73–4). 'Time' seems to be the predator in 12, but in 13 it is the 'fell' (fierce) rage of heaven which assumes responsibility. The two operate differently, the former suggesting duration, whereas the latter often chooses to show its power through the immediacy of its effect. In so far as heaven's judgement is

Time had not scythèd all that youth begun,
Nor youth all quit, but spite of heaven's fell rage,
Some beauty peeped through lattice of seared age.

Oft did she heave her napkin to her eyne,   15
Which on it had conceited characters,
Laund'ring the silken figures in the brine
That seasoned woe had pelleted in tears;
And often reading what contents it bears,
As often shrieking undistinguished woe,   20
In clamours of all size, both high and low.

Sometimes her levelled eyes their carriage ride,
As they did batt'ry to the spheres intend;
Sometime diverted their poor balls are tied
To th'orbèd earth; sometimes they do extend   25
Their view right on; anon their gazes lend
To every place at once, and nowhere fixed,
The mind and sight distractedly commixed.

---

14 lattice] *Gildon²;* lettice Q

touched on, the lines imply that her beauty fades
for a moral and not just a natural reason. The severity of the image perhaps suggests the plight of one
who bears the entire guilt for an action (i.e. breach
of chastity) for which she is only partly to blame.
Compare the description of Hecuba (*Luc.* 1450–6).

  14 lattice Her ravaged and wrinkled face is
likened to the criss-cross pattern in lead on a lattice
window. Compare *Son.* 3.11–12.

  14 seared withered, blighted (Onions). Angelo
uses the word ('seard' in the Folio text) to describe
how his sense of duty has palled in his sudden lust
for Isabella (*MM* 2.4.7–12).

  15 heave See *Ven.* 351n.

  15 napkin handkerchief.

  16 conceited characters emblematic devices
(Pooler²); line 19 indicates their literary nature.
The handkerchief is presumably her lover's gift and
the 'characters' a means of declaring his passion.

  18 seasoned (1) matured, (2) salted.

  18 pelleted i.e. formed into balls or round
drops. 'Pellet' normally conveys hardness, as most
notably at *Ant.* 3.13.165. Following this, Steevens

(Malone), detects a culinary image in 'seasoned'
('pellets' being meatballs); the association is irresistible but surely inadvertent since it vitiates the
pathos of the idea (which is less concentrated but
more successful at *Luc.* 796).

  20 undistinguished i.e. of undistinguishable
purport.

  22 i.e. her eyes seem trained on a target like a
gun battery (the image is from ordnance); see its
recurrence at 281–2 (and compare *Son.* 121.9–10).

  23 As As if (see *Ven.* 323).

  24 diverted turned in another direction.

  24 tied The spherical resemblance of the 'orbèd
earth' appears to exert an influence on the eyeball.
The Pythagorean theory of interconnected spheres
may be in play. For beams as strings compare
Donne: 'our eye-beames twisted, and did thred /
Our eyes, upon one double string' ('The Exstasie',
lines 7–8).

  26 right on straight ahead.

  28 i.e. in the confusion of her grief she gazes as
much with her mind as her eyes.

Her hair, nor loose nor tied in formal plat,
Proclaimed in her a careless hand of pride;   30
For some, untucked, descended her sheaved hat,
Hanging her pale and pinèd cheek beside;
Some in her threaden fillet still did bide,
And true to bondage would not break from thence,
Though slackly braided in loose negligence.   35

A thousand favours from a maund she drew,
Of amber, crystal, and of beaded jet,
Which one by one she in a river threw,
Upon whose weeping margent she was set,
Like usury applying wet to wet,   40
Or monarchs' hands that lets not bounty fall
Where want cries some, but where excess begs all.

---

37 beaded] *Gildon²; bedded* Q   41 monarchs'] *Capell MS;* Monarches Q

29–35 Walker (*Critical Examination*, 1860, 3, 370) detects the influence of Sidney's *Arcadia* (1590):

In the dressing of her haire and apparell, she might see neither a careful arte, nor an arte of carelessness, but even left to a neglected chaunce.   (Feuillerat², 1.376)

. . . she had cast on a long cloake . . . with a poore felt hat, which almost covered all her face, most part of her goodly heare . . . so lying upon her shoulders as a man might well see, had no artificiall carelesnes.
                                                (Feuillerat², II.168)

30 a . . . pride a hand unconcerned with the vanity of appearance. Maxwell and others detect pride even in the unconcern, but such an observation seems unwarranted. The line resembles the passages quoted from Sidney above in evoking unselfconscious humility.

31 descended came down from under.

31 sheaved straw.

33 threaden fillet ribbon binding her hair.

34 true to bondage The description of hair which stays in place interestingly evokes an upright spirit which will not trespass despite tempting circumstance ('slackly . . . negligence'); 'bondage' signifies 'a proper sense of limits'. In portraying the varying action of the girl's hair, the poet seeks to distinguish between her evident fallen self and a part of her which none the less remains pure. Though seduction inevitably calls into question the morality of the victim, the distinction outlined here is not dissimilar to that insisted on by both victim and poet in *The Rape of Lucrece*.

36 favours gifts received from a lover.

36 maund wicker basket (or some form of woven basket).

37 beaded jet beads made of jet. Wyndham accepts Q's 'bedded' as meaning 'imbedded in jet'.

39 margent margin, bank. The water lapping the bank seems to be 'weeping' as if empathising with her tears (as the following line makes clearer). The 'weeping margent' recalls the opening of Lodge's *Scillaes Metamorphosis* (1589): 'Within a thicket nere to *Isis* floud / Weeping my wants, and wailing scant relief' (Alexander, p. 33). Kerrigan (pp. 393–4) connects this image with Desdemona's willow song and the drowned Ophelia.

40 i.e. tears begetting tears (playing on the idea of increase through investment). Although usury was regarded with mixed feelings (deriving in part from Deut. 23.19–20), poetically it could be applied in a neutral way for images of growth and expansion. See also *AYLI* 2.1.47–9.

41–42 The idea is of regal power bestowing its generosity not on the needy, whose requests are modest, but on the greedy, who already have too much.

41 monarchs' This could be singular or plural (see collation and 41n below); but the concept indicates monarchs in general. The pronoun 'that' most likely relates to 'hands' (see next note).

41 lets See Abbott §333–7 who notes the frequent recurrence in the Folio of inflected 's' following a plural noun ('hands'), and ascribes it possibly to a surviving form of early English. (This edition notes several examples in the other narrative poems, e.g. *Ven.* 517.)

Of folded schedules had she many a one,
Which she perused, sighed, tore, and gave the flood,
Cracked many a ring of posied gold and bone,   45
Bidding them find their sepulchres in mud;
Found yet moe letters sadly penned in blood,
With sleided silk feat and affectedly
Enswathed, and sealed to curious secrecy.

These often bathed she in her fluxive eyes,   50
And often kissed, and often 'gan to tear;
Cried, 'O false blood, thou register of lies,
What unapprovèd witness dost thou bear!
Ink would have seemed more black and damnèd here!'
This said, in top of rage the lines she rents,   55
Big discontent so breaking their contents.

A reverend man that grazed his cattle nigh,
Sometime a blusterer that the ruffle knew
Of court, of city, and had let go by

---

51 'gan] *Malone;* gaue Q

43 **schedules** papers, letters (as at 47). See *Luc.*
1312.
45 **posied** i.e. inscribed with posies, or mottoes.
47 **moe** more. Normally used for 'more' where
number or quantity is concerned.
47 **sadly** i.e. in the mood of a despairing lover.
48 **sleided silk** According to *OED* (sv *sb* 'sleave-
silk'), a variant of 'sleaved silk', silk which can be
separated into filaments for embroidery. See *Per.*
4, Prologue, line 21; 'Be't when they weav'd the
sleided silk'.
48 **feat** delicately. For the elision, 'feat(ly)', see
Abbott §397.
48 **affectedly** lovingly.
49 **to . . . secrecy** with fastidious care over the
safety of the contents.
50 **fluxive** flowing (with tears). Unrecorded
pre-Shakespeare, and in Shakespeare occurring
uniquely here. Compare 'flux' in *AYLI* 2.1.52 and
3.2.68.
51 **'gan** ''gan' is Malone's emendation of Q's
'gave'. Porter (1912) retains 'gave' and interprets
the sense as 'gave to be bathed in her flowing eyes'.
Along similar lines, 'gave herself over to tearing
(weeping)' is also possible. But 'tear' as in 'rip'
contrasts effectively with 'kissed', following the
usual antithetical manner (see also 55). The reading
accepted here otherwise accords with Wyndham,
who retains 'gave' as meaning 'made a motion as if

to tear'.
52 **register** record, witness (as in legal terminology).
53 **unapprovèd** unqualified, false.
54 i.e. because of its black colour, ink would have
been a more appropriate means of expressing the
author's perjury.
55 **in top of** at the height of.
55 **rents** rends.
56 i.e. the strength of her fury vents itself on
the letters (and the feelings expressed in them).
Kerrigan's identification (p. 18) of the letters, etc.
as those of his mistresses (see 218–31) advocates a
pleasing dramatic symmetry but ignores the force
of the accusation 'false blood', which insists that the
young man must be their author. 'Big' also conveys
the sense of 'pregnant', as in *MV* 2.8.46: 'his eye
being big with tears'.
57 **reverend** i.e. made respectable by virtue of
his age (not a clergyman); see 62.
58 **Sometime** Formerly.
58 **blusterer** boisterous type.
58 **ruffle** 'ostentatious bustle or display' (*OED*
sv *sb²* 3, citing this example).
59–60 **had . . . flew** The meaning seems to
be that he had misspent ('let go by') his youth
(when intense activity makes time go quickly – 'the
swiftest hours') but that he had learnt ('observèd')
something.

The swiftest hours observèd as they flew,   60
Towards this afflicted fancy fastly drew,
And privileged by age desires to know
In brief the grounds and motives of her woe.

So slides he down upon his grainèd bat,
And comely distant sits he by her side,   65
When he again desires her, being sat,
Her grievance with his hearing to divide:
If that from him there may be aught applied
Which may her suffering ecstasy assuage,
'Tis promised in the charity of age.   70

'Father', she says, 'though in me you behold
The injury of many a blasting hour,
Let it not tell your judgement I am old:
Not age, but sorrow, over me hath power.
I might as yet have been a spreading flower,   75
Fresh to myself, if I had self-applied
Love to myself, and to no love beside.

'But woe is me, too early I attended
A youthful suit – it was to gain my grace;
O one by nature's outwards so commended   80

---

79 suit – it] *this edn;* suit it Q   80 O one] Q; O, one *Capell MS;* Of one *Tyrrwhitt conj. (Malone)*

---

61 afflicted fancy girl agitated in mind. 'Fancy', which specifically means the mind or imagination, stands for the whole girl in her condition of emotional disarray. See 5n.

61 fastly closely, rapidly (Onions). Maxwell, discounting alliteration, supposes a metathetical error for 'softly' ('saftly').

62 privileged by age with the authority of venerable years (implicit may be the suggestion that as an old man he presents no threat of seduction or violation and may therefore be allowed to approach her).

63 motives causes. Compare *Ham.* 2.2.561.

64 slides he down i.e. he uses his staff to ease himself down.

64 grainèd bat i.e. a staff or stick worn and darkened with age (reflecting the condition of its owner). For 'grainèd' compare *Ham.* 3.4.89–90: 'Thou turn'st my eyes into my very soul / And there I see such black and grainèd spots' (F).

65 comely distant at a discreet distance.

67 with . . . divide i.e. the burden of her grief will be somewhat relieved ('divide' = share) if she imparts it to his ears.

68 applied administered (medically); compare

WT 3.2.152–3: 'Beseech you tenderly apply to her / Some remedies for life.'

69 suffering ecstasy i.e. the state of being beside herself with misery. 'Ecstasy' literally means a standing forth (as of the self or soul from the body). Compare *Ven.* 895.

70 charity of age i.e. age through experience acquires a kindly disposition to others' suffering.

71 Father See 57n.

72 blasting blighting, ruinous.

75 spreading flourishing, still opening.

76–7 self-applied . . . myself The use of the double reflexive form for emphasis is characteristic of Shakespeare (see *Ven.* 161, 763, and *Luc.* 160).

78 attended paid attention to, listened to.

79 grace favour. The verb 'was' is probably intentional (i.e. he sought to gain, etc.) though the secondary, prophetic sense (it was going to eventually) is also available.

80 O Q's exclamation (see collation), paralleling the opening of 78 is preferred to the emendation 'Of' (adopted by many editors). But 'O one' could mean 'O' one' (i.e. 'Of one'), allowing for a dropped apostrophe.

80 nature's outwards external appearance.

That maidens' eyes stuck over all his face.
Love lacked a dwelling and made him her place;
And when in his fair parts she did abide,
She was new lodged and newly deified.

'His browny locks did hang in crookèd curls,   85
And every light occasion of the wind
Upon his lips their silken parcels hurls.
What's sweet to do, to do will aptly find:
Each eye that saw him did enchant the mind,
For on his visage was in little drawn   90
What largeness thinks in Paradise was sawn.

'Small show of man was yet upon his chin,
His phoenix down began but to appear
Like unshorn velvet on that termless skin,
Whose bare out-bragged the web it seemed to wear;   95
Yet showed his visage by that cost more dear,
And nice affections wavering stood in doubt
If best were as it was, or best without.

'His qualities were beauteous as his form,
For maiden-tongued he was, and thereof free;   100
Yet if men moved him, was he such a storm

81 stuck . . . all were glued to ('over all' =
'all over'). Compare *Tim.* 4.3.261–3: 'The mouths,
the tongues, the eyes, and hearts of men . . .
That numberless upon me stuck'. The expression
seems idiomatic (like the modern 'glued to') and
was probably no more startling for a contemporary
reader than 'I could not take my eyes off him.'

82–4 Compare *Ven.* 241–6.

85 browny brown (disyllabic for the scansion).

85 crookèd twisted, artfully curled.

86 occasion occurrence, movement.

87 parcels particles.

88 to do will . . . find will be done readily (the
verb 'to do' is the subject).

89 i.e. the mind of each beholder was enchanted.

90–1 'His face showed in miniature what is supposed to have existed in full magnitude in Eden'
(Smith). 'Largeness' means both man's and God's
capacity for large-scale imagination – God execut-
ing the design, man comprehending it.

91 sawn seen (irregular past participle, for the

rhyme); some editors (after Boswell) conjecture the
meaning is 'sown'.

92–103 A commonplace Elizabethan portrait of
perfect male beauty. Compare Jonson's 'Her man
by her own dictamen' in 'A Celebration of Charis'.

93 phoenix down Compared to the bird's covering because of its rare, delicate texture.

94 termless inexpressible; compare 'phraseless'
(225).

95 'Whose naked smoothness claimed to surpass
(in beauty) the downy hair that was just apparent' (Lee). Here 'seemed' means that the slightness
of his beard raised doubts whether it was real or
merely adornment.

96 cost ornament, expense (with play on 'dear').
Mackail spots a pun on Fr. *coste, côte* = 'coat'.

97 nice affections discriminating tastes.

100 maiden-tongued modest or innocent in his
speech; 'free' equally means 'innocent' (and not
'loquacious' or 'liberal') – compare *Ham.* 2.2.564:
'Make mad the guilty, and appal the free'.

As oft 'twixt May and April is to see,
When winds breathe sweet, unruly though they be.
His rudeness so with his authorised youth
Did livery falseness in a pride of truth.   105

'Well could he ride, and often men would say,
"That horse his mettle from his rider takes:
Proud of subjection, noble by the sway,
What rounds, what bounds, what course, what stop he
    makes!"
And controversy hence a question takes,   110
Whether the horse by him became his deed,
Or he his manage by th'well-doing steed.

'But quickly on this side the verdict went:
His real habitude gave life and grace
To appertainings and to ornament,   115
Accomplished in himself, not in his case.
All aids, themselves made fairer by their place,
Came for additions; yet their purposed trim
Pieced not his grace, but were all graced by him.

'So on the tip of his subduing tongue   120
All kind of arguments and question deep,

---

118 Came] *Sewell;* Can Q

---

102 'twixt . . . April i.e. between April and May;
the inversion is for the metre. The speaker has in
mind the occasional bouts of unseasonal weather
between late spring and summer. For this and 103,
compare *Son.* 18.3: 'Rough winds do shake the dar-
ling buds of May.'

104–5 His youthfulness licensed his unpolished
behaviour, disguising falseness as a proud declaration of truthfulness. Note the play on 'livery' and
'pride' (show).

104 authorised Accent on second syllable.

108 noble . . . sway noble in being ruled.

108 rounds turns (the terms are all from
manege: see 112).

110 i.e. it is a moot point.

111 by . . . deed thanks to his rider, went cleanly
through his paces.

112 Or whether his horsemanship owed something to the skill of the horse. In connection with
'manege' (horsemanship) see *Ven.* 598n.

113 on this side in his favour.

114 real habitude regal bearing.

115 appertainings appurtenances (trimmings,

costume); a nonce-use (*OED* sv *vbl. sb.*).

116 case dress, adornment.

117 aids i.e. coiffure, costume, etc. The general
sense is that *he* embellished his adornments rather
than being made beautiful by them. The conceit is
a typical one, though more often applied to female
beauty. Compare the description of the princesses'
undressing in Sidney (*NA*, ed. Skretkowicz, pp.
189–90).

118 Came Nearly all editors follow Sewell in
substituting this word for Q's 'Can'. (*Macbeth* (F)
3.1.98 erroneously has 'Can' for 'Came'.)

118 for additions for the purpose of beautify-
ing him.

118 purposed trim intended adornment.

119 Pieced Pieced out, improved.

120–6 Steevens (Malone) comments: 'These
lines, in which our poet has accidentally delineated
his own character as a dramatist, would have been
better adapted to his monumental inscriptions, than
such as are placed on the scroll in Westminster
Abbey.'

120 subduing masterful.

All replication prompt, and reason strong,
For his advantage still did wake and sleep.
To make the weeper laugh, the laugher weep,
He had the dialect and different skill,   125
Catching all passions in his craft of will:

'That he did in the general bosom reign
Of young, of old, and sexes both enchanted
To dwell with him in thoughts, or to remain
In personal duty, following where he haunted: 130
Consents bewitched, ere he desire, have granted,
And dialogued for him what he would say,
Asked their own wills, and made their wills obey.

'Many there were that did his picture get
To serve their eyes, and in it put their mind,   135
Like fools that in th'imagination set
The goodly objects which abroad they find

---

135 in it put] Q; put it in *conj. Pooler*²

---

122 replication prompt repartee.

122 reason strong powerful or convincing argument.

123 For his advantage As suited his needs; i.e. these qualities waited upon him at all hours like servants.

125 dialect capacity of speech.

125 different skill (1) conversational versatility (lending pleasing variety to his remarks), and perhaps (2) skill that is *unlike* (and so superior) to that of others.

126 i.e. snaring those suffering love for him ('passions' = lovers personified) and subduing them to his carnal appetite. The meaning turns on the symmetry and antithesis of 'passions' and 'will', 'will' being the degenerate form of 'passion', while the latter means, in this context, an involuntary or innocent feeling. 'Craft of will' is a dense phrase meaning 'shrewd application of appetite'.

126 Catching For catching, in order to catch.

127–33 This stanza could stand as a description of the impression made by the young man of the *Sonnets*.

127 That So that.

127 general bosom hearts of all.

128 sexes . . . enchanted The implication is perhaps not so much that of bisexual appeal but rather that men, who would not be expected to fall for his charms as easily as women, were none the

less deceived by his innocent posture. The idea is borne out by the first half of the line, which states that the old (and presumably wise) are as much taken with him as the young.

129 dwell . . . thoughts keep him in their minds.

129–30 remain . . . duty attend him personally.

130 following . . . haunted accompanying him wherever he went ('haunted' = frequented).

131 Consents bewitched Those charmed into consenting to him (for the personification of 'Consents' compare 'passions': 126).

132 dialogued . . . say put his argument for him in advance.

133 wills . . . wills Here, 'will' means inclination or feeling and suggests half-conscious instinct rather than the studied cultivation of carnality of 'craft of will' (126).

135 in . . . mind invested it with their imagination (e.g. imagining that the figure in the portrait might be their lover – see 142). Pooler² conjectures rearranging the syntax as 'put it in', but the ensuing meaning (the picture serving as an aid to memory) contradicts the idea of 128–9 that he impressed himself effortlessly on the imagination.

136 set set out for inspection.

137 objects objects of view (i.e. 'lands', mansions', etc.).

Of lands and mansions, theirs in thought assigned,
And labouring in moe pleasures to bestow them
Than the true gouty landlord which doth owe them. 140

'So many have, that never touched his hand,
Sweetly supposed them mistress of his heart.
My woeful self that did in freedom stand,
And was my own fee-simple (not in part),
What with his art in youth, and youth in art, 145
Threw my affections in his charmèd power,
Reserved the stalk, and gave him all my flower.

'Yet did I not, as some my equals did,
Demand of him, nor being desirèd yielded;
Finding myself in honour so forbid, 150
With safest distance I mine honour shielded.
Experience for me many bulwarks builded
Of proofs new-bleeding, which remained the foil
Of this false jewel, and his amorous spoil.

'But ah, who ever shunned by precedent 155
The destined ill she must herself assay?

138 **theirs . . . assigned** imagining them to be their own.

139–140 **labouring . . . them** enjoying the task of making gifts of them more than would their real owner, whose pleasures are cut short by the gout. (The image is of a nobleman who has various properties 'in his gift' to bestow on those who have performed meritorious service for him.)

140 **owe** own.

142 **them** themselves.

144 **my . . . fee-simple** owner of myself (the term is feudal: 'fee-simple', as opposed to 'feetail', denotes absolute possession).

144 **not in part** not part-owner.

146 **Threw . . . in** Entrusted my feelings to ('My woeful self' at 143 is the subject of the verb 'Threw').

146 **charmèd power** power to charm, charming power. See Abbott §374 for passive participle with active intention.

147 Kept the bitter part ('stalk') for myself and let him enjoy my loveliness (with an evident sense of de*flowering*).

148 **equals** peers, girls of my age and status.

151 **With . . . distance** By keeping at a safe distance.

153 **proofs new-bleeding** newly-broken hearts. There is perhaps a double play on 'proofs' as (1) 'things experienced' and (2) 'things proof against

experience' (from 'bulwarks' in 152).

153 **foil** setting. A portrait (more usually female) framed by broken hearts would serve as a characteristic emblematic device (as in 16). Jackson (pp. 23–4) further notes the submerged wordplay in 'foil' (i.e. sword, as well as that which parries or repulses) and suggests that 'proofs' acts in a secondary sense as a temporary obstacle to the designs of the 'false jewel'. Being 'newbleeding' from his expert, heart-breaking thrusts, they further activate the sense of 'foil' as in swordsmanship. This demonstration of the poem's quick-fire mental activity reminds us, however, of the need to distinguish if possible between puns which are fully integrated into the meaning and the striking of associations which remain in an incomplete or potential condition; otherwise, the overstrained logic impedes narrative function. Such is the risk borne here by condensed expression, which in *LC* more than the other narrative poems resembles the practice of the dramas (see p. 73).

154 **amorous spoil** Governed by 'remained'.

155 **shunned** avoided.

155 **precedent** warning example.

156 **assay** undergo, experience. The maid may be thinking of the Pauline obligation (later expressed by Milton in *Areopagitica*) requiring virtue to test itself against evil.

Or forced examples 'gainst her own content
To put the by-past perils in her way?
Counsel may stop a while what will not stay;
For when we rage, advice is often seen   160
By blunting us to make our wits more keen.

'Nor gives it satisfaction to our blood
That we must curb it upon others' proof,
To be forbod the sweets that seems so good
For fear of harms that preach in our behoof.   165
O appetite, from judgement stand aloof!
The one a palate hath that needs will taste,
Though reason weep, and cry it is thy last.

'For further I could say this man's untrue,
And knew the patterns of his foul beguiling,   170
Heard where his plants in others' orchards grew,
Saw how deceits were gilded in his smiling,
Knew vows were ever brokers to defiling,
Thought characters and words merely but art,
And bastards of his foul adulterate heart.   175

161 wits] Q; wills *conj. Maxwell*   169 For further] Q; For, father, *Staunton conj.*

157 **forced** urged.
157 **content** contentment, satisfaction, wishes.
158 **by-past perils** i.e. dangers which others have experienced and which now serve as examples or warnings to those newly setting forth.
159 **stop . . . stay** Both words mean 'hold back' (transitively and intransitively); 'will not' means 'does not wish to'.
160–1 This is similar to the cast of mind of Tarquin as he anticipates the rape. The maid represents the passive, female converse: i.e. imagining she can dally with temptation without being imperilled.
161 **blunting** dulling.
161 **wits** activities of mind (operating perversely). The plural form is frequently used by Shakespeare. Maxwell emends to 'wills' on the grounds that 'passions' is meant overall (see 162n). But 'wits' helps convey the sense of a self-deceptive mind as well as being satisfactorily antithetical to 'blunting'.
162 **blood** will, emotions.
163 **upon . . . proof** as a result of others' experience.
164 **forbod** forbidden (compare the past definite form at *Luc.* 1648).
164 **seems** Another example of singular usage

for plural ('seems' is probably guided in its choice of form by 'sweets'; see Abbott §333.)
165 **behoof** benefit, advantage (Onions).
166 **judgement** reason.
166 **stand aloof** keep away (do not interfere with).
167 **The one** i.e. appetite.
168 **thy last** your undoing.
169 **further** furthermore.
169 **I . . . say** I was able to tell that.
170 **patterns** (1) examples, (2) methods.
171–2 Compare *WT* 1.2.195–6, and *Ham.* 1.5.106–8.
171 **orchards** gardens.
173 **brokers** panders. Brokers were commercial agents, as now; a pun on 'broken' may be present, following on 'vows'.
174 **Thought** Understood, realised.
174 **characters** letters (compare 16).
175 **bastards** illegitimate creations. But 'bastards' looks back to 'plants' (171) in an intricate image of grafting, and (see also 171–2n) recalls *WT* in the argument over 'Nature's bastards' (4.4.83 and context). Also 'foul adulterate' symmetrically completes the cycle begun in 'foul beguiling' (170). (Compare 'false adulterate eyes' in *Son.* 121.5.)

'And long upon these terms I held my city,
Till thus he 'gan besiege me: "Gentle maid,
Have of my suffering youth some feeling pity,
And be not of my holy vows afraid.
That's to ye sworn to none was ever said;   180
For feasts of love I have been called unto,
Till now did ne'er invite nor never woo.

'"All my offences that abroad you see
Are errors of the blood, none of the mind.
Love made them not; with acture they may be,   185
Where neither party is nor true nor kind.
They sought their shame that so their shame did find;
And so much less of shame in me remains,
By how much of me their reproach contains.

'"Among the many that mine eyes have seen,   190
Not one whose flame my heart so much as warmed,
Or my affection put to th'smallest teen,
Or any of my leisures ever charmed.
Harm have I done to them, but ne'er was harmed;

---

182 woo] *Capell MS;* vovv Q

176 **city** Compare *Luc.* 469.
179 **holy vows** protestations of pure love. Part of the lover's strategy is to imply that his passion is consistent with religious faith (compare *Son.* 31.5–6). As if to secure the point, he cites a nun's love for him a little later (232–3).
180 **That's to ye** That which is to you.
182 **woo** Q has 'vow' (see collation). The emendation to 'woo' as adopted by most editors appears to be straightforward. *Ven.* rhymes 'woo' and 'unto' in 5–6 and 307–9. Either the printer's eye caught 'vows' in 179 or printer (or transcriber) or author may have been influenced by the repetition of 'v' in this line coupled with 'now' at its beginning.
183 **my . . . abroad** public testimony of my wrongdoing. The context requires something less definite than the illegitimate offspring conjectured by Wyndham, so 'offences' probably means broken-hearted mistresses (as in 'proofs newbleeding' in 153). Lines 169–75 may support Wyndham, but note the metaphoric nature of 'bastards' (175).
184 The lover distinguishes between platonic love ('mind') and carnal passion ('blood'), thus keeping up the impression that his feelings are pure (see his argument in 179).

185 **with . . . be** they may be limited to action without involving conscious intention. 'Acture', which occurs nowhere else in Shakespeare, seems to mean 'act'. Compare *Ven.* 1006, where Venus pleads that she is an agent only and innocent of any intention to slander.
186 **nor . . . kind** either faithful or loving. The idea is that merely instinctual behaviour does not carry the obligations of finer feeling. The double negative 'nor . . . nor' is applied, in a characteristically Elizabethan manner, as emphatic negation.
188–9 i.e. the more they reproach me the less I am to blame.
192 **affection** feelings, passion.
192 **teen** grief, affliction (compare *Ven.* 808).
193 **leisures** leisure moments.
193 **charmed** (1) made pleasant, (2) held spellbound; (2) would imply an element of danger.
194 **Harm** i.e. moral or spiritual harm – not physical. None the less, this self-exculpation carries a degree of self-indictment, without its being quite clear from the tone whether the poem intends to register it as such. Our view of the speaker never emerges precisely enough from his own utterances, which remain enigmatic.

Kept hearts in liveries, but mine own was free,   195
And reigned commanding in his monarchy.

"'Look here what tributes wounded fancies sent me,
Of pallid pearls and rubies red as blood;
Figuring that they their passions likewise lent me
Of grief and blushes, aptly understood   200
In bloodless white and the encrimsoned mood:
Effects of terror and dear modesty,
Encamped in hearts but fighting outwardly.

"'And lo, behold these talents of their hair,
With twisted metal amorously empleached,   205
I have received from many a several fair,
Their kind acceptance weepingly beseeched,
With th'annexions of fair gems enriched,
And deep-brained sonnets that did amplify
Each stone's dear nature, worth, and quality.   210

---

198 pallid] *Gildon²;* palyd Q; paled *Malone²*   204 hair] *Benson;* heir Q   208 th'] Q; the *Capell MS*

---

195 in liveries in servitude (livery is worn by servants – see also 105).

197 wounded fancies As at 61.

198 pallid palyd (Q). Q's reading has occasioned a tradition of editorial indecisiveness: perhaps Gildon's emendation 'pallid' (see collation) over-concentrates and limits the range of possible meanings, but it contrasts effectively with 'red as blood'.

199 Figuring Signifying by their colours (compare 16n).

199–200 passions . . . blushes the genitive part of the phrase merely fills out and repeats the sense of 'passions', though with the difference that while 'grief' (pining) is itself a passion, 'blushes' are the sign of passion and denote either the heat of desire or embarrassment at feeling it.

200 aptly understood suitably depicted.

201 mood form (as in *Ham.* 1.2.82).

202 Effects Manifestations, signs.

202 terror i.e. the conventional lover's heartquaking condition in the presence of the beloved (usually attributed to a male lover).

202 dear precious, worthy.

203 Seated in the heart but reflected in the features. Note the conventional use of military metaphors for erotic conflict or intensity of feeling (see *Ven.* 103–14n).

204 talents treasures (*OED,* citing this line), tresses. The shining or glistening hair combined with the ornamental metal which frames it brings out the other meaning of talent as unit of gold or silver (as in Matt. 25.14–30).

205 twisted i.e. intricately wrought.

205 amorously i.e. arranged with loving care, but also suggesting the intimate coupling of hair and brooch.

205 empleached intertwined.

206 fair fair one (compare *Ven.* 1083, 1086 for 'fair' used as a noun).

207 Their . . . acceptance That I should receive them favourably.

208 annexions additions. Some editors, along with Maxwell, emend to 'the annexions' for metrical regularity. But in favour of the graphic elision (see collation) is the fact that in Elizabethan practice '-ion' words habitually stress the 'i', as in *R2* 1.1.155: 'Deep malice makes too deep incision' (see Cercignani, p. 295). The word then has four syllables with stress on the first and third.

209 deep-brained inspired, full of profound thought (Onions).

209 amplify illustrate in detail, embellish (referring to the rhetorical idea of 'copia'; see Trousdale, pp. 43–55).

210 dear precious.

'"The diamond? why, 'twas beautiful and hard,
Whereto his invised properties did tend;
The deep-green emerald, in whose fresh regard
Weak sights their sickly radiance do amend;
The heaven-hued sapphire and the opal blend   215
With objects manifold; each several stone,
With wit well blazoned, smiled or made some moan.

'"Lo, all these trophies of affections hot,
Of pensived and subdued desires the tender,
Nature hath charged me that I hoard them not,   220
But yield them up where I myself must render:
That is, to you, my origin and ender;
For these, of force, must your oblations be,
Since I their altar, you enpatron me.

'"O then advance of yours that phraseless hand,   225
Whose white weighs down the airy scale of praise;

---

212 his its.

212 invised invisible, imperceptible (a nonce-word). Porter (1912) suggests 'inwardly seen', but the more likely meaning is that the diamond has certain properties such as durability which do not manifest themselves immediately.

213 fresh regard restorative sight.

214 sickly radiance dulled lustre. 'Radiance' refers to the eye's natural brightness. Craig² quotes Holland's *Plinie* (1601): 'if the sight hath been wearied and dimmed by intentive poring upon any thing else, the beholding of this stone doth refresh and restore it againe'.

215 blend Probably 'blended'. It all depends on whether 'blend' is a past participle ('blended'), or a present indicative (Maxwell), or a substantive. (Q's punctuation admits each possibility.) In favour of 'blend-ed' is the usage noted by Abbott, §342, plus the symmetry with 'heaven-hued' (an undoubted participle).

216 objects manifold Either objects (of view) (i.e. the various images discernible in the opal) or various other jewels besides those named.

216 several different.

217 wit . . . blazoned Referring most probably to the 'sonnets' (209), which proclaim (blazon) the stones' properties in an imaginative (witty) manner. The conceit is then continued so that the stones appear to respond appropriately ('smiled . . . moan') to the various descriptions of themselves.

218 affections passions.

219 pensived melancholy. For the passive form see Abbott §294.

219 subdued humble (voluntary rather than compelled submission). Though passive in form, 'subdued' functions like 'pensived' (see previous note).

219 tender gift.

220 Nature . . . me i.e. his appeal is from natural law.

220 charged commanded.

222 origin and ender beginning and end. Compare Heb. 12.2 ('the author and finisher of our faith') and Rev. 1.8 ('I am Alpha and Omega, the beginning and the ending'). The speaker's echoing of one or other biblical phrase accords with his expression of love as religious submission (as at 179).

223 of force perforce, necessarily.

223 oblations offerings (in the religious sense).

224 Since I am the altar (on which these gifts have been bestowed), I receive them in your name. 'Enpatron' means to have under one's patronage (Onions).

225 phraseless i.e. for which no description is adequate. Compare 'termless' (94).

226 This witty compliment makes use of nominalism (the idea that words have no reality or point of reference). The colour 'white' none the less has substance uniquely with respect to her hand, for it proves too much for ('weighs down') insubstantial, false, *weightless* ('airy') flattery.

Take all these similes to your own command,
Hallowed with sighs that burning lungs did raise:
What me your minister for you obeys
Works under you, and to your audit comes   230
Their distract parcels in combinèd sums.

"'Lo, this device was sent me from a nun,
Or sister sanctified, of holiest note,
Which late her noble suit in court did shun,
Whose rarest havings made the blossoms dote;   235
For she was sought by spirits of richest coat,
But kept cold distance, and did thence remove
To spend her living in eternal love.

"'But, O my sweet, what labour is't to leave
The thing we have not, mast'ring what not strives,   240
Paling the place which did no form receive,
Playing patient sports in unconstrainèd gyves?

228 Hallowed] Hallow'd *Capell MS;* Hollowed Q   233 Or] Q; A *conj. Malone*   241 Paling] *conj. Malone;* Playing Q;
Planing *Capell MS*   242 unconstrainèd] *Gildon²;* unconstraind Q

227 similes i.e. the elegant expressions or tokens of love he has received from his mistresses. A simile works by comparison: the speaker thus refers to the habit of finding rare terms of expression by which to extol someone's beauty.

227 to . . . command into your own service (as if referring to your own charms).

228 Hallowed Q has 'Hollowed', but 'Hallowed' (made holy) better fits the prevailing religious imagery. 'Hollowed' has little to recommend it, despite Porter's ingenious technical explanation: 'as the artificer uses the blowpipe with molten glass or metal'.

228 burning Perhaps with a suggestion of incense-burning.

229 What . . . you Whoever obeys me obeys you, I being your deputy. 'What' is equivalent to who (see Abbott §254).

230 audit (1) account, (2) hearing. The second of these senses suggests that the gifts come to be assessed and not merely received.

231 distract parcels separate parts.

232 device favour.

233 sanctified most holy (perhaps distinguished from a novice who has not yet taken her vows).

234 Which Who (see 229n).

234 noble suit i.e. the courtiers who attempted to woo her ('suit' playing on 'suitor').

234 shun avoid.

235 rarest havings special qualities, accomplishments (perhaps with the added sense of

material advantages).

235 blossoms young courtiers (the image is explained by 'richest coat' in the following line).

236 spirits Monosyllabic, as in 3 and in *Ven.* 882.

236 coat As well as stylishness (see 235n), the word denotes lineage (as in coat of arms).

237 cold temperate, chaste.

238 living (1) life, (2) benefice. Ecclesiastical livings were in the gift of wealthy proprietors and had a temporal significance, being sought by poor or needy clergy. By contrast, the nun has intended to use her living for purely spiritual ends.

239–40 what . . . have not i.e. it is easy to depart when nothing detains our interest.

240 mastering . . . strives overcoming a nonexistent opposition.

241 Paling Enclosing. Q's 'Playing' is surely the result of compositorial error in setting up the word twice (see 242). Malone's emendation has been generally followed. (But see Sisson 1.215–16.)

241 form i.e. of an animal. Another possible meaning is 'lair' (see *OED* sv *sb* 21, which cites Turberville's *Venerie*).

242 patient i.e. not active, not serious.

242 unconstrainèd unconstraining. (Q has 'unconstraind', but the metre requires an extra syllable, even though it produces an odd hendecasyllabic line.) For this passive form of an active participle, see Abbott §374.

242 gyves fetters.

She that her fame so to herself contrives,
The scars of battle scapeth by the flight,
And makes her absence valiant, not her might.   245

"'O pardon me in that my boast is true:
The accident which brought me to her eye
Upon the moment did her force subdue,
And now she would the cagèd cloister fly.
Religious love put out religion's eye,   250
Not to be tempted would she be immured,
And now to tempt all liberty procured.

"'How mighty then you are, O hear me tell:
The broken bosoms that to me belong
Have emptied all their fountains in my well,   255
And mine I pour your ocean all among.
I strong o'er them, and you o'er me being strong,
Must for your victory us all congest,
As compound love to physic your cold breast.

---

251 immured] *conj. Gildon;* enur'd Q   252 procured] *Gildon;* procure Q

243 fame . . . contrives i.e. she keeps herself to herself and does not risk her reputation in an encounter.

248 Upon the moment At once.

249 cagèd Either (1) 'like a cage', or (2) 'encaging' (another example of an active participle taking a passive form – see 242n).

250 Religious love Love which has the force of religion (compare 222n).

250 put . . . eye deprived religion of its proper vision. Compare *Son.* 31.6.

251 immured Q has 'enur'd', which Benson retains as 'inur'd'; but the Folio and early quartos show that 'immured' could be spelt 'emured' (see *LLL* 3.1.131 (Q1)), which would argue that Q's reading results from a single changed letter.

252 now to tempt i.e. in order to exercise her own powers of temptation. The phrase balances antithetically 'Not to be tempted' above. However, this reading is questioned by the uncertain function of 'all', which may be the object of 'tempt' (giving the meaning 'try all experience') but more likely qualifies 'liberty' (i.e. 'all liberty' = every freedom).

252 procured Q has 'procure', which is grammatically acceptable, but the rhyme insists on the emendation. G. Blakemore Evans reminds me that in Secretary hand final 'd' is often misread as 'e'.

254 bosoms hearts. The bosom, properly speaking, contains the heart (though metonymically identified with it here), which enables the subsequent heart-as-receptacle image. The controlling idea of these lines closely echoes that of *Son.* 31 (see also 250n), except that there Shakespeare pays this compliment to the young friend, with the further implication that the poet's 'lovers gone' appear to be literally deceased and not emotionally destroyed.

255 emptied . . . fountains poured out their hearts. Here 'fountains', as well as perhaps carrying the sense 'tearful emotions', means the heart proper rather than what contains it.

255 in my well in my own heart.

256 your . . . among entirely into your sea (i.e. capacious heart). The use of the preposition 'among' indicates that 'ocean' is conceived of as plural.

257–8 I . . . congest I, who am their superior and your inferior, must according to the terms of your victory reduce myself and them into a single (subordinate) force. 'Congest' means to form into a single mass.

259 As To serve as.

259 compound i.e. formed from simples (herbs) for medicinal purposes (with play on 'congest').

259 physic treat medically.

259 cold Punning on (1) chaste, (2) chill-ridden.

'"My parts had power to charm a sacred nun,   260
Who disciplined, ay, dieted, in grace,
Believed her eyes when they t'assail begun,
All vows and consecrations giving place.
O most potential love, vow, bond, nor space
In thee hath neither sting, knot, nor confine,   265
For thou art all, and all things else are thine.

' "When thou impressest, what are precepts worth
Of stale example? When thou wilt inflame,
How coldly those impediments stand forth
Of wealth, of filial fear, law, kindred, fame.   270
Love's arms are peace 'gainst rule, 'gainst sense, 'gainst
          shame,
And sweetens, in the suff'ring pangs it bears,
The aloes of all forces, shocks, and fears.

' "Now all these hearts that do on mine depend,
Feeling it break, with bleeding groans they pine,   275

---

260 nun] *Capell MS;* Sunne Q   261 ay, dieted] *Capell MS;* I dieted Q   270 kindred, fame] *Benson;* kindred fame Q   271 peace] Q; proof *Capell MS*

---

260 nun. See collation. Wyndham defends Q's 'Sunne' as meaning 'a very sun of sanctity', but he has not been much followed. Most editors prefer Capell's emendation to 'nun', both because of the word's appearance in 232 and in view of the general context.

261 disciplined fortified, strengthened by spiritual exercise.

261 dieted . . . grace i.e. took spiritual grace as her nourishment.

262 Believed . . . eyes The nun confuses graceful appearance with inner grace (spirituality), presumably because her confined religious life has ill prepared her to distinguish between the two. It is a further irony that, according to the terms of Neoplatonic love as set forth by Castiglione, outer beauty ideally heralds inner virtue (Castiglione, p. 309).

262 when . . . assail Again, according to Neoplatonic love theory, the eyes perform their assault on their owner by communicating an image of the beautiful object to the heart (Castiglione, p. 314).

264 potential powerful.

265 In thee Upon you.

265 sting force, harmful effect.

265 confine limitation.

267 impressest press or force into service (militarily).

268 stale worn-out (lacking conviction).

269 impediments An allusion to the marriage service may be ironically intended: 'if either of you know any impediment why ye may not be lawfully joined together in matrimony . . .', (see also *Son.* 116.1–2)

270 filial fear A child's (more likely a daughter's) fear of defying parental will.

270 kindred Either family wishes or the inhibitions imposed by family ties.

270 fame concern for reputation.

271 peace i.e. means of defence. Malone emends to 'proof', but 'peace' (as in officer of the peace) makes effective sense and further supports the irony whereby legality favours love and such virtues as orderliness ('rule'), reason ('sense'), and modesty ('shame') are outlawed.

272–3 sweetens . . . fears i.e. so sweet is love's suffering that it makes pleasant even those effects ('forces . . . fears') which would normally deter and act as bitter remedies ('aloes').

272 sweetens The verb is singular, probably because 'Love' (from 'Love's arms') is intended on its own, the image requiring 'arms' now being complete (see also Abbott §333).

275 bleeding groans Fashionable love theory held that each sigh drew a drop of blood from the heart. Compare *MND* 3.2.97 and *3H6* 4.4.22.

And supplicant their sighs to you extend,
To leave the batt'ry that you make 'gainst mine,
Lending soft audience to my sweet design,
And credent soul to that strong-bonded oath,
That shall prefer and undertake my troth."   280

'This said, his wat'ry eyes he did dismount,
Whose sights till then were levelled on my face;
Each cheek a river running from a fount
With brinish current downward flowed apace:
O how the channel to the stream gave grace!   285
Who glazed with crystal gate the glowing roses
That flame through water which their hue encloses.

'O father, what a hell of witchcraft lies
In the small orb of one particular tear!
But with the inundation of the eyes,   290
What rocky heart to water will not wear?
What breast so cold that is not warmèd here?
O cleft effect! cold modesty, hot wrath,
Both fire from hence and chill extincture hath.

293 O] *Gildon²*; Or Q

276 **supplicant** in supplication.
277 **leave** leave off.
279 **credent** (1) credible, (2) believing. The two meanings are likely because the broken hearts both continue to believe his words and by their sincerity make them believable. (For the active participle used passively, see *WT* 1.2.142–3: 'Then 'tis very credent / Thou mayst co-join with something.')
279 **strong-bonded** Combining the senses of (1) tightly bound, and (2) fully contracted (hence 'conveying a strong obligation' (Onions). The play on 'bond' (1) has something in common with 'hoops' (*Ham.* 1.3.63).
280 **prefer** put forward, present.
280 **undertake** be surety for.
281 **dismount** As of a gun or cannon (note 'sights', 'levelled' in 282).
284 **brinish** salty (as of tears – compare *Luc.* 1213).
285 **channel** i.e. the cheek down which his tears run.
286 **Who** Which (see Abbott §264).
286 **glazed . . . roses** framed or enclosed his red cheeks with crystal.
286 **gate** enclosure, barrier (perhaps playing on 'flood-gate' as at *Ven.* 959). The image conceives

of it as transparent.
287 **water . . . encloses** i.e. the tears act as a glassy frame to the colour of his cheeks ('encloses' governs 'hue'). The image more or less repeats the idea of 286.
288 **father** See 71.
289–90 Compare *Son.* 119.1.
289 **small orb** little world. But because it is a world it makes possible such global effects as 'inundation' in the next line. Either 'orb' or 'particular tear' provides the point of reference for 'here' (292) and 'from hence' (294).
289 **particular** Suggesting smallness (i.e. little part) and so reflecting back on 'small orb'.
290 **But with** Merely with.
291 **to water . . . wear** will not be worn down by water (i.e. tears). A recurrent proverbial idea (compare *Ven.* 200, *Luc.* 560, 592, and 959).
292 **not warmèd** i.e. does not respond passionately.
293 **cleft** divided, twofold.
294 i.e. modesty is inflamed while indignation ('wrath') is cooled or tempered – both caused by tears ('from hence').
294 **extincture** extinction (usage not recorded before Shakespeare).

'For lo, his passion, but an art of craft,   295
Even there resolved my reason into tears;
There my white stole of chastity I daffed,
Shook off my sober guards and civil fears;
Appear to him as he to me appears,
All melting; though our drops this diff'rence bore: 300
His poisoned me, and mine did him restore.

'In him a plenitude of subtle matter,
Applied to cautels, all strange forms receives,
Of burning blushes or of weeping water,
Of sounding paleness; and he takes and leaves,   305
In either's aptness, as it best deceives,
To blush at speeches rank, to weep at woes,
Or to turn white and sound at tragic shows.

'That not a heart which in his level came
Could scape the hail of his all-hurting aim,   310
Showing fair nature is both kind and tame;

305 sounding] Q; swooning *Capell MS*   308 sound] Q; swoon *Capell MS*

---

295 an . . . craft clever dissembling.
296 there at that, then.
296 resolved dissolved. Compare *Tim.* 4.3.439–40: 'whose liquid surge resolves / The moon into salt tears'.
297 stole A stole is an outer covering – more specifically a priest's vestment worn over the shoulders – and is carefully preferred to dress or robe for this delicate image of discarded ('daffed' = 'doffed') chastity. Robe might have suggested a compromising readiness to undress.
298 Shook off Dismissed.
298 sober . . . fears The two nouns have cleverly exchanged epithets (we would normally expect 'sober fears' and 'civil guards') in order to register more fully the image of the city or citadel of chastity at the point of submission (note the image of the 'city' in 176). As it stands 'civil fears' suggests fear of civil war which is apt for the image of a city on the point of self-betrayal.
298 guards defences.
299 Appear . . . appears The use of present tense effectively establishes her recalling or reliving of the moment. (For changes of tense within the narrative compare *Ven.* 43ff.)
300 All melting All tearful (see 296n).
300 drops teardrops.
302 plenitude completeness, fullness.
302 subtle matter treachery. 'Subtle' generally means crafty or treacherous (see *Luc.* 957n), and

'matter' is substance (with here ironic play on the Aristotelian theory of substance and 'forms'). The line means that he is full of deceit.
303 Applied to Applicable to, apt for. Probably another example of the participle form yielding a passive sense (Abbott §375).
303 cautels tricks, deceptions. See *Ham.* 1.3.15–16: 'And now no soil nor cautel doth besmirch / The virtue of his will').
303 all . . . receives assumes unexpected disguises.
305 sounding swooning (see variant form at 308).
305–6 takes . . . aptness uses each selectively according to its suitability.
307 blush . . . rank show embarrassment at lewd or improper remarks.
308 shows appearances (i.e. things that seem tragic).
309 level sights (resuming the imagery of 281–2).
310 scape escape, avoid.
311 Demonstrating that a good disposition ('fair nature') is generous and acquiescent. The insertion of 'both' before the hendiadys 'kind and tame' misleadingly suggests a distinction of meaning where there is none. The line is parenthetical to the main drift of the stanza and refers to the 'heart' (with a pun on 'hart'), which is as game to his marksmanship.

And, veiled in them, did win whom he would maim.
Against the thing he sought he would exclaim;
When he most burnt in heart-wished luxury,
He preached pure maid, and praised cold chastity.   315

'Thus merely with the garment of a grace
The naked and concealèd fiend he covered,
That th'unexperient gave the tempter place,
Which like a cherubin above them hovered.
Who, young and simple, would not be so lovered?   320
Ay me, I fell, and yet do question make
What I should do again for such a sake.

'O, that infected moisture of his eye,
O, that false fire which in his cheek so glowed,
O, that forced thunder from his heart did fly,   325
O, that sad breath his spongy lungs bestowed,
O, all that borrowed motion, seeming owed,
Would yet again betray the fore-betrayed,
And new pervert a reconcilèd maid.'

312 **veiled** disguised.

312 **in them** i.e. referring back to the 'strange forms' (303) adopted as disguises.

312 **would** wished to, intended to.

313 **exclaim** With 'against' this means 'denounce', 'rail at' (compare *Luc.* 757).

313–15 This is the condition experienced by Angelo, though more as a dilemma, in *MM* 2.2–2.4.

314 **heart-wished** wished for from the depths of his being.

314 **luxury** lust.

315 **preached . . . maid** spoke like a chaste or virginal young girl. Compare *AYLI* 3.2.214–15: 'Speak sad brow and true maid.'

316 **garment** outer show.

316 **grace** (1) graciousness, comeliness, (2) spiritual favour (prompting 'fiend' below).

317 **concealèd** Proleptic usage in that present nakedness anticipates being covered.

318 **unexperient** inexperienced (not used elsewhere by Shakespeare).

318 **gave . . . place** let the tempter in.

319 **Which** Who (Abbott §265).

319 **cherubin** guardian angel (though 'cherubin' is the plural form of cherub, the two are not much distinguished, and practice is often, as here, determined by metre).

320 **simple** innocent, artless.

320 **be . . . lovered** similarly accept him as a lover. For the use of a noun-based participle see Abbott §294 (quoting this example).

323 **infected** infectious, poisonous (for the form see Abbott §374).

325 **from** that from (Abbott §394).

326 **spongy** i.e. capable of squeezing out quantities of sighs ('sad breath'). The heavens are often likened to a great sponge producing noxious effects such as rain or damp (see *Ant.* 4.9.13).

327 **borrowed motion** imitated or feigned show of feeling. A 'motion' was a puppet-show or mime, as in *WT* 4.3.96–7.

327 **seeming owed** apparently genuine ('owed' = owned).

329 **pervert** lead astray.

329 **reconcilèd** reformed, repentant. Pooler[2] points to its specific meaning as of one who has been readmitted to the church after excommunication. It is consistent with the seducer's appropriation or debauching of the patterns of religion (see his glib reference to his 'holy vows' at 179 and his declared success with the 'sacred nun' at 260) that the maid should express her despair in terms of spiritual failure.

SUPPLEMENTARY NOTES

VENUS AND ADONIS

97–100 Popular mythology had it that Mars and the boar were closely allied if not interchangeable. Comes, in his *Mythologiae* (1551), records that Mars set the boar on to Adonis out of jealousy, and Alciati (*Emblemata*, 1531) goes so far as to report that the boar was Mars in vengeful disguise. Shakespeare does not incorporate such details directly into his own narrative, but the description of Mars's neck and the account of his ferocity bears out the resemblance (see 619). While it would be a mistake to insist on these equivalences in the poem, which manages its allusions always with discretion, the physical likeness between the boar and Venus's legendary lover helps maintain the balance and symmetry of the whole while keeping in play such subordinate motifs as the potential destructiveness of the erotic instinct.

161–2 Much discussion has gone into establishing both Shakespeare's source for Narcissus and whether he dies by drowning. His most probable source is Ovid, whose Narcissus dies by languishing for his own image in a pool (Golding 3.522–4) – a fate consistent with Venus's admonition. This would explain 'died' as dying (i.e. longing) for as well as merely dying. In contrast, *HL* 1.74–6 and *Luc.* 266 both depict Narcissus as drowning.

Root (*JEGP*, pp. 454–5) first suggested the biographical relevance of John Clapham's Latin poem *Narcissus* (1591), dedicated to Southampton; and Akrigg (pp. 33–4) has further argued that Clapham, Burghley's secretary, may have written the poem to impress his employer, who was chafing over Southampton's disinclination for Burghley's granddaughter, Lady Elizabeth Vere. For general information, see Vinge.

697–702 Pooler (1927) shows how closely these lines resemble two passages from Edward Topsell's *Historie of Four-footed Beastes*: 'When she [the hare] hath left both hunters and Dogs a great way behind her, she getteth to some *little hill* or rising of the earth, there she *raiseth herself upon her hinder legges*, like a Watchman in his Tower, observing *how farre or neare the enemy approacheth*'; and; 'So was hir flight and want of rest like a *sicknesse before her death*, and the Foxes [presumably an error for 'dogs'] presence like the voice of a *passing bell*.' The 'Historie' was published in 1607, fourteen years after *Venus and Adonis*, but its material may have been derived from sources that pre-date the poem: the title page reads, 'Collected out of all the volumes of Conrad Gesner, and all other writers to this present day' (the latter unfortunately have not been identified).

1110–16 The Greek poem on the death of Adonis via the boar's misdirected affection is by an unidentified author and exists in a single manuscript (Codex Vaticanus 1824). Malone thought it was by Theocritus and cited Idyll 30. However, he was following an error perpetrated by H. Stephanus's 1566 printing and not corrected until the nineteenth century. Shakespeare very likely knew this 'Theocritus' through E. D.'s translation of *Sixe idillia*, published in 1588. There are also any number of French and Italian sixteenth-century versions (see Rollins, pp. 390–1). But it should also be recognised that the idea of the boar's love of Adonis just prior to his death grows naturally out of the Orphic interpretation of the youth which Venus establishes from 1075 onwards, and that this is more significant for an appreciation of the 'kiss–kill' antithesis than the 'Theocritan' echo. (For the history of the Theocritan ascription, see the edition and translation by Gow listed in the List of abbreviations.)

LUCRECE

The Argument Shakespeare himself may have wished to advertise that this was indeed the 'graver labour' which he had promised in his dedication to *Venus and Adonis*, so that there should be no mistaking in advance the nature of the work. The argument also differs in points of detail from the poem, and Bush (p. 139) has shown that it corresponds uniquely in certain respects to Painter's story from *The Pallace of Pleasure*, which in turn is extracted from Livy (see Introduction, pp. 35–6). The author of the summary seems therefore to have cribbed from Painter – whose short novella yields a convenient *prose* digest – rather than paraphrasing from the poem. This could not have been done if the action of the two had not closely resembled each other. A likely explanation is that Shakespeare, some time after composing the poem, went back to Painter as a handy guide, knowing that nothing in the other's account would differ essentially from his own. Specific instances of diction at the end of *Lucrece* resemble Painter closely, which supports the view that Shakespeare himself wrote the 'argument' (with one eye on Painter) shortly after finishing the poem. J. R. Tolbert, however, argues plausibly enough that its author was not Shakespeare but someone called in, at a late date by the publisher, to provide an epitome or abridgement of the story. According to Tolbert, this person adapted his account from Livy. See Tolbert's article, 'The Argument of Shakespeare's *Lucrece*', *TSE*, 29 (1950), 77–90.

The proportion of the argument dealing with the story of Lucrece as opposed to the historical and political events matches that of the poem as well as Painter's account. The political framework, here and in the poem, carries far less importance than it does in Livy – despite some interpretations that would prove otherwise (see Introduction, pp. 32–3) – and acts as an internal means of pointing up the gravity of the rape and of ensuring that it is not to be a focus of lascivious enjoyment.

307 Night . . . weasels Ascham's *Toxophilus* (1545) is a possible source:

For on the nighte tyme & in corners, Spirites and theves, rattes and mice, toodes and oules, nyghtecrowes and poulcattes, foxes and foumerdes, with all other vermine, and noysome beastes, use mooste styrrings, when in the daye light, and in open places, which be ordeyned of God for honeste thynges, they darre not ones come, whiche thinge Euripides noted verye well, sayenge. *Il things the night, good things the daye doth haunt and use.*   (ed. Arber, 1895. pp. 52–3)

Foumerdes (foumarts) and polecats belong to the weasel family. Allen (*S. Sur.*, *15* [1962], 92) notes that Alciati (*Emblemata*) observes weasels to be a sign 'of evil to those whose house they infest', which further identifies Tarquin with the animal. Dyer (p. 189) makes a similar point about their ominous significance but adds: 'it appears weasels were kept in houses, instead of cats, for the purpose of killing vermin'. The two ideas are contradictory and the second one unlikely; it seems not to have been substantiated.

680 Porter's objection that bed linen is not worn is insufficient, since 'that she wears' is vague enough to be a line-filling pleonasm. Wyndham argues on behalf of 'bedclothes' observing that 'linen' cannot mean bed-time attire since night-gowns were not worn: Shakespeare's night-gown is the modern dressing-gown. However, discussing the question of domestic custom, Elizabeth Burton (*The Elizabethans at Home*, p. 92) distinguishes between night-gowns (as Wyndham) and 'night-smocks', which she says women slept in. This seems to be demonstrated by Othello's, 'O ill-starr'd wench / Pale as thy smock!' (*Oth.* 5.2.272–3). William Barksted's poem *Hiren, or the faire Greeke* (1611) contains the following description which further supports the idea of a garment as opposed to bedclothing:

> And lo indeed, the purple hangings drawne,
> In came faire *Hiren* in her night attire,
> In a silke mantle, and a smocke of lawne,
> Her haire at length, the beams of sweet desire
> Her breasts all naked, ô enchanting fire!

(*The Poems of William Barksted*, ed. A. B. Grosart (1876) p. 81)

1366–1568 It has long been agreed that Shakespeare's inspiration is literary rather than pictorial, and that the scene that greets Lucrece's eyes in the painting more or less reproduces that of *Aen.* 1.453ff. Both Virgil and Shakespeare confront the reader with an ecphrasis – a moment of pause within the narrative in which the inspection of a visual object becomes the means of meditating on a larger theme. Spenser often creates such moments, as in his description of the tapestries depicting the story of Venus and Adonis in Malecasta's castle (*FQ* 3.1.34–8). Given the consensus in favour of a literary source (the very form of ecphrasis is that of literary narrative), scholars are still concerned to define more exactly the relevance to the poem of the visual arts. Hence, in his useful summary (pp. 141–94), Hulse suggests that Shakespeare *may* have had the composition of a tapestry in mind in creating the Troy-scene ecphrasis (p. 180). But he acknowledges that the point is incidental, whereas earlier art historians such as Colvin and Fairchild had seriously proposed a tapestry as the germinating principle of Shakespeare's meditation; another, Margaret Thorp, had along similar lines proposed a panel painting (Rollins, pp. 224–8). Heckscher (see Hulse) points out that Shakespeare is very detailed in constructing scenes from the imagination (as here) and vague in recounting any work of art he may have seen.

Finally, Gent (pp. 15–16) has recently demonstrated that in the 1590s English lacked the sophistication to comprehend or render the terms of Italian art criticism (Hoby's translation of Castiglione is a case in point), and that knowledge and understanding of Continental painting was correspondingly very limited. By contrast, the power of dissimulation, including the *artistic* delight afforded by the depiction of evil, was being understood as a property of poetry as well as painting (Gent, pp. 45–6). In the depiction of Sinon, *Lucrece* uncovers the principles common to both arts (as Horace and Sidney each saw them).

THE PASSIONATE PILGRIM

18.0 Despite the evident resemblance between the two, no convincing demonstration has been made linking the author of this poem with canto xlvii of *Willobie his Avisa*, published in 1594. The said canto is addressed to H. W. and is attributed tantalisingly to W. S. De Luna (pp. 106–7) disposes of the theory that H. W. is Henry Wriothesley (Southampton) but keeps an open mind as to whether W. S. may be Shakespeare. Claims of Shakespeare's authorship have never been seriously entertained, though commendatory verses preceding it place it in the tradition of *Lucrece*, published the same year (De Luna, p. 128). Stanzaically, metrically, in terms of advice given, and even in occasional lines, the canto from *Willobie* resembles 'When as thine eye hath chose the dame'; but it adopts a more conventional Petrarchan tone (while acknowledging 'She is no Saynt, She is no Nonne', line 3) and carefully avoids the more scurrilous imputations to female nature which are found in the *PP* poem. For example, when W. S. advises the use of gifts he says:

> Apply her still with dyvers thinges,
> (For giftes the wysest will deceave)
> Sometymes with gold, sometymes with ringes,
> No tyme nor fit occasion leave,
> > Though coy at first she seeme and wielde,
> > These toyes in tyme will make her yielde.

The corresponding stanza in *PP* (also the third) echoes the sense of *Willobie*'s, but less straightforwardly:

> And to her will frame all thy ways;
> Spare not to spend, and chiefly there
> Where thy desert may merit praise,
> By ringing in thy lady's ear:
> > The strongest castle, tower and town,
> > The golden bullet beats it down.

'And to her will' echoes the construction of 'Apply her still', thereafter things going differently. However, 'gold' is picked up in 'golden bullet', and 'ringes' is heard again in 'ringing'. The final couplet of each version of the stanza argues the overcoming of resistance, though in quite different images. The versions are like and unlike. But *Willobie's* may explain the not always easy sense of *PP*. What does *PP*'s 'ringing (line 16) mean? Echoing, as of words? But why then his own 'desert' rather than her merits? (This of course continues the problem of *PP*'s line 12, where the printed version and the manuscripts disagree over whether his or her person is to be 'set forth to sale'.) Both 'ringing' and 'golden bullet' suggest the sound of flattering speech, but they could, following *Willobie*'s sense, accommodate the meaning of gift-giving, though in a cruder, more aggressive form (the deliberate jingling of coins, etc.). It is in fact likely that *PP* is playing on innuendo in precisely this way, and that *Willobie* acts as a source for the idea.

It is further conceivable that the canto became popular independently of the rest of *Willobie* (giving rise to the various manuscript versions), the signature 'W. S.' causing readers to suppose that Shakespeare was the author. Jaggard would have needed no more evidence than this to justify its appearance in *PP* as authentically Shakespearean.

TEXTUAL ANALYSIS

Venus and Adonis

Venus and Adonis was first printed in 1593 and entered in the Stationers' Register on April 18 of that year:[1]

[Ornament] / VENUS / AND ADONIS / *Vilia miretur vulgus: mihi flavus Apollo / Pocula Castalia plena ministra aqua.* / [Device, McKerrow 192] / LONDON / Imprinted by Richard Field, and are to be sold at / the signe of the white Greyhound in Paules Churchyard. / 1593. /

This edition is Q1 and exists in a single copy now in the Bodleian Library. It belonged formerly to Malone, who, though convinced of the 1593 Quarto's existence, only came to possess it after he had prepared his editions of 1780 and 1790.[2]

Because the text of Q1 is so clean and carefully prepared, it has often been fancied that Shakespeare saw it through the press personally. There are reasons for doubting this, however, as the discussion of *Lucrece* below (p. 299) will show. Shakespeare's part may have extended no further than choosing to sell the work to Richard Field, a highly efficient printer with a reputation for honesty and scrupulousness, and who was furthermore bound to take special care when he saw that the book was dedicated to the Earl of Southampton. After no doubt having added to his reputation with the publication, Field sold the copyright the very next year to John Harrison, Sr, assigning it to him on 25 June 1594 (Arber, II, 655), but remained as Harrison's printer. This edition is the last known quarto, and it survives in four copies in the British Museum, the Bodleian, the Huntington Library, and the Elizabethan Club, Yale. Thereafter the poem was printed in octavo, a further seven surviving editions appearing in Shakespeare's lifetime and one more in the year following his death (for convenience, all these editions are referred to by Q plus the number). They are:

Q3 (1595? lacks sig. A; unique copy in the Folger Library); Q4 (1596, copies in the British Museum and Bodleian; Field is again the printer for Harrison); Q5 (1599, unique copy in Huntington; copyright transferred to William Leake, and the printer is Peter Short);[3] Q6 (1599, unique copy in Folger, part of the Burton–Longner volume; printed for Leake from the press of Richard Bradocke); Q7 (1602?: only copy in Bodleian; lacks title page, which is supplied in manuscript with the date 1600, but Farr (p. 244)

---

[1] Arber, II, 630.

[2] Malone has written in his copy: 'Bought from Mr William Ford, Bookseller in Manchester, in August 1805, at the enormous price of twenty-five pounds. 'Many years ago I said, that I had no doubt an edition of Shakespeare's *Venus and Adonis* was published in 1593; but no copy of that edition was discovered in the long period that has elapsed since my first notice of it, nor is any other copy of 1593, but the present, known to exist.'

[3] Either this or the following printing has bearing on the 1599 publication of *The Passionate Pilgrim*; see below, p. 303. For the history of printers and stationers concerned with *Venus and Adonis* and *Lucrece* see Henry Farr, *Library*, March 1923, pp. 225–50.

thinks that this may be the original 1602 edition on which Q8–9 are based); Q8 (1602 (1607/8); unique Bodian copy, printed for Leake). Farr (pp. 235–45) demonstrates most effectively that this edition was printed by Robert Raworth in 1607 or 1608 and dated 1602 in order to avoid running the risk of appearing to bring out a new edition of a 'licentious' work during a period (1604–10) when the particularly zealous Archbishop Bancroft was likely to punish such offences. (A further argument may be that with the accession of James I poets – and their printers – felt discouraged from producing light-hearted, 'wanton' works and began to cultivate a more melancholic style.) At the same time (1607) Raworth was 'supprest' for printing 'another's copy' of *Venus* (Arber, III, 701, 703ff.). Leake was then warden of the Stationers' Company, and Farr explains the appearance of yet two more 1602 editions (Q9 and an edition known only by its title page), both also printed for Leake (but not by Raworth), as the copyright-holder's appropriation of Raworth's idea, even while having the latter suppressed for theft! Farr's hypothesis, which is faultless in every detail, explains the disproportionate number of editions dated 1602.

Q9 (1602 (1608/9?), copies BM, Shirburn Castle, Oxon, printed for Leake probably, according to Farr (p. 244), by Humphrey Lownes); Q10 (1617, unique Bodleian copy; printed by William Stansby for William Barrett to whom Leake had assigned copyright on 16 Feb. 1617 (Arber, III, 603)).

A further edition of 1620 survives in a single copy, formerly belonging to Capell, in Trinity College, Cambridge, and in 1627 it was printed at Edinburgh, the first publication of a work by Shakespeare outside London. The 1630s saw several reprintings, but from then on they begin to decrease markedly. The unofficial Cotes–Benson edition of 1640 ignored both *Venus* and *Lucrece* but perhaps only because copyright was too secure; and the next recorded printing is not until 1675 – apparently the last one of the seventeenth century.

In 1707 both the narrative poems appeared, curiously enough, in the anthology, *Poems on Affairs of State*, and Bernard Lintott produced quite a good text (at least one that was free from the whimsy of personal emendation) in 1709. Various eighteenth-century editions were published, each more or less derived from its predecessor; and it was not until Malone, using a copy of Q7, that the first modern critical text was edited in 1780. He improved matters ten years later by borrowing Thomas Warton's copy of Q4 for the 1790 edition. Then, as noted above, he finally acquired the unique copy of 1593, which enabled him to bring out the then definitive critical edition in 1821 (posthumously in Boswell's *Variorum Shakespeare*, vol. XX).

The history of the editions of *Venus and Adonis* (and similarly *Lucrece*) shows that all subsequent printings derive from Q1 and that they depart from it almost always along the predictable lines of corruption or vulgarisation that accompany any large exercise of reprinting. In some cases, later quartos emend or try to improve the sense of certain of Q1's readings, but in so doing they have no more apparent authority than any reader has who finds himself stumbling with an awkward or obscure meaning. Of the subsequent quartos, only Q6 of *Lucrece* – and to a lesser degree Q5 of *Venus* – intervened more decisively between Q1 and its successors, some of the new readings being retained more or less throughout the later editions. We should remind ourselves that none of the quartos can be considered a critical edition: later printers and proof-readers were not editors in the sense that Malone was when he tried to establish as nearly as possible what Shakespeare may have written. Only exceptionally (e.g. Q6 of *Venus* and Q5 of *Lucrece*) does it appear that a printer used any quarto other than the one immediately preceding his own. Sometimes, when his copy was evidently corrupt, he simply deduced the original reading for himself without bothering to seek out an earlier version (as in *Luc.* 1214, in which Q2 misprints Q1's 'cals' as 'calds', leaving Q3 to guess wrongly between 'calls' and 'called' – an error which was followed by all succeeding quartos). At best, printers were concerned to provide a clear and attractive text, and were quite prepared to interfere in order to smooth out problems. But this does not, as may be supposed, signal Shakespeare's return to the scene with second thoughts about his composition. Prince in his edition (see pp. xiii–xx) has analysed the changes and emendations between the quartos of both *Venus* and *Lucrece* and concludes persuasively that all of them are to be attributed to the ordinary hazards of reprinting (as it multiplies opportunities for misreporting). It is instructive as well as amusing that two of the most famous cruxes of the narrative poems (in *Ven.* 466 and *Luc.* 1662) went unheeded by all the quartos and only became issues as a result of nineteenth-century scholarship. But the question whether Shakespeare contributed anything further by way of emendation once he had surrendered his manuscript to the publisher can better be answered by a consideration of *Lucrece*.

The Rape of Lucrece

Lucrece was first published in 1594:

[Ornament] / LUCRECE. / [Device, McKerrow 222] / LONDON. / Printed by Richard Field, for John Harrison, and are / to be sold at the signe of the white Greyhound / in Paules Churh-yard [*sic*]. 1594. /

There are eleven known copies: BM (two); Bodleian (two: Malone 34 and Malone 886); Sion College, Huntington, Folger (three), Elizabethan Club, Yale, and Kraus (see *STC*).

Of these, Malone 34 and Yale differ from the other copies in certain readings. What would have happened is that corrections were made in the type after some sheets had been printed, but the uncorrected sheets would still be offered for sale.[1] This being so, it is possible to inspect those variant readings between the copies of Q1 and ask whether they signal Shakespeare's intervention in the printing-house. They are on three formes: inner B (six), outer I (two), and outer K (one). The most significant ones are those on

---

[1] Willoughby explains the process clearly and succinctly: 'the author would usually visit the shop and read the proofs taken from the page galleys before they were locked up in the forme. If he were delayed, however, the proof-reader would mark the proof as best he could, the type would be corrected, the forme put on the press and the printing would be commenced. Should the author later arrive at the office after some sheets had been printed off, he would be allowed to correct any serious errors which remained, but the impressions from the uncorrected forme usually would not be destroyed, but would be bound up with their later printed fellows. It is because of this practice that some of the pages of the same edition of an early printed book differ so greatly from each other' (p. 25).

sig. B. In line 4 the place-name is given as 'Colatium' (as in 'The Argument', line 23); but on B2 (or line 50) only two copies (Malone 34 and Yale) give 'Colatium', while the rest have 'Colatia' (see collation). In Malone 34 and Yale, sig. B seems to be in the earlier state, which would signify that the other copies carry the corrected reading. Sisson (I, 207–8) points out that 'Colatia' is the classical form of the name (Livy, 1.58, gives the accusative form 'Colatiam') and that an educated (and no doubt pedantic) press-reader is likely to have emended it. But if this had been Shakespeare, he would surely also have emended line 4 ('The Argument' he may have ignored, especially if he was not its author). Why was 'Colatium' not picked up as an error at the very beginning of the poem? The likely answer is that what first caught the proof-reader's eye in line 50 was not the place-name but the misspelt 'arived'. This drew his attention to 'Colatium', which on reflection he also changed; but he did not search for other examples of the name. Perhaps a more telling example is that of line 24, which in Malone 34 and Yale has 'morning silver melting dew' and in the other copies 'mornings silver melting dew'. The additional genitive 's' following 'morning' is perhaps grammatically more sound, but it produces too sibilant an effect. The earlier reading is more fluent, while security of grammar was hardly ever Shakespeare's aim. Finally, in Q1 sig. B we find an example of characteristic Shakespearean usage (in the two earlier copies):

> And everie one to rest himselfe betakes,
> Save theeves, and cares, and troubled minds that wakes,

which in the rest has been emended to:

> And everie one to rest themselves betake,
> Save theeves, and cares, and troubled minds that wake.   (125–6)

But as Abbott (§333) insists, the inflected 's' of 'wakes' occurs all over the Folio, while the present edition notes several examples of it in the poems, including this from *Venus*:

> She lifts the coffer-lids that close his eyes,
> Where lo, two lamps burnt out in darknesse lies.   (Q1, 1127–8)

    There seems every reason to agree therefore with Maxwell, Prince, and the Sisson of *New Readings* that the early versions of Q1's variants are what Shakespeare wrote and that whoever corrected them was not the poet (and not *a* poet). Furthermore, there is nothing in the nature of the many variants and corrections occurring in the later quartos to suggest that Shakespeare ever intervened again in any subsequent publication of either of the narrative poems. Once his carefully prepared manuscript was in the hands of the printer he most likely entrusted the enterprise to the professional competence of others, pausing over the printed copy only long enough to make sure that all was well with the dedication page.
    All editions after the first are in octavo (but convention refers to them as Q2, Q3, etc.). They are:

Q2 (1598, printed by Peter Short for John Harrison; Capell's copy, Trinity College, Cambridge, unique); Q3 (1600, printed by John Harrison, Jr, for his father; the Burton–Longner copy, i.e. in the same volume as Q6 of *Ven.* and the fragment of *PP* 01 (see below, p. 301); Q4 (1600, again printed by John Harrison, Jr; based on Q3 but apparently done hastily, introducing many new errors; two Bodleian copies); Q5 (1607, the printer was now Nicholas Okes – for Harrison *fils* – and he worked hard at removing the corruptions of Q4. Rollins (pp. 408–9) confesses that he is unsure which text he adopted as his copy, and while noting the presence of Q3 concludes that he may have used an edition now unknown between 1598 and 1600. Copies: Huntington, Trinity College, Cambridge); Q6 (1616, printed by Thomas Snodham for Roger Jackson to whom Harrison *fils* had assigned the copyright on 1 March 1614 (Arber, III, 542). Copies: BM (imperfect), Bodleian, Huntington, New York Public Library).

Q6 is worth a little more attention. It appeared in the year Shakespeare died and is accordingly the last edition to which he might have contributed any second thoughts. That he did not do so is firmly argued by Prince, who points out (p. xx): 'if Shakespeare went to the trouble of inserting the very small number of new readings that can be described as good, how are we to explain why he did not eliminate the far greater number of those that are gratuitous, inferior, or downright bad?' But the influence it had over seventeenth- and eighteenth-century publishers and editors indicates that there was once a tradition of accepting it as Shakespeare's own last words. Subsequent quartos are dated 1624, 1632, and 1655, and the printers of these would feel progressively less confident about challenging an edition produced while Shakespeare was still alive, especially one which had issued forth with such a self-important air.

Among the things that are new in Q6 is the title, *The Rape of Lucrece*, replacing *Lucrece* on the title page (though it had served as the running title as early as Q1).[1] Q6 also describes itself as 'newly revised', though this might more accurately read 'newly presented', for Snodham added a 'Contents' page listing the twelve main phases of the narrative (as in the later practice of listing chapters in a novel): e.g. (1) 'LUCRECE praises for chaste, vertuous, and beautifull, enamoreth *Tarquin*'; (2) '*Tarquin* over-throwes all disputing with wilfulnesse', and so on. He also added twelve marginal notes corresponding more or less to the contents headings, and took to italicising many of the 'key' words of the narrative. Such confidence on the part of the printer in the matter of presentation extends as far as occasionally regularising the metre (as in line 26) and 'improving' diction (as, for example, substituting 'shuts' for 'stows' in line 119 and 'fowle' for 'prone' in 684). Unlike Q4, which is simply badly produced,[2] the changes introduced in Q6 are performed by somebody seriously if naively concerned to 'improve' the poem. A case in point is the substitution of 'sad source' for 'mother' in line 117. This is evidently the correction of a reader who jibs at the association of things dark and terrible with the maternal instinct (which presumably ought to be comforting), and feels safer with the less disturbing, impersonal 'sad source'. But this

---

[1] When, however, the 1594 Quarto was first registered it was entered as 'a booke intituled *the Ravyshement of Lucrece*' (Arber, II, 648). Rollins (p. 406) attributes this to clerical error.

[2] It would seem that Harrison, Jr, having served as printer to his father, saw the wisdom thereafter of concentrating on the publishing side and leaving the printing to more able men.

throws the poem badly out, since the original image sets a mood which is to recur
and intensify following the rape, particularly at those moments when the distraught
Lucrece accuses night of complicity in phrases like, 'nurse of blame' (767), 'Night's
child' (785), and 'Night's black bosom' (788), where the maternal and the destructive
are deliberately set against each other. If Shakespeare had been the reviser of line 117
he would certainly have amended his thoughts on all of this.

There are three more surviving quartos from the seventeenth century: Q7 (1624),
Q8 (1632), and Q9 (1655). The last of these adds as an appendix John Quarles's poem,
'Tarquin Banished: or, the Reward of Lust'. The Stationers' Register indicates that
there were no more editions of the poem until the appearance of *Poems on Affairs of
State* in 1707, after which the history of *Lucrece's* publication more or less co-exists
with that of *Venus and Adonis*.

The Passionate Pilgrim

Three octavo editions of *The Passionate Pilgrim*, all printed by William Jaggard,
appeared in Shakespeare's lifetime. O1 exists in only two sheets and lacks a title page.
It was discovered in 1920 by Richard Francis Burton, the owner of Longner Hall,
Shrewsbury, 'among some venerable books which had been preserved in his muniment
room for over 200 years' (Adams, p. xvii). It was acquired by the Folger Library, and is
known as the Folger or Burton–Longner copy. O1's two sheets were stitched together
with quires of the 1599 edition, or O2, and bound in a book containing five works, the
other four being: *Lucrece*, dated 1600 (the only copy); Thomas Middleton, *The Ghost of
Lucrece*, dated 1600; E. C., *Emaricdulfe*, dated 1595 (one other copy known), and *Venus
and Adonis*, dated 1599 (again unique).

Until Adams's decisive edition of 1939 there was some doubt as to which element
of Burton's hybrid discovery constituted the first edition, for, as indicated, of the three
editions of *The Passionate Pilgrim* only two (in their surviving copies) bear title pages:

THE / PASSIONATE / PILGRIME. / *By W. Shakespeare.* / [Ornament] / *AT LONDON* /
Printed for W. Iaggard, and are / to be sold by W. Leake, at the Grey- / hound in Paules
Churchyard. / 1599. /

8°, sigs. A–D⁸.

There are two extant copies of this edition, known as O2, one in Trinity College,
Cambridge, and the other in the Huntington Library.[1]

THE / PASSIONATE / PILGRIME. / OR / *Certaine Amorous Sonnets,* / *betweene* Venus
and Adonis, / *newly corrected and aug-* / *mented.* / *By W. Shakespere.* / The third Edition. /
Where-unto is newly ad- / ded two Love-Epistles, the first / from *Paris* to *Hellen*, and / *Hellens*
answere backe / againe to *Paris.* / Printed by W. Iaggard. / 1612. /

8°, sigs. A–H⁸ (A1, H8 blank).

---

[1] It is best consulted in the facsimile reproduction issued by the Yale Elizabethan Club of the earliest editions
of Shakespeare's poems – see Reading List.

There are two extant copies of this edition, one in the Folger Shakespeare Library, with the title page as above, and the other in the Bodleian (formerly Malone's copy) with the above title page (defective) – and also a cancel title page, reset and omitting '*By W. Shakespere*' (Adams, p. xvi).[1] Both editions carry a supplementary title page, which in each case precedes poem 15 in the collection. In 1599 this was:

SONNETS / To Sundry notes of Musicke. / [Ornament, identical with that on A2] / *AT LONDON* / Printed for W. Iaggard, and are / to be sold by W. Leake, at the Grey- / hound in Paules Churchard. / 1599. / [from same setting of type as on A2]

The 1612 version is less detailed:

SONNETS / To Sundry notes of Musicke. / [Ornament, changed from that of 1599 (the 1612 principal title page carries no ornament)] / *AT LONDON* / Printed by W. Iaggard. / 1612. /

The later version of the title page, which makes no attempt to insist on the contract to sell at St Paul's through Leake, reminds us of Jaggard's ploy, according to Adams (pp. xiv–xv), of selling *The Passionate Pilgrim* at the same bookshop that in 1599 was also furnishing copies of the newly printed *Venus and Adonis* (Q5). By 1612 this stratagem was evidently no longer serviceable.

It is clear from the 1612 main title page that another, previously missing edition had either preceded that of 1599 or intervened between it and 03. Scholars used naturally but perhaps not very thoughtfully to suppose the latter, and gave various approximate dates such as 1604 or 1606 (see Adams, pp. xvi–xvii). But the Burton–Longner discovery put an end to such speculation. It was clear that this composite copy was made up of sheets belonging to two editions which had been issued very close together, raising, as we have seen, questions of precedence. Rollins in the Variorum edition of *The Poems* (1938) tentatively assigned precedence to what is now 02 (thereby giving later editors cause for extra care in distinguishing his 02–01 references from the now accepted 01–02 order). But Adams's brilliant analysis in the 1939 edition of *The Passionate Pilgrim* put the sequence surely beyond dispute. Following Adams, we should therefore examine the make-up of the Folger or Burton–Longner copy.

This copy carries four quires equivalent to signatures A–D. However, it only bears B and D signatures, sheets A and C being unsigned. A is further defective, lacking the equivalent of A1, A2, and A8, though not A7 (corresponding to A2); C1 and the corresponding leaf C8 are also lacking. The leaves of B and D are all intact. The poems contained in A and C (i.e. the fragment of the first edition) are:

$1 = \text{A3}^{\text{r}}$
$2 = \text{A4}^{\text{r}}$
$3 = \text{A5}^{\text{r}}$
$4 = \text{A6}^{\text{r}}$
$5 = \text{A7}^{\text{r}}$
$16 = \text{C2}^{\text{r}}$
$17 = \text{C3}^{\text{r}}, \text{C3}^{\text{v}}, \text{C4}^{\text{r}}$
$18 = \text{C5}^{\text{r}}–\text{C7}^{\text{r}}$, on both r and v.

---

[1] For facsimiles of the two title pages of the Bodleian copy, see Rollins (1612), pp. 128–9.

The rest of the collection is on B and D, apart from those poems which are missing entirely: numbers 6 (presumably on the absent A8), 15 (perhaps on C1, though that may have carried the supplementary title page – if the first edition had one),[1] and 19 (presumably on C8).

Adams establishes that the printer used by Jaggard for the first two editions was Thomas Judson. House style is almost indistinguishable in both of them, and the horizontal row of ornaments at the top and (doubled) at the bottom of each page is the same. Since Judson was recorded as having illicitly set up printing again in September 1598 (nothing suggesting activity between 1584 and 1599 survives), and since an entry in the records of the Stationers' Company shows that he was no longer printing after the end of 1599, that was probably the year in which both editions appeared (Adams, pp. xxi–xxv).

It is in fact likely that the one followed the other in a very short space of time while demand kept up. As noted above (p. 293), Jaggard probably used William Leake's shop to profit from his sale of the new and timely printing, in 1599, of *Venus and Adonis*.

The difference between the two pairs of quires is that A and C had, as stab marks show, previously been stitched, whereas B and D (corresponding to the second edition) were stitched only for the volume in which they now found themselves, the Burton–Longner volume, handsomely bound in vellum with the initials 'G. O.' on the cover.

There is an interesting irregularity in the sequence in which the poems towards the end of the Burton–Longner *Passionate Pilgrim* are printed. Poem 18, 'When as thine eye hath chose the dame', is printed on C5–7, both recto and verso. Then, as we have observed, C8 is missing, after which the poem begins again on D1, printed on the recto only. Both editions appear to have restricted the use of the verso to the later pages, partly in order to make as much as possible of a slender volume while at the same time serving economy by not using more than four quires. It is deduced (see Adams's scheme, pp. xxxiii–xxv) that O1 occupied three quires and half a sheet as against the four quires of O2. What probably happened is that the binder of G. O.'s volume discovered some defective pages on leafing through the original (O1) pamphlet of *The Passionate Pilgrim*. He sent the copy to the bookseller for it to be made good, and the latter (here Adams's argument is necessarily conjectural but none the less plausible and worth giving in full) decided that only quires B and D really needed replacing, since, although A and C were defective in parts, they were not in bad shape.

Since the first edition had been sold off, B and D were replaced from the second edition, as the difference in the order of stanzas between the doubly printed versions of poem 18 shows. The third stanza, beginning at the top of C5^v, reads 'And to her wil frame al thy waies', whereas the corresponding stanza on D3^r is *fifth* in sequence (see text and notes). Editors in general agree that C5's order is the correct one and that the second edition jumbles its pages. Quite likely the printer, copying from the first edition and at this stage printing on the recto only, followed O1's recto sequence and printed stanzas five and six after one and two, only then taking account of the fact that stanzas three and four intervene on C5^v. It is a confusion that occurs naturally enough when

---

[1] For his persuasive argument that O1 had no supplementary title page, see Adams, pp. xxxv–xxxvi.

setting up recto sheets from a copy using both rectos and versos. The printer made good his mistake by placing stanzas three and four after five and six on the following recto, assuming that the rearranged sequence did not affect the sense, or not enough to matter.[1] He seems to have determined to use the versos at the last possible moment and indeed uses only those of D5–D7 (A1 and D8 being blank cover-leaves) for poems 19 and 20. O1, in contrast, made use of the versos much earlier, beginning most likely with poem 14 on B8 (Adams, pp. xxxiii–xxxv).

This brings us again to G. O's binder. He would have got quires B and D back in perfect form from the bookseller and incorporated them into the binding, scrutinising them only for their appearance and not for their effect on narrative sequence. The result, as we have seen, was a double version of 'When as thine eye hath chose the dame'. In addition, the insertion of quire B chops off the end of poem 14, which (see above) O1 would have printed on the verso.

Quires B and D of the Folger copy, when collated with those of the Huntington and Trinity College copies of O2, show variation only in D. As with Trinity, quire D of Folger has its outer forme in the 'later state' and corrects the following errors (all examples of turned letters) in poem 18 – as evident in Huntington: D1, line 7 ('thou' for 'thon'), D3, line 28 ('ringing' for 'ringiug'), and D3, line 36 ('though' for 'thongh').[2] Otherwise the three quartos show little correction. For example, they each give line 28 of poem 17, 'Nimphes blacke peeping', unchanged, whereas surely the correct version, '*back* peeping', is given by Weelkes' *Madrigals* (see text and notes). Similarly, poem 9 (for which O2 serves as copy-text since this poem is not included in the Folger fragment of O1) apparently lacks the whole of the second line – an omission ignored by O3 and Cotes–Benson, and only noted by the ever-reliable Malone. A third example is provided by lines 45–6 of poem 18:

> There is no heaven (by holy then)
> When time with age shall them attaint.

Again, this reading is observed unchanged by all three quartos, and yet sense requires some emendation. Folger MS 2071.7 helpfully renders the phrase 'by holy then' as 'be holy then', but less helpfully changes 'When' in the next line to 'till'. Folger MS 1.112 reads

> here is no heaven, they holy then
> begynne when age doth them attaynte,[3]

which makes perfect sense but challenges 2071.7's exhortatory 'be'. Accordingly, the present edition (for which the manuscripts have been freshly consulted) is made up of those readings which seemingly most respond to the overall tone of the poem.

In 1612 Jaggard brought out his final edition of *The Passionate Pilgrim*. The only difference between this and the first two editions is the massive presence in the volume

---

[1] O1's order is supported by that of both manuscript versions of the poem. See below, and collation.
[2] See Adams, p. xiv, and Willoughby, quoted above, p. 298, n.
[3] For transcripts of the various manuscript versions of poems from *The Passionate Pilgrim*, see Adams, pp. liv–lxiii.

of poems by Thomas Heywood.[1] These additional poems do not interrupt but follow the sequence of twenty poems corresponding to that of o2,[2] Otherwise, the third edition is based on that of o2, as the printing of signatures A3–C8 on the recto only would indicate. According to Rollins (*PP*, 1612, p. xvi) it shows some improvement in spelling and punctuation, and corrects a number of misprints while making some others.

Finally, in 1640 the first edition pretending to be the 'Poems' of Shakespeare appeared. This was *Poems: written by Wil. Shakespeare, Gent.*, an octavo printed by Thomas Cotes for John Benson. Notably absent from it is any trace of *Venus and Adonis* or *Lucrece*, presumably because the copyright to the narrative poems was indisputably in the hands of others (an argument also sometimes advanced to explain the omission of the poems from the Folio). By contrast, no copyright ever existed for *The Passionate Pilgrim*.[3] Benson's collection contains 146 of Shakespeare's sonnets, which are rearranged according to no discernible order as 72 'poems' with titles; *A Lover's Complaint*; the whole of the third edition of *The Passionate Pilgrim* (evidently, Heywood's protests were either unknown to Benson or they went for nothing in his eyes), with the sole difference that poem 19 follows the longer versions of *Englands Helicon* (1600); *The Phoenix and the Turtle*; and poems by Milton, Jonson, Beaumont, Herrick, Cartwright, Carew, Strode, and other authors who have never been identified.[4]

---

[1] For Heywood's quarrel with Jaggard see pp. 58–9.

[2] For an analysis of the Heywood 'contribution' to o3 see Rollins (1612), pp. xvi–xxi.

[3] See J. W. Bennett, 'Benson's alleged piracy of Shakespeare's *Sonnets*', *SB* 21 (1968), 235–48.

[4] For this and subsequent publishing history see Rollins (1612), pp. xxxviii–xl, and Rollins, Var., pp. 604–19.; also Klein, pp. xi–xxi.

READING LIST

This list includes some of the works referred to in the Introduction or commentary and may serve as a guide to anyone wishing to undertake further study of the poems.

Akrigg, G. P. V. *Shakespeare and the Earl of Southampton*, 1968

Allen, Don Cameron. 'On *Venus and Adonis*', in *Elizabethan and Jacobean Studies. Presented to F. P. Wilson*, 1959, pp. 100–11

Axton, Marie. *The Queen's Two Bodies: Drama and the Elizabethan Succession*, 1978

Baines, Barbara J. 'Effacing rape in early modern representation', *ELH* 65 (1998), 69–98

Bal, Mieke. '*The Rape of Lucrece* and the Story of W', in *Reclamations of Shakespeare*, ed. A. J. Hoenslaars, Amsterdam, 1994

Bate, Jonathan. *Shakespeare and Ovid*, 1993

Belsey, Catherine. 'Love as *trompe-l'œil*: taxonomies of desire in *Venus and Adonis*', *SQ* 46 (1995), 257–76

'Tarquin dispossessed: expropriation and consent in *The Rape of Lucrece*', *SQ* 52 (2001), 315–35

Bembo, Pietro. *Prose e Rime*, ed. Carlo Dionisotti, Turin, revised edn, 1966

Bennett, J. W. 'Benson's alleged piracy of Shakespeare's *Sonnets* and some of Jonson's works', *SB* 21 (1968), 235–48

Berry, Philippa. 'Woman, language and history in *The Rape of Lucrece*', *S. Sur.* 44 (1992), 33–9

Berry, Ralph. *Shakespeare and the Hunt*, 2001

Bradbrook, M. C. *Shakespeare and Elizabethan Poetry*, 1951

Braden, Gordon. *The Classics and English Renaissance Poetry*, 1978

Breitenberg, Mark. *Anxious Masculinity in Early Modern England*, 1996

Burrow, Colin. 'Life and work in Shakespeare's poems', *Publications of the British Academy* 97 (1997), 15–50

Bush, Douglas. *Mythology and the Renaissance Tradition in English Poetry*, 1932, revised edn, 1963

Camino, Mercedes Maroto. *'The Stage am I': Raping Lucrece in Early Modern England*, 1995

Campbell, Lily B. (ed.). *The Mirror for Magistrates*, 1938

Charney, Maurice. 'Marlowe's *Hero and Leander* shows Shakespeare in *Venus and Adonis* how to write an Ovidian verse epyllion', in *Marlowe's Empery: Expanding his Critical Contexts*, ed. Sarah M. Deats and Robert A. Logan, 2002

Colvin, Sidney. 'The sack of Troy in Shakespeare's *Lucrece* and in some fifteenth-century drawings and tapestries', in *A Book of Homage to Shakespeare*, ed. Sir Israel Gollancz, 1916

Cousins, A. D. *Shakespeare's Sonnets and Narrative Poems*, 2000
   'Subjectivity, exemplarity and the establishing of characterization in *Lucrece*', *SEL* 38 (1998), 45–60

Craik, Katherine A. 'Shakespeare's "A Lover's Complaint" and early modern criminal confession', *SQ* 53 (2002), 437–59

Cunningham, J. V. '"Essence" and *The Phoenix and Turtle*', *ELH* 19 (1952), 265–76

Daigle, Lennet. '*Venus and Adonis*: some traditional contexts', *S. St.* 13 (1980), 31–46

Donaldson, Ian. *The Rapes of Lucretia*, 1982

Dubrow, Heather. *Captive Victors: Shakespeare's Narrative Poems and Sonnets*, 1987

Duncan Jones, Katherine. 'Much ado with red and white: the earliest readers of Shakespeare's *Venus and Adonis* (1593)', *RES* 44:176 (1993), 479–501
   'Ravished and revised: the 1616 *Lucrece*', *RES* 52 (2001), 516–24
   'Playing fields and killing fields: Shakespeare's poems and sonnets', *SQ* 54 (2003), 127–41
   'Was the 1609 *Shakes-peares Sonnets* really unauthorized?', *RES* 34 (1983), 157–71

Elliott, W. E. Y. and R. J. Valenza. 'Glass slippers and seven-league boots: C-prompted doubts about ascribing *A Funeral Elegy* and "A Lover's Complaint" to Shakespeare', *SQ* 48 (1997), 177–207

Ellis, Jim. *Sexuality and Citizenship: Metamorphosis in Elizabethan Erotic Verse*, 2003

Ellrodt, Robert. 'An anatomy of *The Phoenix and the Turtle*', *S. Sur* 15 (1962)

Empson, William. Introduction to the Signet *Poems* 1972 (also collected in his *Essays on Shakespeare*, ed. David B. Pirie, 1986)

Fairchild, A. H. R. '*The Phoenix and Turtle*', *Englische Studien* 33 (1904), 337–84

Fineman, Joel. 'Shakespeare's *Will*: the temporality of rape', *Representations* 20 (1987), 25–76

Gent, Lucy. *Picture and Poetry 1560–1620*, 1981

Hadfield, Andrew. *Shakespeare and Renaissance Politics*, 2004

Hawkins, Harriet. 'The poetic and critical *Rape of Lucrece*', in *The Devil's Party: Critical Counter-Interpretations of Shakespearean Drama*, 1985

Hendricks, Margo. '"A word, sweet Lucrece": confession, feminism and *The Rape of Lucrece*', in *A Feminist Companion to Shakespeare*, ed. Dympna Callaghan (2001), 103–18

Hobday, C. H. 'Shakespeare's Venus and Adonis sonnets', *S. Sur.* 26 (1973), 103–9

Honigmann, E. A. J. *Shakespeare: The 'Lost Years'*, 1985

Hulse, Clark. *Metamorphic Verse: The Elizabethan Minor Epic*, 1981

Hyland, Peter. *An Introduction to Shakespeare's Poems*, 2003

Jackson, MacDonald P. *Shakespeare's 'A Lover's Complaint': Its Date and Authenticity*, University of Auckland, Bulletin 72, English Series 13, 1965

Kahn, Coppélia. 'The rape in Shakespeare's *Lucrece*', *S. St.* 9 (1976), 45–72

Kay, Dennis. *William Shakespeare: Sonnets and Poems*, 1998

Keach, William. *Elizabethan Erotic Narratives*, 1977

Kiernan, Pauline. 'Death by rhetorical trope: poetry metamorphosed in *Venus and Adonis* and the sonnets', *RES* 46 (1995), 475–501

'*Venus and Adonis* and Ovidian indecorous wit' (Taylor, 81–95)

Kietzman, Mary Jo. 'What is Hecuba to him or [s]he to Hecuba?: Lucrece's complaint and Shakespearean poetic agency', *Modern Philology* 97 (1999), 21–45

Kolin, Philip C. (ed.). '*Venus and Adonis*': *Critical Essays*, 1997

Kramer, Jerome A. and Judith Kaminsky. '"These contraries such unity do hold": structure in *The Rape of Lucrece*', *Mosaic* 10 (1977), 145–55

Kuhl, E. P. 'Shakespeare's *Rape of Lucrece*', *PQ* 20 (1941), 352–60

Laws, J. 'The generic complexities of *A Lover's Complaint* and its relationship to the Sonnets in Shakespeare's 1609 volume', *AUMLA* 89 (1998), 79–97

Lanham, Richard A. *The Motives of Eloquence*, 1976

Lever, J. W. 'Shakespeare's narrative poems', in *A New Companion to Shakespeare Studies*, ed. K. Muir and S. Schoenbaum, 1971

Levin, Richard. 'The ironic reading of *The Rape of Lucrece* and the problem of external evidence', *S. Sur.* 34 (1981), 85–92

Lewalski, Barbara K. (ed.). *Renaissance Genres*, 1986

Lewis, C. S. *English Literature in the Sixteenth Century, Excluding Drama*, 1954

Lindheim, Nancy. 'The Shakespearean *Venus and Adonis*', *SQ* 37 (1986), 190–203

McDonald, Joyce Green. 'Speech, silence, and history in *The Rape of Lucrece*', *S. St.* 22 (1994), 77–103

Maguin, Jean-Marie and Charles Whitworth (eds.). *William Shakespeare, 'Venus and Adonis': Nouvelles Perspectives Critiques*, 1999

Matchett, W. H. '*The Phoenix and the Turtle*': *Shakespeare's Poem and Chester's 'Loues Martyr*', 1965

Maus, Katherine Eisamen. 'Taking tropes seriously: language and violence in Shakespeare's *Rape of Lucrece*', *SQ* 37 (1986), 66–82

Miola, Robert. *Shakespeare's Rome*, 1983

Monsarrat, G. D. '*A Funeral Elegy*: Ford, W. S., and Shakespeare', *RES* 53 (2002), 186–203

Mortimer, Anthony. *Variable Passions: A Reading of Shakespeare's 'Venus and Adonis'*, 2000

Muir, Kenneth. *Shakespeare the Professional*, 1973

Muir, Kenneth and Sean O'Loughlin. *The Voyage to Illyria*, 1937

Nass, Barry. 'The law and politics of treason in Shakespeare's *Lucrece*', *Shakespeare Yearbook* 7 (1996), 291–311

Newman, Jane O. '"And let mild women to him lose their mildness": Philomela, female violence and Shakespeare's *The Rape of Lucrece*', *SQ* 45 (1994), 304–26

Partridge, A. C. *The Language of Renaissance Poetry*, 1971

Platt, Michael. '*The Rape of Lucrece* and the republic for which it stands', *CR* 19 (1975), 59–79

Rabkin, Norman. *Shakespeare and the Common Understanding*, 1967

Roberts, Sasha. *Reading Shakespeare's Poems in Early Modern England*, 2003

Roe, John. '*Willobie his Avisa* and *The Passionate Pilgrim*: precedence, parody, and development', *Yearbook of English Studies* 23 (1993), 111–25

'Pleasing the wiser sort: problems of ethics and genre in *Lucrece* and *Hamlet*', *Cambridge Quarterly* 23 (1994), 99–119

Shakespeare Survey 15 (1962) (a volume largely devoted to the poems of Shakespeare)

Shakespeare's Poems: Venus and Adonis, Lucrece, The Passionate Pilgrim, The Phoenix and the Turtle, The Sonnets, A Lover's Complaint. A Facsimile of the Earliest Editions. Published for the Elizabethan Club, New Haven and London, 1964

Schmitz, Götz. *The Fall of Women in Early English Narrative Verse*, 1990

Scholtz, Suzanne. 'Textualising the body politic: national identity and the female body in *The Rape of Lucrece*', *Shakespeare Jahrbuch* 132 (1996), 103–33

Shohet, Lauren. 'Shakespeare's eager Adonis', *SEL* 42:1 (2002), 85–102

Simone, R. Thomas. *Shakespeare and 'Lucrece': A Study of the Poem and its Relation to the Plays*, Salzburg, 1974

Sister Miriam Joseph. *Shakespeare's Use of the Arts of Language*, 1947

Smith, Hallett. *Elizabethan Poetry*, 1950

Straumann, Heinrich. *Phönix und Taube*, Zurich, 1953

Swärdh, Anna. *Rape and Religion in English Renaissance Literature*, Uppsala, 2003

Taylor, A. B. (ed.). *Shakespeare's Ovid*, 2000

Tipton, Alzada. 'The transformation of the Earl of Essex: post-execution ballads and "The Phoenix and the Turtle"', *SP* 99 (2002), 57–80

Tolbert, J. M. 'The Argument of Shakespeare's *Lucrece*', *TSE* 29 (1950), 77–90

Trousdale, Marion. *Shakespeare and the Rhetoricians*, 1982

Tuve, Rosemond. *Elizabethan and Metaphysical Imagery*, 1947

Underwood, R. A. *Shakespeare's 'The Phoenix and the Turtle': A Survey of Scholarship*, Salzburg, 1974

Vickers, Brian. *'Counterfeiting' Shakespeare: Evidence, Authorship, and John Ford's 'Funerall Elegye'*, 2002

Vinge, Louise. *The Narcissus Theme in Western Literature*, 1967

Wall, Wendy. *The Imprint of Gender: Authorship and Publication in the English Renaissance*, 1993

Watkins, W. B. C. 'Shakespeare's banquet of sense', in *Elizabethan Poetry*, ed. Paul J. Alpers, 1967

Williams, Gordon. 'The coming of age in Shakespeare's *Adonis*', *MLR* 78 (1983), 769–76

Wilson, Richard. *Secret Shakespeare*, 2004

Ziegler, Georgianna. 'My lady's chamber: female space, female chastity in Shakespeare', *Textual Practice* 4 (1990), 73–100

Praise for *Embracing Excellence in the Public Sector*

Far more than simply a "Leadership Story," the book speaks the language of the public sector and provides an easy to understand five step process leaders and teams can use to drive amazing results. I found it to be an exceptional guide for delivering measurable, performance oriented results in a truly tough environment – the public sector.

Sean J. Byrne
Assistant Administrator for Human Capital
Transportation Security Administration

Just when you thought you could not learn another lesson as a leader – Patrick takes the time to create a one of a kind idea and book that everyone in the public sector should want to read and they will be pleasantly surprised by the valuable lessons they learn along the way. Great Job!

Gwendolyn Sykes
VP for Business & Finance/Chief Financial Officer,
Morehouse College
Chief Financial Officer, National Aeronautics and
Space Administration (2003-2007)

Today America is full of those who want to condemn the public sector but offer no solutions, ideas, or creative thought to address the challenges we all face. People forget that government includes our first responders in any emergency, those who educate the future generation, public health personnel who care for us, and the military who protect us.

What Patrick has done is to use a story to show a path to excellence; leading toward restoring pride in the words PUBLIC SERVICE. All who care about the public good – from the city hall to the White House – from a school board election to presidential race must have these ideas in their heads and put them into practice.

Andrew "Skipper" Martin
Chief of Staff to the Governor of the Commonwealth of Kentucky
(1995-2003)
Chief of Staff to Lt. Governor of the Commonwealth of Kentucky
(1992-1995)

In this highly readable fable, seasoned business coach Patrick Leddin addresses five key leadership steps to sharpen focus and elicit results. Leddin widens the aperture commonly employed in business writing to spotlight the public sector, with insights easily translatable to the nonprofit sector. Teams which employ a *qualitative* balance sheet – like a government agency or a nonprofit – can immediately implement Leddin's steps to refine priorities, map strategy, increase and monitor productivity, and enhance communication.

Rev. Dr. Nancy Graham Ogne
Presbyterian Pastor

The 5 Ps workshop session was terrific. It gave us great clarity. All of our directorates should go through this process.

Gordon Cox
Chief, Human Capital
Deputy Under Secretary of the Air Force, International Affairs

Embracing Excellence in the Public Sector truly captures the unique essence of working in government and the issues we face. Dr. Leddin's message is right on point and is a great resource for any government manager/supervisor.

Mike Rodman
Assistant Executive Director
Kentucky Board of Medical Licensure

I have worked with Patrick and the Wedgewood Group for years. They take 'out-of-the-box' thinking and implementation to another level. The 5 P's is yet another example of their innovative thinking.

Patrick E. Fox
Deputy Comptroller for Security Assistance
Defense Security Cooperation Agency